A Basic Guide to Throwing and Grappling

JUDO
FORMAL TECHNIQUES
The Essentials of Kodokan Free Practice Forms

Donn F. Draeger
Tadao Otaki

With a new foreword
by **Neil Ohlenkamp**
author of *Judo Unleashed*

TUTTLE Publishing

Tokyo | Rutland, Vermont | Singapore

"Books to Span the East and West"

Tuttle Publishing was founded in 1832 in the small New England town of Rutland, Vermont [USA]. Our core values remain as strong today as they were then—to publish best-in-class books which bring people together one page at a time. In 1948, we established a publishing outpost in Japan—and Tuttle is now a leader in publishing English-language books about the arts, languages and cultures of Asia. The world has become a much smaller place today and Asia's economic and cultural influence has grown. Yet the need for meaningful dialogue and information about this diverse region has never been greater. Over the past seven decades, Tuttle has published thousands of books on subjects ranging from martial arts and paper crafts to language learning and literature—and our talented authors, illustrators, designers and photographers have won many prestigious awards. We welcome you to explore the wealth of information available on Asia at www.tuttlepublishing.com.

First published by Tuttle Publishing, an imprint of Periplus Editions (HK) Ltd.

www.tuttlepublishing.com

Library of Congress Control Number: 2018966794

ISBN: 978-0-8048-5148-0

26 25 24 23   5 4 3 2   2308TP
Printed in Singapore

Distributed by

North America, Latin America & Europe
Tuttle Publishing
364 Innovation Drive, North Clarendon
VT 05759-9436 U.S.A.
Tel: 1 (802) 773-8930
Fax: 1 (802) 773-6993
info@tuttlepublishing.com
www.tuttlepublishing.com

Japan
Tuttle Publishing
Yaekari Building 3rd Floor 5-4-12 Osaki
Shinagawa-ku, Tokyo 141 0032
Tel: (81) 3 5437-0171
Fax: (81) 3 5437-0755
sales@tuttle.co.jp
www.tuttle.co.jp

Indonesia
PT Java Books Indonesia
Jl. Rawa Gelam IV No. 9,
Kawasan Industri Pulogadung
Jakarta 13930, Indonesia
Tel: 62 (21) 4682 1088
Fax: 62 (21) 461 0206
crm@periplus.co.id
www.periplus.com

Asia Pacific
Berkeley Books Pte. Ltd.
3 Kallang Sector #04-01
Singapore 349278
Tel: (65) 6741-2178
Fax: (65) 6741-2179
inquiries@periplus.com.sg
www.tuttlepublishing.com

Table of Contents

Acknowledgments

Since this book deals with a highly technical area of Judo training, the Kodokan Randori no Kata, the authors have been quite anxious to have the most authoritative reading of the manuscript possible. We are therefore deeply indebted to Sumiyuki Kotani, former Chief Instructor of the Kodokan International Division; to Takashi Uzawa, Kodokan historian and former administrative assistant-secretary to Jigoro Kano; to Yoshizo Matsumoto, head of the Kodokan Editorial Section; to Teizo Kawamura and Toshiro Daigo, members of the Kodokan technical and instructional staff; and to Nobuo Nishimori, an outstanding high-ranking Judo teacher in the U. S. A. All gave generously of their time and provided valuable technical suggestions.

Special thanks are extended to the Kano family, whose permission to peruse and quote from the personal diaries and technical notes of Jigoro Kano has given this text its core. The classical Japanese work on *kata*, Murakami's *Randori no Kata*, fourth edition (Kodokan Bunkakai), originally edited by Jigoro Kano, provided many of the technical data which are to be found in this book. Thus it has been possible to recapture the original spirit and intent of Kodokan *kata* from its source, and to explain it so that its importance may be discovered by the reader. Technical details have also been taken from the contemporary *kata* standard of Kodokan, and many high-ranking Judo teachers have therefore made distinctive individual contributions. However, it is the authors who assume full responsibility for any technical errors of substance or omission.

Excellent cooperation in demonstrating skills for the pictures in this text was given by Isao Inokuma, two-time All-Japan Judo Champion, 1964 Olympic Heavyweight Judo Champion, and 1965-66 Unlimited and World Judo Champion, who performs as Tori; and by T. Matsukawa, a teacher of physical education in Tokyo and instructor in the Kodokan International Division, who performs as Uke. Additional thanks are extended to Joel Stewart and Howard K. Alexander, Canadian former Judo *kenshusei* at the Kodokan, who demonstrate many of the technical key points. Daniel Wacksman and Navon Doron of Israel, students at the Kodokan, demonstrate some special technical matters. Tsunemori Kaminoda, senior combatives instructor for the Metropolitan Tokyo Police Department, served as model for the illustrations concerning the relationship between swordsmanship and Judo.

The pictorial appeal of this book is largely due to the great photographic skills of A. Jinguji. Pascal Krieger was responsible for the outstanding accuracy of the graphics, without which the work's technical complexity would prove a burden to the reader. A great debt is owed to Dr. John B. Hanson-Lowe for the care and time which he devoted to conscientious proofreading of the manuscript as well as the many valuable suggestions he made in preparing it for publication. Trevor P. Leggett, the senior-ranked non-Japanese judoist, too, has been most helpful in identifying classical Japanese texts used in preparation of the manuscript. The work of the Yale University Library staff, which cooperated in certain phases of the research, is also much appreciated. Finally, the authors wish to thank Yasuko Nagazumi and Sakiko Odajime for their long and faithful hours in the tedious work of interviewing and translation.

Foreword

No other book on Judo, and very few teachers, can offer the comprehensive instruction available from *Judo Formal Techniques*. The exhaustive research and training undertaken by Donn Draeger and Tadao Otaki to produce this book has resulted in a resource so important that no serious exponent of Judo can afford to be without it.

Even after practicing diligently for 50 years, I find mastery of Judo technique elusive. But Judo training offers all of us occasional glimpses of its inherent beauty — the surprisingly effortless, yet powerful, throw applied in contest; the Olympic champion taking a fall for a nine year old who manages to apply proper technique; the student who builds the confidence to turn his life around. Nowhere is this beauty more evident than in the intrinsically Japanese practice of *kata*, the formal exercises containing idealized movements illustrating specific combative principles. To practice *kata* is to seek the perfection of technique, and ultimately the self. Draeger and Otaki delve deeply into the technical details of Judo to remind us just how much meaning is embodied in the techniques we study.

Kyuzo Mifune, 10th dan, wrote, "Judo is, after all, a living thing; something that is constantly undergoing growth and development." Over the years, I have seen the development of popular new techniques, evolving competition rules, improved training methods, and revisions to the basic syllabus of Judo. *Judo Formal Techniques*, however, provides the means to understand the immutable foundational principles of Judo techniques.

Donn Draeger and Tadao Otaki came from entirely different backgrounds but shared a love of Judo. Their collaboration produced a book that is exceptionally well researched and demonstrates a rare understanding of the art. They had previously co-authored *Judo for Young Men* (1965) and established themselves as famed instructors. As a professor of physical education at Tokyo Education University, Tadao Otaki was engaged in historical and technical research concerning the role of judo in education. Donn Draeger was an instructor in the foreign section of the Kodokan in Tokyo where he specialized in the study and teaching of Kodokan Judo *kata*.

Born in Wisconsin in 1922, Draeger started Judo training as a child Already a fourth degree black belt when he moved to Japan, he competed in the All-Japan High-Dan-Holders Judo Tournament. He was the first non-Japanese to demonstrate *kata* at the All-Japan Judo Championships and the 1964 Olympic Games. He was also the only foreigner to have been awarded official *kata* teaching licenses by the Kodokan.

As a recognized authority on Asian martial arts, Draeger authored more than 20 books along with numerous articles for a variety of publications. His books (including *Judo Training Methods* with Takahiko Ishikawa and *Weight Training for Championship Judo* with Isao Inokuma) greatly influenced training in Japan, and around the world. Indeed, Isao Inokuma credited Draeger's training methods for his success in winning the gold medal at the 1964 Olympics. His most comprehensive book was the three-volume masterpiece, *The Martial Arts and Ways of Japan*, but *Judo Formal Techniques* has been equally influential in regards to its more finite subject.

This book primarily examines Kodokan Judo *nage no kata* (forms of throwing) and *katame no kata* (forms of grappling), which together form the *randori no kata*. The original *randori no kata* (free practice forms) were codified in the 1880s, mostly based on techniques and methods Jigoro Kano, the founder of Kodokan Judo, studied in *Tenjin Shin'yō-ryū* and *Kitō-ryū jujutsu*. These combat techniques were adapted to conform to the principles of modern physical education, and played a key role in the formulation of the larger principles of Kodokan Judo. In addition to throws and pins, these *kata* include Judo techniques as varied as strikes, blocks, escapes from submissions, and joint locks to both the elbow and knee.

The *randori no kata* formed the technical basis for Judo training in the early development of the Kodokan, serving as a necessary balance to *randori* (free practice). By practicing with a cooperating partner prepared to offer a specific action for us to, we complement the more unpredictable competitive training of *randori* and *shiai* (contest). A *kata* partner is not just a compliant dummy or actor though; he or she must challenge us with real attacks and reactions in order to hone our skills, both mental and physical. The discipline instilled by such practice prepares the *kata* expert for a range of situations with instinctive responses that achieve maximum effect.

Judo Formal Techniques was groundbreaking when Tuttle first published it in 1983. There were few other *kata* resources available in English, and none as comprehensive. Knowledgeable *kata* instructors were not widely accessible, and other books and articles on the subject were limited. Tournament preparation was the primary objective of most judo classes in the West. The publication of this book was a significant factor in changing the environment and building a greater appreciation for the benefits of *kata* practice.

Kata competition has become increasingly popular since this book was published. Most Judo tournaments now include a *kata* component where each move is judged for conformance with established standards. While occasional revisions to these judging standards may result in minor deviations from the information in this, it still reflects the best research available on the original intent of *kata* and is an essential resource for improving performance.

Shortly after *Judo Formal Techniques* book was first published, I relied on it to prepare for *kata* competition at the U.S. Senior Nationals in Honolulu. This book significantly advanced my understanding of Kodokan *kata*, even though I had previously completed several *kata* courses and earned certifications in *nage no kata* and *katame no kata*. Part historical, part theoretical, and a large part instruction manual, it filled in the blanks and provided the required context and detail to train successfully. It also sparked a lifelong appreciation of Judo *kata* by enhancing my understanding of how to practice.

Fans of mixed martial arts, grappling, and self-defense training sometimes criticize the role of *kata* in Japanese martial arts arguing combat effectiveness is better achieved through free practice with full resistance. Similarly, some Judo competitors and coaches argue that other training methods are more suitable for tournament success, claiming *kata* is useless, or even counter-productive to high-level performance.

Draeger and Otaki counter that the Western view of *kata* is somewhat distorted. It is not, as some believe, a stereotyped, phony, performance of useless techniques in unrealistic situations. *Judo Formal Techniques* addresses these concerns by explaining how *kata* training must be realistic and effective in every respect. A full chapter is devoted to powerful testimony from 24 of the world's top competitors and instructors who explain how practicing *randori no kata* improved their competitive performance and their understanding of vital combative principles like engagement distance (*maai*), unbalancing (*kuzushi*), awareness (*zanshin*), and body shifting (*tai sabaki*).

Kata training provides an opportunity to focus on understanding and mastering technique; it is not limited to the formal techniques in *randori no kata*. Most Judo classes incorporate some type of *kata* into their workout as a necessary step in learning. The popular prearranged, repetitive practice called *uchi komi*, is an example of the less formal kind of *kata*, which can be adapted for any level of experience including beginners learning their first throw.

Judo Formal Techniques lists other Kodokan *kata* for studying self-defense, physical education, and theory, but the subject of this book covers the most relevant type of practice for the majority of Judo participants precisely because it improves the throwing and grappling techniques utilized in free practice and competition. The value of studying these *kata* is recognized by the requirement to demonstrate *nage no kata* and *katame no kata* for the early black belt promotions, even though this is often during the trainee's peak competitive years. Studying this book offers a complementary balance to other training, and it may continue well beyond a competitor's prime.

The Kodokan *randori no kata* preserves a worldwide standard for Judo theory and technique. Practicing these forms of throwing and grappling provides us with a direct connection to Jigoro Kano who devised them for the benefit of all Judo students. This book contributes the complete instructions needed to make this valuable training accessible for English-speaking trainees.

Kata is only a part of what Judo has to offer; yet it embodies the essence of what Judo is. That essence is captured and revealed by Donn Draeger and Tadao Otaki so it can be applied in practice. Real progress does not come without serious training, but thirty-five years after it was first published, *Judo Formal Techniques* can still be savored today, providing inspiration and guidance for those seeking to unravel the mystery and meaning of Judo.

NEIL OHLENKAMP
Author, *Judo Unleashed*
Santa Barbara, California

Preface

This book has been prepared as a technical manual for all judoists, whether trainees or instructors. It describes the basic formal techniques of Kodokan Judo, the Nage and Katame no Kata. The primary purpose of this book is to give judoists an adequate source of reference for the study and practice of these basic *kata*. It contains the most recent amendments and modifications made by the Kodokan in arriving at the formulation of a definitive *kata* standard. Additionally, this book extrapolates from Jigoro Kano's technical notes in order to remove the appearance of uselessness which is often projected by modern interpretations of *kata*.

It will be readily seen that this book is unique in several major areas. The precision with which *kata* must be performed requires that an adequate description of it be somewhat lengthy and detailed. *Kata* must be given its just place in a full-length text without trying to cram too many types of *kata* and too little about each into the limitations of a book. Therefore, this book provides more pages of illustrated text than are usually found in a work on this subject.

Heretofore, books on Judo *kata* have been mainly concerned with describing the actual techniques of throwing and grappling. They have concentrated mainly on the role of Tori, almost to the exclusion of the role of Uke, which is very vital to *kata*. We object to this method of presentation as being full of technical gaps which weaken learning. These gaps have made *kata* study from most existing books a loosely connected series of performances and next to impossible. In *kata* the connecting movements are highly significant, and need to be practiced as correctly as the individual techniques. This book gives a full and accurate description of the roles of both Tori and Uke, making the whole *kata* understandable as a continuous process, without omitting the technical details necessary for a smooth and complete performance. Understanding the direction of movement and the rhythm involved in the performance of each technique places the strength climaxes properly and makes them easily identifiable. The "in-betweens," or transitional movements from the completions of techniques to the subsequent techniques required of the performers, are described so that the physical positions and attendant movements can readily be practiced throughout the whole range and depth of their fields. Additionally, the positional attitudes taken by Tori and Uke from start to finish of each technique are clearly illustrated and explained. Emphasis is also given to the correct spirit and etiquette of *kata*, without which *kata* is meaningless.

This book stresses, in progressive steps, the necessity for the integration of the objectives *of kata*. The primary intention of this stress is to contribute to the overall Judo education of judoists. The book also deals with the many components to making *kata* interesting and learnable; specifically it discusses the unification of *kata* into the realm of practical Judo training. It is this portion of the book that should appeal most to the reader. A stereotyped and inflexible curriculum of demonstrational *kata* will see many judoists grow bored, and rightly so. The student's distaste for *kata* ill-presented can be turned into a love for *kata* correctly presented. *Kata*, as indicated in this book, is concerned with real throwing, real falling, and energetic grappling; the suggested application of *kata* in training is the basis for the development of a judoist's skills so that they may endure.

Incompetent or, at best, indifferent Judo instructors who indict the practice of *kata* as slavish adherence to the traditionalist approach, and condemn it as meaningless form, are irrefutably rebutted by documentary testimony to the value of *kata* training. Some of the most outstanding Japanese judoists, famous in international circles as contest champions and high-ranking teachers, give their opinions about *kata* here. It is evident from their testimonies that only the judoist with rich past experience appreciates and understands *kata*, and that it is the inexperienced judoist who lacks an ability to enlarge and make meaningful the course of *kata* study.

TADAO OTAKI
DONN F. DRAEGER

Note: It is deeply regretted that one of the authors, Donn Draeger, did not live to see the publication of this book. We are fortunate that Mr. Draeger did find an opportunity to check the printed proofs and layout of this work, the fruit of his lifelong devotion to martial arts.

How to Use This Book

There are many sound approaches to the use of this book. You may of course choose your own procedure; but one way which makes full use of this text, and the one which we think best, is as follows:

Read Chapters 1 through 3 inclusive; you may also begin reading Chapter 10. You may do all this before taking your first *kata* instruction, or you may read along as you train. However, it is perhaps best to have the information in those chapters in mind prior to your actual lessons. If you are already familiar with *kata*, these chapters will add to your store of knowledge.

When you begin your actual practice of *kata*, turn directly to Chapter 8 or 9 as appropriate, and begin reading the technical descriptions of the techniques you will practice. As you read and as you practice in the *dojo*, certain technical points are bound to confuse you. You may be able to understand them as they arise by reading Chapters 5 through 7, which give detailed insight into many of your potential problems. You will notice that this book contains a unique structural presentation of *kata* in Chapters 8 and 9; that is, the roles of Tori and Uke are given a two-column arrangement. This arrangement has much in common with a musical score in that each part may be read and practiced independently, or may be practiced in concert with the other to produce the desired whole. It will be greatly helpful to have a third training partner read the text, step by step, as you and your training partner follow his spoken instructions; "walk" through your first few such training sessions without completely applying the techniques—that is, omitting the throw and resultant fall, or the struggle on the mat—until you have the familiarity with the mechanics of the techniques which permits you to give a complete performance. Other judoists can sit and watch your performance, criticizing by noting any differences in it from what has been read in the text. When you have the technical details firmly in mind, you may then practice without the aid of these additional training partners.

This book contains action photographs of all the techniques of Nage and

Katame no Kata, exactly as they are performed, by two young, leading world *kata* experts, one of whom (Tori) is not only a two-time All-Japan Judo Champion but also an Olympic and World Champion. There are no posed photographs in the technique sequences. You may note some minor inconsistencies between the pictures and the text; this may be due to photographic difficulties (angles, timing, etc.) in obtaining exactly what the text requires, rather than a technical deficiency in the performers. At any rate, when such differences are detected, follow the text.

Rereading any portion of this book will always greatly improve your Judo study and practice. Refer to the appropriate chapters by consulting the Table of Contents and the Glossary-Index, which will help you to find what you are searching for. For ease of reference, the Glossary-Index has been divided into three parts: Nage no Kata Techniques; Katame no Kata Techniques; and General.

Those judoists who may criticize this text as being too involved and detailed are reminded that the book has been written precisely with the idea of including such detail. *Kata* cannot be correctly performed without strict attention to detail, and adequate explanations *of kata* must discuss indispensable detail. Casual reading is not desirable; this text is meant to provide a basis for the study and practice of Nage and Katame no Kata for the Judo lifetime of any dedicated judoist. Would those who criticize its length expect a book on equally technically difficult subjects to be brief? A dictionary, a text on anatomy and physiology, a text on electrical theory or automotive mechanics given in summary form would be of little or no value to the user. The old adage "One picture is worth ten thousand words" often gives rise to the design of books which are based on explanation by pictures. Magnificent books have been so published, lavishly pictorial but sparse in textual content. They make their appeal to the lazy reader. These books cannot impress the reader deeply, even when elaborately and carefully planned. They appeal only to curiosity of a superficial nature, because unless the reader can correctly interpret the pictures, he cannot learn the intricacies and technical precision that are required by *kata* or any other complex subject; important details in the photographs will escape his untutored eye.

Read and reread the text, often and carefully. You will always find something new to improve your *kata* ability and knowledge. But, beyond that, in all techniques described herein and their related counters, neutralizations, and escape procedures, are values that should be applied when practicing *randori* and *shiai*.

CHAPTER 1
Historical Background

There is no art without originality;
there is no originality without personality.
—R. ALDINGTON

The Combative Roots of Kodokan Kata

The Japanese concept of *kata*[1] is as old as Japan itself. This concept stems from the activities of the earliest Japanese people as they struggled for group identity and social stability. The application of kata in various ways to the establishment and maintenance of the Japanese nation was, and continues to be, an active force, an intrinsic element of Japanese culture.

Kata is an expression of the Japanese spirit intimately connected to the artistic achievements of the Japanese people; it is virtually their "form language." Kata touches almost everything in the Japanese sphere of daily activities—writing, architecture, bearing and demeanor, etiquette, and art included. Art is the form language of humanity without exception, and therefore, on the Japanese scene, art traditionally includes the classical *bugei* (also called *bujutsu*), the martial arts or formalized martial disciplines; it also includes the classical *budo*, the martial ways or spiritual disciplines which stem from martial sources. Within the classical martial arts and ways are found the elements of simplicity, natural efficiency, harmony, intuition, economy of movement, and "softness" of principle that characterize all traditional Japanese art forms. It is important to grasp this significant relationship in order to com-

---

1. The Japanese read the ideogram 形 as *katachi* or *kata*, words for which more than one approximate English equivalent may be found: form, shape, size, style, type, a cut, a make, pattern, design, mold, cast, model, convention, tradition, security, pledge, stereotype. In our opinion, none of the English equivalents suitably covers the various implications of the ideogram for *kata*. But inasmuch as the root idea of that ideogram refers to form, we accept the word "form" as adequate and meaningful for the purposes of this book. *Kata* is a word that may be used as either singular or plural, without the addition of *s* to form the plural. Like the word "form," *kata* may be used either as a count noun or as an abstract, mass noun. The ideogram 形 always conveys an animate idea, and therefore it must not be confused with the ideogram 型, also read *kata*, which connotes dull, inanimate, inert, spiritless form.

Chikara kurabe, an ancient combat method. Nneteenth-century artwork from the Draeger collection.

prehend the true meaning and fullness of the Japanese martial arts and ways, and, further, to understand their ancestral relationship to Kodokan Judo kata.

The Japanese people have always placed a high value on weapons and fighting arts. Various systems of hand-to-hand combat were developed in the Japan of old. One of the first records indicating the existence of Japanese-style combative arts in early days is found in the *Nihon Shoki (Chronicles of Japan)*, written in A. D. 720. Passages in this literary classic tell of the *chikara kurabe*, or "strength comparison" contests, allegedly conducted in still earlier times. The combatants, naked or clad only in loin cloths, would fight furiously, as the price of losing was usually dishonor, loss of tribal identity, or even death. Other documents dating from the tenth century describe the spirit and mechanics of similar combative methods. Such fighting skills were passed down through the ages and were brought to fruition by the classical warriors who made up an aristocratic and privileged stratum of Japanese society. These fighting men were known as *bushi*, and they were active in the government of their nation up until the late nineteenth century.

It was the *bushi* who made a thorough study of many kinds of weapons and developed fighting methods that employed a wide range of lethal instruments. These enterprising warriors were truly professional fighting men. They were responsible for the development of the classical martial arts. In the twelfth

Two warriors engaged in yoroi kumi-uchi on the battlefield. Nineteenth-century woodblock print by Ichieisai Yoshitsuya, from the Draeger collection.

century, when the reins of government passed from the imperial family to the warriors, fighting skills made possible and supported the latter's position of leadership. One of the skills destined to have a strong effect on Kodokan Judo kata was the fighting art called *yoroi kumi-uchi*, a method of grappling designed to be used by two enemies fully dressed in battle armor. *Yoroi kumi-uchi*, in turn, had evolved its stances, postures, movement, and tactics from primitive methods of combat such as those in the *chikara kurabe* contests.

A great proliferation of styles accompanied the development of the classical martial arts. Powerful socio-political units either adopted existing styles of combat or sponsored capable warriors who designed new systems for them, in order to bolster their influence on Japanese society. By the early sixteenth century many thousands of martial *ryu* had been established. The *ryu* may be thought of as a "martial tradition," that is, an organization specially established to perpetuate the martial teachings of its founder. Some *ryu* had a considerable effect on the development of Kodokan Judo, especially those *ryu* which included methods of hand-to-hand combat in which the practitioner was minimally armed or chose to rely less upon his weapons than he would normally on the battlefield.[2] Some of these systems of combat include: *yoroi kumi-uchi, kumi-uchi, kogusoku, koshi no mawari, yawara-ge and yawara-gi, hakuda, shubaku, kempo, taijutsu, wajutsu,* and *torite*. To some extent *sumo*, at this time in Japanese history a method of combat with a sports flavor, also influenced the design of Judo kata.

In the seventeenth century Japan entered a long period of domestic peace. Under the domination of the Tokugawa family, the warrior class lost its once predominantly martial role; it degenerated into a meaningless and unproductive stratum of Japanese society. The upshot was the final collapse of the warrior class and the rise of the common man to a place of prominence in the affairs of his nation. These vast social and political changes brought about considerable cultural dislocations. One of the dislocations involved the classical martial arts. The martial arts (*bugei*), originated by the warriors, became less important and were to a large extent relegated to a secondary position by the development of spiritual disciplines, the martial ways (*budo*), founded by commoners.

"Jujutsu" is a generic term that is commonly applied to all Japanese systems of hand-to-hand combat in which the operator is minimally armed. In a broad sense, from the seventeenth century onward the term included such

2. The *ryu* of combative arts that most directly influenced the development of Kodokan Judo kata are: Fukuno Ryu, Jikishin Ryu, Kashin Ryu, Kito Ryu, Kyushin Ryu, Miura Ryu, Sekiguchi Ryu, Shibukawa Ryu, Shin-no-shinto Ryu, Tenjin-shin'yo Ryu, and Yoshin Ryu.

distinctly different systems as *kumi-uchi, kogusoku, koshi no mawari,* and others. Originally, however, jujutsu was but one manner of waging hand-to-hand combat through the use of techniques that utilized the principle of *ju,* or "flexibility." The warrior considered jujutsu to be a secondary system of combat, always attached to some major system involving the use of the sword; nor did he insist that the techniques of jujutsu be applied only to empty-hand combat. But as the warrior class became less important in Japanese society, and eventually an anachronism, the meaning of jujutsu changed. With the rise of the common man, jujutsu became more and more a product of his needs, characterized by methods of unarmed combat such as were useful in civil life. In fact, many of the applications of jujutsu were focused on altercations that took place in tea rooms, houses of prostitution, gambling dens, and the other places for entertainment frequented by the commoners.

By the nineteenth century jujutsu styles were largely a collection of tactics that could be used without weapons against either an armed or an unarmed adversary. Jujutsu styles became so numerous that professional jealousy between them caused many of the most prominent *ryu* to divide into still more individual styles. Many jujutsu styles divorced themselves entirely from the study of weapons; *ryu* were founded to feature unarmed methods of combat. Practitioners of all jujutsu styles vied with each other for technical perfection

The sumo technique of uchi-gake (the inner hook). Late nineteenth-century woodblock print from the Draeger collection.

and many sought favor for their style by attaching themselves to important families or influential governmental agencies. Over seven hundred different styles of jujutsu had emerged by the end of the nineteenth century. The development of jujutsu is indicative of a rise in freedom of expression among the Japanese people, and an important sign of the vast social changes which were sweeping Japan.

Peace had a profound effect on jujutsu, for it was peace that married jujutsu to art and brought about tremendous technical refinements. Though the underlying purpose of all warrior styles of jujutsu was a martial one, and remained unchanged, many other styles lost their combative vitality due to the lack of practical experience of their practitioners; what combative integrity remained lay only in applications for self-defense in civil life. Yet all jujutsu styles, warrior- or commoner-founded, found it difficult to satisfy the ardor of their practitioners, especially those styles in which a lethal array of weapons was used. It occurred to many practitioners that if jujutsu were to be conducted in an entirely unarmed or empty-hand manner, certain modifications could be made in technique which would allow practitioners to use their skills against one another without having recourse to drastic conclusions. A primary training method of the classical martial arts, that of kata, or prearranged formal techniques, was borrowed by advocates of empty-hand jujutsu styles to broaden their technical bases and to provide practical outlets for their practitioners.

Traditionally, all Japanese classical martial arts called for complete mastery of technique. Only through training carried out over a period of many years was a practitioner able to become an expert. Zealous, dedicated practice led the warrior to maturity of technique and mental acuity. Kata was the only method of training through which the warrior could safely practice his fighting arts with the members of his *ryu*. Primary kata called *omote* were to be learned, then polished by engaging in more advanced kinds. Intuitive learning (*kaen*) was the key to all progress. Silent communication between master and trainee was the basis of all teaching; the trainee learned by following example. Through repetition of prescribed exercises the trainee brought his initially crude imitation of action to the desired level of skill, in which a conditioned reflex governed his every action. Casual training was not tolerated, and every training session approximated the conditions of the battlefield. Through use of kata the warrior harmonized himself in the simple sense of developing efficient motor skills, and gained courage by deepening his confidence in himself. By harmonizing himself in this fashion, the warrior embodied the nobility of his spirit.

The developers of empty-hand jujutsu styles were not always attracted to the idea of using kata as a primary training method. They declared that actual fighting was the only way to develop and maintain fighting skills; in the absence of opportunities to fight, they encouraged their followers to seek fights with practitioners of other *ryu*. Some jujutsu styles, they pointed out, were developing kata that had little combative value, such kata being little more than collections of movements to be made in an artistic manner; these movements pleased the aesthetic sense by giving an abstract quality to the performance.

The Formulation of Kodokan Kata

Jigoro Kano, the founder of Kodokan Judo, was an extraordinarily perceptive man; he was also extremely inquisitive about the jujutsu of his time. Kano first studied the jujutsu of the Tenjin-shin'yo Ryu in his late teens, and several years later, as a newly graduated university student, he studied the system of *ran* of the Kito Ryu.[3] He could not help but notice that the former type of jujutsu was martially oriented, and the latter somewhat aesthetically inclined rather than combatively practical.[4] Kano was both an idealist and a pacifist. He formulated a plan for the founding of a reformed jujutsu, and moved with intellectual vigor to foil the tendency of the classical martial arts and ways to be either exclusively martial or aesthetic in nature.

Kano had a strong dislike for the misuse of jujutsu, for example against defenseless citizens. His insatiable thirst for knowledge about jujutsu led him to probe into its lore. From this research he was able to draw the information he needed. Jujutsu, as an object of culture, had been developed by people of widely differing outlooks. Kano disagreed with many of its precepts, both mechanical and ethical. But it is obvious that Kano was greatly impressed with the strong degree of attachment to tradition exhibited by all classical martial arts and ways. In Kano's notes we find frequent statements, such as the following, which characterize his thinking along the lines of tradition:

> Nothing is of greater importance than education; the teachings of one virtuous man can reach many, and that which has been learned by one generation can be passed on to a hundred.

---

3. Kan'emon Terada, the founder of the Kito Ryu, clearly distinguished jujutsu from his system, *ran*.

4. Kano studied the Kito Ryu teachings under Tsunetoshi Iikubo. By that time, the Kito Ryu had undergone severe changes that removed most of its combative integrity.

From his experience with the teachings of the Tenjin-shin'yo Ryu, Kano developed his *katame* and *ate waza* skills; from the Kito Ryu teachings he derived his finesse with *nage waza*. He studied the kata of these *ryu* carefully, adding ideas from other sources, developing some ideas of his own, and discarding that which he thought superfluous or dangerous, or not in accord with laws of statics and dynamics. The methods of grappling which stemmed from the *chikara kurabe* contests, known in Kano's day mainly through the sport of *sumo*, were also researched. From *sumo* techniques Kano gleaned valuable technical information. He evolved and championed the all-permeating Principle of Judo, the Principle of Maximum Efficiency, which can be stated thus: Whatever be the object, the best way of attaining it is the most efficient use of mental and physical energies directed to that goal. That which did not conform to this Principle was regarded by Kano as unsuitable for inclusion in Kodokan Judo. Thus, by welding physical techniques to this ideal, he produced a synthesis of tremendous importance to Japan and the world. In 1882 Kano publicly brought forth his brainchild, a reformed jujutsu which he called Judo. To prevent it from being confused with the Judo of the Jikishin Ryu, which had been using the word more than two centuries before Kano's time, Kano founded his Kodokan at the Eishoji, a temple in Tokyo, and thus established Kodokan Judo. Kano followed the lead of the founder of the Jikishin Ryu in making the transition from a *jutsu* form, primarily concerned with martial matters, to a *do* form, where emphasis is on character development and the perfection of the individual.

Kano borrowed liberally from jujutsu kata; both their disclosed teachings (*omote waza*), which are but introductory exercises, and such secret doctrines (*okuden*) as he had been able to get access to or actually learn. But he took an unorthodox approach. He sought to clarify those complicated aspects that surround secret teachings, substituting logical thinking and scientific analysis for the psychological learning patterns of the classical martial arts and ways. Kano's thoughts and methods, in this respect, were heretical. He depended largely on his knowledge of the teachings of the Tenjin-shin'yo Ryu and the Kito Ryu to bridge the gap. Kano also understood that idealism is an essential ingredient in all classical Japanese martial arts and ways; and he was well aware of the failure of some jujutsu styles to confront combative reality. Thus, any idealism that he might impart to Kodokan Judo had to be balanced by realism if Kodokan Judo was to survive the tests which it would be subjected to by practical-minded persons. But most of all, Kano, as a well-informed educator of his time, proved his intellectual mettle through a bit of foresight which was to cinch the public's approval for his Kodokan Judo.

The birth of Kodokan Judo came as an accretion, not as an eruption. An imperial edict issued in 1868 had announced the Meiji Ishin, a course of modernization, commonly translated as "the Meiji Restoration" and named for the restoration of official control of the government to the emperor. It was the most drastic change that Japan had ever experienced, and it eventually brought Japan to a position of equality with Western countries. The important question of education for all Japanese citizens was paramount in the minds of the Meiji governmental leaders. Emperor Meiji ordered all Japanese to seek knowledge from all sources throughout the world. The underlying idea was to equip the nation, which had been intellectually starved for centuries, with the knowledge necessary for carrying out the obligations of its new and prominent political role. Primary and secondary education were emphasized as much as they were in the West, and higher education was modeled after Western patterns.

Kano sensed the turning political tide and slanted his Kodokan Judo teachings according to the situation at hand. He was quick to realize that many of his Judo techniques would be seen by the untrained eyes of the general public as almost identical to those of the jujutsu styles. He could not hope to gain popular support for Kodokan Judo if the stigma of jujutsu colored it. Kano knew that in spite of similar outward appearances, Kodokan Judo and jujutsu had many striking differences. Kodokan Judo techniques could be more safely practiced; they also followed his Principle. But something more would have to differentiate Kodokan Judo from jujutsu.

Kano therefore gave his Kodokan Judo educational substance in tune with Meiji times. Above all, he insisted on a strict code of ethics for all Kodokan members. Examples of good character were set by himself and his instructors. This brought Kodokan Judo to the level of a medium for moral education. By additionally requiring lectures and energetic debates on the technical and philosophical essences of Judo study, Kano brought his Judo to the level of an intellectual endeavor. He further rounded out his system and met the criteria of physical education by creating kata patterns of his own. The Ju no Kata and the Seiryoku Zen'yo Kokumin Taiiku are two examples of formal techniques which brought a balance between exercise and systematic physical education to Kodokan Judo.

Kodokan Judo, in its formative days, had three objectives: (1) to develop the physical body, (2) to train the mind, and (3) to develop combative efficiency. In Kano's words (1889):

> [Judo] is the study of techniques with which you may kill if you wish to kill,

injure if you wish to injure, subdue if you wish to subdue, and, when attacked, defend yourself.

Kano sought to spread his Kodokan Judo teachings throughout the world. By the time of his return from his first trip abroad (1889) he had broadened his thinking. Judo education had to dovetail into the democratic ideal.

The spiritual aspect of Kodokan Judo gradually matured and emerged in 1924 as Kano gave his Principle social significance:

> Judo is not a method of making the best use of energy for purposes of attack and defense alone, rather it is a method by which this principle can be assimilated and applied in all spheres of life.

He elaborated on the social significance of Kodokan Judo by making use of the maxim "Mutual prosperity." This referred to the highest level of Kodokan Judo philosophy, the attainment of a state of perfection in an individual where the differences between him and others have been transcended. Kano believed that while practicing Judo techniques one assimilated the Principle and, further, eventually reached the state of mutual prosperity. So important were the Principle and the concept of Mutual Prosperity to Kano that he regarded the diffusion of these things as his great mission in life.

It was intended by Kano that Kodokan Judo be a balanced and practical entity, composed of physical and spiritual aspects. Kata plays an important role in the achievement of this balance.

From the records available, one cannot be certain as to whether Kano intended *randori* (free exercise)[5] or kata (prearranged exercise) to be foremost in the development of Kodokan Judo. Some historians of Judo maintain that if one considers carefully the general line of Kano's thought, it becomes evident that kata takes precedence over *randori*. Others, however, point out that although Kano was certainly an idealist, he was also an extremely practical man. Thus, although kata must have played an important part in the early stages of his Judo planning, it is more likely that *randori* held first place in his scheme.

Nevertheless, we know for certain that the technical bases of Kodokan Judo have their origins in the jujutsu kata. Most of Kano's ideas sprang from a consideration of the Tenjin-shin'yo Ryu and the Kito Ryu. Furthermore, records clearly show that kata lay at the very core of Kano's Judo.[6]

---

5. Kano's design of a method of free exercise was undoubtedly influenced by the training method of the Kito Ryu's *ran* system, in which trainees fought without restrictions as are the basis of kata practice. The *ran* method of the Kito Ryu was modified by Kano, who renamed it *randori*, meaning "to take freedom."

6. The *Judo Nenkan* (Judo Yearbook) of 1888 refers to Kodokan Ju no Kata, Katame no Kata, and Itsutsu no Kata. From this reference most Judo historians surmise that Nage no Kata, as the fundamental kata, preceded all others. However, this may not be so, inasmuch as the *nage waza* form the bulk of the Kodokan techniques,

Kano trained his first judoists by *randari*, using the techniques of *nage* and *katame waza*. As they progressed, they were encouraged to study and practice kata as a complementary training method. Kata then became part of a process based on natural learning. This proved workable for only a short time, since it depended entirely upon the judoist's own initiative. As Kodokan enrollments increased, this method, we are told in the founder's diaries, proved impractical. By the late 1880s Kano was giving more weight to kata by separating it from *randori* and requiring all judoists to study it as a supplement to *randori*.

It was obvious to Kano, as an educator, that *randori* alone could not guarantee physically balanced Judo practice, and we can see from his own words his desire to make Kodokan Judo a balanced educational subject:

> I drew up, in 1882, my Kodokan Judo, assimilating all the good qualities found in all the jujutsu schools and formulated a method of instruction in conformity with the teachings of modern sciences. In this I did not attach exclusive importance to the contesting side of the exercise, as had been the case formerly [in jujutsu], but aimed at a combination of contest exercises and the training of the mind and body.

Kano categorically opposed a training philosophy depending on the "survival of the fittest." According to him, the word "Judo" had two connotations: "Judo in the wide sense" (*jodan judo*), and "Judo in the narrow sense" (*gedan judo*). He explained:

> Judo in the narrow sense is that form which has evolved from the ancient military art of jujutsu.

The narrow interpretation of Judo did not satisfy Kano, for it limits Judo to the mere acquisition of physical or motor skills. For him there was much more than this at the core of Judo, and he continued:

> Although Kodokan Judo begins with the kata and randori, unlike jujutsu, it is based on the principles of physical education and lays stress on the harmonious development of the body muscles.

We may also note the priority given to kata over *randori* in this quotation.

It is evident that Kano was unshaken in his belief that physical education must be performed not for the sake of physical culture alone, but as a means of properly guiding the young in the development of a wholesome personal-

---

and thus it may have taken Kano longer to complete them and formalize a kata based on these techniques. This thesis is somewhat reinforced when we realize that Kano entered the Kito Ryu after completing his study of the Tenjin-shin'yo Ryu teachings; it was from the former that Kano derived his *nage waza* skills.

ity. He established Judo as an integral part of school physical education on the basis of what he called the Three-Culture Principle. This suggests a balanced approach to education, and consists of intellectual, moral, and physical disciplines. Kano's emphasis was on the harmony of the three elements; he was against any form of education which lacked this harmony. His notebooks are replete with critical observations which are applicable today:

> Not all those practicing Judo are doing it in earnest as a means of promoting physical education.... Special attention must be paid in order not to over-exert any part of the body. The formation of untoward habits or functional disability must be carefully avoided. In order to practice Judo as a means of physical education, special attention must be paid to the care of the health.

Modern-day Judo training, in disregard of Kano's cautions, has come to have only the purpose of developing contest skills and the contest champion. By such a deliberate narrowing of the founder's intention for Judo, untold harm is being done to its practitioners. Not only are trainees unable to get the fullest benefits from Judo, but often they suffer injuries. Only when the emphasis on contest Judo is lessened and returned to its proper perspective, as intended by the founder, will Judo function as healthful physical education.

Through an emphasis on kata, Kano was able to transform mere exercise for the development of skills into beneficial and purposeful physical education. The modern-day Judo practitioner must respect the rightful place of kata training within his Judo training methods. We learn from the founder's notes:

> In order to practice Judo with the object of physical education in mind, one must choose the techniques which allow uniform motion in every part of the body.... What is deficient in randori must be supplemented by kata.

From such a lucid notation we can see the importance which Kano attached to Kodokan Judo kata. He obviously did not limit his Judo to the narrow kind, which is a Judo built solely on a basis of *randori* and contest; rather Kano laid stress on the harmonious inclusion of kata in all training programs.

When Kodokan Judo was to be demonstrated to a distinguished audience, Kano favored kata as the medium. One such recorded incident took place on September 20, 1900. Professor G. T. Ladd of Yale University, a lecturer at Tokyo University (then Teikoku Daigaku), was invited to the Kodokan by Kano to attend his lecture and to see various demonstrations of Judo. Kano himself demonstrated the theory of *nage, katame,* and *ate waza*; he followed with a performance of the Koshiki no Kata. Some of Kano's outstanding disciples then followed his performance with the Katame and Nage no Kata.

Despite such displays of Judo kata, Kano never meant kata to be exclusively a show-piece or to be exhibitionary in nature. Ideal as kata is for demonstrating Kodokan Judo in its total scope, Kano emphasized its practical applications to training. Those technical difficulties which arose in *randori* were often solved by breaking a technique down into its component parts. For throwing situations, these include breaking balance (*kuzushi*), fitting the thrower's body to his opponent's state of unbalance (*tsukuri*), and the execution of the throw (*kake*); grappling situations include a comparable set of components.

The Nage no Kata, as well as the Kime no Kata, largely formed the technical province of the Kodokan until 1908, when, on the demand of adherents of various jujutsu styles who were dissatisfied with Kodokan technical dominance over kata, a large meeting of teachers and instructors was held in Kyoto by the Dai Nippon Butokukai (Japan Military Virtues Association). At this meeting the Kodokan kata were studied and the Nage no Kata was accepted as designed by Kano; the Katame no Kata underwent some modifications. Both kata were formalized and announced as standard for all Japanese practitioners of Judo.

In April 1920, Kano declared his awareness of the need for more kata study to improve the grappling skills of Kodokan judoists. He records in his diary:

> [I] consulted with Mifune concerning the student's deficiencies in katame. We agreed to intensify all kata study and to make kata instruction a regular teaching function at Kodokan, on a twice-a-week basis. All students will specially take part in the practice of *katame-uchi awase* [Katame no Kata].

It is significant that scheduled weekly kata practice under direction of Kodokan teachers took place in the period during which kata flourished and reached its technical peak (see chart, p. 30).

Kano had a specific plan in mind when designing kata. He was aware that jujutsu practice was almost always carried out in kata style, and that the remarkable fighting skills of the warrior were due to a concentrated study of kata. Fighting skills did not come about simply from free fighting, but from knowing how to fight against an enemy under all conditions of terrain and weather; such concentrated study was made possible through the application of kata. Yet some practitioners of jujutsu, especially those employing empty-hand styles, were, to Kano's mind, less efficient than they should be. This resulted from training that failed to develop the whole body. Nor did any jujutsu styles give their techniques application as sports.[7] Worst of all, to

---

7. Various *ryu* had, before Kano's time, developed kinds of free-exercise training, but no sports aspect attached

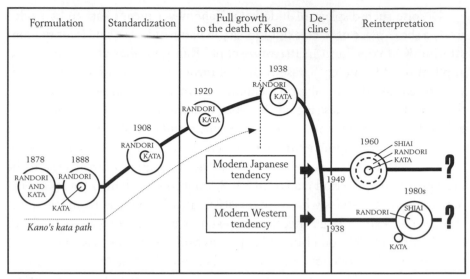

Evolution of Kodokan Judo kata.

Kano's mind, the practice of jujutsu, by any means, always disregarded personal safety in training.

Jujutsu kata were executed in a crude, dangerous manner. Thus, it was difficult, at best, for trainees to practice without sustaining injuries. In addition to the hazards to health, jujutsu kata contained so much formal conventionalism that progress toward expert skill was only possible after many years of training.[8] Most of all, Kano criticized jujutsu kata for ignoring his Principle of Judo; they were filled with uneconomical movements and were not designed with the conservation of energy as all-important to their purpose.[9] Having such deficiencies as were noted by Kano, jujutsu kata were incapable of meeting the requirements for physical education of Meiji society.

Kodokan kata, on the other hand, were designed to operate on the founder's Principle. All techniques serve as guides to the economizing of energy prescribed by the Principle; by stressing strict control of energy, the Principle reduces the element of danger in actual practice.

---

to it. The element of sports appears to have had its first connection with classical martial ways (*budo*) in some forms of swordsmanship in the nineteenth century.

8. Kano may have overlooked the fact that warriors practicing jujutsu-like tactics did so with battlefield applications in mind. There one mistake could have been fatal. The degree of expert skill that guaranteed personal safety could not be developed in a short time. The jujutsu kata that Kano referred to were not martially oriented, but their requiring a long period of study was nonetheless justified for their purpose of developing the practitioner's spiritual qualities—a never-ending, lifetime pursuit.

9. Kano appears not to have understood that the purpose of many kata in classical martial arts is to force the trainee to exert his body severely. This is done along the lines of sound physical education, which holds that hard exercise conducted over a protracted period of time improves physical fitness; it further fits the realities of combat, in which ideal actions cannot always be achieved.

Through careful attention to the detailed planning of Kodokan kata, Kano sought to stylize technique and to express the power of Judo in controlling an opponent's attack. Kata was meant to be an expression, an experience of humility, an object lesson which minimized subjective artistic effect. The Kodokan kata is designed for practical application; it is firmly structured on a combative foundation. Attack-defense relationships cover all aspects from self-defense against an aggressor to tactics to be applied in contests. But in spite of the apparently formidable finish of kata, it will also be found to contain artistic elements. Kano preserved the artistic quality of kata, for if there were no aesthetic element, kata would be no more than a highly conventional manner of practicing Judo techniques, a dry and uninteresting training method. Kata was meant by Kano to be decorative, but only to the extent that it makes the asymmetrical symmetrical and the irregular regular. Kano never meant to impose on judoists any hard and fast rules merely for the sake of rules, but hoped that, by specifying minute details, physical and mental effort could be reduced to a minimum, while at the same time the highest degree of grace, safety, and efficiency could be achieved. This must be understood by all judoists who undertake serious study of kata.

Kodokan Kata Today

A judoist needs technical distance, that is, technical maturity, to see kata as something which is both an art form and of practical value. In other words, the meaning of kata eludes all but the most experienced judoists, and it is therefore the obligation of those experienced judoists to demand kata study of all students in their charge. Kata must not be left to the student's choice, but must be correctly taught on a regular basis.

Kano saw kata as something plastic and limitless in expression and application. To him kata was definitely a measure of the vitality of Judo and an indication of its elastic strength. Kodokan kata today has become an expression of the combined experience of Judo experts of the past,"speaking" to the judoist of today. The more kata training a student undergoes, in carefully determined proportion to his total training time, the more he is able to benefit by that experience, which far exceeds the amount any one individual can amass in a lifetime. The less kata experience a judoist has, the less Judo experience he shares, and the shallower his technical knowledge is; the shallower a judoist is technically, the less prepared he is to understand Judo and to pass on its teachings correctly as an instructor.

Sufficient kata study and practice impose a well-defined technical discipline upon the judoist, one that is unattainable by only *randori* and contest methods. This discipline, instead of hampering the judoist, actually frees him from undue restrictions, liberates his bodily expression in movement, and best teaches him economy of mental and physical energy. This process can only be understood through experience, and only through kata performance can judoists come to appreciate Judo in its fullest sense.

The chart on page 30 shows the progress of Kodokan kata in relation to the whole scope of Judo. For convenience the entire span of Kodokan Judo history has been divided into five periods of kata progress.

During the first period, one of conception and formulation, the founder quickly realized that his original idea of including kata in Judo without specific regulating policies concerning its study and practice, depended largely upon a natural type of learning in which the student took initiative to learn without direction. But this proved unworkable as Kodokan enrollments increased. It was therefore necessary to give kata a position of its own within the scope of Judo. It should be noted that *randori* and kata, with *randori* predominating, were the only two forms of physical Judo practice officially recognized; the contest aspect of Judo was considered only a kind of *randori*.[10] In spite of its importance, kata nevertheless was the core entity in Kano's training methods.

The second period, that of trial and standardization, was significant in that the first truly national Japanese kata standardization was realized (1908); this event stands as a monument to the awareness of the importance of kata in Judo training methods. In this standardization not only were the technical aspects of kata specified, but a pattern of teaching was established. *Randori* and kata continued as the two recognized forms of Judo study; contest applications remained a part of *randori*.

It was during the third period, one of study and growth, that Kodokan kata reached its technical peak, a zenith which was realized through meaningful practice and application in Judo. During this period the importance of kata was instilled in all Japanese judoists. Kodokan kata committees were organized by the founder to further develop kata; still further efforts resulted in standard kata being taught throughout Japan. *Randori* and kata continued as the two forms of recognized Judo study, and the contest was still only a part of *randori*.

A period of kata decay and decline came upon Kodokan Judo, caused by

---

10. Kodokan Judo also recognizes, in addition to *randori* and kata, lectures (*ko*) and questions and answers (*mondo*) as legitimate methods of study.

the circumstances of world politics. This period began shortly after the death of the founder (1938).

Kodokan Judo kata is now in a period of reevaluation and reinterpretation; it has not yet run its full course. Generally speaking, it has taken two distinct courses, a Japanese trend and a Western or foreign trend. As far as the Japanese trend is concerned, the decline of kata was slowed down and gradually stopped altogether, beginning about 1949; a slow climb back to the technical heights of old was begun. Along with the gradual realization that kata is important to the health of Kodokan Judo came two significant events: the design and acceptance of a new kata-like form, the Goshin-jutsu, in 1956; and the meeting of a national kata-standardization committee in 1960. These events indicated a partial recovery of kata. But the concept of the unity of Judo seems to have undergone change. Kata, while still treated as a core entity for Judo training, has nevertheless been given less importance than was intended by the founder. Moreover, whereas both *randori* and kata continue to be officially recognized as the two main methods of Judo study, there has been a distinct emergence of *shiai*, or contest Judo, as an entity of intrinsic importance.

The Western opinion of kata, unfortunately, is a distorted one, which therefore does not coincide with the founder's concept of the unity of Judo. For the Westerners who became intensely interested in Judo about 1950, kata was not understandable; they avoided performing it. Kata has been removed by Westerners from its position as the core training entity of Judo, and has been made an appendage to the sphere of Judo unity. Thus, though kata is recognized by Westerners, it is taught infrequently as a strange and separate item and not as part of the normal training program. *Randori* has become the core of Western Judo training methods, and *shiai* has taken on an importance beyond what the founder declared healthy to the essence of Kodokan Judo. This trend is continuing today in the 1980s, largely due to the immense emphasis being placed on competitive Judo at international and Olympic levels. There is even some evidence that the Western opinion of kata is staining Japanese minds. The logical consequence of this trend will be the narrowing of Judo, though what is confined within those narrow limits of technical overspecialization will receive amplification beyond what has ever been known before.

Some modern-day judoists have criticized Kodokan Nage no Kata for not containing techniques which require Uke to perform *ukemi* in a backward direction. Practical Judo, these critics maintain, is filled with ample opportunities to throw an opponent backward, and kata, if it is to be practical, must contain techniques which call for that type of *ukemi*. But there are several good reasons why the founder did not choose to include such techniques.

First of all, techniques which throw Uke backward into *ukemi* are generally of the *kari waza* or "reaping technique" type; they must be chosen from the *ashi waza* or "leg technique" category (*osoto-gari, kosoto-gari, kouchi-gari,* etc.). A limited few can also be chosen from the *sutemi waza* or "sacrifice technique" category (*tani-otoshi, yoko-otoshi,* etc.), or from the *te waza* or "hand technique" category (*sukui-nage*). *Kari waza* are predominantly *ko-waza,* that is,"minor techniques," which require less body action in performance than is the case for *o-waza,* or "major techniques." It is from the *o-waza* category that Kano chose techniques to ensure the use of big body actions. Further, the *kari waza* are relatively abrupt actions which do not easily lend themselves to graceful application; Uke's *ukemi* is usually a small action and it is difficult for Tori to maintain balance during *kake.* Kano definitely wished to minimize the *ko-waza.* He included only *okuri-ashi-harai* in the kata, and only such *sutemi waza* as produce big body actions. Techniques that produce big body actions are more virile and better meet the requirements of physical education.[11]

Secondly, the attitude of self-defense that is intrinsic to Nage no Kata is, to Kano's way of thinking, generally provoked by an attack which brings the attacker forward against his intended victim. Kano reasoned that seldom does an attacker move backward in offense. In Nage no Kata, Kano permits only one attack incident in which Uke is moved backward, and that movement is not made by Uke's choice. This is in *tomoe-nage,* where Tori's application of quasi-*sen* (attack initiative) causes the defeat of Uke, who is compelled to retreat in the face of Tori's push before being thrown forward. Three other techniques (*uchi-mata, sumi-gaeshi,* and *uki-waza*) have Uke intending to move (perhaps backward), but he never gets the chance to do so. Thus the criticisms of Tori's actions in *tomoe-nage* are less valid. At the onset of *tomoe-nage,* as Tori pushes Uke backward, various opportunities arise for Tori to apply *kari waza;* but Tori ignores them in favor of a large-action *sutemi waza.* Kano's intention here is clearly to demonstrate *hando no kuzushi* (breaking of the opponent's balance) by utilizing Uke's reaction to a diversionary action; this is a very deliberate attempt to set up the *tomoe-nage,* and nothing more. When we investigate Kano's choices of techniques for Nage no Kata, we find they are reasonable and logical within the categories they represent.

---

11. Kano originally included *sukui-nage* as the last technique of the *te waza* category. Abrupt and less virile than Kano wished, it was replaced with *kata-guruma,* which ensures big body actions and graceful control in both the Tori and the Uke roles. It has not been proved that Kano's original design excluded *kari waza,* but it is evident that, if included, they did not remain in the kata for any substantial length of time.

CHAPTER **2**

Outline of Judo Kata

Style is the man himself.
—BUFFON

Kodokan Patterns and Scope

Nine different kata have been established as traditional standards of, and are regularly taught at, the Kodokan. In this book, only the Nage and Katame no Kata are explained in detail, but it is important that you add to your Judo knowledge by having some familiarity with the others. The following list summarizes all the standard Kodokan kata. They have been divided into groups to enable you to better interpret the original purpose, scope, and spirit of each kata.

Free Exercise:
    Nage no Kata (Forms of Throwing)
    Katame no Kata (Forms of Grappling)
Combat:
    Kime no Kata (Classical Forms of Self-Defense)
    Goshin-jutsu (no Kata) (Modern Forms of Self-Defense)
    Goshin-ho (no Kata) (Modern Forms of Women's Self-Defense)
Physical Education:
    Seiryoku Zen'yo Kokumin Taiiku (no Kata) (Forms of National Physical
        Education)
    Ju no Kata (Forms of Flexibility)
Theory:
    Itsutsu no Kata (Forms of Five)
    Koshiki no Kata (Forms of Antiquity)

The groupings do not imply that every kata strictly adheres to the idea that names its group. You will recall from Chapter 1 that all kata are based upon a framework of attack and defense and are further applicable as exercise within the scope of physical education. Yet these groupings do give a hint as to how best to apply each of the kata in modern training programs.

You will note that in the names of some kata, the suffix "no Kata" is not considered necessary. This is indicated by placing the suffix in parentheses.

Non-Kodokan Kata

There is some tendency among practitioners of Kodokan Judo to narrow their thinking concerning kata styles and interpretations. Many think that only Kodokan kata exist or are legitimate; all others are thought to be "wrong" and therefore best avoided. This kind of thinking is definitely in error, and all judoists should realize that while the Kodokan has standardized and systematized its kata to a high degree of perfection, streamlining them over the years, the Kodokan kata are not the only Judo kata. They are, however, perhaps the best known and stand as excellent examples of the dynamics and psychological spirit of Judo. They are the traditional standards and should receive their due recognition and respect, while the just place of others is acknowledged.

Different practices and uses for kata have been established by judoists outside of the Kodokan, though the majority of these versions hinge on the unchanged fundamental Principle of Kodokan Judo. These kata can be referred to as private variation patterns. Included here are those which have been developed by qualified Judo teachers; some of these teachers are Kodokan men. Because these kata have definite qualities and characteristics meaningful within the realm of Judo, they are most certainly worthy of preservation and use. Perhaps the best-known example is the Nage Ura no Kata (known also as the Go-no-Sen no Kata), or "Forms of Counterthrowing," originally designed and developed by the legendary Kyuzo Mifune, a late tenth-*dan* master-teacher of the Kodokan. Other Go-no-Sen no Kata exist, however, and have sound training value; judoists should make every effort to become familiar with them and thereby add to their Judo knowledge. It is not within the scope of this book, however, to deal technically with them.

It is most important for judoists to bear in mind that other aspects of Judo and jujutsu as well as other Japanese combative systems are linked with kata in countless patterns. Kata may be likened to handwriting. There are many types and many standards; it is less a matter of being "right" or "wrong" than a matter of preference when it comes to choosing a style to suit oneself. Equally important, kata is an expression of one's personality, style, capabilities, and limitations. However, when dealing with Kodokan Judo we are primarily concerned with the technical aspects of Kodokan kata, and should center our study on that area. The latitude with which each kata may be performed serves to permit each person to express himself without losing the value of the kata. Yet we are bound by certain technical requirements to ensure meaningful practice of the greatest possible value to the judoist.

CHAPTER **3**

Understanding Kata

Tradition is not a heritage;
it is rather an active principle, a principle
we apply to solve particular problems.
—HERBERT READ

What Is Kata?

Kata is the fire in which Judo was, and is being, forged. It stands as the epitome of the great Principle which underlies Judo. Yet, due to a lack of comprehension of what Judo really is, most students of Judo, and some instructors, regard kata as vague and having only a casual relationship to the Judo of the day. On account of this unawareness, kata has been placed on the margin of Judo knowledge.

The complete meaning of kata cannot be expressed by words alone, for it becomes understandable only through experience with the performance of kata. This matter will be expanded on in Chapter 5; but for the moment it is essential to begin to understand kata through words alone.

Begin your study with the idea that Judo is a system of physical education. This was the founder's idea, and it allows you to interpret kata in various ways as he did. Let us examine the most important of those ways.

◆ KATA IS A DELIBERATE THING
You have seen from its historical genesis (Chapter 1) that kata is a very important part of Judo and that it was deliberately designed by the founder to be the core of Judo. As a supplement to *randori*, kata greatly aided in developing Judo from the level of a crude martial art (jujutsu) to that of a system of physical education. All the original Kodokan Judo instructors were required to be kata experts before Professor Kano would approve them for graduation as instructors. Through kata, additional interest in study and usefulness in

application are established and maintained, as kata permits the safe practice of certain techniques which cannot be practiced safely under the conditions of *randori*. The best examples of these are, of course, the techniques of self-defense, which are much too dangerous to apply except under the controlled conditions of kata. Without kata these valuable techniques, a substantial part of Judo, would wither and eventually die, destroying the self-defense value of Judo in the process.

◆ KATA IS A SYMBOL

Inasmuch as the founder of Judo liberally borrowed from the ideas and techniques of the ancient and later Japanese fighting arts, kata can be regarded as preserving the traditional or classical styles of combat of Japan. This generalization, however, is not completely accurate because the founder modified and redesigned old techniques, even adding new ideas and techniques of his own. In fact, there are some modern kata-like entities, formulated long after the founder's death. Much of what is contained in kata is based directly upon jujutsu and its antecedents, and is preserved, as intended by the founder, as a symbol of the constant elastic strength of Judo. This symbolism is somewhat obscure and is of more importance to the Judo historian and master teacher than to you; therefore you need not trouble yourself unduly about it.

◆ KATA IS A LIVING THING

Though designed and established many years ago, kata is not an anachronism. It has, many times over the years, been reexamined, modified, and improved upon by technical masters of the Kodokan, giving it new life and bringing it into harmony with modern needs and the dictates of the current Judo world. All these modifications and flexions, however, have been made within the all-pervading Principle of Maximum Efficiency. This assures today's judoist that the kata he studies and practices, while being a touch of the old, is also at the same time a touch of the new. The effective time-proved methods ofjudo have been given over to you for study and practice in today's world, but need your continued study and practice so that they may remain alive and be passed on as living things to the generations of judoists which will succeed you. Kata is representative of certain inviolable laws of nature, such as those determining balance, movement, posture, and concentration of forces; thus, kata can be considered truth. Truth cannot be changed. It can only be forgotten—or accepted and applied.

◆ KATA IS THEORY

Within the broad scope of Kodokan Judo kata, and all techniques so formalized, lies a firm basis for the variations and modifications of technique that each judoist may perhaps utilize as an expression of his own individual style. This is possible only because the techniques within each kata are fundamental in nature, and all else in Judo proceeds naturally from them. As fundamental techniques they can be used as building blocks upon which to construct your advanced Judo skills. Think of kata as being related to Judo as grammar is to prose. More will be mentioned about this later in this chapter when you read why kata must be studied and practiced.

◆ KATA IS AN EXHIBITION

This is true only when kata is used for that purpose; it is not the primary one. You will learn more about exhibitionary kata later in this chapter, but for now you should regard kata as a very good method by which to show how Judo works and what its elements are. As you become more expert, you may be called upon to perform kata as an exhibition or at a ceremony. Bear in mind that as you perform, your kata has two aspects. First, you are in part demonstrating what Judo is, and secondly, you are demonstrating your individual skill. To the casual observer kata appears purely exhibitionary in nature, like something performed to entertain. If well done, kata looks so easy that onlookers find themselves thinking they could almost immediately repeat what they are seeing. If poorly performed, kata is a frightful thing to observe, and leaves the audience not only with a bad impression of kata and Judo in general, but with a low opinion of your skill. To the trained observer, kata must exemplify fundamental representative techniques of Judo, and clearly show the systematic theory of attack and defense as applied through efficient use of mind and body. If you succeed in conveying this information, your skill is admirable. If you do not, it indicates that you must practice more. Kata must never be used only to give a beautiful performance. But correct kata performances will be beautiful in terms of the efficiency and bearing of the performers.

◆ KATA IS BOTH PHYSICAL AND MENTAL

Kodokan kata are the formal techniques which demonstrate a basic style and method of Judo performance. They are also the conveyers of a spirit which reflects the Principle of Maximum Efficiency. Kata is therefore not to be considered solely a physical performance, for it is the spirit of the performance which houses the essence of all kata. Trainees must be in the correct mental state for effective kata practice. If attention is paid only to the mechanics of kata, without a sincere attempt to merge one's identity with the whole of kata spirit, the essence of kata escapes and the entire performance becomes pallid, without truth or meaning. Kata is really a contest with yourself; you work for control of your mind and body in Judo performance. You will learn more about this later in this chapter and in Chapter 5. Finally, you must understand that the spiritual and mental grasp of kata as a whole must accompany detailed knowledge of individual techniques. This prerequisite actually conditions the assimilation of the physical techniques. Of those judoists who believe that it is better to learn the mechanics first and then add the spirit of the performance, it can be said that they will never learn kata properly.

◆ KATA IS PRACTICAL

Kata was designed to be used as a training method or manner of practice through which a solid technical base is given to the judoist. As a supplement to *randori*, kata becomes a prearranged exercise in the performance of selected Judo techniques. Each partner has a specific role which must be executed in harmony with the other so that the kata will achieve its purpose. We will investigate those purposes a little later in this chapter, but at this point it is enough to realize that kata was designed and developed with certain technical points in mind, to develop specific abilities in judoists; kata enables the discovery of technical errors in *randori* and *shiai*. Kata, by setting up certain conditions and situations and exposing the judoist to them repeatedly, trains him to arrive at the necessary state of mind to react properly within the Principle of Maximum Efficiency. Kata is a rigorous discipline, both mental and physical. Kata is cooperation, but not anticipating cooperation. The prearrangement of the techniques, and of the conditions under which they are to be performed, presupposes cooperation by both training partners. However, this cooperation only requires both partners to be at a certain place, in a certain position, at a certain time—nothing more. There must be no excessive cooperation by either partner falsifying the action; anticipation of the technique and aiding it superfluously is never correct kata action. Then, too, we can see how much practical value the founder attributed to the fundamental kata by the way he named them. Professor Kano referred collectively to the Nage and Katame no Kata as Randori no Kata, implying that they were the fundamental techniques of free exercise. Each technique of the Nage and Katame no Kata contains valuable lessons by which *randori* may be improved. A qualified instructor can easily point these lessons out to you, but it is a challenge to discover them for yourself; Chap-

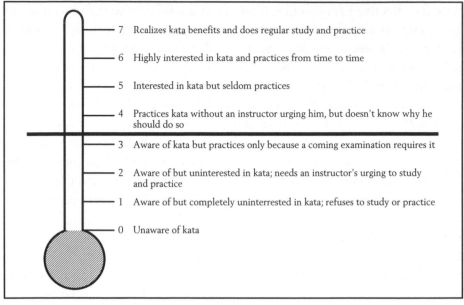

7 Realizes kata benefits and does regular study and practice

6 Highly interested in kata and practices from time to time

5 Interested in kata but seldom practices

4 Practices kata without an instructor urging him, but doesn't know why he should do so

3 Aware of kata but practices only because a coming examination requires it

2 Aware of but uninterested in kata; needs an instructor's urging to study and practice

1 Aware of but completely uninterrested in kata; refuses to study or practice

0 Unaware of kata

The Judo barometer.

ter 10 will guide you in this respect. Kata which is purely exhibitionary in nature, or kata done for form's sake alone, is never substantially useful. Too often the judoist will practice kata simply because he must; his instructor orders him to do so. It is this judoist who would never practice kata on his own initiative and who, when performing it, does so grudgingly. He practices lifelessly and without benefit, but worst of all, he only practices and never really studies kata. To be of practical use and immense benefit, kata must be studied intently and investigated for the valuable lessons it contains. This takes mental effort and requires that the judoists have an inquiring mind.

Why Study and Practice Kata?

Many relatively inexperienced Judo instructors report that when they direct their Judo trainees to begin kata study, they have no confidence in urging the necessity for it. This attitude is found especially outside of Japan, though Judo's native land is sometimes remiss, too. Furthermore, student judoists, if left to themselves, lack motivation for kata study and practice. This lack of interest and, therefore, lack of proper attention to training methods are due almost entirely to inexperience and ignorance about the purposes of kata and its direct value in aiding the wholesome, full development of judoists.

Where do you stand in your opinion of kata? Make an honest analysis of yourself in regard to your motivation for kata study and practice. The "Judo barometer" above can forecast your future "Judo weather"—the final degree of your total Judo skill.

Consult the barometer and find your numerical position. If your reading lies below the heavy black line, your technical level is weak and your future Judo weather will be bad. If your reading lies above the heavy black line, your Judo is on a sound technical footing, and your Judo weather will become better as the reading climbs.

If the barometer has indicated that your kata motivation is weak, you should want to correct it. To aid your motivation for kata study and practice, consider the following major purposes of kata; at least one of them will be meaningful for you.

Ten chief purposes of kata:

1. To afford a basic training method for Judo
2. To develop representative basic Judo techniques
3. To ensure harmonious technical development and a wide range of Judo techniques
4. To ensure a harmoniously developed body
5. To improve mental control
6. To display the mechanics and spirit of Judo by exhibition
7. To promote the development of the Judo spirit
8. To ensure the development of self-defense principles and values
9. To provide a suitable kind of Judo practice for all
10. To ensure the preservation of the traditional symbolic values of Judo

PURPOSE 1. Kata was primarily intended by Kano to serve as the basic training method for Judo as a whole. In the truest sense, kata is considered the core training method of Judo. This is not to say that kata is the central Judo training method in terms of time allotted to study and practice. But since, through its essential nature, kata alone can best satisfy the requirements of a core study as defined by the criteria of physical education, kata study and practice must take its rightful place. We need only turn to the exact words of Kano to substantiate this:

> Following the principle of physical education we will observe the rule that a moderate exercise should come before a strenuous exercise, as well as a symmetrical exercise before an irregular exercise.

Of the three major basic training methods of Judo (kata, *randori*, and *shiai*), only kata can meet the requirements of moderation and symmetry. In this sense, kata can be considered the core training method for Judo. In modern training methodology, kata can include the normal *uchikomi* method. Chapter 10 elaborates on this idea.

PURPOSE 2. It is axiomatic that to be effective with any given skill, one must understand the nature and function of the component parts of its mechanics. Thus, the judoist cannot be completely effective in Judo unless he understands all of its aspects. Kata is full of representative basic Judo techniques which, when practiced and understood, form the basis for all other Judo skills; kata anticipates solutions to most situations that can arise, by application of Judo techniques. Through proper use of kata, these representative basic techniques may be thoroughly studied, practiced, and learned under ideal conditions. By ideal conditions are meant those circumstances under which kata should be practiced, since they afford the best possible opportunity to study and practice techniques without confusion. Since kata dictates cooperation in a prearranged manner, the performers have the best chance to concentrate fully on what they are doing, and have a predetermined time in which to react and perform their roles without any distractions. None of the circumstances under which *randori* is practiced guarantees such opportunities to judoists, and therefore basic learning of a technique can better be achieved through the use of kata. On the other hand, Judo training based only on kata can never lead to full Judo maturity. There must be sufficient practice of *randori* for judoists to be able to apply basic knowledge and skills in a free fashion. This is discussed further in Chapter 10.

PURPOSE 3. The harmonious development of Judo techniques cannot be ensured through overemphasis on *randori. Randori,* as a basic major training method of Judo, can lead to the harmonious technical development of Judo techniques, but judoists are prone to use it only in the narrow way which centers their practice solely around their best or pet technique, or, at best, a few techniques related to their pet technique. The common training weakness of almost exclusive practice of only right- or left-hand techniques results in a lack of development of techniques on the other side. A one-sided or "sugar-sided" technique, once firmly established, can only be extended to the other side through unremitting energy and application, and even then not without great difficulty. Kata practice allows one to study under ideal conditions and therefore encourages a judoist to experiment and broaden his skills over a wide range of techniques on both sides.

Kata ensures that the whole range of Judo techniques will be covered in depth, and not solely a few contest techniques. Techniques which have been developed only for *randori* and *shiai* are usually narrow in scope, superficial and shallow in motivation and purpose. Important as they may be within their limited spheres, they constitute but a small part of Judo, and the judoist who possesses only such techniques is not truly well rounded. His active Judo life and usefulness to other judoists is quite limited. Think of your Judo knowledge and skills as a tree. At all stages of its growth, the "Judo tree" below must be planted in a soil which permits adequate growth. Your training spirit is this soil. Given a good start by strong and continued motivation for training, this tree sprouts from its tap root (kata) and auxiliary roots *(randori)*. Soon the development of trunk, branches, and foliage takes place. These represent your Judo skills and techniques. They are dependent upon the soil (training spirit) and strong roots *(kata and randori)*. Cut off a limb and do what you will with it. Use it as decoration to satisfy yourself or others (win awards, win contests), and the foliage and branches (your techniques) will soon wither and die. Those techniques, so isolated from their root source of life (kata and *randori*), are technically dead the moment you make the cut, even though they appear to be alive. Their life is just temporary and cannot be prolonged. Furthermore, if one develops a tree without a tap root (kata) by using the auxiliary roots *(randori)*, a tree will grow, but it can never have the sturdy

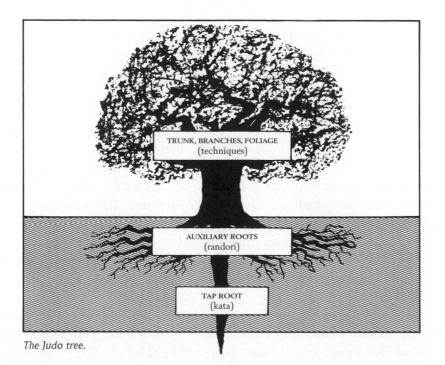

The Judo tree.

rooting and potential grandeur of development that belongs to a tree with a full root system; it will always be scrubby. Likewise, the true and full Judo development of a judoist cannot be attained without thorough knowledge of, and ability in, kata.

PURPOSE 4. The regular practice of kata ensures a harmoniously developed body and fulfills the vital purpose intended by the founder, who purposely designed Judo to meet the requirements of a sound system of physical education. Judo without kata cannot fulfill those requirements. A full discussion of this matter is beyond the scope of this book and is not necessary for your study of kata at this time. However, you should think about this point in relation to the discussion of *randori* under Purpose 3. You will readily notice that the restricted manner in which *randori* is usually practiced can lead to inadequate stimulation of some muscles and thus result in disproportionate development of the body. Proper physical education must permit and stimulate harmonious body development. Kata was designed to bridge the gap between adequate and inadequate exercise; it provides a sounder foundation and wider area of practice than the jujutsu systems. Thus, through kata as designed by Kano, Judo was brought into tune with modern society and its ideas of and need for physical education.

PURPOSE 5. Kata also serves to heighten mental control. Through the thorough study and practice of formal techniques, oriented so as to be of practical use, the judoist is able to gain confidence in meeting a wide variety of imposed situations; confidence will generate self-control. Too often kata is thought to be nothing more than a stiff exercise in etiquette, a formality with little evidence of individual imagination or original thought. Yet even the most anti-kata judoists will not deny that there is a beauty of movement displayed by the control of power in the effortless style of the kata expert, which belies the fact that kata is a mental and physical performance much harder to learn than the less precise and harsher movements of *randori*. It is difficult to present a physical explanation of kata and to point out its practical applications. But it is even more difficult to explain kata in terms of its spirit and the mental processes involved; such discussions border on the realms of psychology and philosophy. However, a brief introduction to such aspects is important for a better understanding of kata.

We have seen that the practice, of kata imposes a wider range of situations on the performers than does either *randori* or *shiai*. The performers must, therefore, develop specific reflexes to meet the challenges of these situations.

Certain other mental processes, such as the display of proper spirit *(kiai)*, judgment of engagement distance *(ma-ai)*, performance of appropriate action *(rial)*, and establishment of a special kind of alertness by which to dominate the opponent (*zanshin*), must accompany these reflexes. Mere physical reaction to an imposed situation, governed by application of Judo techniques in a conscious fashion, is a mechanical process similar to everyday thinking. A judoist applying such a mechanical process to his Judo operates somewhat like this: My opponent is doing such-and-such, and so I will do such-and-such. Only when the judoist can dispense with this mechanical process will he be practicing correct Judo.

Kata is a primary method by which a judoist can be trained to do Judo without knowing that he is performing a specific action. When he does Judo in this "unconscious" fashion, he is an expert. Such a level of expert skill makes use of a mental circuit and a process based on a conditioned reflex; mechanical thought is not relied on since there is not time enough to think about what is to be done. Kata is the tuning mechanism for the mind. It trains the mind to operate in "faster than thought" fashion. If one wishes to be a master of Judo, mere technical knowledge is not sufficient, nor is the ability to mechanically apply techniques. It is necessary to transcend technique so that the art becomes an "artless art," a product of the unconscious mind.

Perhaps an analogy will make all this a bit clearer. Consider, for example, a person who decides to learn to type. At the start he cannot type. He begins to acquire technical skill by practicing and learning certain prearranged exercises (a typewriter kata, if you will) to become familiar with the keyboard. He continues practicing for some time and eventually attains a limited knowledge of typing. But we cannot say that he really knows how to type; nor can we honestly say that he *cannot* type. In further practice new prearranged exercises are used (new typewriter kata), and these gradually give way to the typing of actual words and phrases, and, finally, to sentences also typed in a prearranged manner. With more practice, the typist is able to use the whole keyboard and needs only an occasional glance at the keys to ensure accuracy. We can now say that he knows how to type and that he is normally skillful, but he is still *conscious* of the keyboard, as his occasional glances at it indicate. With further practice he manages to type skillfully *without* conscious effort and without the need to look at the keyboard. He types because he has "forgotten" the positions of the keys, as shown by the difficulty he has in verbally identifying the position of each key (as a beginner he once knew those positions clearly from memory). He has transcended technique and we can say that he has forgotten to think about typing, but we cannot say that he cannot type. He types as an artless art. He has mastered his art.

PURPOSE 6. Kata is exhibitionary only inasmuch as it demonstrates the mechanics and spirit of Judo. Even when it is used to display Judo, kata must
never lose its more practical values. Though an exhibition of kata may carry
with it a note of entertainment for the audience, kata is in fact a medium by
which the audience may be informed about Judo. The members of the audience see Judo in action and this stimulates their desire to learn more about
it. A running commentary by a qualified judoist will aid them in understanding what is taking place. The performers, for their part, should be training
themselves and not simply entertaining the audience.

PURPOSE 7. Kata helps to preserve the true spirit of Judo for posterity. Every
movement of kata and the very spirit of performance are based upon the
underlying Principle of Judo: making the best use of mental and physical
energies directed to a purpose or aim. Kata is thus based on a solid foundation of logical body dynamics. For the judoist, kata becomes the springboard
for the expression of the Judo spirit, which is one of cooperation, give and
take, and mutual concession. Sufficient kata study and practice result in a
transfer of this spirit to the judoist's very personality. Kata is a means by
which the judoist's spirit is forged and tempered to a more mature and socially acceptable level.

PURPOSE 8. The theory of attack and defense in self-defense situations forms
the basis for the psychology, philosophy, and mechanics of Judo. The practice
of *randori* and *shiai*, in spite of the regulations which govern their functions,
lacks safety features, which makes the thorough and realistic practice of
self-defense impractical. Only through kata are the intended self-defense
values of Judo developed and maintained. Kata is a self-contained, responsive
method of self-defense which tempers combative ardor. It seeks not to provoke attack, but to avoid attack; it allows the judoist to face an unavoidable
attack with confidence. Through application of the Judo Principle, kata
demonstrates the correct manner of meeting an attack and of dominating an
insistent attacker. If kata practice is neglected, almost all the practical self-defense values of Judo will be laid aside. Judo itself will suffer a narrowing
influence and kata will eventually be forgotten.

PURPOSE 9. Judo is based on flexibility of mind and body. Its core entity, kata,
reflects this duality of flexibility inasmuch as it is designed to allow those

who, though poor in health, of advanced age, or lacking access to training facilities, wish to continue their study and practice. The physical demands of kata are less than those imposed by *randori*, and therefore kata allows judoists to practice over a protracted period without undue fatigue. Kata is an ideal way for injured or older persons to continue healthful activity. In addition, it may be practiced outside the *dojo* and without any special costume. It may even be beneficial when practiced without a training partner.

PURPOSE 10. The founder, out of respect for his former teachers and their styles of jujutsu, built a monument to them in the form of Kodokan Judo kata. As you already know from the historical discussion in Chapter 1, Judo drew many of its features from jujutsu. As a just tribute to Judo's roots, Kano made kata a symbol of tradition, a cornerstone of the "Judo building." For Orientals, formulas of respect for tradition are familiar, but for most Westerners, there is a strong tendency to forget tradition or to neglect it. It is perhaps best for the Westerner to think of form as the guardian of past or traditional substance; kata is thus a symbol of unchanging truth. Respect for form shows a sincere state of mind and makes possible correct study of Judo; the Judo champions and great teachers of Judo all manifest the spiritual and educative values of Judo.

Limitations of Kata

This book, or any other for that matter, would not be playing fair if it were to leave you with the impression that kata is by itself the most important thing you can learn when you study Judo. So far, this text has presented the positive arguments in favor of kata, yet you should know its limitations.

Judo involves study of mental and physical balance, which depend upon a well-adjusted relationship between component parts. Kata, as one of these components, must be performed in a technically correct manner if it is to be of any value for the judoist. Kata must be considered a complement to the other major Judo training methods, *randori* and *shiai*, and all three should be developed equally throughout the training years of the judoist. It can be said of kata that its form and practice offer only hints for the full development of the judoist; much depends upon the methods of utilization if such development is to be realized at all. The utilization of kata in training is discussed in Chapter 10.

Kata, when compared to *randori*, is often criticized as being a less effective method for obtaining sound mental development. Whereas kata, which provides numerous situations and responses which are applicable to *randori*, has more value as pure physical education than *randori*, it nevertheless fails to heighten the excitement of the judoist to the degree of *randori*. The study and practice of *randori* involves a mental and physical relationship between the participants that kata cannot achieve. Each participant is competing with the other, and does not know what the other will do. Each must, therefore, be prepared to take quick decisions and prompt actions to meet any sudden emergency. Each must be alert in order to detect the weak points of his opponent and to launch an attack or counterattack of his own. Through *randori*, an attitude of mind is developed that enables the possessor to be earnest, sincere, thoughtful, cautious, and deliberate in his actions. If enough *randori* has been experienced, this attitude becomes part of the judoist's everyday life. This criticism of kata, though substantially valid, is somewhat blunted by the fact that kata is intended to be an individual affair, that is, a competition against oneself. *Randori* (or *shiai*), on the other hand, features competition with an opponent. Then, too, if kata is practiced along the lines intended by the founder, and as described in this book, the criticism is still further weakened.

Kata feebly presented and based on sketchy knowledge will produce little or no benefit for the judoist. The judoist, therefore, especially if competent instructors are not available, must rely upon the written word. There are few books available that deal with the Randori no Kata, especially authoritatively written and detailed books in the English language. Judoists will find that this textbook has been prepared with the objective of being as complete as possible. While based on the standard modern interpretation of Judo kata of the Kodokan, as approved by the All-Japan Judo Federation, the description of kata in this book may nevertheless vary in details with Japanese publications. Some of these differences are due to the fact that the Japanese publications are incomplete and lack descriptions of the practical applications of kata. The authors of this book have attempted to recapture the traditional essence of Judo kata by including much of the technical data found in classical Japanese works on Judo kata. Unfortunately, most of these sources are now out of print. Discerning judoists are urged to make use of two fine works by the British master judoist Trevor P. Leggett, which are translations of the modern Kodokan kata standards combined with notes translated from the Japanese classics and other vital sources.[1] This text, together with these two books, will remove the technical limitations that are usually present in Randori no Kata study and practice.

---

1. Leggett, T. P., *The Demonstration of Throws* and *The Demonstration of Holds* (London: W. Foulsham & Company Ltd., 1963).

CHAPTER 4

Famous Japanese Judoists on Kata

When we look back in later life and we think of these dry,
dull lessons we had to learn, then only can we understand,
how each task which then had seemed so trivial and
meaningless had its own share in opening our minds,
in training our memory, in fitting us for the great struggle of life,
which lay before us.

—F. H. LEE

Introduction

An untrained person can make a few crude attempts to draw a picture, using line and shading; even a baby can achieve some semblance of a drawing. But it takes a trained person, one with a wide variety of experience, to draw a really good picture, a product of line and balance. So it is with Judo. Take a close look at all the judoists you know or have heard or read about, no matter what their experience and competence, on a worldwide basis. You will find one thing to be true. Those who are highly skilled in Judo technique and mature in the application of its Principle to daily living, those who are famous internationally, really know kata. Of course kata alone has not made them what they are; they are what they are because of their dedication to balanced Judo training.

Kata, used as a training method, has played an important part in their study and practice of Judo. It is interesting to note that they did not first become champions and later learn kata. Their technical skills developed naturally, and kata was never external to their training programs. On the other hand, those judoists who are not highly skilled or not well known can be shown to be deficient in kata ability. Keep in mind that the virility of your

Judo depends on technical depth. This is not necessarily measured in terms of contest skill, but in ability to demonstrate and understand the full range of Judo subjects. It is a sure sign of inexperience when a judoist fails to demonstrate such technical depth; an inexperienced judoist also usually declares that kata has no bearing on the development of Judo technique.

To better judge whether or not serious study and practice of kata is worthy of your time and effort, let the following world-famous Japanese judoists tell you what kata means to them. (Their ranks are given as of the publication of this book.)

High-Ranking Kodokan Teachers

HIKOICHI AIDA, 9th Dan: In retrospect I can say that great changes have been made in the interpretation and use of kata for Judo training over the years, that is, from the days of my youth up till the present day. Whereas in my time there was a harmonious balance of training components, in which kata was given a prominent position, today an overemphasis on the contest masks this fundamental training method. In my time, it was technique plus contest results and not solely contest points which determined promotion in Judo rank. I can well recall when my status as vice-captain of my university team gave me sufficient contest points for advancement, but in Kano Shihan's opinion I was not yet sufficiently mature to be promoted to fourth *dan*. I had studied kata assiduously during all my early training days, concentrating on the Nage and Katame no Kata. At one Kagami-biraki ceremony, as a second *dan*, I demonstrated the Kime no Kata. Not until I was proficient with Ju no Kata did Kano Shihan see fit to promote me to fourth *dan*. All instructors of Kodokan had to master these kata prior to being graduated as instructors. The most important things about kata today, I believe, include the understanding that it is a valuable training method when correctly used. It is essential to practice kata so that *taisabaki* and *kuzushi* blend as one movement, rather than letting them appear to be separate. Kata must provide the chance for one to perform in passive and active roles in uninterrupted action; we "feel," "grip," "yield," and "resist," all in proportion to the execution of honestly executed technique. Kata must not give a false portrayal of Judo mechanics.

SUMIYUKI KOTANI, 9th Dan: The formal techniques are fundamental in Judo, and all other Judo techniques are only modifications of these. It is impossible to understand the essentials of Nage no Kata unless it is studied and practiced in accordance with the Principle of Judo and its application to disturbing an opponent's balance. The Katame no Kata can be effectively studied and practiced only in accordance with the Principle of Judo; the whole opponent, not just some isolated part, must be controlled. These two kata are basic and therefore essential for all judoists who aspire to become expert.

SEIICHI SHIRAI, 9th Dan: Though I have over 40 years of kata experience, it is only in the past two decades that I have made an intensive, almost full-time study of kata. I began serious kata study, however, when I was a third *dan* and practiced faithfully about four hours per week. I consider kata an essential part of Judo, one through which a judoist can come to understand each and every technique of throwing (not just the 15 techniques in Nage no Kata) and every technique of grappling (not just the 15 techniques in Katame no Kata). Kata certainly is a way of developing swift reactions [nerve-and-muscle synergy]. Kata allows a judoist to gain confidence in his skill and permits him to bring his full power and skill to *randori* and *shiai*. It is a mistake to concentrate only on throwing to the exclusion of grappling, or the opposite; through kata the connection between the two can be achieved. Progress in *renraku-henka waza* is necessary, and aspects almost neglected today are the connections between *tachi* and *ne waza*, and between *nage* and *katame waza*. I believe that the *ashi-garami* of Katame no Kata should remain an element of this kata, as it exemplifies the transition from *tachi* to *ne waza*, and it should serve to remind thinking judoists of our present-day deficiency. The practice of kata develops better-balanced judoists than is possible without it.

MASAMITSU KINEBUCHI, 8th Dan: I studied kata with the late master Kawakami, and I have almost 50 years of experience. I began serious study of kata as a second *dan*, practicing an hour each day. As I gained some knowledge of and skill with kata, I cut my practice to about one or two hours per week, a schedule which I still keep to this day. Many judoists concentrate on practice only for *shiai*, but kata practice is absolutely necessary if one wishes to become strong and to make progress, and if one expects to achieve all-around Judo skill. I believe that unless one knows the correct form of the techniques, one cannot win consistently in contest. All the skilled contest judoists I know are expert in kata. Through kata you learn to handle many techniques freely, far more than you would in the practice of *randori*. Thus one can develop the balanced body so desired by all. A body which is well developed and proportionately balanced in musculature is an asset and one important goal of physical education. Judo is physical education. Kata is also necessary to understand and skillfully perform the correct use of power in *rial, kuzushi, tsukuri*, and *kake*. The basis of kata practice is to let the student learn to attack the opponent freely with a wide variety of skills. Uke, of course, learns how to manage his body correctly, and how to adapt himself to Tori's actions. Kata should be taught to *kyu*-rank judoists who want to become *yudansha*. I teach all techniques, first analyzing them in kata style, by emphasizing *kuzushi*, *tsukuri*, and *kake*; then I teach how to apply them in various forms suitable for each student.

Champions, Famous Coaches, Instructors

YOSHIHIKO YOSHIMATSU, 8th Dan; All-Japan Judo Champion, 1952, 1953, 1955: When I was young, kata held little real importance for me. I began Nage no Kata when I was 16 years of age, just prior to being examined for first *dan*. I began to study Katame no Kata when I was about to be examined for third *dan*, at the age of 18. I was required, against my inclinations, to spend about one and a half hours per week exclusively on kata practice, usually each Wednesday. I now realize that kata is essential for all judoists who hope to understand the importance of *riai*, *kuzushi*, *tsukuri*, and *kake*, and *taisabaki* no less. I take it for granted that kata is the basis of Judo. As in the case of a good actor playing on the stage, prearranged practice techniques become a real part of your freedom of expression. Judoists come to understand Judo theoretically through kata practice; there is no thorough understanding without practicing kata. But I think it would be better to include techniques such as *osoto-gari* and *ouchi-gari* and the like, as they are highly efficient contest techniques which could be still further improved by kata study. Skilled instructors should reconsider kata training values and perhaps make new kata for new purposes. Kata is excellent for beginners, who may perfect their *ukemi* through being thrown by a skillful Tori.

YASUICHI MATSUMOTO, 8th Dan; All-Japan Judo Champion, 1948; Japanese Olympic Judo Team Coach, 1964; Japanese World Judo Championship Coach, 1965: Without a doubt kata is important for the development of a judoist. Without sufficient kata practice his full potential cannot be realized. I began Nage no Kata study just prior to being examined for first *dan*, and I have continued my practice ever since. It is perhaps due to this kata that I became fascinated by *harai-goshi*, a technique which I have used in contest with good effect. As for Katame no Kata, I am sure that there can be no real understanding of grappling without a thorough study of this kata, especially the methods of holding. Today, as an instructor, I insist upon kata study for all of my trainees, and find it particularly good as a "cooling down" exercise in the course of a day's training.

MAHIKO KIMURA, 8th Dan; All-Japan Judo Championship Co-holder, 1949: Kata, to be of training value, must be realistic. I began Nage no Kata at a young age and could practice all the techniques by the time I was a first *dan*. By continuing my study, it became obvious to me, I could widen my throwing abilities and thus improve my contest proficiency. I paid special attention to *seoi-nage* and *okuri-ashi-harai*. Katame no Kata is a fine source of firsthand technical strength for any judoist who hopes to become proficient in grappling. The emphasis in my training days was on immobilizing an opponent through holding techniques. When this was mastered, choking and armlocks were found easy to apply. As an instructor, I require kata study of all my students—All-Japan University Champions included—but not to the point where it replaces *randori*. I believe that kata must become an important part of all training programs, so that the trainee has the best possible chance to experience the full scope of Judo techniques. Without such serious study, his Judo could become narrowed around one or two favorite techniques, and this would greatly detract from his chances of becoming a champion. A champion is a champion because of his superior qualities. In the contest, it is the champion alone who counts.

TAKAHIKO ISHIKAWA, 8th Dan; All-Japan Judo Championship Co-holder, 1949, 1950: My first introduction to kata came at a late age, after my Judo skill had already developed. I first seriously began kata study around the age of 20, while a college student. My original Judo instructors did not lay much stress on kata training, so I cannot say that my techniques were greatly influenced by the kata method, at least during my younger days. However, no doubt some important improvements in my skills were made through kata practice. Frankly speaking, I think that kata, unless done with a high degree of repetition and regularity when training, has little value for those concerned only with championship performances. It is the repetition of kata that produces benefits, not occasional practice. There is no need to change the traditional kata; in fact, I stand against any move which tends to modify or destroy them. I think that kata must be preserved as a sign of the wholeness and perfection of Judo. Nor am I in favor of creating new kata; for what already exists is sufficient, containing all the basic principles of Judo. Rather, we should practice to seek to apply that which exists. Kata seems to work well for some judoists and not so well for others. In my own case I did not train intensely in its methods until my competitive college days were over, though of course I could do both Nage no Kata and Katame no Kata in a fluent manner.

TEIZO KAWAMURA, 8th Dan; Kodokan *kenshusei* instructor: Since I was about to become a first *dan* I have always studied and practiced kata. For over 25 years I have managed to spend on the average two to three hours per week on kata. I believe that Judo training should include about 20 to 30 percent kata practice as compared to 70 to 80 percent *randori*. My preference has always been for right-hand techniques, but through kata I learned to bring off left-hand techniques. It is important to any serious-minded judoist to learn techniques on both the right and left sides. Kata is also the best way to learn the *rial* of throwing techniques. Kata is best taught to those judoists who will *becomeyudan-sha*; they should begin their study at the middle [third] *kyu* rank. We may have to reconsider the present kata structure for future Judo progress, building new kata as necessary. Kata is essential for all judoists who will become teachers.

TOSHIRO DAIGO, 8 th Dan; All-Japan Judo Champion, 1951, 1954: My study and practice of kata began with the Nage no Kata at the age of 15; therefore I confine my comments to that kata. It was an essential item in my training for third *dan*, a rank which I achieved at the age of 18. Nage no Kata continued to be an important training method for me while I was developing my throwing skills for the grades of fifth and sixth *dan*. Since maturing, I have used kata to perfect my throws for contest and for various teaching and coaching assignments. Most important, I think, is the proper use of kata. It must be practiced side by side with *randori*, and not treated as a separate and strange item; this is especially true for young judoists who are attempting to develop an all-around technique. By practice of *randori* a judoist usually develops only his *tokui waza* [pet technique]. I think kata gives a judoist an excellent chance for strengthening his attacking power by gaining skills for throwing, on both sides, and for extending his ability through a wide range of techniques. Especially important is the acquiring of *sutemi waza* skills, which are never brought off in *randori* or contest unless they have been well learned through the use of kata. Kata gives us the only good way to achieve *sutemi* skill for contest use. Kata also serves to teach the importance of the *rial*, or proper meeting of the opponent's strength, so that we are best able to apply our techniques. Finally, an instructor must be proficient in kata; without this skill he is not capable of being an effective teacher.

SHOKICHI NATSUI, 8th Dan; World Judo Champion, 1956; All-Japan Judo Champion, 1957: Kata is necessary for learning the correct techniques of throwing and grappling. Especially important are the *taisabaki, kuzushi, tsukuri, kake,* and *riai*. I have always practiced kata, beginning my serious study of Nage no Kata when I was a second *dan*, and my Katame no Kata when I was a third *dan*. The earlier the better for kata training. About two hours a week is sufficient for study and practice, but kata must never be neglected. When I teach I first show the technique in kata style, emphasizing the fundamentals; then I teach the various styles applicable to *randori* and contest.

YOSHIMI OSAWA, 8th Dan; Tokyo Champion, 1952: I have about 20 years' kata experience. Kata study and practice began for me as a *kyu* judoist when I was a student in junior high school. At our school, kata was not emphasized and was left more or less as a secondary practice method. Through kata, however, I learned to make great progress in my techniques. Kata can serve to bring a student into the path of harmonious development of technique. Nage no Kata develops rounded throwing abilities, and Katame no Kata correct form in attacking and defending in grappling situations. Today, emphasis in university Judo is on the contest and kata is being neglected; young judoists have little understanding of kata's beneficialness to training. If Judo is to be interpreted only as "pure sport," we must revitalize kata. For example, the striking by Uke in Nage no Kata is rather useless and the *ashi-garami* in Katame no Kata is meaningless when considering pure sport. There must be some serious consideration of this in the future.

YASUJI SONE, 8th Dan; World and All-Japan Judo Champion, 1958: Kata was forced on me whether I wanted to do it or not. My instructors insisted on my performing it and gradually, as I developed proficiency, I was able to enjoy it. I think that without kata a judoist cannot develop his fullest potential. It is one thing to use a single technique effectively; but without a wide range of skills the chances in contest are less than encouraging. Kata is one important method by which the judoist can develop a wide range of attacks. At Meiji University, all students are required to practice Nage no Kata and Katame no Kata. This school, holder of more national collegiate team championships than any other in Japan, has developed a strong line of judoists, all of whom are capable kata performers. Now, as an instructor, I, too, insist that my students practice kata, and I take special pains to point out the fundamental aspects of each technique in this method.

MASAI KAWANO, 7th Dan; All-Japan Police Judo Champion, 1960: It is said that Judo *tachi waza* and *katame waza* are the wheels of a vehicle, both being essential in developing Judo skill. I have had about 22 years experience in Nage no Kata and about 21 years in Katame no Kata, and I consider them both absolutely essential to the proper development of a judoist. I began Nage no Kata when I was a beginner of *kyu* rank, but did not begin Katame no Kata until I was a first *dan*. I was required to spend about five hours a week on kata, a habit I manage to keep up even today. Through Nage no Kata a judoist gains a sound understanding of *taisabaki, kuzushi*, and *kake*, for a wide variety of throwing techniques, as well as right- and left-hand performances. It offers a judoist a chance to actually feel the Principle of Judo in action and thus easily learn the theoretical divisions in which the throws are categorized [*te, koshi, ashi*, and *sutemi waza*]. All of this speeds up technical progress. Even Uke can learn to perfect his *ukemi* and thus reduce his chance of injury in falling from a wide variety of throws. A judoist learns more than his *tokui waza* by kata and can develop a greater throwing ability for use in contest. My *tokui* is *tsurikomi-goshi* and it is through Nage no Kata that I have learned many things about it. First, it became evident to me that the "pulling arm" was a key feature for unbalancing the opponent, and the control of the shoulder and neck of the opponent had to be achieved with the "assist arm." I have also learned the use of the *age-goshi* [lifting hip] to throw an opponent who is defending against my *tsurikomi-goshi* done in the normal manner by trying to escape by moving to the side, or perhaps trying to counter me with *uchi-mata*. Katame no Kata has taught me the correct form for controlling an opponent on the mat, and how to keep my body in balance while grappling. I require my students to study kata as long as possible, usually after each *randori* session of each day. I emphasize the importance of *riai, kuzushi, tsukuri*, and *kake* and how to use the "pulling arm." In Katame no Kata, I stress to those whom I am teaching the manner of controlling an opponent according to his movements.

AKIRA KAMINAGA, 7th Dan; All-Japan Judo Champion, 1960, 1961, 1964: My kata skill was built up during my university days because my instructors required me to practice Nage no Kata even as a first *dan*. Katame no Kata was practiced after reaching the second *dan* rank. I enjoyed both very much, but it was not until I was selected to be a special member of the *kenshusei* [Kodokan research division] that I realized the true importance of kata. At the Kodokan, members of this group would spend each Saturday practicing both Nage and Katame no Kata for as much as three hours without interruption. I am certain that this kata instruction gave strength to my techniques and brought me a better understanding of Judo.

ISAO INOKUMA, 7th Dan; All-Japan Judo Champion, 1959, 1963; Olympic Heavyweight Judo Champion, 1964; Unlimited and World Judo Champion, 1965, 1966: My kata experience is very shallow because I am quite young, but I began Nage no Kata as a sophomore in high school and Katame no Kata as a junior in college. I averaged about one hour per week at school and an additional two or three hours at the Kodokan as a member of the *kenshusei*. Kata taught me correct form for representative Judo techniques; I applied it to improving my *randori*. The critical aspect of Nage no Kata is, in my opinion, within the *riai*, and, if correctly studied, it can improve every judoist and guarantee his progress. I developed one of my favorite throws, the *kata-guruma*, from my study of Nage no Kata; I have been able to bring this technique off against strong opponents in contest. My *tokui waza are te waza*, which the mechanics of kata clearly revealed to me. The Nage no Kata has no meaning unless Tori really throws Uke, and Uke does not jump for him but concentrates instead on his *ukemi* form. My Katame no Kata study enabled me to develop my *tokui* of *yoko-shiho-gatame*; I used this with continual success in contests.

YUSHINORI TAKEUCHI, 7th Dan; All-Japan Judo Champion, 1962: Kata was a training method for me every day in the *dojo*, and I concentrated on kata for four years during my university days. My impression of kata is that it teaches the correct basis of form for all techniques of throwing and grappling, and it is especially useful for a judoist to help him achieve good *taisabaki*, of either *tachi* or *katame* type. My *tokui waza, tsurikomi-goshi*, was developed and polished for contest application through intensive kata practice.

HIROYUKI HASEGAWA, 7th Dan; All-Japan Heavyweight Judo Champion, 1963: I began kata study earnestly while in college, at 18. I averaged about one period [two hours] per week, but I feel now that this was not enough time to devote to such an important study. I gained additional experience with kata as a member of the Kodokan *kenshusei*. I am able to say that through kata I learned the basis of throwing and grappling and sharpened my techniques. My Judo skill has become rather well rounded, but I am constantly seeking contest applications during my kata study and practice. To my way of thinking the Nage no Kata is especially useful and I have learned *sutemi waza* through such practice. Both *yoko-guruma* and *uki-waza* are efficient techniques in contest, and I use them frequently with success. I achieved my ability with these throws by blending what I learned about them in kata into *nandori* action. My students spend about 15 minutes per day on Nage no Kata, with emphasis on *sutemi waza*, which we adapt for contest use.

SEIJI SAKAGUCHI, 5th Dan; All-Japan Judo Champion, 1965: I began my study of Nage no Kata just prior to reaching first *dan*. Kata was interesting, but due to my great height [6'6"], I was always self-conscious about performing it; it was difficult to get a training partner who fit my size, especially when it was my turn to be Tori. As a student of Meiji University I was also a member of their national championship teams, and I practiced kata at every training session. From this practice I developed my feeling for *harai-goshi* and for holding techniques. I believe that it is absolutely necessary for contestants to study kata, though not all can become expert at it or in contest. Attention must be given to the development of *taisabaki* and the timing of the execution of the throws. In Katame no Kata I believe that the immobilizations through holding techniques are basic and should be stressed when studying kata. The level of a judoist's Judo skill cannot rise without sufficient kata study.

MITSUO MATSUNAGA, 7th Dan; All-Japan Police Judo Champion, 1964; All-Japan Judo Champion, 1966; Unlimited and World Judo Champion, 1967, 1968: My first experience with kata was when I was a first *dan*; both Nage and Katame no Kata were practiced. In my school usually only one period per week was devoted to this study. I was especially interested in the *ashi waza* section of the Nage no Kata and the *shime waza* section of the Katame no Kata. From the Nage no Kata I learned how to move my body correctly in order to take advantage of my opponent's unbalance, and I improved my timing greatly. It is said that my favorite throws, the *uchi-mata* and the *sasae-tsurikomi-ashi*, are effective in contest. I owe much for such strength to a study of kata. Basically I am right-handed, but through kata practice I learned to execute throws on the left side as well. As a police instructor, I now make good use of kata in teaching students, and put all introductory teaching of judo techniques on a kata-first basis. Later, I use varied methods of teaching.

ISAO OKANO, 6th Dan; Olympic Middleweight Judo Champion, 1964; World Middleweight Judo Champion, 1965, 1966; All-Japan Judo Champion, 1967, 1969: Kata training was important in the development of my right- and left-hand *seoi-nage*. From the study of rim in Nage no Kata I have been able to improve my technique. Because of the strictness of my Judo instructors at my university, I had early experience of Nage no Kata. Usually, all students devoted a total of about three hours per week to this study. Katame no Kata was begun later, at about the time I was a second *dan*, and I liked the chance to study grappling techniques, especially the *shime waza*. For those contest judoists who wish to become champions, both of these fundamental kata are essential studies because of the wide range of techniques they employ. When a judoist decides what his *tokui* will be, if it is in the kata he can reap direct benefit by special study of that technique in kata style. If his *tokui* is not in the kata, then the method of kata should be extended to apply to the *tokui*. Now, as an instructor, I am always looking for new ideas to explain techniques, and I use kata as a basic method of expression.

Toshiyuki Murata, 6th Dan; All-Japan Police Judo Champion, 1959-63: My Judo experience included kata when I was a *kyu* judoist; by the time I became a first *dan*, I could perform the Nage no Kata, though not with polished skill. Nage no Kata has taught me the essentials of a wide range of techniques, but I was especially attracted by *harai-goshi*. From the kata study of this throw, I learned the correct *taisabaki*, *kuzushi*, *tsukuri*, and *kake* principles together with the *rial*. I then adapted those teachings to my own particular style, and through contest application learned to perform this technique as a *sutemi waza* by adding a *maki-komi* action. During my early Judo years, I made it a point to practice about two hours of kata weekly, a habit which I still manage to keep up. Katame no Kata contains all the fundamentals for the development of good and efficient grappling. My *tokui* is *kesa-gatame*, and I use all variations of this technique, developing my understanding of them through the application of kata study. Now, as a police Judo instructor, I insist that all my students practice kata without fail and seek new ideas to improve their contest abilities through a better understanding of kata.

Nobuyuki Sato, 6th Dan; World Light-Heavyweight Judo Champion, 1967, 1968: My Judo experience is not much over 20 years, but during this time I have been aware of the necessity for kata study. All of my Judo instructors have been strict about the study of kata, especially the use of Nage no Kata in training. From my study, I have learned the importance of the correct application of the *rial* in making a technique successful. I devote about three hours per week to kata and perhaps most of this time goes into Nage no Kata. However, I am especially interested in grappling, and I can say that through a thorough study of the Katame no Kata my understanding of grappling has improved. Taking the kata pattern as a guide, I have been able to devise unusual ruses which make the standard techniques work in contest. I believe that this kind of progress is needed to make Judo as a whole more effective in contest. My biggest test of kata came at the Kodokan Kagami-biraki [in 1968] when I was called upon to demonstrate my skill with Nage no Kata. It is said that I did well.

TAKESHI MATSUZAKA, 6th Dan; All-Japan Judo Champion, 1968: My reputation lies mainly in being known as a contestant. My effective contest throws are *uchi-mata, tai-otoshi,* and *kouchi-gari.* The study of Nage no Kata has aided the development of the first of these techniques in a direct manner. Through constant practice I was able to understand the mechanics of *kuzushi, tsukuri, kake,* and *ri ai.* The latter two techniques were only indirectly affected by my practice of Nage no Kata in that they do not appear in that kata. I did, however, apply the method of kata to the study of these throws, practicing the fundamental mechanics for each of them until I was proficient enough to attempt the techniques in free exercise. My experience with kata began while I was a student in high school; several periods per week were devoted to the practice of Nage no Kata. Being a naturally right-handed judoist, I found it difficult to attempt techniques on the other side, but through the practice of kata I have been able to improve my left-hand techniques. It probably would be better to begin Katame no Kata study earlier than I did in college, so that the judoist can parallel the development of his throwing techniques with those of grappling.

The Judo education of the Japanese champions from 1969 to 1982 has been largely directed toward winning international competition. A twenty-year study of the influence *oi kata* on Japanese Judo Champions is being conducted by the junior co-author and will be reported on elsewhere upon the completion of the study.

Note: It is greatly to be regretted that Hikoichi Aida, Seiichi Shirai, and Yasuji Sone, whose comments are recorded above, did not live to see the publication of this book.

CHAPTER 5

Kata Fundamentals

Spirit carries the mind and controls the body.

—ISSAI CHOZAN

Certain aspects of the Nage and Katame no Kata are fundamental in nature, and are common to both kata. The special discussion given these aspects of spirit and mechanics in this chapter shows clearly that they are far more than just decoration or "window dressing." Failure to recognize the intrinsic value of these fundamentals as connecting links in the correct practice of kata can lead to the almost complete destruction of kata training values. It is our purpose here to examine these fundamentals carefully as subjects that often require as much study as do the actual techniques of throwing and grappling.

Theoretical and Spiritual Facets

♦ **ROLES**

Traditionally, the roles of the training partners who perform kata have been designated as *tori*, the "taker," and *uke*, the "receiver." There is no need to change these designations, but you must have no doubt about the requirements of each of the roles. Various English equivalents have been suggested to convey the meaning of each. Among these are, for *tori*: thrower, defender, victor; for *uke*: attacker, opponent, victim. While the words "thrower" for *tori* and "opponent" for *uke* are useful, some of the other terms can cause confusion through ambiguity. The roles of "defender" or "attacker" are frequently, if only temporarily, exchanged between Tori and Uke; much of the time Tori can even be considered to be the intended "victim" of Uke's actions. Thus it is manifestly better to use the traditional terms "taker" for *tori*, and "receiver" for *uke*. The following memory aid may prove useful:

Tori is the taker; that is, he takes his partner into a throwing or grappling technique. Notice that the Japanese word *tori* and its English equivalent, "taker," both begin with the letter *t*.

Uke is the receiver; that is, he receives the throwing or grappling techniques performed by his partner. Notice that Uke performs *ukemi*, or comes "under" Tori in a general sense, and that the Japanese word *uke*, and the words which describe Uke's final action or result, begin with the letter *u*. Never make the mistake of saying *uki* (*u* and *ki* as is *cookie*), which has an entirely different meaning, for *uke* (*ke* as in *kettle*).

◆ SPIRIT

A correct kata performance cannot be ensured by technically correct mechanical body actions alone. It is the mental attitudes of the persons performing kata that establish the *kiai* or "union of spirit," which constitutes the true essence of kata. *Kiai* is not well understood by Westerners; you may even think of it only as the shout that is emitted by a judoist when he executes a technique. This is an extremely narrow meaning. There is no single word in the English language which is precise enough to explain what *kiai* is. But for your purposes you may think of it as an aura of controllable, plastic nervous energy that can be made to "flow" physically, as it is perceived by the mind. It is essential that you witness *kiai* as generated by an expert kata instructor so that you may come to understand the spirit of kata. But giving some fine points about spirit here will substantially aid you to gain this end.

First of all, regardless of whether your role is Tori or Uke, your individual *ki* or "nervous energy" must never fail to be strongly apparent. Preliminary movements, as well as the techniques of throwing and grappling themselves, must be performed with a dignified, precise attitude. Your mental attitude must lead your physical actions, setting the stage for your postures and movements, thus conveying a unified dignity of demeanor. You must clearly exhibit composure, quiet alertness, and confidence. Your *ki* and that of your training partner must unite and blend as *kiai*, which in turn articulates a mental state referred to as *muga-mushin*. *Muga-mushin* has deep psychological implications and is a most difficult thing to define, but something can be shown of its Japanese-culture-bound nature.

Understand *muga-mushin* as an ideal state, one which is attainable only by those with long experience in the study and practice of kata. It is not something which, though necessary to kata performance, is attainable immediately for the judoist who seeks to "turn it on" as he performs. It is actually a major goal made possible by long training in Judo.

The inexperienced kata trainee will find it impossible to fake despite his most strenuous efforts; because it cannot be faked, it is the badge of the true expert and the failing of the less skilled. *Muga-mushin* comes in varying degrees of recognizability and intensity, and matches the level of the judoist's overall Judo attainment. In its highest state, it is a sign of a high level of technical development in Judo (and in the Japanese martial arts as well), and is an expression of the masterly mind.

Muga-mushin literally means "no self, no thought," implying "without mind and without minding." It is a state of indifference which frees one from the thought "I am doing this." Jujutsu technicians often equated it to *fudo-shin*, which translates literally as "immovable mind" and indicates a trained mind which is always at ease and never ruffled or troubled by external occurrences. In the state of *muga-mushin* or *fudo-shin*, the mind can involuntarily dispose of problems imposed upon it; it is the automatic ability of the mind to be alert, perceive, act, and react. It guarantees an always ready mind which can meet any emergency with reasonable assurance of success, and thus it becomes an important development for self-defense and sports considerations.

A less abstract way for judoists to understand *muga-mushin* and *fudo-shin* is, paradoxically, through their seeming opposites. Think of "presence of mind" and "movable mind." Thus the understanding of an ever-prepared mind in a state of relaxed alertness becomes possible; this "flexible" mind is aware of and responsive to external events without fear, anxiety, or concern over success or failure, and easily meets situations imposed upon it. Means to aid the development of *muga-mushin* must rest upon experience, but some directing forces will be discussed in Chapter 10.

Secondly, in your study of the spirit of kata, you should realize that all kata must represent reality. Any tendency to think, before the execution of any technique, that Uke is going to "lose" must be avoided. Uke must be neither a "jumper" nor a "vegetable." His role is vital to keeping the kata from becoming one-sided, a dead and meaningless practice of techniques by Tori against a "dummy" or "punching bag."[1]

Finally, since these kata are expositions of the principles of throwing and grappling and contain elements of attack and defense, there must be a high degree of *zanshin* (alertness) in the performers. Tori must always appear alert to and anticipate the coming attack. Further, after the execution of his technique, especially the throws in Nage no Kata, Tori must exhibit combative

---

1. Uke's importance is borne out historically in that during the early days of Judo it was generally the senior judoist, the more skillful one, who took the part of Uke, since that role is technically more difficult.

ardor, which is continued alertness exhibited by a postural form which would permit speedy action to deal with any continuance of Uke's attack. Uke must be filled with vigor, life, and energy, without giving a "ham" or overdone performance. A lack of alertness on the part of Uke in particular gives rise to feeble actions which provoke a sense of dullness, and fails to show real reason why Tori must make his required responses.

◆ ETIQUETTE

This is closely related to kata spirit, but is given separate attention here because etiquette is a process of preparing the right frame of mind and maintaining it so that kata may flow in its intended manner. Visually identifiable as a system of mechanical movements, etiquette in kata is nevertheless more than just a physical entity. There is in kata etiquette a scientific principle tied to a philosophical and psychological framework which compels the performers to exert themselves mentally. Courtesy and serenity are essentially embodied in this etiquette and permit harmony and refinement in the technical details of the whole performance. Without an understanding of this, kata etiquette is a meaningless formality. There are some instructors and students of Judo who insist too severely on observing minute details of formal etiquette during kata performance, or require the blind following of hard and fast rules without fully knowing what is below the surface.[2]

Kata etiquette can be observed in the preliminaries in "courtesy positions," as well as in the conduct of the techniques. What often is seen as courtesy is in fact an extension of *zan-shin*, which shows that combative ardor must permeate etiquette.

Practical Facets

◆ WEARING THE JUDOGI

The *judogi* worn for kata performances should be of legal size, clean, and in good repair, and must be worn correctly. You have already learned about proper dress during your early training days. For kata, it is well to take some extra precautions against the *judogi's* coming undone during your performance. This is especially important when kata is being demonstrated.

The drawstring which adjusts the waist size of your trousers should be drawn up until the trousers fit snugly but comfortably; the drawstring is then

---

2. Nothing is more contrary to the Judo ideals taught by the founder than to follow rules for the sake of rules alone and thereby reduce kata to a sterile exercise for etiquette training. Such kata is designated by the ideogram 型 (see p. 17, n. 1).

knotted with a bow tied over it to take up the loose ends. The belt must not only be of proper length, but should not be ragged. The usual *randori* style of tying is permissible, but a special style also exists and is considered better.

Wrap the belt around you in normal fashion, but begin with it off-center; hold the short tail end in your right hand. After taking the belt around your body twice, bring the short tail end in front of you, holding it in your left hand. Insert it under the main body of the belt, which is now around your body. Work the belt bands together and tighten the belt to the desired degree. Then pass the tail end held in your left hand over the tail end in your right hand, and tie the usual square knot. A little practice will permit you to make both tails hang evenly (Figs. 1-8). This gives a neat appearance, as the belt looks like a continuous loop running around your body, as opposed to the separated two-band appearance produced by the *randori* method.

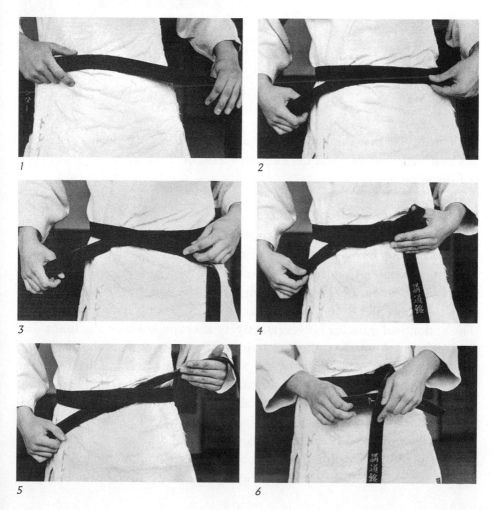

7

8

Tying the belt.

8 (second view)

If you fear that the knot may slip and come undone during your kata performance, you may wet the knot area a bit before tying it. This will keep it from slipping.

◆ BREATHING

The method and rhythm of breathing in kata are identical for both Tori and Uke, and cannot be overemphasized. Breathing must be well down into one's abdominal region. Care must be taken to avoid a heaving rising action in upper chest expansion. Physiologically, of course, breathing is accomplished with the lungs, and so this "abdominal breathing" is only a matter of feeling. The abdominal muscles, however, actively exert pressure on the lungs. The lungs take a passive role as they are activated by the pressure of the diaphragm which, in turn, is acted upon by the abdominal muscles. In inhalation, the abdominal muscles are relaxed as the breath "sinks" to swell that area just as peak capacity is reached. Exhalation is produced by tensing the abdominal muscles and shrinking the abdominal area to push the air out forcefully, but as silently as possible. Breathing is deep, slow, and quiet.

The breathing rhythm must be controlled so that all moments of performance, which require maximum unification of body power, fit the following

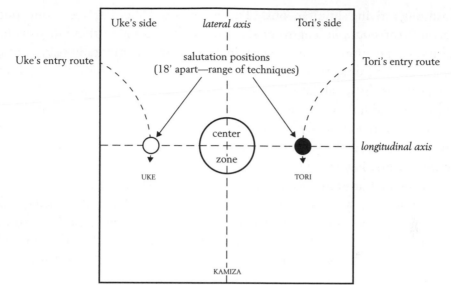

(a) Approaching the starting positions.

relationships. Inhalation commences with movement to distinct positions, maximum inhalation being reached as the position is assumed. Exhalation commences during minor transition movements and execution of techniques, arriving at maximum exhalation at the climax of the technique. Under no circumstances do either Tori or Uke make major exertions in attack or defense while in the process of inhalation.

◆ OPENING REQUIREMENTS

The approach to starting positions for demonstrations of kata is made from outside the performance area. You and your partner must each arrive at a precise spot in the performance area and stand facing the *kamiza*.[3] Tori positions himself on the right, with Uke on the left (as seen from the *kamiza*). Figure (a) shows the standard manner in which you approach your starting position for demonstrations. (In ordinary training sessions, you merely start at this position without preliminary approach to it from outside the mat area.) The routes to the starting positions for demonstrations may be modified if the physical layout of the mat area requires it; both Tori and Uke may come in on the same side and proceed directly to their respective starting

---

3. The performance of all Japanese martial arts and ways, whether for training or for demonstration, is always oriented to a seat or place of honor. Various names identify that position, *kamiza*, *shinden*, and *shomen* being the most commonly used. The first two terms reflect Shinto and Buddhist elements inherent in the martial arts and ways. In this book preference is given to the first term.

positions, arriving simultaneously. Position yourself about 18 feet from your partner (three *tatami* lengths or six widths). You are now standing in your salutation position on the longitudinal axis. Mark it mentally using lines, cracks, designs, or spots on the mat surface. The distance between the kata partners sets the ideal limit for the performance of the techniques; all techniques should fall inside these positions. This becomes a bit difficult when the judoists are extremely tall. In such cases 18 feet is the minimum starting distance between the performers, and is occasionally exceeded if the kata contains throwing actions.

When mat limitations force a decrease in the starting distance, take care to minimize the shrinkage, for it tends to weaken the force of the kata. It is also a good idea, when possible, for you and your partner to position yourselves on a line running between you, a longitudinal axis such as that formed by the edges of the *tatami*. This can serve as a valuable guide to keep your performance from running off track. Top kata experts, however, do not use this guide, as they are proficient enough to perform within the width of a *tatami* used as the longitudinal axis.

◆ OPENING STANDING SALUTATION

This salutation, the *ritsurei*, should be familiar to you from your basic training days.[4] It need not be described in detail here, but it is your first action in

9   10   *Ritsurei.*   10 (second view)

4. The *ritsurei* was originally performed from the *shizenhontai*, that is, with feet apart. You may still see some of the older, high-ranking teachers using this open stance when they perform *ritsurei*; it is a habit ingrained from their youthful training days. You, however, should hold your heels together, with toes naturally pointing slightly outward, as required by the modern standard.

11

kata performance, and is made toward the *kamiza* from your salutation position just after you and your partner arrive there. Tori and Uke perform the *ritsurei* together; it is Uke's obligation not to precede Tori's actions nor to lag noticeably behind them (Figs. 9-11).

◆ OPENING FACING ACTION

Your opening *ritsurei* completed, you and your partner pause momentarily with composure and quiet alertness, then face each other by turning inward (toward each other) in place, in a natural manner. Turn as though you had an axle running through your body from head to feet, and come to rest with your feet together as they were a moment before during the *ritsurei*. Here, too, Uke must not precede Tori's actions but must seek to blend with them. As you turn, do not wobble about or change your relative position. Turn your body as a unit without stiffness. As you face your partner, make visual contact with concentration but without tenseness.

◆ OPENING SITTING POSTURE

Your facing actions completed, you and your partner pause momentarily with composure and quiet alertness, maintaining visual contact, and simultaneously assume the *seiza*, the kneeling-sitting posture with which you became familiar during your basic training days (see Appendix). Notice that when you assume *seiza* or leave it to stand up, your insteps rest on the mat only at the instant of sitting, when your buttocks actually settle down onto your legs. At all other times during the lowering or rising action of your buttocks, your feet rest standing on their toes for stability (Figs. 12-16).

12

13

14

14 (second view)

☒ Wrong.

15

16

16 (second view)

X *Wrong.* **X** *Wrong.*

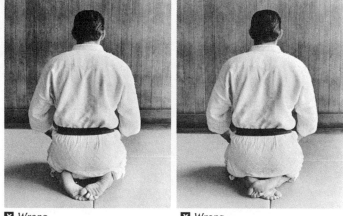

X *Wrong.* **X** *Wrong.*

◆ OPENING SITTING SALUTATION

After arriving at *seiza*, you and your partner pause momentarily with composure and quiet alertness, maintaining visual contact, then perform the *zarei*, the sitting salutation (see Appendix). This etiquette form was also required in your basic training days and this book is no place for a description of its mechanics. However, take care that Uke stays with Tori's movements and does not precede them (Figs. 17-20).

17   17 (second view)   18

19   20   20 (second view)

◆ OPENING RETURN TO STANDING

Upon completion of the *zarei*, both you and your partner pause momentarily in *seiza* with composure and quiet alertness, keeping up visual contact, then simultaneously rise to assume a standing position. This is a reverse application of the lowering action to the sitting posture (see p. 71).

◆ ENGAGMENT POSITION

You and your partner are now standing with your feet together in your respective salutation positions, about 18 feet apart on the longitudinal axis. Take another momentary pause with composure and quiet alertness, maintaining visual contact, then simultaneously with your partner advance one

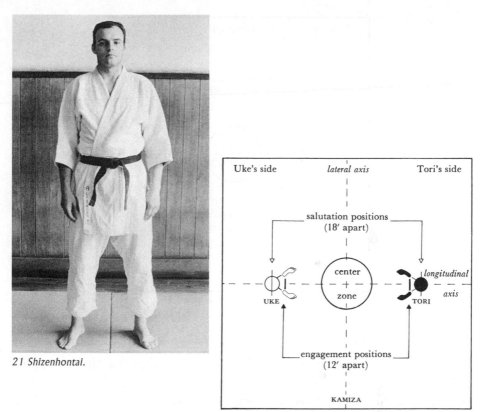

21 Shizenhontai.

(b) Engagement positions.

pace with the left foot, and then the right, putting both feet in line to assume the *shizenhontai* (Fig. 21). The *shizenhontai*, too, is a carry-over from your early days and there is no need to describe it. The step forward, however, is a slightly lengthened and exaggerated one which makes your body motion resemble a wave coming up onto a smooth beach. This action is important to the spirit of the kata and not just a step which "dribbles" you forward; it is a motion which clearly shows good balance, power, and determination in both roles. You and your partner now stand in what is known as the engagement position; it is very important to mark it mentally and remember just where it is. It is distinct and different from the salutation position. It brings Tori and Uke to a position slightly more than 12 feet apart (Fig. b). After this point, the Nage and Katame no Kata differ (see Chapters 8 and 9). Do not confuse this engagement position with the engagement distance used with each technique (see p. 96).

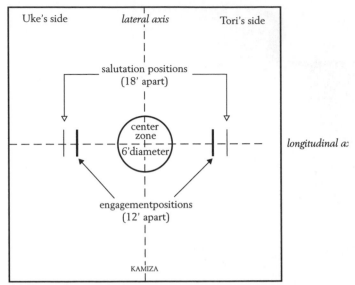

Uke's side   *lateral axis*   Tori's side

salutation positions
(18' apart)

center
zone
6'diameter

longitudinal ax

engagementpositions
(12' apart)

KAMIZA

(c) Kata performance in the center area.

◆ CENTER PERFORMANCE

This aspect often confuses participants but it is essential that those engaging in kata understand what is meant by "center performance." This will be elaborated on in the descriptions of aspects of each kata in Chapters 6 and 7, as well as in the descriptions of actual techniques in Chapters 8 and 9. However, a general discussion of the subject is not out of place here.

The kata area, when kata is performed for demonstration purposes, should be centered on the main portion of the *kamiza* and may be either the actual geometrical center of the mat area or a bit off-center and somewhat nearer to the *kamiza*. The ideal kata area is at least the area of 50 *tatami* (approximately 30' X 30'). In ordinary training, availability of *dojo* space must determine the kata area.

Within the area, the kata must be performed along a longitudinal axis and a lateral axis. The longitudinal axis is bounded by the respective salutation positions of Tori and Uke. The lateral axis bisects the longitudinal axi, and the point of intersection is centered on the *kamiza* (Fig. c).

Preliminary movements and actions preceding the technique's execution may or may not be centered, but the climax of every technique takes place in the center. This "center" refers to a zone, *not* a point. It is an imaginary circle with a 3-foot radius, and is of course centered on the *kamiza*.

In the Katame no Kata, each technique performed is a "leadoff" technique by virtue of being performed only on the right side. No great linear displace-

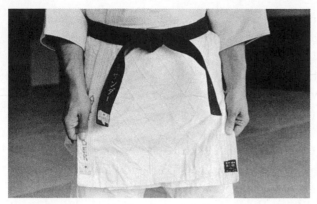

22 Adjusting the judogi

ment is thus required and all techniques are executed within center zone. In the Nage no Kata however, due to there being both right- and left-hand techniques with the attendant linear displacements, the moment of technique execution does not always coincide with the area of completion, and the term "center performance" becomes less easy to understand (see pp. 98, 147).

"Center performance" in kata suggests symmetry, but it is not precisely so. Partners can only strive to achieve as much symmetry as possible. This is required not for the sake of form alone, but as an additional technical hurdle to test the accuracy of judgment and action of the performers. Furthermore, the physical limits of the *dojo* or demonstration area may affect symmetry.

◆ SOUNDS AND GESTURES

These kata are performed as silently as possible and with a poker-faced expression. Attempts to liven up the performance with loud sounds, even in *kiai* fashion, or facial grimaces, are not necessary.

◆ ADJUSTING THE JUDOGI

The excessive disarrangement of *the judogi* in kata practice is a sure sign of less than expert skill. Only the most skillful of judoists can achieve a kata performance with a minimum of disarrangement. At that level of performance, Tori demonstrates a minimum use of energy (the control factor), and Uke confidence and relaxation.

Some disarrangement is bound to occur during a kata performance. The rule is that there must be a minimum of costume adjustment in spite of this disarrangement. If the *judogi* is properly worn, less adjustment will be needed.

You are permitted to make adjustments to your *judogi*, provided that they are minor and unobtrusive, at any time. If possible, however, avoid the adjustment actions while performing within any one category; adjust only after finishing the category,[5] and then in this very simple, special manner. Upon completing the last technique in each category (details are described in Chapters 8 and 9), simply grasp the tail corners of your jacket, inner tail in the fingers of your left hand and outer tail in the fingers of your right hand. Grasping firmly, pull downward once or twice. This must be done with the least possible arm action (Fig. 22).

◆ CLOSING DISENGAGMENT
After completing all of the techniques of either kata, you and your partner are required to move to a closing position (the precise movements are described in Chapters 8 and 9), and stand facing each other in *shizenhontai*. You stand at the same spot as at the opening of the kata, that is, at your engagement position. It is now your disengagement position.

◆ CLOSING SALUTATION POSITION
After a momentary pause at the engagement position with composure and quiet alertness, still maintaining visual contact, you and your partner move backward simultaneously to the precise positions you held at the opening of the kata, that is, your salutation positions. Do this by retreating one pace, beginning with your right foot and then the left, bringing your heels together, toes naturally pointing slightly outward. This is your closing salutation position.

◆ CLOSING SITTING POSTURE, SITTING SALUTATION, AND RETURN TO STANDING
After a momentary pause showing composure and quiet alertness, with visual contact, you and your partner perform the kneeling-sitting posture (*seiza*) and the sitting salutation (*zarei*), and then return to a standing position just as at the opening of the kata. The actions should be precisely as described on pages 72-74.

◆ CLOSING FACING ACTION
This action, performed simultaneously by you and your kata partner after a momentary pause with composure and quiet alertness, with visual contact, is identical to the facing action which you performed at the opening of the kata (see p. 70), but the direction of your rotation is outward (away from

---

5. Traditionally, no adjustment of the *judogi* was permitted until the end of each category of technique, when partners returned to prescribed positions, pausing to make adjustments before continuing with the kata. Adjustments so made were final and were expected to last through the next category.

your partner), bringing both of you to a standing position facing the *kamiza* once again.

◆ CLOSING STANDING SALUTATION

As you and your partner face the *kamiza*, you both pause momentarily with composure and quiet alertness, but your visual contact with each other is now broken. Then you perform the *ritsurei* simultaneously, without haste. This action is identical to that performed at the opening of the kata (see p. 70). Upon completion, pause once more momentarily with composure and quiet alertness, and then take a few short steps backward while still facing the *kamiza*. Leave the demonstration area without delay by reversing the route you took into the kata area (see p. 69).

CHAPTER **6**

Technical Aspects of Nage No Kata

So that the end of law is not to abolish or restrain,
but is to preserve and enlarge freedom.
—JOHN LOCKE

There are numerous important technical details of Nage no Kata that cannot be clearly presented along with descriptions of how to perform the actual techniques. It is, therefore, the purpose of this chapter to examine these technical aspects, and to categorize them in a manner useful to the judoist. You will find it useful to read Chapters 5 and 8 in connection with the material presented here.

Theoretical Facets

◆ **THE CATEGORIES OF THROWING TECHNIQUES**
This kata takes in 15 model throwing techniques, divided into 5 categories composed of 3 techniques each. The categorization is based on the body dynamics involved in the throwing actions. Each technique is performed in both right- and left- hand applications before proceeding to the next technique; all except *uki-goshi* are executed first on the right (see pp. 180, 452).

NAGE NO KATA (Forms of Throwing)

Tachi waza (standing techniques)
  1. *Te waza* (hand techniques)
     Uki-otoshi (floating drop)
     Seoi-nage (shoulder throw)
     Kata-guruma (shoulder wheel)

2. *Koshi waza* (hip-loin techniques)
   Uki-goshi (floating loin)
   Harai-goshi (sweeping loin)
   Tsurikorni-goshi (lift-pull loin)
3. *Ashi waza* (foot-leg techniques)
   Okuri-ashi-harai (accompanying foot sweep)
   Sasae-tsurikomi-ashi (blocking lift-pull foot)
   Uchi-mata (inner thigh)

Sutemi waza (sacrifice techniques)
  4. *Ma sutemi waza* (back sacrifice techniques)
     Tomoe-nage (whirl throw)
     Ura-nage (rear throw)
     Sumi-gaeshi (corner overturning)
  5. *Toko sutemi waza* (side sacrifice techniques)
     Yoko-gake (side hook)
     Yoko-guruma (side wheel)
     Uki-waza (floating technique)

The names of the categories of throwing as well as those of the actual techniques must be learned in Japanese as that is the international standard.

◆ ATTACK-DEFENSE THEORY

Nage no Kata, as an exposition of the dynamics of throwing, often is not recognized by Judo trainees as a *randori-oriented* training exercise which rests solidly, as intended by its founder, on a foundation of self-defense (see Chapter 1). Without knowing this basic concept and without sound understanding of how it is woven into the theory of the Nage no Kata, it is impossible to derive the fullest training benefits. Not knowing if there is to be an attack, or how and when the attack is to be made, or by whom—that is, how Tori and Uke apply their energies in a synergetic fashion (*riai*) —will increase the chances that training may be misused. Nage no Kata then degenerates from an important exercise in self-defense plus throwing skills, in which Uke really attacks or intends to attack a responding Tori, to a meaningless use of Uke as a "guinea pig" meekly submitting to the actions of Tori, who in turn is just trying to "practice some throws."

One key failure which causes misinterpretation of this kata is the general lack of realization that the Nage no Kata exemplifies both facets of the Principle of Judo, namely, yielding and resisting. By this complete Principle,

Tori either yields to or resists Uke in a certain way to unbalance him, and then throws Uke down by the use of a throwing technique. Uke, by the same Principle, resorts to both yielding to and resisting Tori in prescribed ways.

When to yield and when to resist is precisely prescribed in the founder's technical notes on this kata; but much of this technical clarity has been obscured or lost, and misinterpretations have arisen which lead to variations in Nage no Kata practice from what was originally intended. Much modern-day instruction, and consequently today's study and practice of kata, is conducted on the basis that Tori responds to all of Uke's actions with purely defensive yielding for most techniques of this kata. This gross mistake is easily shown up by turning to the founder's written words:

> By giving way, a contestant may defeat his opponent, and as there are so many instances in Jujutsu [Judo] contests where this principle is applied, the name Jujutsu, the "gentle" or "giving way" art, became the name of the whole art.

> Such is the principle of Ju. But strictly speaking, real Jujutsu is something more. The way of gaining a victory over an opponent by Jujutsu is not confined to gaining victory only by giving way.

Here we have conclusive evidence that the founder did not consider "softness" or "yielding" as the entirety of his Principle; there is still another facet. The founder continues:

> Sometimes an opponent takes hold of one's wrist. How can someone possibly release himself without using strength against his opponent's grip? The same thing can be asked when somebody is seized around his shoulders from behind by an assailant. If thus, the principle of giving way cannot cover all the methods used in Jujutsu contests, is there any principle which really covers the whole field? Yes, there is.... There is one principle which consistently emerges; in any form of attack, to attain our objective we must make the best use of our mental energy and physical strength. This is also true in defense.

Thus, the founder did recognize the necessity of using strength, and included it within the Principle of Judo. The Nage no Kata logically applies this Principle by using strength to resist an opponent where yielding is inappropriate or fails to meet the situation.

Another failure which causes misunderstanding of Nage no Kata is due to the erroneous argument that the theory of attack and defense applies only within the narrow limits of *randori* and its contest applications. Even a superficial glance at Uke's actions show intent otherwise; four clear-cut occasions require Uke to make direct striking attacks at Tori (*seoi-nage, uki-goshi, ura-nage,* and *yoko-guruma*). None of these precise attacks is permissible in *randori,* and judoists who misunderstand the founder's purpose argue that these four techniques are not realistic and should be removed from the kata or so modified as to bring them closer to *randori* practicability. Removal of these techniques is not necessary inasmuch as the techniques, executed as they now stand in this kata, are replete with applications for practical self-defense as well as for contest or *randori*. In the former application, the techniques deal with striking attacks which could occur in self-defense situations; in the latter application, a charging opponent, reaching for his grip, can be dealt with in these manners of throwing.

Still another failure to get the most from the Nage no Kata in training occurs when this kata is taught and practiced on the basis of what can be called a "passive attack" theory. By this theory, Uke actually behaves somewhat inconsistently with the normal circumstances surrounding attack and defense situations. Uke is acknowledged as an "active" attacker only in the 4 cases already mentioned (*seoi-nage, uki-goshi, ura-nage,* and *yoko-guruma*). The remaining 11 techniques of this kata require Uke to operate in a relatively passive attack role.

Uke, upon engagement with Tori in these 11 techniques, merely wants to take either a right or left *shizentai* or modified *jigotai*, as the case may be. This implies that Uke intends only to advance one of his feet about one-half pace, leaving his trailing foot in place, as he grips Tori; he intends no other movement against Tori. It further implies that this is the sum total of his attack: mere stance and gripping of Tori. With no intent or attempt to push or pull Tori upon this initial engagement, the attack is thus at best very weak and less than realistic.

By this passive-attack theory, insofar as these 11 techniques are concerned, the responsibility for action and the attack is switched over to Tori who, upon initial engagement with Uke, takes advantage of Uke's limited movement into *shizentai* or the modified *jigotai* and pulls Uke forward so that Uke must advance his lead foot a full pace, instead of the intended half pace, to preserve balance. Uke must also bring his trailing foot up a half pace to improve his balance.

One exception to this pattern (in form, not principle) comes in the technique of *okuri-ashi-harai*, where Uke stands fast in *shizenhontai* and merely intends to statically grip Tori. Here Tori is required to push-pull Uke to the side preparatory to the throw.

Passive-theory advocates argue that since the techniques of *okuri-ashi-harai, uchi-mata, tomoe-nage, sumi-gaeshi,* and *uki-waza* operate with Uke passive, carried along by Tori's initiation of force after initial gripping, it is reasonable to expect all remaining techniques in which Tori and Uke couple through gripping to operate the same way. The error of this thinking rests in implications of *sen*, the quality of "attack initiative," which is explained on page 85.

The "passive" role of Uke can be interestingly analyzed in six similar techniques of Tori and Uke: *uki-otoshi, kata-guruma, harai-goshi, tsurikomi-goshi, sasae-tsurikomi-ashi*, and *yoko-gake*. In all of these techniques, Uke is coupled onto Tori through gripping and is moving forward as Tori moves backward. The entire matter becomes confusing after the initial stepping and gripping actions. Assuming, as the passive theory does, that Uke merely wishes to adopt *shizentai* on engagement with Tori, with Tori responding by retreating and gripping in *shizentai* to pull Uke a full step, what would be their respective roles through the completion of Tori's throw?

Uke, already being in *shizentai*, obviously cannot initiate a similar second movement, to cause Tori's next response and the next step, without becoming active and therefore violating the theory. To make continued movement, Uke must either remain completely passive (not in accord with his initial movements) and allow Tori to be completely active by pulling Uke into full steps (not in accord with his initial movements), or Uke must turn fully active (contrary to his initial intent and movements) and push Tori backward as Tori switches into a completely passive role (in opposition to his original role).[1]

By the passive theory, Uke's actions are not only inconsistent with the normal circumstances surrounding attack and defense, but further prohibit the formation of a precise pattern of repetitious movement. Because of these factors, as we shall see, the passive theory does not reflect the intent or design of the founder, who wished to show a normally active Uke through an extended pattern of movement in these six techniques.

It is interesting and essential to compare the passive theory with that originally intended by the founder. The difference is somewhat subtle, but is relevant for those judoists who seek kata interpretation in its original form. Again it is necessary to turn to the words of the founder (italics ours):

> It is generally concluded that Jujutsu [Judo] is an art of attack and defense based on the old theory that "softness controls hardness," and that this was the only reasoning employed in Jujutsu contests. If the latter were true, it would imply that Jujutsu techniques were useless unless the opponent attacked first and if this were so it would indeed be a restricted *form of combat*.

In this comment the founder reiterates that Judo is of a combative origin and not a pure sport; the full value of Judo can only be realized when Judo

---

1. In theory, one other possibility can be conceived, by which Tori alternates between active and passive roles, but this idea becomes cumbersome and somewhat absurd when applied in practice. There is no technical evidence to substantiate this possibility.

is studied and practiced as originally intended. We learn also that the founder did not wish Judo to be based on the narrow concept of defensive response made only after an attack is well launched, that is, a *go no sen* or "late initiative" action by Tori. We may surmise that the "passive" concept was not intended to be the sole basis of judo, for obviously if two passive judoists faced each other, each waiting for the other's attack which would in theory never come, *nothing could happen*. The founder continues:

> On the other hand, if we consider how many theories are, in fact, involved in attack and defense, we realize how difficult it is to explain them simply.... It may be said that, interpreting the meaning of Ju in a broad sense, its principle is applicable where one resorts to *a positive feat of attack* at the most appropriate moment.

Here it is quite evident that license to attack is not given solely to either Tori or Uke; either may initiate "a positive feat of attack" when appropriate. The spontaneity intrinsic to attack-defense situations (in combat or sports), and the appropriateness of responses made in such situations, is acknowledged in the founder's use of the expression *hobo-ichi*, which expresses the oneness of an attack and an appropriately active response to that attack. For Kano, an attack and its proper defensive response were instantaneous, harmonious, and active forces for an attacker or defender; that is, an attacker may be a defender, and a defender an attacker. The roles are interchangeable at any time.[2] *Zanshin* makes this possible by allowing *sen*.

Kano recognized three levels of combative initiative (*sen*): (1) *go no sen*, the "late" form of attack initiative, usually characterized as a defensive move or counteraction; (2) *sen*, the attack initiative that is also defensive but launched simultaneously with the aggressor's attack; (3) *sen-sen no sen*, a supraliminal attack initiative, also defensive but appearing to be offensive, through which the aggressor's attack is anticipated and "beaten to the punch" by an appropriate action. A judoist who can execute his techniques with all three forms of attack initiative is a master technician. Judo that contains all three kinds of initiative is a tremendously flexible art, and is therefore applicable to any attack-defense situation. The Nage no Kata, however, clearly utilizes only *go no sen*, and what is debatably quasi-*sen*. Nevertheless, the

---

2. The attack-defense concept is an arbitrary division enabling the layman to analyze and better understand the role of an attacker as contrasted with that of his intended victim. This dichotomy is rejected by combative specialists inasmuch as attack-defense is always a unity (*kobo-ichi*). Kano retained the dichotomy in order to conform to the limits of the nonspecialist's knowledge of combat. In this book, we have retained the dichotomy for similar reasons.

founder ensures an active role for both Tori and Uke by requiring them to utilize the two facets of his Principle—yielding and resisting—as appropriate to the situations prescribed in the Nage no Kata.

The advocates of the passive theory sometimes insist that Kano's recognition of different levels of *sen* actually supports their theory. Taking the techniques analyzed earlier (*uki-otoshi, kata-guruma, harai-goshi, tsuri-komi-goshi, sasae-tsurikomi-ashi,* and *yoko-gake*), they first argue that Uke is permitted to be passive, that is, to merely adopt a grip in *shizentai*; it is Tori who becomes active by stealing the attack initiative from Uke through the power of quasi-*sen*, just as he does in the techniques of *okuri-ashi-harai, uchi-mata, tomoe-nage, sumi-gaeshi,* and *uki-waza*. Uke is active only in the techniques of *seoi-nage, uki-goshi, ura-nage,* and *yoko-guruma*, where Tori utilizes *go no sen* to defeat Uke.

Passive-theory advocates secondly argue that because of Tori's active role in applying quasi-*sen* in the majority of the techniques of this kata, their theory is not in fact passive at all; any passivity assigned to Uke has nothing to do with the theory as his is the minor role. On the other hand, by accepting the converse "active" theory and thus making Uke always active, it is Tori who becomes passive and therefore nothing is really accomplished. "Passivity" is relative passivity and is found in both theories.

But this does not get at what the founder had in mind for the Tori-Uke relationship in Nage no Kata, nor what the active-theory supporters attack in the passive theory. The passive-theory advocates' first argument would require that Uke make one weak attack through his initial gripping and movement into a new posture; thereafter, by Tori's active stepping and pulling or pushing, the movement is continued without maintaining the precise spirit and pattern Uke had established at the onset of the engagement. The founder, however, very definitely designed this kata as a series of repetitious patterns of action, where possible prolonging the final throwing action deliberately so that all mechanics would be visually discernible. Uke is thus given repeated chances to attack Tori and Tori's responses are also repeated. This procedure is not strange when it is recalled that this kata is a training method, and by repetition the judoist learns more effectively than by varied movements. The training method *uchikomi* is an outstanding example of this. Of course in *randori* application this kata's techniques need not depend upon a repeated pattern of movement, though they often do, and may be executed immediately upon contact; but it is not desirable for the purposes of either training or exhibition, both of which require clarity in execution, to bring the action to an instantaneous climax.

The second argument of the passive-theory advocates shows misunderstanding of Tori's character. The founder was firmly against an aggressive use for Judo, insisting always upon the proper moral application of Judo in society.[3] The "appropriate moment" which gives license to attack must, by the founder's socially concerned thinking, be carefully defined to conform to ethical practice. Tori must not be an aggressor no matter how active he is in the kata; rather he responds to attack (in intent or action) in a defensive manner. He thus represents what may be regarded as "good," while an actively attacking Uke portrays "bad."

Tori's role is merely what the founder referred to as an exercise of *riai*, or the correct use of Uke's attack strength in the management of Tori's body as he responds in defense and climaxes his actions by a throwing technique against Uke. In the passive theory, Tori cannot be passive; he must be clearly active as an "aggressor," and thus contradicts the founder's deep concern for the proper application of Judo in a civilized society. In the founder's theory of the Nage no Kata, Tori's role is passive only as one facet of the Principle, when he yields to Uke's active attack by backing up, in seeking to unbalance and throw Uke as a defensive response in the techniques of *uki-otoshi*, *kata-guruma*, *harai-goshi*, *tsurikomi-goshi*, *sasae-tsurikomi-ashi*, and *yoko-gake*.

In the founder's theory, Tori is active, too, in these techniques in that he is launching his own attack in response to provocation by Uke. Therein lies the chief difference between the founder's theory and the passive-attack theory. In the founder's theory, Uke is actively attacking Tori; he is an aggressor. Tori responds and recovers the attack initiative by use of *go no sen*; Tori is active, but not aggressive. In the passive-attack theory, Uke is passive; he is not an aggressor. Tori is not yielding, but activating Uke through a pulling action and applying quasi-*sen* to defeat Uke; Tori is an outright aggressor. These six techniques were designed by the founder to operate by similar methods, with Uke attacking actively and Tori applying the *riai* and recovering the attack initiative by distinct *go no sen*.[4]

---

3. It is documented in the founder's technical notes that he removed all traces of martial aspects (jujutsu in particular) and terminology from Judo; he substituted the idea of ' 'opponent' ' for that of "enemy."

4. We know that the founder designed the *tsurikomi-goshi* to exemplify this group. Kano originally required Uke to lose his active attack initiative as Tori attempted a first throwing technique, but Uke quickly regained it with a successful though momentary stiffening action; Tori then regained the attack initiative by a second, successful throwing action. Tori's first attempt at throwing was clearly not a *tsurikorni-goshi*, but a *koshi-nage* much like *harai-goshi* in nature. We know this from the deliberate high placement of Tori's body and his quick change of hip position to execute the final throw (*tsurikomi-goshi*). The technique was later redesigned to be taken directly, but is *go no sen*.

The techniques of *okuri-ashi-harai*, *uchi-mata*, *tomoe-nage*, *sumi-gaeshi*, and *uki waza* operate under the concept of Tori's utilization of quasi-sen.[5] Passive-theory advocates are guilty of misunderstanding these techniques and often point out that the active theory must fail here. Admittedly it is not easy to portray Uke as active in these techniques, which appear to require Tori, operating as an aggressor, to take the initiative and unbalance a more or less static Uke in preparation for the coming throw. But only when the founder's ideas are forgotten or unknown and Uke is allowed to be passive *in both thought and deed*, that is, when Uke is allowed to merely adopt *shizentai* or modified *jigotai* or just stand in place in *shizenhontai*, without any specific attack in mind, can the active theory fail to apply here.

In these five techniques, by the founder's thinking, Uke is active in that he couples onto Tori by gripping with *intent* to attack, not merely to adopt a stance. Tori defends himself actively, but not as an aggressor, and steals the attack initiative away from Uke before Uke can get into his intended action. The founder made this clear by choosing *sumi-gaeshi* from the *ma sutemi waza* and *uki-waza* from the *yoko sutemi waza*. to exemplify this important concept.

It is essential to understand that both of these *sutemi waza* make use of the second facet of the Principle of Judo, that is, resistance. Both Tori and Uke are active here, but Tori's activity is nonaggressive and comes as a response to Uke's aggression. Uke couples into modified *jigotai* and is attempting to pull Tori forward; Tori meets that pull with resistance, to develop a temporary condition of equilibrium between the bodies, by a pulling action of his own (which is explained further at pp. 244 and 271). Under no circumstances does Uke just take up the modified *jigotai* insipidly or depend upon Tori to hold him up; nor should Tori and Uke lean against each other for mutual support.

It is only in the four striking actions of Uke, in the techniques of *seoi-nage*, *uki-goshi*, *ura-nage*, and *yoko-guruma*, that passive-theory advocates find no variance or argument with the founder's active theory; this is, of course, due to the obviously active and aggressive actions of Uke which cannot be otherwise explained. These techniques operate at a *go no sen* level, with *yoko-guruma* being perhaps the best example of this concept.

The underlying key to the understanding of the founder's theory of the Nage no Kata is found in the mechanics of "push-pull." Uke always operates so as to make, or with intent to make, an attack in each technique of this kata.

---

5. The founder's original kata design had *okuri-ashi-harai* operating as pure *go no sen* and thus joined to the techniques of *uki-otoshi*, *kata-guruma*, *harai-goshi*, *tsurikomi-goshi*, *sasae-tsurikomi-ashi*, and *yoko-gake*. Subsequent redesign brought *okuri-ashi-harai* to the quasi-*sen* status we know today.

Uke is always active and the aggressor in this sense. His action is always either a push or a pull executed, or intended, against Tori. At times Uke makes his initial pushing attack by gripping, colliding with, or striking Tori, or intending to push-pull Tori in couple; at other times Uke actually pulls in couple by gripping Tori, or with intent to pull Tori in couple by gripping. In each case the push-pull relationship is always present. Uke is always active, by action or intent; Tori displays *riai* by yielding or by resisting, following the Principle of Judo, as the case requires.

Still further clarification of the attack and defense roles for Tori and Uke is given in the technical descriptions of each technique in Chapter 8. For now, it should be borne in mind that the very essence of this kata depends upon a clear understanding of the founder's active theory. Whether judoists utilize Nage no Kata as a less meaningful, less vital sequence of motions through the passive theory, or whether they charge their performances with the intended spirit and mechanics through the active theory, will be determined by their understanding of the view of attack and defense upon which this kata is founded.

Practical Facets

◆ POSTURES

The postures used by Tori and Uke for the practice of this kata are of two basic types. The first, the natural posture or *shizenhontai* and its right and left variations (right and left *shizentai*), should be well known from your early training in Judo. Maintain this posture (or variations) throughout most of the kata techniques unless instructed otherwise. The second type, the defensive posture (*jigohontai*) and its right and left variations (right and left *jigotai*), may be new to you. These postures are called *kamae* (combative engagement postures).

Assume the. *jigohontai* by learning how to establish the correct distance between your feet. Place your feet, toes to heel, in a straight line (Fig. 1). Then step a foot length (Fig. 2). Pivot on the balls of your feet and face forward naturally so that both your feet come into line, toes pointing outward at a 45-degree angle (Fig. 3). Lower your hips by bending your knees, which point outward a bit. Let your arms hang naturally at your sides, palms resting flat on your upper thighs (Fig. 4). This is *the jigohontai*.

Now move into the right *jigotai* simply by sliding your right foot about two foot-lengths forward in the direction those toes are pointing. Settle your hips a bit lower by slightly increasing the bend in your knees. Adjust your left

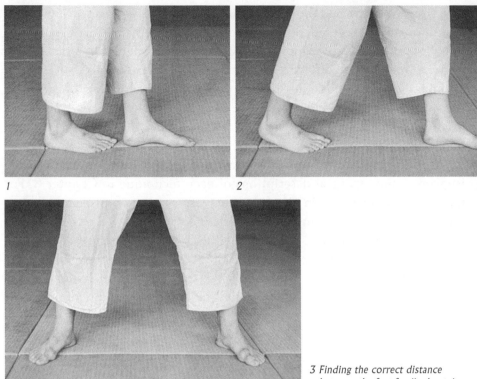

3 Finding the correct distance between the feet for jigohontai.

foot by turning the toes a bit outward (Fig. 5). The left *jigotai* is taken by reversing these instructions, substituting "left" for "right."

Judoists who lack experience with the standard *jigotai* are prone to position their feet either too close or too far apart. Note that your shoulders fall inside of the spread of your feet. Figure 6 shows the proper relationship of two partners engaged in right *jigotai*. Also note that they are using the standard grip, which you learned in your basic Judo days. The rather upright positioning of their bodies and the distance between them are also important details. For this kata, you are required to modify these latter two details when you use the *jigotai*, and you will use this modified form only for the techniques of *sumi-gaeshi* and *uki-waza*. It will be referred to as the "modified *jigotai*."[8]

---

6. The engagement posture used by Tori and Uke for the techniques of *sumi-gaeshi* and *uki-waza* is combative and is not the standard *jigotai* of Kodokan Judo. The standard *jigotai* was developed later, based on a modified engagement posture developed in primitive types of grappling. The modified *jigotai* used in this kata in Japan has an interesting background. It comes out of the ancient Japanese *chikara kurabe* contests (see Chapter 1) in which unclad enemies, locked in a desperate struggle, were unable to secure a normal grip because of the lack of garments. It served well for *sumo* (a kind of grappling in loincloths) and was also used by warriors who applied it to their art of *kumi-uchi*, a style of combative grappling which permitted armor-clad enemies to engage, also without gripping. The proper distance between the bodies of enemies had to be maintained to avoid the tangling and

4 Jigohontai.

4 (second view)

5 Right jigotai.

6 Opponents in right jigotai (standard grip).

Figures 7-10 show the modified *jigotai* correctly taken. Do not stand too close to your opponent when you assume this stance. Face him about 3 feet away to allow for forward movement. Simultaneously you and your training partner advance your right feet and assume the body position of the right *jigotai*. The modification comes as you extend your arms for contact. Note that "gripping" is applied without actually gripping your partner's garment. Your right palm is applied *flat* to his left shoulder blade by threading your hand through his left armpit. Your right hand does not grasp, but exerts flat palm pressure against his rear-and-top shoulder-blade area. Cup his right arm by placing your left hand high above his elbow and a bit on the underside of that arm. Practice this modified *jigotai* until you can assume it smoothly and without hesitation.

In the modified *jigotai*, no grasping of the jacket is permitted, especially by the hand pressing against your opponent's shoulder blade. However, in the interests of safety, the hand which cups your opponent's elbow may grasp the sleeve of his jacket when you assume the role of Tori and apply the techniques of *sumi-gaeshi* and *uki-waza*. Two points are important here. If either partner or both are inexperienced in throwing or falling, it is well that Tori actually grasp Uke's sleeve to better guide the throw. (Uke must never grasp, for he must quickly detach his hands at the proper moment and execute *ukemi*.) However, even the continued practice of Tori's grasping Uke's sleeve may hinder the acquisition of a correct throwing technique. Through gripping, inexperienced judoists are prone to lose the motivating force for this throw, the momentum of Tori's falling body; they are apt to depend upon the power of the arm to tug and heave Uke into his *ukemi*.

In this modified *jigotai*, the forward lean of your body is important. It is somewhat more pronounced than in the standard *jigotai*, but ideally it should not bring your body and your partner's into tight contact. You may even leave a little "daylight" between the upper bodies. Carefully note the head positions in Figure 10. They permit you and your opponent to see over each other's shoulders. Do not lay your head on your partner's shoulder, using it as a "pillow"; keep your eyes to the front, and the side of your face near that of your opponent.[7]

---

snagging of armor, which was inevitable should they press together. Modern sport *sumo* utilizes this old combative posture, as does Kodokan Judo, albeit with less emphasis on the distance between the opponents. *Sumo* refers to it as *yotsu-gumi*, indicating four-handed symmetrical gripping. It is this posture that you are actually using when you assume the modified *jigotai* for this kata.

7. If you are fortunate enough to see photographs of some of the old masters of Judo demonstrating the techniques of *sumi-gaeshi* and *uki-waza*, you may see them in *jigotai* postures that position them closer to their opponents and with head positions different from those recommended in this book. Such is the natural evolution of Judo. We are here concerned with restoring combative vigor to the *jigotai*.

7

8

9

❌ *Wrong.*

❌ *Wrong.*

❌ *Wrong.*

❌ *Wrong.*

Once you assume this posture, you and your opponent must keep some tension between you by a simultaneous, steady, light pulling action. Keep equilibrium as you stand engaged in the modified *jigotai*. If you are engaged properly, both you and your opponent will fall backward, away from each other, if you release your hand positions at the same time (and, of course, do not move your feet). Think of this as a *resistance* posture.

Part of the correct approach to posture is eye position. Generally speaking, in Nage no Kata Tori and Uke must try to achieve head positions which enable them to look directly at each other's faces, even in the modified *jigotai*. Eye-to-eye visual contact is a must. For Uke, it is a simple matter. Too often, however, Tori feels the need to look at his own or his partner's feet. Head movement must be minimized; it should be more a matter of "eye gymnastics" than a deliberate tilting of the head. Tori must not bury his eyes in Uke's feet. Tori of course strengthens his body positions by drawing his chin in as he sets up the throw and actually throws. The importance of not leaving the chin jutting outward from the body cannot be overemphasized, but judoists must also be careful to avoid the opposite extreme of too rigidly holding the chin in.

◆ STEPPING MOVEMENTS

Your basic Judo training taught you two types of stepping movement. This kata makes good use of both types. The normal walking, or one-foot-ahead-of-the-other, type is called *ayumi ashi* or *tsuzuki ashi*; and the "follow-foot" method, in which your trailing foot never catches up with or passes your lead foot, is called *tsugi ashi*. It is essential in this kata to slide all your stepping movements lightly over the surface of the mat. Do not lift your feet unduly before placement on the mat, as you would in "prancing" actions. Stepping movements are unfortunately not as simple as they look. Much practice is needed to make them efficient in kata. Learn to grip the mat with your toes; don't simply stand *on* it.

Ayumi ashi is not only performed in a straight advancing or retreating fashion, but also in a semicircular stepping or "arc step" fashion, both in advancing and in retreating. The straight manner is used by Tori and Uke in the preliminary movements, such as opening or closing the engagement distances (see p. 96), or in separating between the categories of techniques. It is also used by Uke in performing *seoi-nage*, *uki-goshi*, *tomoe-nage*, *ura-nage*, and *yoko-guruma*; Tori also uses it in *tomoe-nage*. Arc-step *ayumi ashi* is used by Tori in *ura-nage*, *sumi-gaeshi*, *yoko-guruma*, and *uki-waza*.

Tsugi ashi is performed in three distinct ways. The first is used in most of the techniques of this kata. It is a straight movement for advancing or retreating, and is used simultaneously by Tori and Uke in *uki-otoshi, kata-guruma, harai-goshi, tsurikomi-goshi, sasae-tsurikomi-ashi*, and *yoko-gake*. The second involves a straight sideways movement, used simultaneously by Tori and Uke only in *okuri-ashi-harai*. The third is a rotary movement and is used simultaneously by Tori and Uke only in *uchi-mata*.

Practice stepping movements by the self-practice method (see p. 446), then with a training partner. In the practice of kata techniques requiring *tsugi ashi* in either role, *do not anticipate* the coming throw. Especially, as Tori, do not anticipate the turning movement (*taisabaki*) preparatory to the throw. There are always at least two clear-cut steps in *tsugi ashi* before the throw. You must remain facing your Uke, your belt knot centered on him. On your third "step," or during the time at which a third step could be taken, you are permitted the *taisabaki* necessary to make the throw. Often, inexperienced judoists will be seen turning during their first or second steps. Uke must face Tori throughout all stepping actions and not show that he knows the throw is coming, or that he wants to aid Tori, by turning. Actually, when Uke anticipates, Tori will have a more difficult time executing a proper throw.

In the techniques of *uki-otoshi, kata-guruma, harai-goshi, tsurikomi-goshi, sasae-tsurikomi-ashi*, and *yoko-gake*, Tori and Uke couple together by gripping and move by *tsugi ashi*. Uke's attack would appear to the casual eye to be made in precisely the same manner for each technique; that is, his intentions and actions are apparently repeated identically. However, this is not the case.[8] Subtle differences exist and have a strong effect on the proper practice of these techniques.

In *uki-otoshi*, Uke's attack is carried out without inhibition as he drives forward unhesitatingly into Tori; in this first technique of the kata, Uke has no prior engagement experience with Tori and is a bit unreserved in the management of his body. In *kata-guruma*, Uke draws on his past experience of "defeat" and hangs back a bit cautiously, bracing lightly with a slightly bent advancing leg; Tori also adds to the difference in movement by not permitting Uke to move forward as he did in *uki-otoshi*, for Tori changes his grip during the second step and "floats" Uke. In *harai-goshi*, Uke, still fresh from defeat by *kata-guruma*, softens his body to make a similar attack difficult, and perhaps anticipates stepping around a similar throwing action by Tori; Tori manages to get Uke to stiffen his body regardless, by changing his grip and

---

8. Stereotyped stepping actions by Uke in these techniques produce less-meaningful kata. Evidence shows that the founder did not intend such stepping actions. However, no agreement has yet been reached in modern teaching at the Kodokan on the precise differences to be employed. Possibilities suggested herein are based on early Kodokan technical notes and the authors' preferences.

floating Uke upward during the second step. In *tsurikomi-goshi*, Tori never lets Uke start stepping; Tori grips unusually high with his assist-arm hand at the very onset of their engagement. This induces Uke to hang back against a possible throw like the previous *harai-goshi*, this time with extreme body stiffness. Tori, in *sasae-tsurikomi-ashi*, gets Uke to stiffen immediately after the second step by its prolonged action, unexpectedly breaking the timing of the usual stepping pattern; Uke never gets a chance to take a full third step. In *yoko-ga-ke*, Uke gets only one step of the usual pattern going, when Tori accentuates Uke's bracing action by imparting an inward twist and forward raking action to Uke's body; this turns Uke forward and inward during the second and third steps, preparatory to the throw.

◆ ENGAGEMENT DISTANCE

A good sense of distance perception by both Tori and Uke is essential to the success of this kata. Perhaps the most critical judgment is selecting the correct distance between the performers just prior to the beginning of their engagement in a technique. This can be called the "engagement distance," *ma-ai* in Japanese. Don't confuse engagement distance with engagement position (see p. 75).

The importance of the engagement distance cannot be overemphasized. Its essence is combative, and while today in this kata we are faced with a matter less serious than life or death, to attain the maximum training benefit it is essential to apply the engagement distance as if one were engaged in actual combat.[9]

Both Tori and Uke must stand in *shizenhontai* when positioning themselves for each engagement distance. In this kata there are four different engagement distances, which must be used in their appropriate places and at the proper times.

The near position, in which Tori and Uke face each other about 2 feet apart, makes it possible for them to simultaneously move into *shizentai* (Uke moving forward in attack and Tori backward to yield defensively until he can manage a throw) and to take the standard grip. The near position is used only in conjunction with the techniques of *uki-otoshi*, *kata-guruma*, *harai-goshi*, *tsurikomi-goshi*, *sasae-tsurikomi-ashi*, and *yoko-gake*.

---

9. The engagement distance is combatively significant in that by its correct application the *kime*, or decisive finalizing action, the "kill," is guaranteed. Improper stationing might not only negate the *kime* one can deliver, but bring one into the *kime* of the enemy. Elaborate tactics and ruses to gain proper engagement distance and to prevent the proper taking of engagement distance by the enemy permeate the teachings of the classical martial arts, and are applicable in Judo to defeating an opponent.

The far position, in which Tori and Uke face each other about 6 feet apart, makes Uke's forceful striking attacks possible. The far position is used only in conjunction with *seoi-nage*, *uki-goshi*, *ura-nage*, and *yoko-guruma*.

The semifar position, with Tori and Uke facing each other about 3 feet apart, makes it possible for them to take the standard grip as they move into *shizentai*, both coming forward, or to grip specially in the modified *jigotai*. The semifar position is used only for *uchi-mata*, *tomoe-nage*, *sumi-gaeshi*, and *uki-waza*.

The closed position requires Tori and Uke to stand about 1 foot apart and permits them to take the standard grip in *shizenhontai* preparatory to the *okuri-ashi-harai*. This is the only application of the closed position in this kata.

These distances work well for all but the shortest and the tallest judoists, who may need to modify them slightly to accommodate their sizes. They are not fixed, and nothing can be more harmful to positioning than blind adherence to these distances if they are wrong for a particularly large or small performer. The only rule in determining these distances is to make them combatively meaningful and technically sound.

Generally speaking, it is Uke rising from *ukemi* who has the responsibility of adjusting the engagement distance, fixing on Tori, who is already waiting in *shizenhontai* to receive Uke's next attack. Tori is thus charged with the responsibility of stationing himself oil the correct spot prior to Uke's arrival for engagement. This permits the technique to be carried out within the prescribed limits, that is, the 18-foot span between the starting (salutation) positions (see p. 71). Often Tori and Uke appear to station themselves at the same time.

The only difficulty in this manner of engagement comes at the beginning of each category of technique. The first category (*te waza*) and the last (*yoko sutemi waza*) find Uke moving a considerably shorter distance to the point from which the first technique (*uki-otoshi* and *yoko-gake*, respectively) will begin. Uke moves about one-third the distance between the points where he and Tori stand at their respective engagement positions; Tori must move about two-thirds of this distance. This arrangement is necessary to climax the techniques in the center of the center zone, and to keep them within the confines of the kata area. If both Uke and Tori move at the same pace, Uke will find himself at his appointed position much earlier than Tori. It is essential that Uke delay his first step as much as he can and that he take slower steps than Tori; Tori, however, must not try to beat Uke there by rushing his forward movement. If this is done skillfully, it is possible for them to appear to arrive together, Uke just coming to a dead stop in *shizenhontai* a fraction of a second later than Tori. The second category (*koshi waza*) sees both Tori and Uke on the move; no stopping occurs and the engagement distance must be judged accurately by Uke on the move, as Tori arrives at the correct station (approximately the edge of his side of the center zone). Since they both move the same distance from their engagement positions along the longitudinal axis, there is no timing problem. The third (*ashiwaza*) and fourth (*ma sutemi waza*) categories also should present no timing problem since Tori and Uke move the same distance and come to a dead stop prior to engagement.

Crowding too close together at the engagement distance causes weak movements in the execution of the technique, while overextending the distance makes it awkward for Tori and Uke to make and maintain the necessary contact.

◆ SYMMETRY AND CENTER PERFOMANCE
The tremendous task of keeping kata movement symmetrical in relation to the center zone hinges upon Tori's responsibility for determining the exact spot from which each technique begins. Ideally, this kata requires an area of 50 *tatami* arranged as a 30'x30' expanse. Smaller *dojo* which cannot offer such spacious accommodations may require certain modifications. This area requirement is more important when kata is given as a demonstration; kata in training may be somewhat more confined but safety requirements must be met.

Generally speaking, except in the most restricted mat areas, this kata is performed somewhat symmetrically on each side of the center zone. It is primarily activated along the longitudinal axis, that imaginary line running parallel to the *kamiza* for approximately 18 feet, there bounded by the respective salutation positions of Tori and Uke. One technique, *okuri-ashi-harai*, moves along the lateral axis, the imaginary line through the center of the center zone and perpendicular to the longitudinal axis.

Starting positions for each technique may be classified as outside the center zone, on opposite edges of the center zone, or within the center zone. Regardless of where a technique begins, in both its right- and its left-hand applications each technique climaxes in the approximate center of the center zone; that is, the transition from *tsukuri* to *kake* takes place there. In spite of this, it must be realized that the final resting place of Uke in *ukemi* is not always at the place of technique climax and therefore is not always within the center zone (see *ukemi* map, p. 109).

Techniques which start outside the center zone are: *uki-otoshi, kata-guruma, harai-goshi, tsurikomi-goshi, sasae-tsurikomi-ashi, sumi-gaeshi, yoko-gake,* and *uki-waza*. Tori and Uke face each other in *shizenhontai* at a point just a

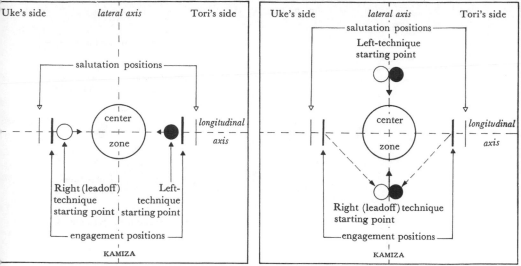

| (a) Starting points outside the center zone. | (b) Starting points for okuri-ashi-harai. |

bit forward of Uke's engagement position, in the right technique. They move along the longitudinal axis to a technique climax in the approximate center of the center zone. The left technique begins at a point just forward of Tori's engagement position (toward the center) and moves back along the longitudinal axis in the opposite direction to that taken for the right technique, to climax in the approximate center of the center zone (Fig. a).

While this "outside" principle applies also to *okuri-ashi-harai*, that technique is a bit different in that it moves along the lateral axis. Tori and Uke face each other in *shizenhontai* on the lateral axis but at a point outside the center zone, near the *kamiza*, and move for the right technique to a technique climax in the approximate center of the center zone. The left technique begins at a point outside the center zone, away from the *kamiza*, but on the lateral axis, and moves back in the opposite direction to that taken for the right technique to its climax in the approximate center of the center zone. Thus, to take the correct stationing action for the right technique, Tori and Uke leave their engagement positions (at which they ended the *koshi waza* category) and walk toward the lateral axis on a diagonal from the longitudinal axis on the *kamiza* side. After the climax of the right technique and as Uke comes to rest in *ukemi*, Tori shifts very slightly to his right along the lateral axis (away from the *kamiza*) to station himself in *shizenhontai* prior to Uke's arrival; this slight adjustment permits the left technique to climax in the center zone (Fig. b).

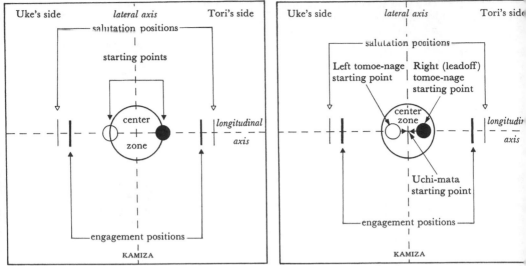

(c) Starting points on opposite edges of the center zone.

(d) Starting points within the center zone.

The techniques of *seoi-nage*, *uki-goshi*, *ura-nage*, and *yoko-guruma* see Tori and Uke face each other at opposite edges of the center zone. The climax by collision is in the approximate center of the center zone. In the right technique Uke and Tori operate from their own edges, while for the left technique they reverse sides. Only *uki-goshi* is peculiar. Its first peculiarity is that the first attack is performed with both Tori and Uke moving; the other three techniques operate from static positions. Secondly, while Uke attacks with his right arm, Tori's first response is in fact a *left* technique in that Uke is thrown around his left loin; the next attack, initiated by Uke's left arm, makes Tori respond with a right technique. In spite of this, the first attack begins with Tori and Uke moving into climax from their respective edges of the center zone; the second attack begins with them static at exchanged positions on the edges of the center zone (Fig. c).

Only two techniques, *uchi-mata* and *tomoe-nage*, begin within the center zone. *Uchi-mata* offers no difficulty in that it also climaxes and ends with Uke's *ukemi* within that zone. For the right technique, Tori and Uke stand within the center zone but on their own sides; for the left technique, they exchange sides. *Tomoe-nage* is peculiar in that it has double movement. For the right technique, Tori and Uke face each other within the center zone, slightly toward Tori's side, and move away from the center zone toward Uke's engagement position along the longitudinal axis. The climax of the throw sees the movement reversed along the longitudinal axis, takes place within the center zone, and results in Uke being thrown in the direction he faces. For the left technique, Tori and Uke exchange sides within the center zone, stationing themselves a bit toward Uke's side. They first move away from the center zone, along the longitudinal axis toward Tori's engagement position, then come back toward the center zone, with the climax within that zone in the direction opposite to that used for the right technique (Fig. d).

In small *dojo* where the length requirement of the longitudinal axis for this kata cannot be met, often the diagonal dimension of the mat area offers a reasonable substitute. When the width dimension is less than desirable to permit *okuri-ashi-harai*, the longitudinal axis may serve as a substitute: Tori and Uke move from Uke's side of the kata area along that axis, Tori facing the *kamiza*, Uke with his back to it.

◆ GRIPPING

There are several distinct ways of taking hold of one's partner in this kata, but most of them utilize the standard grip which you learned during your basic training days. Exceptions to the standard grip will be discussed under Key Points in each technique, where they occur.

Regardless of the gripping method used, Tori and Uke must hold firmly, but lightly. Tori's grip must be such as to not greatly disarrange Uke's *judogi* during throwing actions, and Uke's grip must not be a frantic clutching as he is unbalanced and thrown and executes his *ukemi*, for similar reasons.

Tori retains his grip on Uke (except in the techniques of *tomoe-nage, ura-nage, sumi-gaeshi, yoko-guruma*, and *uki-waza*) upon completion of each throw. This is essentially a one-handed grip on Uke's sleeve. The other hand, which is relatively free, must not be allowed to dangle uselessly in the air. It should simply be placed on Uke's sleeve at a point near the hand which is actually gripping; place it naturally as Uke settles into *ukemi* during the final moment of the throw. Uke must release his grip on Tori's lapel during all throws as he settles into *ukemi*. By releasing his grip Uke demonstrates skill and confidence in his *ukemi*. Otherwise Tori will have difficulties in balance and *judogi* orderliness.

Gripping for the techniques of *sumi-gaeshi* and *uki-waza* is peculiar, as it is done while the opponents are in the modified *jigotai* posture and there is no actual grasping of the *judogi* by either Tori or Uke. This has already been discussed (on p. 90).

At no time in this kata does either Tori or Uke grip the other's belt.

11   12   ❌ *Wrong.*

◆ UKE'S STRIKING ACTIONS

Four techniques require Uke to face Tori at the far position about 6 feet away, in *shizenhontai*, and attack by stepping forward and striking. These techniques are: *seoi-nage, uki-goshi, ura-nage,* and *yoko-guruma.* Only in his leadoff attack for *uki-goshi* is Uke already moving—all other striking attacks by Uke are started from static positions facing Tori. The first striking action in all the techniques is made with the right arm as follows. Uke steps deeply forward from *shizenhontai* with his left foot and simultaneously raises his right arm, slightly bent at the elbow, backward and upward; the hand is held in a tight fist. The arm is raised upward from the right back corner to a position which brings the fist to head level or slightly higher; the arm remains slightly bent.[10] The fist is positioned so that the ulnar (little finger) side faces Tori. Avoid bad form. This threatening gesture must be made smoothly and not too quickly (Figs. 11, 12).

Uke immediately steps forward with his right foot and strikes directly downward against the top of the front of Tori's head.[11] Uke must time the arrival of his advancing right foot with the blow (Figs. 13). The ulnar portion of the fist is the striking area and is referred to as the "bottom fist" (p. 103).

---

10. The form of this blow was taken by the founder from the jujutsu tactics of *atemi waza* (assaulting techniques), the most effective of which positions the fist directly overhead preparatory to downward delivery to the top of the enemy's head.

11. Originally in this kata, Uke was required to strike on the first step forward, without preliminary stepping. The founder modified this procedure as described to give more combative force to the execution of the technique.

12 (second view)   13   13 (second view)

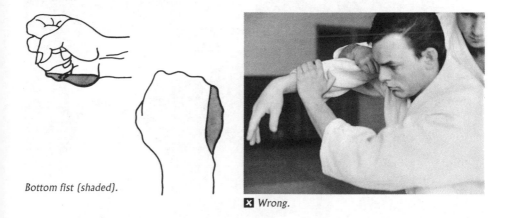

Bottom fist (shaded).

❌ Wrong.

The forward movement of Uke's right foot and the striking action should be made smoothly and a bit more quickly than the initial threatening action. Strike with a slightly bent arm and a tight fist, as if you were hammering something with a mallet. Avoid a limp wrist.

While Uke's striking-attack actions appear stereotyped and may show little combative common sense to the untutored eye, this is not the case. Subtle variations in Uke's body mechanics make this kata interesting and vital.[12] Compare Figures 14-17.

---

12. There is some historical evidence to support the idea of Uke handling his body differently in each of the four striking attacks. But standard Kodokan practice today does not definitively set such patterns.

14 Uke's first striking attack (seoi-nage). *15 Uke's second striking attack (uki-goshi).*

16 Uke' third striking attack (ura-nage). *17 Uke's fourth striking attack (yoko-guruma).*

In his first attack, Uke is met with *seoi-nage*. He attacks somewhat reck-lessly and without prior experience of "defeat" in a striking attack; he collides with Tori, trying to drive Tori backward and down with his blow. Uke's body is thrown fully into this attack and his weight comes well forward, his body leaning a bit with the blow. He is met abruptly, and turned up and over by Tori (Fig. 14).

In his second attack, Uke is met with *uki-goshi*, and he takes his past failure into account as he places his blow against Tori. He is more cautious; he withholds some of his forward momentum but still attempts to drive Tori backward and down. [13] By keeping his body erect and his weight more or less evenly centered, Uke makes his body a bit stiffer than in the first striking attack (*seoi-nage*) in an attempt to avoid being thrown over; but Uke is slung, sticklike, around Tori's loin (Fig. 15).

Uke's third attempt at a striking attack is met with *ura-nage*. Uke can now draw on sufficient past experience in defeats. As he strikes, he drops his weight just a bit downward, facing into Tori as if to drive him into the ground with the blow, much as one would hammer a stake. We know this from the manner in which Uke's arm strikes over Tori's shoulder in full commitment of body force as his fist misses the intended target; his arm does not stop at the horizontal, but continues downward. Tori goes well under him and uproots Uke (Fig. 16).

In the final striking attack Uke, with three prior defeats as sad experience to draw on, and especially remembering the last defeat by *ura-nage*, tries to provoke the same response by Tori without exposing himself to the devastating throw. As Uke strikes, he does not face as fully into Tori as he did for the *ura-nage*, but leaves his trailing leg back a bit so that both feet are more or less on a line parallel to the longitudinal axis, rather than at right angles to it as was the case with *ura-nage*. Tori gets hung up in an attempt at *ura-nage*, which is a genuine attempt to throw; Uke then further complicates Tori's attempt by placing a second attack against Tori which bends Tori over. Tori takes advantage of Uke's new line of unbalance, and by *go no sen* slides under Uke to counterthrow him by *yoko-guruma* (Fig. 17).

◆ UKE "GIVES" HIS BODY

Uke must at all times remember the prearranged spirit of kata and thus "give" his body completely to Tori along prescribed lines, so that Tori is able to execute the required throwing actions in the correct direction. Tori is charged with the responsibility of throwing and depositing Uke's body in a specific direction and area. Any awkwardness or mishandling by Uke of his body, in order to withhold or avoid the coming throw and *ukemi*, greatly hinders Tori and may even destroy the training value of this kata.

---

13. The use by Uke of a "haymaker" or roundhouse-type striking action aimed at Tori's temple is not a standard Kodokan attack method. This type of blow may be used to provoke the execution of this *uki-goshi*; but it cannot be properly utilized for the other three striking attacks, as its direction of force runs contrary to the required throwing responses. Historical evidence indicates that the lateral striking attack was studied by Kodokan teachers but not accepted as standard for the technique of *uki-goshi*, and it remains only in private variation patterns of teaching.

While Uke is expected to cooperate by accepting the technique correct-ly, this cooperation can be overdone. Anticipation of the throw, in which Uke turns to "assist" Tori, is bad: Uke must face into Tori. Tori must unbalance Uke, fit his body to Uke's unbalanced position, and throw Uke by a real throw. Tori must not merely be "in the way" for Uke to jump over or around. By the theory of this kata, Uke is moving from a balanced position at engagement with Tori to unbalance at the last step, where Tori takes advantage of this positional weakness and throws Uke forcefully. Uke must always respect this concept and allow himself to lose balance as a result of the integration of his actions with Tori's. Fighting to stay balanced will destroy the kata when demonstration is the purpose. In training, under special circumstances, Uke may resist if so desired. Yet Uke can overbalance himself by leaning too heav-ily or too prematurely into the coming throw.

With the foregoing in mind, Uke must perfect his body control. This is only possible with considerable experience and then only if Uke first trusts his *ukemi* skills, then has complete trust in Tori's throwing abilities.

◆ THE CLOSED-GATE EFFECT

One device which Uke must be proficient at, one which can really make or break this kata, is the "closed-gate" effect. This action can be found in the majority of techniques, in varying degrees of ease of visual identification, though not in the techniques *oîuki-otoshi, okuri-ashi-harai, sasae-tsuri-komi-ashi, yoko-gake, yoko-guruma,* and *uki-waza.*

Seoi-nage is a good example of a throw which requires Uke to perform the closed-gate effect. In Figure 18, Uke's striking action places him in a pos-ture with his right foot advanced and his left foot trailing behind. Uke per-forms the closed-gate effect by bringing his trailing foot up on an approximate line with his advanced right foot (approximately *shizenhontai* foot placement) as Tori swings in under him to complete the *tsukuri* for the throw (Fig. 19). Uke's movement is much like that of a gate swinging from open to closed position; this action brings Uke closer to Tori and puts the front of his body into tight contact with Tori.

The closed-gate action facilitates the throwing action on Tori's part, Tori being required to throw Uke forward somewhat in line with the longitudinal axis. Note that the palm of Uke's free left hand (the one not used in striking) is placed firmly on Tori's left buttock, fingers pointing downward to stabilize Uke's body during *kake*. At the moment of body contact, as produced by Tori's *tsukuri*, Uke "floats" up against Tori, a condition which is ensured by Tori's pulling Uke and thus compelling him to move his trailing leg forward

18   19

in an attempt to preserve his balance. Uke must not, by himself, drift onto his toes as he performs the closed-gate effect. He is brought into it by Tori.

Tomoe-nage and *sumi-gaeshi* require Uke to perform the foot action only, the hand-bracing action not being necessary.

The importance of the closed-gate effect may be seen in Figure 18, above. If Uke remains in this position, trailing leg behind, it of course means that Tori's unbalancing actions are weak, but another aspect is also important. In this position, Uke has actually brought the direction of the throw off the longitudinal axis (the direction perpendicular to a line drawn between Uke's feet). Uke must bear in mind that Tori is required to place most throws near or on the longitudinal axis (exceptions are seen in *okuri-ashi-harai*, where Uke lands along the lateral axis, and in *yoko-guruma* and *uki-waza*, where Uke follows lines oblique to and away from the longitudinal axis). This is especially true if kata is being used as a demonstration. In training, if it is desired to test Tori's awareness of the proper lines of Uke's unbalance, it is permissible for Tori not to unbalance Uke in the normal way by pulling him, but rather to "go to" Uke in the position before the closed-gate effect would be effected, there to throw Uke in a direction off the longitudinal axis. This, of course, is not a standard practice but has meaning, as though Uke were resisting the efforts of Tori to unbalance him along the longitudinal axis, but at the same time creating a new line of unbalance which Tori must recognize and take advantage of. Only when Tori induces the closed-gate effect in Uke can Uke's *ukemi* coincide with the intended direction of the throw.

The closed-gate effect should be studied in connection with Uke's "giving" of his body.

◆ UKEMI

Uke must perform 30 *ukemi*, that is, one to the right and one to the left for each of the 15 techniques of this kata. *Ukemi* must be performed correctly with emphasis on standard Kodokan form. Proficiency in *ukemi* by the partner-support method (see p. 453) and the *zempo kaiten* method is absolutely essential; you practiced these methods during your basic training days, and they will now stand you in good stead. But some additional requirements must be observed.

It is essential that Uke not allow his feet to vibrate or bounce up off the mat after *ukemi* contact. The feet must be pressed to the mat in all techniques where his body comes to rest on the mat, with the one exception of *yoko-ga-ke*. *Ukemi* from *yoko-gake* is not strictly a side-falling type; the fall deposits Uke flat on his back, legs in the air, but he utilizes a single arm-beating action.

The arm which beats the mat can and should be made to rebound from the mat immediately after impact, to break some of the shock of the fall. Pressing the hand to the mat after impact allows the shock just dispersed by the beating of the arm to be retransmitted into the body. All techniques require Uke to perform *ukemi* first (in the right technique) by beating with the left hand, and then (in the left technique) by beating with the right; the one exception is *uki-goshi*, in which the sequence is reversed.

Falling from the throws of the first three categories (*te waza*, *koshi waza*, and *ashi waza*) offers no confusion concerning final *ukemi* action. The *ukemi* from these techniques always requires that Uke remain lying on the mat. But in the *sutemi waza*, final *ukemi* action can be misinterpreted.

In *ma sutemi* and *yoko sutemi waza*, there are only two techniques in which Uke is required to remain lying on the mat upon *ukemi*: *ura-nage* and *yoko-ga-ke*. Additionally, Uke must come to his feet at the completion of his *ukemi* out of *tomoe-nage* to demonstrate full control of his body by adopting *shizenhontai* without tottering forward. For the remaining *sutemi waza*, Uke is permitted to elect whether he will remain on the mat in a reclining position, or come to his feet in *shizenhontai* to end his *ukemi*. As a matter of symmetry, in standard practice most skillful Uke prefer to come to their feet in those techniques, staying down on the mat only when the force of the throw or body position and balance make rising difficult.[14] Regardless of which final position is taken,

---

14. Historically, masters of this kata believed that if Tori really executes any of the *sutemi waza* correctly and

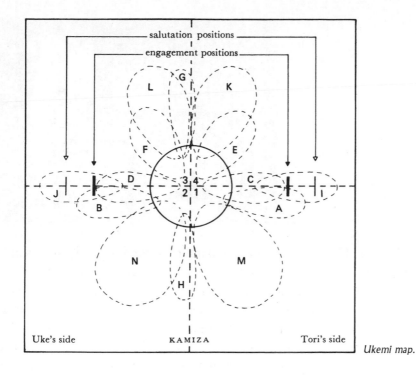

Ukemi map.

KEY:

Right-technique ukemi zone	Technique	Left-technique ukemi zone
A (leadoff)	*Uki-otoshi*	**B**
C (leadoff)	*Seoi-nage*	**D**
A, M (leadoff)	*Kata-guruma*	**B, N**
F	*Uki-goshi*	**E** (leadoff)
A, C. M (leadoff)	*Harai-goshi*	**B, D, N**
C (leadoff)	*Tsurikomi-goshi*	**D**
G (leadoff)	*Okuri-ashi-harai*	**H**
A, C, I (leadoff)	*Sasae-tsurikomi-ashi*	**B. D, J**
3, D, F (leadoff)	*Uchi-mata*	**4, C, E**
I (leadoff)	*Tomoe-nage*	**J**
A. C, I (leadoff)	*Ura-nage*	**B, D, J**
A. C, I (leadoff)	*Sumi-gaeshi*	**B, D, J**
1 and **2** (leadoff)	*Toko-gake*	**2** and **1**
G, K (leadoff)	*Toko-guruma*	**G. L**
M (leadoff)	*Uki-waza*	**N**

it must be matched in the right and left applications of each technique; that is, what is done in *ukemi* on one side must be done on the other.

---

forcefully, as if in a combative situation against an assailant, Uke cannot stand up but must take his *ukemi* lying down. Whether or not Uke would be retained in Tori's grip is not the only consideration here, but also that Tori could guide Uke into a brutal fall and injury. Thus, the old masters thought, only a "fake" throw allows Uke to rise.

20

In all *ukemi*, Uke is approximately parallel to the longitudinal axis in his final *ukemi* position. Exceptions to this occur only in *okuri-ashi-harai, yoko-guruma*, and *uki-waza*. If radical angles to the longitudinal axis are experienced, it is possible, the starting positions of Tori and Uke being correct, that Tori is not executing the throw with enough attention to correct unbalancing of Uke or perhaps the *kake* is lacking in force. The axis along which Uke must fall and his precise position in relation to that axis, the *kamiza*, and Tori, are discussed for each technique in Chapter 8, but the *ukemi* map above should be studied carefully.

◆ TORI'S KAKE BALANCE

Tori must maintain his balance with chin tucked in during all *kake* as Uke hits the mat. He must position himself on both feet for throws of the first three categories. Completing any of these throws with one leg dangling in the air, even though the foot or leg had been lifted from the mat to perform the throw, is incorrect. Additionally, as mentioned on page 101, both of Tori's hands are on Uke at the time of Uke's impact with the mat. Leaving the "free" arm dangling in the air will destroy Tori's balance. Tori's final standing position must be natural without stiffness, slightly bent at the knees and with the back slightly bowed (concave), facing into Uke's *ukemi* position on the mat. Tori's position must convey *zanshin*; his eyes are focused on Uke as if to jam Uke into the mat by his gaze (*mikomi*), except in the technique of *uki-otoshi*. *Uki-otoshi* is done with Tori's fullest confidence as to its outcome; he retains Uke by sleeve grip with two hands and does not turn his head to follow Uke's flight pattern or *ukemi*.

Compare Figures 20-20². They all show Tori immediately after executing a right-hand *seoi-nage* (over his right shoulder) and with Uke just settling

20¹ ☒ Wrong.   20² ☒ Wrong.

down onto the mat in *ukemi*. Figure 20 shows Tori assuming a correct postural balance. While Uke has become purely receptive, Tori's offensive state is unmistakable; he has clearly focused his energies, mental and physical, into Uke. There is a degree of naturalness in Tori which is possible only by an unconscious use of mind and body. He stands with his body squarely centered on the support afforded by his legs, chin in, the power curve of his body (dorsal line) reflecting the efficiency of its application. There is more here, however, than physical application.

This quality, mentioned earlier (see p. 65), is *zanshin*.[15] *Zanshin*, though embodied in a physical posture, is nevertheless a mental process. It is intense concentration, and unswerving awareness by focused alertness which removes any chance for the target to long obtain the initiative. Tori, by extension of his *zanshin*, which permits *sen*, completely dominates Uke.

Figure 20¹ shows Tori with everything gone wrong. Balance, concentration, and thus *zanshin*, are almost totally absent. Correction of throwing posture and mental concentration can remedy this if intensive practice is done along the suggested lines.

Figure 20² shows Tori sincerely trying to achieve what he should, but succeeding only in breaking the unity between himself and Uke. He has done this through the mistaken notion that as Uke is slammed to the mat, Tori

---

15. Historically, *zanshin* has been highly regarded by martial arts masters and jujutsu technicians who practice realistic combative styles. *Zanshin* is indicative of the highest state of training, which enables combatants to survive. *Zanshin*, as the essence of technique, is an unconscious application of body energies developed through intense, regular, correct training. It cannot be faked, and unless it is present, true technique deteriorates into meaningless and mechanical form. The correct posture after the throw, the "jamming" of the gaze into the fallen opponent (*mikomi*), and the holding of the thrower's body motionless for a moment are manifestations of *zanshin* which must appear before Uke is released.

must add some finesse to the technique by snapping his body erect and pulling upward on Uke's sleeve. This is a stiff unnatural habit which is incorrect and, if performed to preserve Tori's balance, indicates that something is seriously wrong with Tori's final actions.

Tori's *kake* balance and *zanshin* are meant to be prolonged momentarily after all action ceases at the end of each technique. Whether you regard kata training as self-defense or contest exercise, *zanshin* is applicable. The self-defense aspect is obvious. The sporting phase is, too, on consideration; it is discussed in Chapter 10.

What has been said so far has been expressly for the techniques of the first three categories, but in the main is applicable to the remaining techniques of this *kata*, the *sutemi waza*. At the time of Uke's *ukemi* from the *sutemi waza*, Tori's *kake* balance is no less defined than in the *tachi waza*. Tori's entrance foot, the one which prepares the "platform" for the throw, must be correctly placed, or not only will Tori's balance be bad on the execution of the throw, but it spells trajectory difficulties for Uke. The precise positioning of this foot must be carefully studied by Tori.

Tori in his recumbent throwing position must stabilize his body by keeping his platform foot or feet firmly against the mat. The knee or knees must be held upright and not allowed to fall outward. The forward portion of the platform foot, not the heel, is pressed firmly against the mat.

In the techniques of *tomoe-nage*, *sumi-gaeshi*, and *yoko-gake*, Tori uses just one foot as a platform to achieve this stabilization, the other foot (or leg) being involved in contact with Uke to assist in throwing. In *ura-nage*, *yoko-guruma*, and *uki-waza*, Tori uses both feet as a platform. In the final stage or *kake* of all *sutemi waza*, some more visibly than others, Tori's body action must include an upward bridging surge of the midsection (in *ma sutemi waza*) or an upward and diagonal rear-corner one (in *yoko sutemi waza*). This action follows Uke's trajectory in the direction of the throw. Any tendency by Tori to lie limp on the mat, or to collapse in his midsection with buttocks resting comfortably relaxed on the mat, will negate the throwing action. Additionally, feet weakly positioned on the heels, or with the knees dropped outward, make for incorrect throwing forces. Tori should not try to make deliberate visual contact with Uke in the *ma sutemi waza*, as this requires him either to lift his head straight back, losing the compression force of a tucked-in chin which ensures body unity, or to look around to one side or the other, which tends to destroy the back-down position required by this category. However, in the *yoko sutemi waza* Tori can achieve visual contact without disturbing either his body unity or the throwing form.

As in the *tachi waza, zanshin* must prevail, but some judoists find it harder in those *sutemi waza* which do not feature direct visual contact between Tori and Uke. Direct eye-to-eye contact is not necessary to *zanshin*,[16] and the lack of it in certain of the *sutemi waza* is no different from that in *uki-otoshi*, where Tori radiates confidence in the outcome of the technique and *zanshin* is established by what can perhaps best be described as a "hearing contact," or, perhaps, peripheral vision.

Arm actions in the *sutemi waza* must be in concert with the throwing forces, and always are secondary to the momentum created by Tori's falling body. Efforts to "chuck" Uke by arm-and-hand action alone, or by that action preceding the falling of the body, are improper technique. Yet, in the *kake* and the final position with *zanshin* prevailing, certain requirements must be met.

In the technique of *tomoe-nage*, Tori's arm actions follow a circular pattern. While they do extend in the direction of the throw, the arms must be snapped into the chest as Uke goes over beyond Tori's reclining position; they do not remain stretched out in the air. In *ura-nage* and *sumi-gaeshi*, both arms remain outstretched in the direction of Uke's trajectory. *Toko-gake* offers no arm problem for Tori, who must keep both hands on Uke. *Yoko-guruma* sees Tori extending both arms in the direction of Uke's flight. *Uki-waza* however is a bit like *tomoe-nage* in that the arm action is circular; while the arms extend in the direction of the throw, they must be snapped into the body as Uke goes over, out and away from Tori's outstretched position on the mat. This is especially true in the case of the hand or arm that is in contact with Uke's sleeve.

◆ MAIRI SIGNAL

As you have already learned, this kata is done in a rather serene manner insofar as *kiai* sound and facial gestures are concerned. There is, further, no need for Uke to visually indicate surrender by the usual tapping action of Judo, for it is the *ukemi* itself which is indicative of the *kake*, or conclusion; Uke has "lost" in that particular sense in each situation portrayed by each technique.

◆ RISING AND FACING ACTIONS

Both Tori and Uke have many occasions, after the execution of the individual throwing techniques, to get up from a more or less recumbent position on the mat. Tori has this opportunity 14 times, or once each on the right and

---

16. To understand this, think of viewing a star-studded sky at night. If the star you wish to view is looked at directly, it is difficult to keep in focus; by simply gazing intently a bit away from that star in any direction, you bring it into better focus. And it is the same with combative situations; the movement of the enemy can more easily be seen by less-than-direct visual contact.

left sides for *uki-otoshi, tomoe-nage, ura-nage, sumi-gaeshi, yoko-gake, yoko-gu-ruma*, and *uki-waza*. Uke must rise and/or face Tori a total of 30 times, once each on the right and left sides for each of the kata's 15 techniques. Of course, in some cases in *sutemi waza*, Uke is carried to a standing position after striking the mat in *ukemi* by the force of the throw; he need not then make any special effort to rise, but only turns and faces Tori.

Regardless, the rising actions constitute a major share of the in-between-technique movements, as they are executed from static positions of completed *ukemi*, and are intimately connected to the responsibility for determining most of the engagement distances. Both Tori and Uke must be certain about what to do. Opportunities for facing actions by Tori and Uke are still greater than for the rising actions; they are performed not only in connection with the techniques, but also separately to bring the performers back from where they stand in *shizenhontai*, at their respective engagement positions, at the end of each category.

Rising and facing actions involve a basic feature of Judo etiquette which is often misinterpreted and thus misused in this kata. Most judoists know that, as a general rule, proper *dojo* etiquette requires that judoists performing kata not turn their backs to the *kamiza* during facing actions.[17] This custom is not uniquely Oriental and should not be regarded as something foreign and undesirable in modern Judo; it closely follows Western etiquette, in which almost every type of performer tries to maintain as much facial contact with his audience as possible. While this etiquette still holds today, in modern Judo it can be overdone and cause unnaturalness to creep into the facing actions and the kata as a whole.

The key to correct rising and facing actions lies in naturalness. All actions must take into account the *kamiza* and the correct etiquette extended to it, but must give first priority to the need for getting up efficiently, turning naturally in the direction of the body position in *ukemi* or throwing. This naturalness and efficiency must also extend to the route of movement to new stations, which is always the shortest route, thus permitting an uninterrupted continuation of the kata.

Turning to face your partner without turning your back to the *kamiza* should be done *only* when conditions permit it to be done naturally, following the motion and direction of the body as already determined by either throwing or *ukemi*. Uke will have a more difficult time of it than Tori in this respect.

---

17. This custom stems from martial arts etiquette. Demonstrations given before ruling dignitaries, high officials, superiors, or temples and shrines are all oriented toward a seat or place of honor. Out of deference to the place of honor, performers seek to minimize the need to turn their backs to that area.

There are, however, standard procedures for use by Tori and Uke when either partner or both are on the mat, somewhat reclining, at the completion of the *ukemi* by Uke.

The rule may be summarized as follows: from a lying position on the mat (due to throwing or *ukemi*), sit and fold the low-side leg, kneel on the low-side knee, stand, and turn toward the low side. This amounts to rising and turning toward the beating arm in *ukemi* for Uke.

Uke will see that his *ukemi* position on the mat places one leg into contact with the mat; that contact is along the outer surface of the entire leg. This is the side on which he beats the mat and it can be referred to as the "low side" (there is one exception in *yoko-gake*, where Uke lands flat on his back but still performs the single-arm *ukemi* as if falling onto his side). By this type of *ukemi*, one side of Uke's back is somewhat raised from the mat and generally his back points at the *kamiza* (with exceptions in *uki-goshi* and *yoko-gake*).

Figures 21-25 show a completed right *seoi-nage* and Uke rising to turn and face Tori preparatory to stationing himself for the left technique. Uke must sit up and simultaneously fold the low-side leg (the leg farther away from the *kamiza*) (Fig. 22). Uke then rises to a kneeling position by kneeling on the low-side (left) knee without placing the hands or arms on the mat to prop himself into position (Fig. 23). Uke stands up to face Tori by turning more or less in place, his back to the *kamiza*, toward his low-side (left) leg, and moves backward a bit and faces Tori (who is already waiting for him) to station himself for the left technique (Figs. 24, 25).

21   22

23   24   25

An exception to this procedure is found in the already mentioned *uki-goshi*. Tori has, in this technique, led off with a left-hand throw which brings Uke onto the mat in *ukemi*, facing somewhat into the *kamiza*, lying on the right side of his back. This means that on rising and turning in place Uke does not violate the *kamiza*. Notice also that in the case of *okuri-ashi-harai*, facing actions are not identical for the right and left techniques insofar as turning direction and the *kamiza* are concerned. Uke, upon getting up from the first throw by that technique (which is right-handed but with Tori's left leg), finds himself turning without violating the *kamiza*; the left-hand throw (with Tori's right leg) requires him to turn his back to the *kamiza* as he positions himself for the next technique. Uke, after *ukemi*, in order to station himself for certain techniques, cannot simply rise and turn in place to face Tori. He must, upon rising, face the direction of his *ukemi* and move a bit in that direction (usually to an approximate engagement position) before turning to face Tori; that turn should follow the same direction as would be done directly by a turning-in-place action. In right *yoko-gake*, Uke lands approximately parallel to Tori, and the longitudinal axis as well; being flat on his back, legs in the air, Uke has no true low-side leg. He should sit up, fold the leg on the side nearer to the *kamiza* (the beating-arm side), and rise by turning naturally in that direction in order to walk to a new station on the longitudinal axis (approximately Tori's engagement position), there to turn once again naturally to his left (his back to the *kamiza*) to face Tori; Tori has risen similarly and turned naturally into the *kamiza* to station himself for left *yoko-gake*. Rising from *ukemi* out of left *yoko-gake* by folding his right leg, however, Uke backs directly to his new station (his edge of the center zone).

An Uke who has executed *ukemi* from those *sutemi waza* which permit him to come up to *shizenhontai* has no need to sit and fold the low-side leg, kneel on the low-side knee, or stand. Really all he need do is turn to face Tori and adjust to the proper engagement distance. Uke, after executing *ukemi* from *tomoe-nage*, and after *sumi-gaeshi* if he elects to come to his feet, will find himself on the longitudinal axis, facing outward away from Tori. Uke in this momentarily static posture is neutral insofar as the *kamiza* is concerned. He should, therefore, turn into the *kamiza* as he faces Tori. In *yoko-guruma* and *uki-waza*, however, Uke is thrown on a line off the longitudinal axis. In the above cases, if he is standing in *shizenhontai* he must turn toward what is the shortest distance to his new engagement position, where he will face Tori. In *sutemi waza* where he is required to stay down on the mat in *ukemi* (*ura-nage* and *yoko-gake*) or where he elects to stay down on the mat (*sumi-gaeshi*, *yoko-guruma*, and *uki-waza*) Uke is required to follow normal procedure as dictated by the rule.

Tori, finding himself down on the mat at the completion of a *sutemi waza*, simply sits and folds his leg on the *kamiza* side, comes smoothly to a kneeling position (without dependence upon hands or arms to prop him into it), and then stands to face Uke by turning toward the *kamiza* naturally; he can always respect the *kamiza*. Of course, in *uki-otoshi* the throw brings Tori directly into a kneeling position and it is therefore necessary only to stand, turn toward the low-side leg, and face Uke naturally.

On various occasions, Tori must either walk forward or step a bit backward to station himself prior to Uke's arrival so that the next throw can begin; Uke, too, must walk and adjust to the proper engagement distance before the throw can commence. This movement creates a longer axis on which to act, and ensures that the climax of the technique falls within the center zone; the movement sees both Tori and Uke moving independently, but in harmony with each other. This movement in no way effects a change in the rule for facing actions.

♦ **THE RHYTHM OF THIS KATA**
The rhythm of Nage no Kata is not particularly difficult to understand, being fairly evenly paced throughout all techniques. But it always creates difficulties for the training partners performing it, as will be evident when the correct rhythm is sought. Only the most experienced judoists can achieve it correctly. Nothing looks worse and can ruin this kata more completely, for demonstration purposes, than a jerky interrupted performance caused by hesitations and mistakes in positioning for the engagement distances. Bad

timing in these preliminary movements prevents Tori and Uke from combining their actions harmoniously.

This kata is a blend of smoothly executed, formal, preliminary movements and energetically executed techniques. Tori and Uke must use great care to distinguish between preliminary movements (postures and attitudes) and the actual movements used for execution of the throws. There must be a clearly apparent visual difference between them. Preliminary movements are artificial; nevertheless, as stated in the opening of this chapter, they must be considered important connecting links, chaining the actual techniques of throwing together in continuous sequence, and as such they often must be practiced as much as the throws themselves. They are exercises in control of engagement distances (*ma-ai*).

The roles of Tori and Uke must be clearly understood in terms of attack initiative. Who is attacking, or initiating the movement into the technique, is essentially the foundation upon which the kata spirit rests, and further the foundation of all mechanics performed. This is the *rial* in application, the synergy produced by Tori and Uke.

Tori and Uke must move harmoniously together from the engagement distance to couple by gripping and simultaneous movement into the technique, or by collision in a striking attack. Uneven or mistaken gripping, a general pawing at each other, or false starts all detract from proper practice of this kata. Further, Tori and Uke must couple through gripping, in an action which does not stop movement after gripping, but rather grips and moves directly into the technique. Steady pulling, rather than spastic jerking, is essential. The movement itself must be a picture of harmony between Tori and Uke; it must not progress in an oscillating or bobbing-up-and-down fashion. Nor may the movement accelerate into a race between Tori and Uke to see "who can finish first." Rather, Tori and Uke move in couple, as evenly as undisturbed water flows, to the conclusion of the throw.

One of the first and most important things to achieve in preliminary movement is for Tori and Uke to come to the engagement distance with correct steps in *ayumi ashi*. The leadoff" technique for each category of throwing will find both Tori and Uke on their feet and moving together simultaneously to establish the proper engagement distance. They appear to arrive together, but in reality Tori is slightly ahead of Uke. Their last steps in this stationing action are taken in a slightly exaggerated manner as already described for the opening of this kata (see p. 75). With the last pace, the trailing (right) foot is brought into line with the other (left) foot already in place, so that the resultant body motion resembles a powerful wave rolling up onto a smooth beach.

This action demonstrates balance, confidence, and determination, as if each partner faced his opponent for actual combat. It must not be overdone, however. Other techniques will find Tori already stationed and waiting for Uke to rise from *ukemi* and establish the proper engagement distance; Uke does this by coming up to face Tori, also in a wavelike fashion.

Each and every time Tori and Uke station themselves at the engagement distance, they pause momentarily before launching into the technique which follows. The pace of movement leading to the execution of each throw is about the same as the tempo set for the preliminary movements, and must not be slower than that. At this natural and unhurried tempo, the throws develop evenly and give the appearance of an uninterrupted sequence of performance. Exceptions to this rhythm pattern are *okuri-ashi-harai* and *ura-nage*.

Inexperienced judoists always tend to rush the tempo when they perform *okuri-ashi-harai* and conversely tend to slow the tempo when they execute *ura-nage*. Correctly performed, *okuri-ashi harai* begins at the normal pace of stepping in *tsugi ashi* for the first step, gradually picking up speed for the second and third steps into the throw. The rhythm of this technique gives the appearance of unified body motion, like the large wave rolling and breaking on a smooth beach. Likewise, at the completion of the last *tomoe-nage* (a left-hand throw assisted by Tori's left leg), both Tori and Uke come to their feet somewhat more quickly than following the other *sutemi waza* to set the engagement distance and execute *ura-nage* (the right technique, over Tori's left shoulder) without the usual pause for such actions. Uke thus gets up from *ukemi* and must judge an engagement distance on the move. Thereafter, the normal tempo is restored.

It can be generally said of all the techniques that they give the impression of developing by a one-two-three-count progression; there are distinct and identifiable stages as the technique develops within itself. From the engagement distance to the climax at the instant of throwing, these stages may be marked. However, nothing is more artificial and harmful to training than kata which is consciously performed by such a count timing; it makes for a jerky, unnatural performance and leads to little all-around proficiency.

The one-two-three-count rhythm is most easily observed in the techniques of *uki-o1toshi*, *kata-guruma*, *harai-goshi*, *tsurikomi-goshi*, and *yoko-gake*, where Tori is moving backward as Uke moves forward into him; it is also evident in *okuri-ashi-harai*, where Tori push-pulls Uke sideward, and in *uchi-mata*, where the motion is circular. In these techniques, Uke comes from a balanced position at the engagement distance to successively threatened balance predicaments in steps one and two, to final destruction of his balance resulting in the throw on the third step. Both Tori and Uke execute three clear stepping actions. This rhythm sets the entire kata's pattern of rhythm and it should be practiced until the tempo can be positively felt.

Sasae-tsurikomi-ashi, however, with Uke moving against Tori who is moving backward, often eludes identification with the one-two-three-count pattern because Tori deliberately combines his second step with the third, using the same foot in a lagging, sliding way to bring his forward foot backward but beyond the position expected by Uke. This is done to break the lockstep timing with Uke and thus permit the throw on what amounts to Uke's third step.

The striking actions by Uke in attacks met by *seoi-nage*, *uki-goshi*, *ura-nage*, and *yoko-guruma*, which bring Uke and Tori into collision with each other, also follow the one-two-three-count pattern. Uke's preparatory step as he threatens to strike is "one," his step with the strike is "two," and his execution of the closed-gate effect with his trailing leg is "three," in the first three techniques. In *yoko-guruma*, the first two counts arc similarly marked by stepping, but the forcing down of Tori's body by Uke's striking-arm action can constitute the "three" count. Tori's stepping to blend with Uke's attack in *seoi-nage* and *uki-goshi* constitute "one"; the "two" count is his pivotal action to affect *tsukuri*; while the actual throwing motion is "three." For *ura-nage* and *yoko-guruma*, Tori's first entrance step going in low under Uke's blow is "one"; "two" is his step between Uke's legs as he prepares for *ura-nage* in both these techniques. In *ura-nage* itself, "three" is the actual sacrifice of Tori's body to the mat; in *yoko-guruma* it is same, but blended with Uke's motion forcing Tori to bend forward.

Tomoe-nage is a lone wolf in the pattern of stepping movement. With Tori and Uke gripping in couple, Tori pushes Uke backward into mutual *shizentai*, and throws after the third step. Uke actually completes three steps after engagement in *shizentai*, and is brought forward by Tori into a fourth step, and thrown as he is about to complete it.

Sumi-gaeshi offers an interesting contrast to the final technique of *uki-waza*. Both operate from the modified *jigotai*. In the former technique, Uke is pulled forward by Tori for "one," straightens up and takes a step forward with his trailing foot, but never completes it by bringing his feet into line, for "two," and is thrown there; no third count can be established by Uke's stepping actions. Tori however, takes two steps and finalizes the throw by his sacrifice of standing position to lie down for "three."

Uki-waza sees Tori also take only two distinct steps. The first of these is a wide, backward arc step which pulls Uke against his resistance into a full step forward for the count of "one." Tori takes no full second step, merely allowing his other foot to drag slightly as he floats Uke upward by a hand-lifting action. Uke, however, takes a full second step to adjust to this threat to his balance; Tori instantaneously slides his foot, which has been slowly dragging backward (this can be counted as "two"), to its extended position for the throw as he sacrifices himself to the mat. This final sacrifice action, which includes the extension of his leg, can be considered equivalent to a third step, and thus the "three" count.

Separating the throwing techniques into the one-two-three-count rhythm has training value and often helps the trainee to better execution. Experts, however, dispense with this to blend all stages in a smoothly executed performance.

It is the completion of each technique category's final throw (which is a left-hand throw in all but *uki-goshi*) that causes the only intended and clear-cut interruptions in the prevailingly even rhythm, and quality of *zanshin* in this kata. Tori and Uke walk quietly away from each other, timing their arrivals at their respective engagement positions to coincide as they come to a halt in *shizenhontai*.[18] They adjust their *judogi* unobtrusively as they walk to those positions. After a slight pause for final adjustments to their *judogi* and also to compose themselves, they turn in place naturally into the *kamiza*, maintaining *shizenhontai*, and come face to face. If it is the end of any of the first four categories, they pause momentarily and move simultaneously together to take up the proper engagement distance to continue to the next technique of the kata. If it is the end of the fifth and final category, they pause momentarily and then step backward one pace with the right foot, and then bring the left foot in line, heels together, toes pointing outward slightly; this is the salutation position, which is preparatory to their closing actions (see pp. 78-79).

Master kata teachers often say a credible kata performance is one which gives the appearance of being suspended on an invisible thread. The performers are so harmoniously joined that, to the viewer, there appears to be a taut thread linking them as they perform. At no time would the correct rhythm of the kata permit the invisible thread to become slack. This is of course most desirable when kata is being used for demonstration, where visual appeal is important. But even in training, Tori and Uke should strive to achieve such mastery.

---

18. These actions were artificially introduced into the kata by the founder, who desired some relaxation of the need for constant vigilance by both partners. The older jujutsu kata never permitted the loss of visual contact with the "enemy," as the opponent for training was described; *zanshin* was maintained throughout the entire practice. Furthermore, jujutsu kata are not as quietly performed, the *kiai* sounds usually being required not only before engagement of Tori and Uke, but also during actual attack and climax.

CHAPTER **7**

Technical Aspects of Katame No Kata

It is not the accumulation of extraneous knowledge,
but the realization of the self within, that constitutes true progress.
—OKAKURA KAKUZO

Like Nage no Kata, Katame no Kata incorporates numerous important technical details. To simplify the descriptions of the actual techniques in Chapter 9, we will examine some of these technical aspects in this chapter. You can make best use of this chapter by reading it with Chapters 5 and 9.

Theoretical Facets

◆ **THE CATEGORIES OF GRAPPLING TECHNIQUES**
This kata includes 15 model grappling techniques, divided into 3 categories composed of 5 techniques each. The categorization is based on the body dynamics involved in immobilizing actions. The techniques are performed as right-hand techniques only.

KATAME NO KATA (Forms of Grappling)

1. *Osae-komi waza* (holding techniques)
    Kuzure kesa-gatame (irregular scarf hold)
    Kata-gatame (shoulder hold)
    Kami-shiho-gatame (upper holding of the four quarters)
    Yoko-shiho-gatame (side holding of the four quarters)
    Kuzure kami-shiho-gatame (irregular upper holding of the four quarters)
2. *Shime waza* (choking techniques)
    Kata-juji-jime (half-cross choke)

Hadaka-jime (naked choke)
Okuri-eri-jime (sliding lapel choke)
Kataha-jime (single-wing choke)
Gyaku-juji-jime (reverse cross choke)
3. *Kansetsu waza* (joint-locking techniques)
Ude-garami (entangled armlock)
Ude hishigi juji-gatame (arm-crush cross armlock) or *juji-gatame* (cross armlock)
Ude hishigi ude-gatame (arm-crush arm armlock) or *ude-gatame* (arm armlock)
Ude hishigi hiza-gatame (arm-crush knee armlock) or *hiza-gatame* (knee armlock)
Ashi-garami (entangled leglock)

The names of the categories of grappling as well as those of the actual techniques must be learned in Japanese as that is the international standard.

◆ ATTACK-DEFENSE THEORY

The Katame no Kata is a graphic exposition of the dynamics of grappling in which inexperienced judoists often seek for, but fail to find, the foundation of self-defense with which the founder flavored all Kodokan kata. The subtlety of the presence of the self-defense relationships and the extent to which they apply need not, however, weaken or destroy the training benefits to be derived from this kata. The mere fact that here Tori obtains a technique, and Uke attempts to release himself from it, should be enough to guarantee the beneficial working of this kata for practical training applications along sports lines. Exhibitionary Katame no Kata, however, is dependent upon understanding of the self-defense aspects.

This kata sees Tori's techniques applied either against Uke's right side, from behind as he sits or lies on the mat, or while Uke faces Tori directly. The founder never meant to reconcile the performance of this kata with the usual preliminary circumstances in self-defense situations. Instead, he deliberately designed a good portion of this kata as "unreal" insofar as self-defense is concerned; the balance of the kata, however, becomes realistic enough in the style of an honest struggle between both parties. Intended to test the grappling skills of both performers, this kata does just what it was designed to do.

This kata is "unreal" within the sphere of self-defense only to the extent that the prelude to the starting point from which the struggle begins is arbitrary, and requires certain assumptions and concessions in the positions of both performers. There is no debate on how the performers got into contact on the ground, merely a well principled preliminary arrangement which is both mechanical and hypothetical. Reality begins only at the moment when Tori signals that his technique is "on" and ready to be tested by Uke, or when Tori's proximity to Uke invites Uke's attack; Uke is then at liberty to probe Tori's effectiveness by the appropriate escape actions.

An important consideration in reaching a good understanding of this kata is that it is, unlike Nage no Kata, a complete exercise in the methods of continuing an attack and the defenses against it. In the Nage no Kata, Uke, always an aggressor by deed or intent, makes no real attempt to foil or defend against Tori's techniques except along very carefully prescribed lines and with controlled energies; in the Katame no Kata, a real and less restricted defense and continuation of attack is the whole object. At a specific time during the application of each technique of this kata, when the technique has been or is being placed, Uke is required to honestly defend himself by vigorously attacking Tori's techniques for immobilizing him. It is not the one-way affair it was in the Nage no Kata, with Tori being the key figure, but rather an interplay of both roles which makes precise attack-defense relationships difficult to explain clearly.

Tori, during the "unreal" portion of each technique, that is, the preliminary movements which permit him to secure his technique or attempt to do so, can be considered aggressive since Tori not only makes the first movement (his entry step) but obtains his technique and, in reality, places his attack without Uke's doing anything about it. Only two exceptions to this exist, in the techniques of *hiza-gatame* and *ashi-garami*, in which Tori and Uke face each other and come to grips in *shizentai* (kneeling and standing, respectively). This initial "reaching" for a grip is Uke's action, with Tori following suit, but moving quickly, to first obtain a similar grip. Other apparent exceptions in the techniques of *ude-garami*, *juji-gatame*, and *ude-gatame* are really not exceptions at all in that Tori, from the near position on the lateral axis, makes the initial movement by taking his characteristically short entry step. Upon moving closer to Uke (except in *juji-gatame*) Tori must first move Uke's right arm before Uke responds with an attack; in *juji-gatame*, Tori just completes his entry step when Uke attempts to grasp him before he can do more. Regardless, it is Tori who is clearly aggressive if preliminary movement is taken as the starting point in determining aggressiveness. Uke's really aggressive actions do not come until after Tori has taken his preliminary position and thus "notified" Uke that all is ready for him to attempt attack or escape actions, as the case warrants.

After Tori has placed his technique and its effect is evident to Uke, Uke defends himself by attacking Tori's weak points; in control, Tori continues his attack by defending against Uke's escape or neutralization actions. Thus, there is a blend of attack and defense on both sides.

One more consideration is vital here. Alert judoists often question how the socially concerned thinking of the founder can be extended to Katame no Kata, where Tori can, in the sense just discussed, be considered an aggressor (see p. 86). If the founder intended an ethical use for Kodokan Judo, as is the case in Nage no Kata, why does it not apply in this kata?

There is no breach of ethics intended, for Tori's apparently aggressive actions are limited to the artificial or "unreal" preliminary movements, which are not in any way meant to be aggression by Tori against Uke. What has preceded by way of a struggle between Tori and Uke is unknown (and unimportant to this kata), but if we extrapolate back from what happens in the Katame no Kata, we can show it to be a natural continuation of a struggle which started in the standing position. As in the Nage no Kata, Uke in Katame no Kata could have taken some aggressive action which resulted in his being deposited on the mat by Tori's response to his attack. Uke is down due to a complete or partially complete throwing action or entry into a grappling tactic applied by Tori, the aggressor.

We have come in late on the struggle which we now see continuing upon the mat. The arbitrary preliminaries are merely appendages by which logical situations can be constructed without complications of getting into these situations by real combat.

The importance of this extrapolated meaning extends still further. As against the Nage no Kata, the Katame no Kata is often accused of being impractical for self-defense. While it is true that this kata is largely applicable to *randori* and the sports or contest application of Judo, a fact which should delight the practical-minded and contest-centered judoist, nevertheless the grappling actions can be the basis of a self-defense struggle which has already been brought to the mat. No practical methods are offered for bringing the opponent to the mat, except in the techniques of *hiza-gatame* and *ashi-garami*.[1]

This kata, too, utilizes the Principle of Judo in both its facets; yielding and resisting both are found within it, though perhaps not as distinctly as in the

---

1. The severe techniques of *hiza-gatame* and *ashi-garami* were adapted from the rudiments of the Tenjin-shin'yo Ryu of jujutsu, which specialized in *katame* methods. The founder preserved these techniques as a reminder that efficient grappling tactics can begin from an erect posture, a fact which supports the self-defense value of this kata. Because of the potential danger of such techniques and the difficulty of practicing them in *randori*, the founder stripped virtually all similar jujutsu tactics from his Kodokan Judo.

Nage no Kata. Uke's role is largely one of resistance, trying to extricate him-self from a predicament imposed by Tori. This he does by resisting Tori's techniques through avenues of escape directed against Tori's weakest points in his control of Uke. Tori, on the other hand, after taking a technique, may allow Uke to struggle, but blends harmoniously with him and continues ef-fective control if possible. This is especially true and evident in the first cat-egory, the holding techniques, in which Tori may move his body as required to foil Uke's attempts at escape. Yield-resist interchanges are subtle and not precisely patterned as they are in the Nage no Kata.

Practical Facets

◆ THE FAR AND NEAR POSITIONS

There are six precise locations on the mat, relative to Uke's position for re-ceiving Tori's techniques, at which Tori must station and restation himself to engage Uke. These locations, however, may be referred to by only two names: the far position (*toma*) and the near position (*chikama*). There is one of each position on the lateral axis, those locations never changing. The longitudinal axis, however, has two different locations for each of the positions—a total of four positions. All locations, either on the lateral or the longitudinal axis, are critical to a successful performance of this kata and must be well known to both performers, especially Tori. They have some peculiarities all their own.

First of all, the far position may be thought of as a transitory station at which Tori composes himself and prepares for the action at hand. As a pre-liminary position for Tori, it is artificial but nevertheless important to prepa-ration for the techniques to follow. The far position is always located approximately 4 to 6 feet away from the nearest part of Uke's body when Uke is correctly positioned.

The near position relates only very roughly to the relative positions of Tori and Uke as they establish the engagement distance for each technique of the Nage no Kata; it has some important differences. It is always located approximately 1 to 2 feet away from the nearest part of Uke's body when he is correctly positioned. From this position Tori cannot efficiently engage Uke without moving his feet; the distance is too great. Likewise, Uke cannot launch an effective attack without moving the main part of his body; he cannot reach Tori by arm movement alone. This distance, then, is a subtle safety margin which reminds us that this kata contains positive elements of self-defense.

These suggested distances between Tori and Uke, for both the far and near positions, will suffice for all but the tallest and shortest of judoists who perform the role of Tori. Slight modifications to these dimensions may be made, if necessary, to accommodate Tori. These distances of separation are never rigidly fixed for all judoists, even though Japanese descriptions of the kata appear to require precise distances.[2] If Tori stations himself too close to Uke at either position, he will find that movement toward Uke is cramped and the force of his applied energies is reduced; further, at the near position, he is disregarding the safety zone between himself and Uke dictated by the self-defense training values of this kata. A position too far away from Uke makes movement awkward and grossly exaggerated as Tori attempts to approach Uke.

As against Nage no Kata, in the Katame no Kata it is Uke's responsibility to determine the point from which each technique will begin, and it falls to Tori to set the proper engagement distance. Thus, in Katame no Kata Tori has the responsibility for the correct choice and precise location of the far and near positions, guided by Uke's waiting and fixed position. Nevertheless, Tori should make some mental note of physical features (cracks, spots on the mat) to aid him in finding these positions again. For the majority of the techniques, Uke is supine on the mat.

The far and near positions on the lateral axis are used in preparation for the techniques of *kuzure kesa-gatame, kata-gatame, yoko-shiho-gatame, kata-ju-ji-jime, gyaku-juji-jime, ude-garami, juji-gatame,* and *ude-gatame*; and on the longitudinal axis, for the techniques of *kami-shiho-gatame, kuzure kami-shi-ho-gatame, hadaka-jime, okuri-eri-jime, kataha-jime, hiza-gatame,* and *ashi-ga-rami*[3] Thus, other differences between this kata and the Nage no Kata are seen: in this kata the lateral axis is used more than the longitudinal axis, and the lateral axis is not the imaginary line that bisects the kata area. When stationing himself on the lateral axis, Tori must imagine a line extending through Uke's belt toward him, at right angles to the longitudinal axis. Stationing himself on the longitudinal axis requires Tori to take up a position directly behind Uke as Uke lies back on the mat, behind Uke as he sits, or directly facing Uke, as the case may be; both bodies center on the longitudinal axis.

Both Tori and Uke must be aware that twice during this kata, the far and near positions for Tori on the longitudinal axis, where he prepares for a new technique, are not at the same points on the mat as usual; relative to Uke's body, of course, they are the same. (Tori's usual far position lies well outside the center zone.)

---

2. The approximately 4- and 1-foot separations suggested in Japanese texts for the far and near positions, respectively, were set in the days when judoists were generally smaller in stature than now.

3. *Ashi-garami* actually begins with Tori and Uke in *shizenhontai*, about 3 feet apart (semifar position).

1 *Shizenhontai.*   2 *Kyoshi (closed).*   3 *Kyoshi (open).*

The first change of the location of the far position comes upon completion of the *kata-juji-jime*, for which Uke has been lying on his back. Tori moves back to the far position on the lateral axis and then stands up in preparation for his movement to the longitudinal axis where he will continue with the next technique (*hadaka-jime*); simultaneously with Tori's standing, Uke sits up. By his sitting action Uke is waiting for the *hadaka-jime*, but has brought the point at which Tori must station himself, the far position on the longitudinal axis, nearer the center zone. Tori's movement to the longitudinal axis must therefore take this into account; if he simply stationed himself on the same spot on the longitudinal axis that he had been at twice before (in *kami-shiho-gatame* and *kuzure kami-shiho-gatame*), as Uke lay supine, that would now position him too far from Uke, who is in the sitting position. It is up to Uke to sit up as Tori stands at the lateral-axis far position; if Uke waits to sit up after Tori has committed himself to a far position on the longitudinal axis based on Uke's reclining posture, Tori will make a serious misjudgment in establishing a far position which puts him too far away for the technique of *hadaka-jime*. If Uke fails to sit up as required, Tori must be alert and judge a far position which, upon Uke's late sitting action, will be correct.

The second change in locating the far position on the longitudinal axis follows the same reasoning. It occurs upon the completion of *ude-gatame* and the preparation for *hiza-gatame* in the *kansetsu waza*.

◆ POSTURES

This kata involves fewer different postural forms than does the Nage no Kata. You are already familiar with the *shizenhontai* and its right and left derivatives

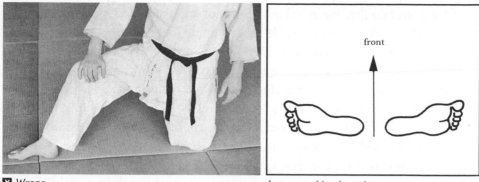

❌ Wrong.

Incorrect shizenhontai stance.

called *shizentai*. You will use the *shizenhontai* in making all opening movements in this kata, and in all movements preliminary to the actual stationing for the techniques when you, as Tori, move to locate and relocate yourself in the far positions on the lateral and longitudinal axes. You will also use this posture for the execution of one technique (*ashi-garami*), and in another (*hiza-gatame*) a kneeling variation, both in their right derivatives. The kneeling variation is also much used as a transitional posture for Tori as he makes his entry step to place every technique but *ashi-garami* (see p. 135).

Utilize the high kneeling posture for all other requirements of this kata. It is referred to as *kyoshi no kamae* (high kneeling engagement posture) or simply *kyoshi*. This posture is important to both Tori and Uke, but especially to Tori, who must use it to initiate all his stepping movements preparatory to stationing himself at the far and near positions. It is always a right posture and has two modes: a "closed" and an "open" form.

Assume the *kyoshi* from *shizenhontai* by kneeling on your left knee, moving your left foot directly backward so that, as you lower your body to kneel, your left knee can be placed in line with your right ankle. Stand your left foot on curled-under toes, with the sole surfaces of the toes in contact with the mat. As you lower your body, place your right hand, with fingers extended and together, so that it cups the big muscle at the inside of your right thigh just above the knee. Allow your left arm to hang vertically, naturally, at your left side; keep your left side vertical to the mat. Hold your head naturally, with chin tucked in and eyes fixed to the front (Figs. 1, 2). This is the closed form of the *kyoshi*, which you will use to move along the two axes between the far and near positions.

Now slide your right foot outward lightly across the mat surface to your right, stopping with the full sole surface on the mat; your right thigh and shin area form slightly more than a right angle with each other. Keep your body erect as you do this. Notice that the toes of your right foot point outward to your right front at a comfortable natural angle. There is great stability in this posture (Fig. 3). This is the open form of the *kyoshi*, which you use as Tori to station yourself at the far and near positions when you compose yourself and prepare for engagement with Uke and for relocation to the far positions on the other axis and on your axis.[4] Uke too uses it to prepare himself for engagement with Tori on occasions when he goes to the mat in a reclining position on his back, and when turning, after rising from the mat, to face Tori. Placing your right foot so that your toes point directly to your right is incorrect and a common mistake; it greatly weakens the stability of the *kyoshi*. Think of it in this way: when you stand in *shizenhontai* do not position your feet as shown above; this would be ridiculous and would weaken your balance. It is the same for the *kyoshi*; to establish stability as well as mobility potential, your right foot must be placed naturally and at a similar angle to what it would be if you were in *shizenhontai*.

When you are at the far position in *kyoshi* and are about to move forward to the near position, or you are about to stand to relocate to the far position on the other axis, fix your eyes at a point on the mat just beyond Uke. In *kyoshi* at the near position you hold this eye direction until you first move to attack; then make visual contact with Uke's head. After completing the technique, keep visual contact with Uke's body as you move back to the near position. For each successive attack from this near position, shift your gaze to his head. When you leave the near position and move backward in *kyoshi* to the far position, keep in visual contact with Uke's body.

Since this kata is permeated with more artificialities than the Nage no Kata, it is of first importance for each trainee to play his role with as realistic a flavor as possible. Tori must restrict himself to postures and body manipulations which express the highest state of composure and quiet alertness. *Zanshin* must be evident. The *kyoshi* is a posture which, in movement, has mechanical intricacies that must be sufficiently practiced before Tori is able to find and give these qualities full play. When assuming the *kyoshi*, Tori must pay strict attention to the establishment of visual contact with Uke. Visual contact with Uke is not necessarily eye to eye, but more a gaze at Uke's body by Tori with no attempt to fix a conscious stare at Uke's eyes.[5]

---

4. When jujutsu was at its technical zenith, and also during the early days of Kodokan Judo, *kyoshi* was often assumed with the left knee up. It was further complicated by requiring the performer to sit down on his right heel; appropriately, it was called the "low kneeling posture." Modern Judo no longer uses this left posture, though it can be found in some jujutsu kata.

5. The old kata masters often gave the impression that Tori should not stare directly at Uke's reclining body. Their instructions were to look "over" Uke's body and concentrate on a spot on the mat beyond him. Actually, they

The qualities of composure and quiet alertness are encouraged by the *kyoshi* which, while dignified, is strictly a combative posture.[6] Tori while in *kyoshi* must generate and maintain these qualities throughout the kata. The descriptions of the actual techniques in Chapter 9 are filled with reminders that visual contact, composure, and quiet alertness are essential. A kata performed without these qualities is a meaningless mechanical repetition of movement, not sound practice; it will be of far less training value than correct practice. Tori is charged with the responsibility of demonstrating these qualities each time he comes into *kyoshi* at the far and near positions, and while he is moving between those positions. Only when he moves between far positions, from one axis to the other, does he forego these qualities somewhat, but even then only because of the necessity imposed by his physical movements, which reduce his visual contact with Uke.

Tori should especially note that each time he assumes the *kyoshi* (open), he must pause momentarily; this applies whether or not he is at the far or near position on either axis. Any slighting of this pause, with movement through the *kyoshi* in a sloppy or hurried manner, is improper; likewise, too long a pause while in that position is detrimental to the rhythm and training benefits of the kata.

Uke has no deliberate eye-to-eye contact requirements with Tori except when he assumes the *kyoshi* to face Tori at the opening and closing of the kata, at the end of each category to adjust his *judogi* preparatory to beginning the next category, and as he engages in the techniques of the *kansetsu waza* category. In his supine position on the mat, he may, as Tori takes his entry step, make eye-to-eye contact with Tori if he chooses to do so.

◆ STEPPING MOVEMENTS

Both *ayumi ashi* and *tsugi ashi* are used in this kata. These movements were taught to you in your basic Judo training days and are important to your practice of the Nage no Kata. The opening movements for coming onto the mat area to practice Katame no Kata, for both Tori and Uke, make good use of *ayumi ashi*, as do all preliminary standing movements between the actual grappling techniques, in which Tori moves to station or restation himself at the far positions on either axis. All other movements require Tori and Uke

---

were simply trying to point out the well-known fact that looking directly at an object often screens its movement or even its location. At the instant of Tori's entry step to engagement, however, eye-to-eye contact is permitted, but not obligatory except in executing the *kansetsu waza*.

6. The *kyoshi* and variations on it may be seen clearly in the various martial arts of Japan. Swordsmanship, spear, bow-and-arrow, halberd, even stick and staff tactics employ this useful posture.

4 Kyoshi (open).   5 Kyoshi (closed).   6 Movement forward (tsugi ashi).

to utilize *tsugi ashi* while in *kyoshi* (closed) and while moving to the kneeling *shizentai* (see p. 128)

Tori's *shizenhontai* from *kyoshi* (open) is preparatory to his movement to the appropriate far position. Standing up from *kyoshi* (open) always terminates in *shizenhontai*; do not bring your feet together. Never rise from *kyoshi* (closed) directly; open it first. To rise correctly from *kyoshi* (open), first slide your right foot just a bit inward, then stand up naturally; do not move your right foot to the *kyoshi* (closed) position.

Tori's stepping off for movement to the far position on either axis commences from *shizenhontai* by pivoting in place toward the direction of his coming movement; he then steps off slowly with his left foot first.

Tori's movement between far positions is performed in straight *ayumi ashi* fashion, taking the shortest course, a diagonal route to the new far position; Tori then turns in place in the direction of the *kamiza* to face Uke, positioning himself in *shizenhontai* (see Fig. d, p. 140).

To move forward one step by *tsugi ashi* while in *kyoshi*,[7] first close that position by sliding your right foot from its extended position at your right, to the inside of your left knee which rests on the mat; bring your right toes into approximate line with your left knee (Figs. 4, 5). Without pause, advance your right foot one natural pace by sliding it directly forward; the length of

---

7. This action derives from the movement of swordsmen of ancient and medieval times, who achieved their powerful effect in cutting from that position by timing the action of the blade with their motion. Expert swordsmen can actually come out of *seiza* into *kyoshi* (closed), simultaneously drawing their swords and making parries or cutting attacks. The founder utilized this posture and movement to strengthen the legs and hips and to impart flexibility to the lower body.

☒ *Wrong.* 7 **☒** *Wrong.*

this pace must permit your right sole to keep contact with the mat as a firm base for the support of your coming weight shift onto that leg to permit movement forward (Fig. 6). Now slide your left leg forward on the knee, keeping the toes of that foot curled with their sole surfaces in contact with the mat and heel upward; slide your knee to a position just alongside the inside of your right ankle (Fig. 7). Assume the starting position, *kyoshi* (open), once again by extending your right leg to your right, sliding it lightly across the surface of the mat to the correct place (Fig. 4).

Backward movement by *tsugi ashi* while in *kyoshi* (closed) is achieved by reversing these elements.

Notice that the closing and opening actions of your right foot, preparatory to either forward or backward movement in *kyoshi*, form a right-angle pattern resembling an L traced on the mat with the stepping movement of your upraised leg. Throughout this L-shaped motion your body must be held erect, with a weight distribution that shows balance and self-control. As you step forward or backward your midsection is thrust forward a bit. This action roughly resembles the exaggerated stepping action in the Nage no Kata by which the performers came into their engagement positions or into engagement at their engagement distances. Both Tori and Uke have occasion to use this action while in *kyoshi* in the Katame no Kata.

All movement by Tori in *tsugi ashi* while in *kyoshi* is referred to as *kurai-dori*. It requires an erect, balanced body, gliding with an easy smooth effort just like *tsugi ashi* in *shizentai*. It is somewhat more difficult to achieve than movement in a standing posture and considerable practice is needed to make

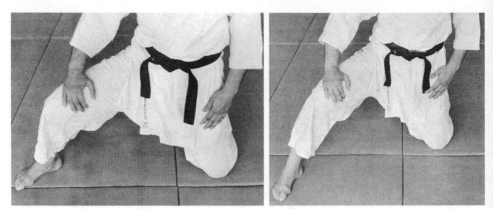

8 Kyoshi (open).   9. Entry step.

such *kyoshi* movement satisfactory. Western judoists are weaker in the lower body regions than Orientals. Bobbing, oscillating, or a bent-forward lurching motion is a sure sign of weakness in those regions.

It is especially necessary not to hunch over as the movement is made. Neither the arms or hands may aid this movement by propping actions on the mat or body. It is the legs that are the correct source of power for this action, and they operate with a firmly fixed midsection as their base. Notice that the trailing left foot always moves on its toes; "glides" is perhaps a better description. It does not move with the instep resting or dragging across the mat. This form is taken for balance purposes and relates to the combative meaning explained on page 132. It is somewhat more difficult to move backward while in *kyoshi* than it is to come forward. (See "Wrong"s on p. 133.)

Movement by Tori from the far position to the near position and his return, on either axis, is always just two steps. This range of displacement must be carefully studied as it depends entirely how accurately Tori stations himself, that is, on the engagement distance he chooses as an interval between Uke and himself.

Tori's entry step is not to be confused with going from *kyoshi* (open) to *kyoshi* (closed) nor with normal movement forward by stepping from *kyoshi* (closed). Study Figures 8-10 to learn the differences. The entry step is a necessary movement performed from the near position only, on either axis, which permits Tori to secure his technique. Tori, correctly stationed at the near position, is too far away from Uke to engage him directly without some kind of movement forward, and too close to require the normal stepping action forward by *tsugi ashi* in *kyoshi* (closed). The safety zone, which exists between him and Uke as a correlate of self-defense, must be broken if engagement is to occur. It is broken by the entry step (Figs. 8, 9).

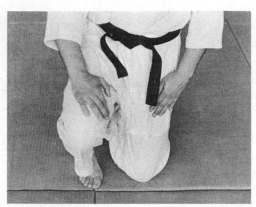

10 Kyoshi (closed). 11 Kyoshi (open).

Tori's entry step is used in making the attack for all techniques but *ashi-ga-rami*; Uke uses it only for *hiza-gatame*. It is taken by taking a short step with the right foot, directly from *kyoshi* (open); the left knee then slides up a bit to keep Tori's balance and mobility as the right foot is weighted in its new position nearer Uke. Tori is now in what can be called a right kneeling *shizentai* (see p. 128). Upon completion of each technique, Tori adjusts and releases Uke from the right kneeling *shizentai*, not *kyoshi* (closed) or *kyoshi* (open); he then reverses this entry-step procedure by taking the same short step backward, his left knee first followed by his right foot, to once again assume *kyoshi* (open) at the near position.

Uke's movement in *kyoshi* is quite limited when compared to Tori's, being necessary only as he moves forward one step from his engagement position at the opening of the kata to assume the lying-ready position (see below) and, finally, to move backward one step to his engagement position at the completion of the last technique, *ashi-garami*, preparatory to closing the kata. Uke matches Tori's entry step only once, when he initiates engagement leading to *hiza-gatame*.

◆ UKE'S LYING-READY AND SITTING-READY POSITIONS
At the beginning of this kata, Tori and Uke face each other in *shizenhontai* at their respective engagement positions. After a slight pause, they simultaneously assume the *kyoshi* (open). After another slight pause, Tori stays motionless in *kyoshi* (open) as Uke moves one step forward by *tsugi ashi* in *kyoshi* (closed), then assumes *kyoshi* (open) (Fig. 11). A pause by Uke and he lowers himself into the lying-ready position supine on the mat, somewhat inside of the center zone along the longitudinal axis, but favoring his side of that area.

12 Uke assumes the lying-ready position.　　　13

He does this by bending forward while in *kyoshi* (open), putting his right palm on the mat with fingers extended and together but pointing to his left, and placing his right hand approximately 1 foot ahead of his kneeling left knee. He stabilizes his body by keeping his chin tucked in and placing his left hand on his left thigh just above the knee (Figs. 11, 12).

Shifting his weight with a steady smooth transfer movement, he assumes a three-point suspension or tripod position with his right hand and his feet firmly on the mat, as he raises his left knee (Fig. 13).

Uke now turns counterclockwise (left) by shifting his weight so it is fully supported by his left foot and right hand; he threads his now free right leg through the opening between his right arm and his left leg (Fig. 14). Extending his right leg straight back past his left foot, he spins smoothly to sit on the mat near his left heel (Fig. 15). Without a pause, he lies down on the longitudinal axis (Fig. 16). This is the lying-ready position.

Note that Uke's hips now rest near his left heel; this is made possible by his bent left leg's resting with its full sole on the mat. His right leg rests outstretched, with the heel on the mat. Uke's body position must be straight at this point, with legs resting naturally together and not splayed in a V-shaped fashion; his arms rest naturally straight along the sides of the body. The chin is tucked in and the head is a bit raised off the mat. This position indicates to Tori that Uke is ready for him to begin the actual techniques.[8]

When properly done, Uke's weight shift and turning to lie down do not

---

8. In early Kodokan Judo, Uke lowered himself similarly but allowed both legs to remain straight for a brief moment as he assumed the lying-ready position. By then bending his left knee, while positioning his left heel near his hips, Uke signaled Tori to begin. Today the movement is direct. Modern-day kata tends to permit Uke the comfort of placing his head on the mat. In this restful position, this kata becomes less lifelike and is furthermore less valuable for physical education. Only when extreme muscular weakness prohibits keeping the head raised off the mat should trainees take the restful position.

14

15

16 Lying-ready position

let the body collapse into a sitting or semilying position. The speed of this complete action is uniform throughout its course and appears as an Uke-controlled action, not as gravity-controlled, abrupt flopping to the mat. Only Uke makes this movement; he uses it in preparation for each category of techniques, that is, three times.

Uke's return to *kyoshi* (open) from the lying-ready position is also required three times. Only Uke makes this movement. The first two occasions come at the end of the first two categories: Uke and Tori assume the *kyoshi* (open) to compose themselves and to adjust their *judogi*. The final occasion comes at the completion of the technique of *ude-gatame* after Tori has moved back to the lateral-axis far position in preparation for movement to the longitudinal-axis far position for the next technique, *hiza-gatame*.

Uke makes this movement distinctly, carefully timing it with Tori's actions. Uke sits up as Tori rises to *shizenhontai* at the lateral-axis far position, but before Tori turns and steps off to move to the far position on the longitudinal axis.

Uke sits up and bends his left knee, to fold the leg's outer thigh surface to the mat and the sole to the inside of his right leg near the knee joint. This

17

18 Sitting-ready position.

19

20

21

22 Kyoshi (open).

is the sitting-ready position; it is used in preparation for the techniques of *hadaka-jime*, *okuri-eri-jime*, and *kataha-jime* (Figs. 17, 18).

As Tori steps off to move to the new far position on the longitudinal axis, Uke reaches with his right hand behind himself, placing his palm on the mat approximately 1 foot straight behind his right buttock, fingers extended and together, pointing to his right (Fig. 19).

Next, smoothly shifting his weight, Uke supports his body with his right hand and left foot, and lifts his buttocks from the mat as he begins to turn clockwise (right) (Fig. 20). Continuing this action, Uke spins himself erect to face Tori, assuming *kyoshi* (open). Uke's free right leg is withdrawn through the opening created by his right arm and left leg. As Uke rights himself, he makes minor adjustments with his right foot (Figs. 21, 22).

When properly done, the weight shift and turning to assume *kyoshi* (open) do not let the body collapse. The speed of this action is uniform from beginning to end and appears as an Uke-controlled action. There must be an effort to make the motion flow smoothly in all phases. It should be completed prior to the moment that Tori lowers himself into *kyoshi* (open) at the longitudinal-axis far position.

◆ OPENING ASSUMPTION OF KYOSHI

The opening movements of Katame no Kata are identical with those of the Nage no Katá from the time Tori and Uke enter the practice area until both stand in *shizenhontai* at their respective engagement positions on the longitudinal axis (see pp. 70-75). From here, while the Nage no Kata progresses

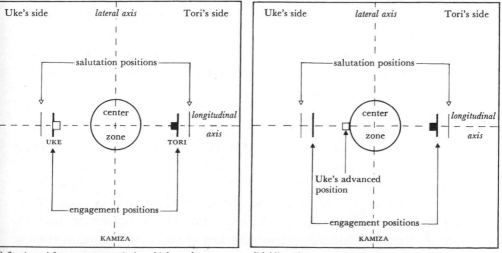

] Stationed for engagement in kyoshi (open).   (b) Uke advances one step.

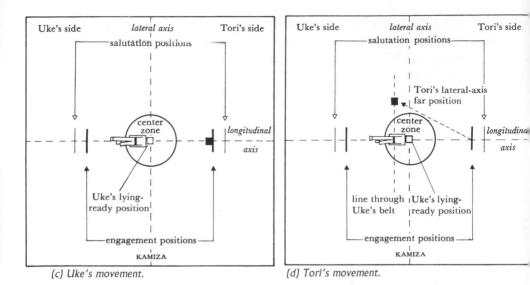

(c) Uke's movement.

(d) Tori's movement.

with Tori and Uke walking in *ayumi ashi* to station themselves for engagement in the first technique along the longitudinal axis, the Katame no Kata follows a distinctly different procedure.

Standing at their respective engagement positions on the longitudinal axis, both Tori and Uke simultaneously lower themselves into *kyoshi* (open) and momentarily pause with composure and quiet alertness, being careful to maintain visual contact (Fig. a). While Tori holds fast, Uke advances one step by *tsugi ashi* in *kyoshi* (closed) and then reassumes *kyoshi* (open); visual contact with Tori is maintained (Fig. b). After another momentary pause, Uke lowers himself to the mat in the lying-ready position, thus signaling Tori that all is ready for Tori to commence the techniques; during Uke's lowering action, Tori holds fast' (Fig. c). Now Tori stands up and proceeds directly to the lateral-axis far position (see p. 128) to assume *kyoshi* (open) (Fig. d). After a momentary pause, keeping composure and quiet alertness, Tori begins the approach for the first technique.

◆ CLOSING PROCEDURES

Upon completion of the last technique of this kata, *ashi-garami*, which takes places within the center zone, Tori and Uke untangle themselves naturally and assume *kyoshi* (open) at the semifar position on the longitudinal axis. Without a pause, Tori retreats along the longitudinal axis by *tsugi ashi* in *kyoshi* (closed) for two steps to take his station at his engagement position in *kyoshi* (open); Uke holds motionless during Tori's retreat and stationing actions. Pausing momentarily to adjust their *judogi*, Tori and Uke maintain

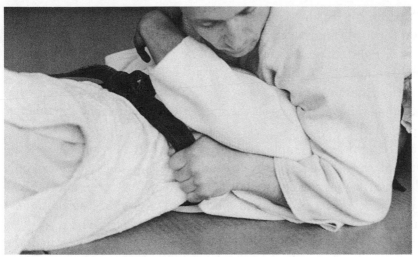
23 Normal grip.

visual contact. Adjustments completed, Uke then retreats one step by *tsugi ashi* in *kyoshi* (closed) along the longitudinal axis to take his station at his approximate engagement position in *kyoshi* (open); Tori holds motionless during these actions. Tori and Uke must begin from the correct points within the center zone, Tori from a position at the center of the center zone, and Uke from his edge of the center zone. Pausing momentarily with composure and quiet alertness, maintaining visual contact, they simultaneously rise to *shizenhontai*. From here on the procedure to complete this kata is identical to that of the Nage no Kata (see pp. 77-78).

◆ GRIPPING

Both Tori and Uke use a wide variety of gripping actions in this kata. As in Nage no Kata, gripping both with and without actually grasping the *judogi* is practiced. There is, however, no overall grip procedure that can be compared to that of the Nage no Kata. In the majority of this kata's techniques, grips are asymmetrical and may vary within the course of any one technique. However, on two specific occasions Tori and Uke bring off techniques using the standard grip as employed in the Nage no Kata.

One occasion comes in *hiza-gatame*, when Tori and Uke couple in what can be called a right kneeling *shizentai*. Carefully distinguish between the *kyoshi* (open) and this kneeling *shizentai*. They are not identical. The *kyoshi* requires that the left knee, which is on the mat, and the extended right foot form a line approximately at right angles to the axis of forward movement. The kneeling *shizentai* permits the extended right foot to project forward beyond that imaginary line. Thus, as a rough comparison it can be said that the *kyoshi* (open) is equivalent to *shizenhontai* and the kneeling *shizentai* is equivalent to right *shizentai*. Thus, the standard grip is used just as if Tori and Uke were standing.

The other occasion comes in *ashi-garami*, when Tori and Uke couple from a right standing *shizentai*. Here, too, the standard grip is used and should offer no complications.

Regardless of the type employed, all gripping actions in this kata must be firm, yet light; they should never become a frantic clutching which can only succeed in disarranging the opponent's *judogi*. All of Tori's gripping on Uke's belt (in *yoko-shiho-gatame*, *kami-shiho-gatame*, and *kuzure kami-shiho-gatame*) is with the normal grip, that is, with the thumb inside (Fig. 23).

Specific gripping procedures are discussed fully in Chapter 9 where the actual techniques of grappling are explained. But because these gripping procedures are generally vaguely understood by judoists, they can lead to inefficient grappling. They are important enough to be described at this point and, so amplified, may directly aid proper training. Only a few of the most troublesome are discussed below.

Among the *osae-komi waza*, the technique of *kuzure kami-shiho-gatame* offers perhaps the most confusing gripping method. After picking up Uke's right arm, Tori threads it under his own armpit, then grips Uke's back collar (lapel), fingers inside but palm upward, the back of the hand (knuckles) resting on the mat (see p. 332). To the inexperienced judoist, this procedure gives the impression of a strange, inefficient, and contortionist-like routine. Because the actual gripping in this manner is a bit painful to the forearm muscles, judoists often believe that they are on the wrong track when they make their first attempts at it. This grip, however, makes use of scientific principles by which the pulling action of the right arm ensures an automatic clamping action of Tori's elbow to his right side. Without this tight clamping action, Tori cannot trap Uke's right arm securely; improperly held, Uke can escape. The grip actually screws the arm clockwise, and when the pull is made the elbow comes in close to the body. To take the improper grip, fingers inside and palm down toward the mat, is easier to be sure, but only the most experienced of judoists can make it functional. By this grip the elbow tends to move away from the body during pulling, thus opening a channel through which Uke's loosely trapped arm can be freed. Study this point carefully and your *kuzure kami-shiho-gatame* will improve greatly.

The preparatory lapel action by Tori's left hand in the rear choking techniques of *okuri-eri-jime* and *kataha-jime* is often confusing. Tori should pull

Uke's left lapel down and slightly outward to create an opening between Uke's neck and his lapel. Into this opening Tori must insert his right hand to grip high on the lapel for the choke. To prepare Uke's left lapel by pulling straight down does not cause an opening, but only difficulty in obtaining a high enough grip. These *shime waza* depend on a right hand placed high.

In the *kansetsu waza*, for the technique of *juji-gatame* Tori must seek to grip Uke's attacking right arm directly; he must not take a sleeve grip. His grasp should be Uke's wrist, at its smallest circumference (where it meets the hand), with the right hand first, then the left; the right hand is on top. The grip resembles a normal right-handed grip on a baseball bat. Gripping the sleeve with both hands enables Uke to slip his arm back out of the sleeve and renders location by Tori of Uke's elbow joint difficult; as Tori lies back on the mat for the lock, he cannot be sure where Uke's elbow really is. If the sleeve must be gripped, Tori may use his left hand only while his right grips Uke's wrist.

Ude-gatame also can be weakened by improper gripping. For efficiency, Tori must grasp Uke's attacking left arm just above the elbow with his right hand first; he must cup-grip just above Uke's elbow with his right hand. Tori adds left-hand action to reinforce his right hand's circular push-pull, the convex side facing him. Inexperienced judoists see little to choose in which hand comes first, and more often than not use their left hands first; Uke can buckle his arm and free it if the left hand is so applied.

Hiza-gatame, too, requires Tori to cup-grip just above Uke's right elbow. The reason is identical to that discussed for the technique *oïjuji-gatame*. Tori should think of his left-hand cup grip as nothing more than a marker, marking the spot upon which to later, by means of his left leg (knee-and-thigh area), apply pressure. Gripping the sleeve will greatly complicate location of Uke's elbow joint and gives Uke plenty of opportunity to escape. Tori's right-hand grip on Uke's left lapel serves a functional purpose which must be carefully studied. It must be tightly held to serve as a base for strong pulling and inward pressing action against Uke's neck. This action will keep Uke from turning to his left and withdrawing his trapped right arm.

◆ UKE "GIVES" HIS BODY

As in the Nage no Kata, Uke must at all times remember the prearranged spirit of kata and thus "give" himself completely to Tori during the initial phase of all techniques, so that Tori is able to execute the required preparatory grappling actions. Any awkwardness or mishandling by Uke of his body, to prematurely avoid or escape from the coming technique, greatly hinders Tori and may destroy the value of this kata. While Uke is expected to cooperate by accepting the techniques correctly, this cooperation can be overdone.

Anticipating the technique by trying to assume the proper position to accommodate Tori's actions, but ahead of those actions, is particularly unhelpful to Tori in spite of the good intentions behind it. Tori must be allowed to secure the immobilization of Uke, who after it is completed formally then tests Tori's control by realistic escape measures, not by a feeble flopping around. By the theory of this kata, Uke is brought into a grappling technique by Tori, who unbalances Uke ("opens" Uke's body), takes advantage of Uke's unbalance by immediately fitting his body smoothly into the prescribed attack position against the waiting Uke, and then brings about the *kime* or effective conclusion by causing Uke to surrender. Uke allows Tori to place his technique, but must nevertheless fight to regain his balance and extricate himself from the technique after that technique has been signaled "on" by Tori. Uke must perfect his body control; this is possible only if Uke trusts Tori's grappling abilities and understands his own role.

Specific actions by Uke which can make Tori's movements preparatory to the technique, and the initial stages of the technique, neater are as follows. In the *osae-komi waza* it is often necessary for Uke to lift his head a bit, as Tori applies the techniques of *kuzure kesa-gatame*, *kata-gatame*, and *yoko-shiho-gatame*, if Uke positions himself in the new restful style with his head lying on the mat. In *kuzure kami-shiho-gatame*, Uke picks his right shoulder up a bit to facilitate Tori's gripping actions. In *kami-shiho-gatame*, Uke should turn his face, putting either ear to the mat, to avoid facial discomfort as Tori settles down on him.

In the *shime waza*, during the techniques of *kata-juji-jime* and *gyaku-juji-jime* Uke may lower his head to the mat as Tori places the form of the chokes; this will facilitate gripping. Uke must further ensure that his raised left knee does not in any way stop Tori from coming astride him as Tori moves aboard for the choke gripping form. If it is apparent to Uke that his leg will hinder Tori, Uke may quietly slide his left foot slightly forward to lower his left knee. Tori should seek to move his right foot across Uke near the belt line, rather than swinging it wide around and over Uke's upraised knee. Uke, in the sitting-ready position for the techniques of *hadaka-jime*, *okuri-eri-jime*, and *kataha-jime*, must not tuck his chin in so tightly so as to prohibit the passage of Tori's arm or his own lapel as the preparations proceed; thereafter, with the choke on, Uke may do so.

In the *kansetsu waza*, Uke must pick his head up off the mat (providing he has chosen to operate in the relaxed head-on-the-mat starting position) and look directly at Tori in the techniques of *ude-garami, juji-gatame,* and *ude-gatame.* In the *hiza-gatame,* Uke must release his right-hand grip on Tori's left lapel as Tori gathers up his arm; Uke must also allow himself to be brought to the mat properly, supporting himself by his left elbow, his left knee, and the toes of the left foot, as well as his extended right leg; he should not collapse face down on the mat. While the technique works no matter what final position Uke assumes, for the purpose of studying the technique it is far better to do it in this neater fashion. In the final technique, *ashi-garami,* Uke likewise must not collapse; he supports himself similarly.

◆ TORI'S ATTACK SIGNAL

In line with the comprehensive nature of this kata, either Tori or Uke may have license to initiate attack action, depending on the technique. Regardless, Tori's actions are always initially accepted by Uke, until Tori has obtained the correct form of the technique and has brought about control and restrictions against Uke's body. Then, at a signal from Tori, Uke is allowed to test the effectiveness of Tori's control by the use of legitimate and forceful escape actions. This signal is unmistakable. Tori achieves it by cinching the form of the immobilization a bit tighter, compressing Uke a bit more, and giving a forceful but almost inaudible exhalation of breath by contracting the abdominal muscles, as he tightens up on Uke. Uke should feel a considerable difference between the moment Tori first applies the form of the technique and the effect of the technique. Tori's technique must provoke Uke's escape actions by threatening him with inescapable holding tactics, unconsciousness, or pain as the category demands.

◆ UKE'S ESCAPE PATTERNS

Uke has the role of honestly trying to escape from Tori's applications of grappling techniques, but only after they have been signaled "on" by Tori and as they begin to take effect. These escape actions are not defined as only certain correct methods. Such rigidity is not required by this kata; in this respect, this kata is far more "real" than the Nage no Kata. While the possibilities for Uke's escape actions will be dealt with in the technical discussions of the techniques themselves in Chapter 9, certain general comments are necessary at this point to avoid misunderstandings in practice.

Practicing this kata with reliance on certain prescribed escape actions by Uke, and only those actions, gives it an unnatural flavor. The kata is thereby reduced to an exercise in purely anticipated movements and subsequently has less training value than intended by the founder.

In correct practice, Tori does not necessarily know what precise methods of escape Uke will attempt. While the avenues of escape are commonly more or less expected by Tori, and there are some escape actions that are best, they are not stereotyped and prearranged as to their identity or the order in which they will be attempted by Uke.

This is especially true in the *osae-komi waza*. Uke in this category is required to make a minimum of three distinctly different escape actions with vigor, ensuring that they are *big* movements. Counterchoking and armlocking should be minimized by Uke, who should rather attempt more appropriate measures involving twisting, bridging, and breaking the immobilization by realistic big motions of his body. The period of Uke's struggles from the onset of the technique until his surrender must be reasonably long and should not be hurried into a one-two-three-count affair, followed by Uke's quickly giving a *mairi* signal. Indeed, 5 to 10 seconds of energetic struggle should be a minimum, even when this kata is used for demonstration purposes; in training, it can be extended to 30 seconds for *osae-komi waza* and actual submission or escape (neutralization) by Uke for the categories of *shime* and *kansetsu waza*.

In the two latter categories, the period of the struggle is considerably shorter because the nature of these techniques generally permits only one escape attempt by Uke and should ensure instant surrender if properly applied. Uke's escape pattern is usually limited to one attempt which becomes more one of neutralization than one of extrication. If the technique is properly applied, Uke will be rather immobile and therefore quite limited in his ability to bridge, twist, and move out of the technique; he can do little more than surrender.

◆ MAIRI SIGNAL

This kata differs from the Nage no Kata also in that it is less serene. Uke makes positive, energetic movements in his attempts to escape from each of Tori's techniques. Another unique feature is that Uke gives the usual Judo signal of surrender at the completion of the *kime* of the technique, to indicate that the technique has effectively immobilized him and that he has lost. You learned about this signal during your basic Judo training days.

The signal must be loud enough to make it clear to Tori that Uke is surrendering. The moment it is given by Uke, both Tori and Uke stop action. Tori then slowly moves out of the form of the technique, but not before adjusting Uke's position to that where the technique began.

Uke gives the *mairi* signal by tapping twice in rapid succession on Tori's body, on his own, or against the mat with the flat palm of either hand. The signal may also be given by tapping similarly with either foot sole on the mat or against the sole of the other foot, or by stamping both soles on the mat if the case warrants it. This procedure is particularly useful in surrendering to the choking techniques of *hadaka-jime*, *okuri-eri-jime*, and *kataha-jime*, where Uke's hands have been and should remain busy in attempts to neutralize Tori's attack.[9]

◆ SOUNDS AND GESTURES

While this kata is correctly performed without a conscious effort to produce audible *kiai* sound or extreme facial expressions, nevertheless there is unavoidably a small amount of each during the close body contact and ensuing struggles made necessary by the very nature of grappling. Tori's initial application of the technique, as he signals Uke to commence escape action, is a cinching action which can be accompanied by an almost inaudible but forceful exhalation of Tori's breath; this is particularly true in the first category, *osae-komi waza*, where Tori's body force is applied almost directly with contact-compressive action. Uke's facial grimaces, as exertion or pain sets in, are unavoidable.

◆ SYMMETRY AND CENTER PERFORMANCE

The more or less statically performed Katame no Kata requires no great linear displacement and thus is easy to perform in almost any *dojo*; no serious regard to restrictions of space need be given. Recall that the center of the kata-practice area may be thought of as a zone about 6 feet in diameter. Generally speaking, all techniques begin within or mostly inside the center zone. There should be no real cause for the performers to fall outside of that zone during technique climaxes.

Symmetry and center performance are much simpler matters here than in the practice of the Nage no Kata, where positions are more fluid. Since Uke is relatively fixed in this kata, it is the obligation of Uke to set the initial position relative to which Tori will station himself. Uke assumes the appropriate position and is waiting before Tori commits himself. Nevertheless there is one peculiar aspect which must be borne in mind, especially if the kata is being performed before an audience and centering on the *kamiza* is a requirement.

The 18-foot range between Tori and Uke as they stand at their respective

---

9. Historically, effective choking action by Tori always precluded Uke's release of hands to signal surrender. Judo masters of old regarded only a "fake" technique as permitting the release of Uke's hands to deliver the *mairi* signal.

salutation positions on the longitudinal axis at the beginning of this kata, if centered on the *kamiza*, tends to bring Uke a short distance off-center as he moves in to take the lying-ready position (see Fig. c, p. 140).

Uke, standing feet together at his salutation position, is about 9 feet from dead center on the longitudinal axis. Stepping forward to *shizenhontai* at his engagement position and assuming *kyoshi* (open) there should bring him to approximately 7 feet from dead center. Moving one step forward in *kyoshi* (closed) and then assuming *kyoshi* (open), to lie down into the lying-ready position, places Uke's body along the longitudinal axis with his head just touching or slightly beyond the center of the center zone, toward Tori's side. Tori is now required to move to the lateral-axis far position and to center on Uke's belt.

This sets his line of advance and retreat in *kyoshi* (closed) along a lateral axis which does not precisely coincide with the center line (lateral axis) running through the *kamiza* at right angles to the longitudinal axis. This new lateral axis is transposed a bit, favoring Uke's side of the center zone (see Fig. d, p. 140).

Uke's movement from his salutation position to his engagement position, as well as his movement in *kyoshi* (closed) from his engagement position to take the lying-ready position, must not be made with overextended stepping actions in attempts to compensate for this discrepancy; such elongated stepping destroys his balance and posture. If centering on the *kamiza* is of vital importance, easy adjustment can be made by permitting Uke to take two normal forward steps in *kyoshi* (closed) instead of the now standard single step; very short judoists will need to do this. With this double stepping, Uke's belt will fall approximately on the center of the center zone and the lateral axis running through that center, as he lies in the lying-ready position.[10]

◆ THE RHYTHM OF THIS KATA

Unlike the Nage no Kata, this kata is a mixture of paces or tempos, easy to recognize, but quite difficult to achieve except for the most experienced judoists. The burden of keeping the proper rhythm rests with Tori, who frequently must move in and out on both the lateral and longitudinal axes as well as between them to apply his techniques. Uke remains relatively motionless during these preliminary movements by Tori; Uke's great concern

---

10. Historically, Tori and Uke stationed themselves 12 feet apart at their respective salutation positions. This caused no symmetry problems, as the lateral axis intersects the center of the center zone. When the 12-foot distance was changed to 18 feet in 1960, Uke's movement forward in *kyoshi* should have been changed to two steps, but this was apparently neglected.

here is to be in the right position at the right time to permit Tori to conform and apply the correct technique. Hesitations and mistakes in positioning by either partner make for bad timing and easily shatter the rhythm of this kata.

As an alternation of slow, smoothly executed preliminary movements and faster, more actively executed techniques, this kata lacks the metronomic rhythm of the Nage no Kata. Tori must be especially careful to display clear distinctions between his preliminary movements, postures, and attitudes, as well as later movements used for the actual taking of the form of the techniques, and the movements used to compensate for Uke's struggles to escape. While all that happens prior to the actual struggle is artificial, it is essential to the kata, acting as connecting links to string the techniques together in a logical pattern. These preliminary movements need to be practiced more than those in the Nage no Kata.

Tori and Uke must clearly understand their roles in terms of who "attacks," or initiates the attempt at first physical contact. The assumption that this procedure is identical for all techniques is erroneous.

There must be a harmonious attitude as Tori is allowed to obtain the form of his technique; Uke is watchful and waiting for Tori's "on" signal, taking no premature action. Uke does, however, anticipate Tori's execution of the technique, and must blend with it and promptly take countermeasures. Uke has ample time to think about his role. Tori, on the other hand, being required to move forward and backward a lot in *kyoshi* (closed) on both the lateral and longitudinal axes between far and near positions there, as well as in *shizentai* between the two far positions, will be greatly mentally occupied. He further must move from *kyoshi* (closed) to *kyoshi* (open), and vice versa, many times. Tori must strive for "automatic" actions; smoothly executed, graceful, balanced preliminary movements are essential and must be mastered to a degree which allows Tori to think primarily about the actual techniques. Preliminary movements must be void of bobbing or oscillating action, and the movement in *kyoshi* (closed) should never look as though Tori were limping along. A very skillful Tori makes such preliminary movements look easy; they appear to move as heavy oil flows along a smooth, flat surface. Uke's biggest task is the smooth execution of the lying-ready position from *kyoshi* (open) and his return to that posture. This movement, too, must be a model of body harmony; it must match the pace of Tori's preliminary movements.

Important for Tori to achieve is an unhurried and deliberate manner of action in preliminary movements. Each change of position must be followed by a very slight pause, for composure and quiet alertness. The standing up from *kyoshi* (open) to *shizenhontai* must clearly show that standing posture, before the turning in place to step off (with the left foot) in *ayumi ashi* on the way to the other far position. Tori, if he tries to rise, turn, and half step off before assuming *shizenhontai*, gives the appearance of trying to rush matters; this is not good kata procedure.

The walking between far positions continues the unhurried pace. As the new far position is reached, Tori turns naturally in place, once again assumes *shizenhontai*, and pauses for composure. His lowering into *kyoshi* (closed) always terminates with his right leg being extended for *kyoshi* (open). A slight pause is then taken before closing that leg and moving forward (in *kyoshi*) by *tsugi ashi* to the near position. At the near position, Tori once again opens his leg for *kyoshi* (open) and pauses momentarily; he is now ready to actually engage Uke.

Taking his very short entry step to get closer to Uke, Tori makes the required hand-and-arm preparations carefully, slowly, and at the same pace as all his previous preliminary movements. Keeping balance, he remains as erect as possible as he moves into the key positions which permit the form of the technique to be applied.

Viewers seated at the *kamiza* must be able to see what is taking place, so Tori's actions are slightly exaggerated. Though all of this preparation is slow and deliberate, once the form of the technique is established Tori signals that the technique is "on" and this breaks the slow-paced rhythm. Uke struggles to free himself. There is no set pace for the struggle actions, in which Uke attempts vigorously to extricate himself as permitted by correct practice procedure, and Tori compensates for those escape actions with appropriate responses and by continuing his immobilization. These actions need only be realistically attempted.

For symmetry and efficient action, the following preparatory hand-and-arm actions will prove helpful to Tori when operating from the near position on the lateral axis. They are used in the approaches to *yoko-shiho-gatame*, *kata-juji-jime*, *gyaku-juji-jime*, *ude-garami*, and *ude-gatame*, where Tori is required to grasp and pick up Uke's right arm, which is resting on the mat alongside Uke's body, and relocate it on the mat alongside his own left leg preparatory to the actual technique.

Tori, from the near position, takes his short entry step (with his right foot, sliding his left knee up) to draw close enough to Uke in the kneeling *shizentai*, which permits him to grasp Uke's arm. Tori reaches down with both hands to grip Uke's right arm; with his left hand, palm up, Tori cups Uke's right arm just above the elbow, while Tori's right hand grips Uke's right wrist from the top, palm down. Tori should not grip the sleeve of Uke's *judogi*. Tori then lifts

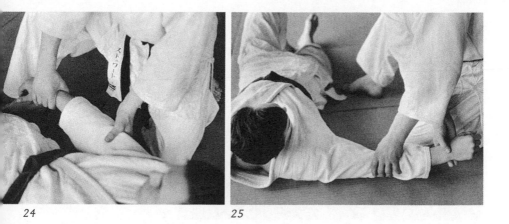

24   25

Uke's right arm off the mat (not by the sleeve), holding it in both hands still grasping as just mentioned, and moves the arm to his left to place it naturally on the mat alongside his own left leg; Uke's right arm is positioned at about right angles to Uke's body, palm down (Figs. 24, 25). Tori also grips the reclining Uke's right arm as in Figure 24 for taking the techniques of *kuzure kesa-gatame* and *kuzure kami-shiho-gatame*; only for *kata-gatame* does he grip as in Figure 26. At the completion of all seven techniques mentioned, as Tori is adjusting Uke's right arm to its starting position on the mat alongside Uke, the procedure is reversed (Figs. 25, 24), except in *kata-gatame* where Uke's right arm must be returned as in Figure 26.

Gripping Uke's right arm and moving it in any way other than the recommended one usually results in clumsy action which does little for the symmetry of this kata, to say nothing of the possibility of transferring such less efficient actions to *randori* grappling situations.

After Uke's *mairi* signal, all actions must stop promptly insofar as the vigor of attack-defense interplay is concerned. Tori must, after the *mairi* signal, relax pressure to adjust Uke's position before releasing Uke and moving to the near position; Uke must cooperate. In techniques where Uke is in the lying-ready position, at the *mairi* signal Uke usually takes care of the placement of his own left arm alongside his body, while Tori readjusts Uke's right arm by returning it naturally alongside Uke's body. If during their struggles they have substantially displaced themselves from their starting point on the longitudinal axis, Tori must retain the form (not the effect) of the technique just completed, and slide Uke back to the starting point on the longitudinal axis and otherwise adjust Uke properly before releasing him and moving back to the near position.

This is slightly modified in *gyaku-juji-jime*, wherein Tori, astride Uke, has

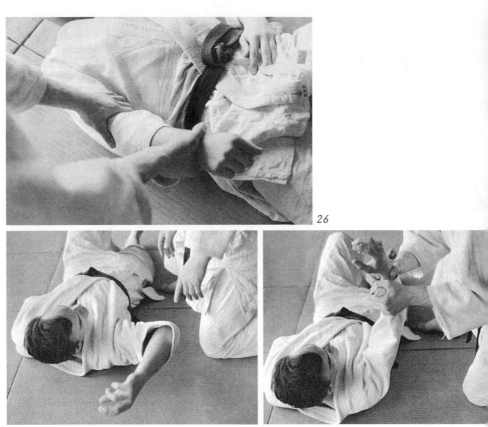

26

❌ *Wrong.*   ❌ *Wrong.*

rolled onto the left side of his back to obtain Uke's surrender. Tori and Uke cooperate to come back to their starting point by rolling into place with Tori once again coming astride Uke. Some master Judo teachers today think that this action is too much to expect, and permit Tori and Uke to disentangle naturally as they do in *hiza-gatame* and *ashi-garami*, the final techniques of this kata. This rolling action takes considerable practice to achieve smoothly without looking ridiculous.

In connection with Uke's adjustment to the lying-ready position after his surrender, Uke will do well to locate some physical feature overhead, if possible, to use as a reference point to judge his positioning. All readjustments of position are made in the unhurried manner of the preliminary movements.

The *shime waza* techniques of *hadaka-jime*, *okuri-eri-jime*, and *kataha-jime* are applied by Tori from behind a sitting Uke (in sitting-ready position). Inexperienced judoists are prone to rush the pace here because these techniques are the only place in the kata where three similarly operating techniques utilize relatively similar positional attitudes of both Tori and Uke; Tori also has a minimum of preparatory movement necessary for engagement. The rhythm operates here unchanged from that throughout the kata.

Tori, from the near position, takes his very short entry step and with slow, careful actions, places his technique; he shows correct gripping, then the application of the technique for effect. The technique is applied by unbalancing Uke slightly backward (straight or slightly diagonally as appropriate to the technique) and shows control of Uke by Tori. Tori does this by moving a very short step back (*tsugi ashi*), while in the form of the technique, in the kneeling *shizentai*. Upon the *mairi* signal, Tori loosens the effect of the technique but, before releasing Uke, returns him to his balanced sitting posture (sitting-ready position) with the form of the technique still on. He does this by moving forward with the same short step. Releasing his grip, Tori then repositions himself at the near position in *kyoshi* (open) by taking the short step backward once again.

Most of the *kansetsu waza* operate with Uke in the lying-ready position and follow patterns similar to all other techniques in the kata insofar as rhythm and responsibility for readjustment of positions is concerned. However, the last two techniques, *hiza-gatame* and *ashi-garami*, can cause problems in rhythm. After completion of each of these techniques, on Uke's *mairi* signal, both Tori and Uke release each other and move efficiently but independently into *kyoshi* (open), facing each other on the longitudinal axis within the center zone; they do so in an unhurried, natural manner. There is no set way of achieving this, except to be natural and to keep the harmony of the kata movement. These actions, too, will take quite a bit of practice to bring off smoothly.

At the completion of the final techniques in each category of grappling, Tori and Uke interrupt their performance briefly to face each other in *kyoshi* (open) outside the center zone on the longitudinal axis. They position themselves about at what amounts to the far position. At this point they compose themselves, keeping quietly alert and maintaining visual contact as they adjust their *judogi*. Then they resume their practice. The actions here should also be unhurried and careful; at the completion of the first two categories, Uke sits up from his lying-ready position and assumes the *kyoshi* (open), blending with the arrival of Tori on the longitudinal-axis far position. However, at the end of the last category Uke comes directly out of his more or less prone position on the mat (the result of *ashi-garami*) and moves directly to *kyoshi* (open) near his edge of the center zone on the longitudinal axis; he does this in an efficient, natural, and unhurried way.

As in the Nage no Kata, this kata must be performed so as to give the appearance of two performers on a single invisible thread. By a harmonious perfection of movement, the performers keep the thread taut and make a highly pleasing visual pattern characteristic of expert skill in kata.

CHAPTER **8**

Nage No Kata

Steep is the way to mastery.

—E. HERRIGEL

For the reader's convenience and understanding, a numbering system has been used in the Engagement section under each technique, to indicate who has the attack initiative at every point. Each technique has been divided somewhat arbitrarily into three or four stages, numbered 1 to 4 in bold face. The number appears in either Uke's column or Tori's depending on who then has the attack initiative. When a number appears in a different column from the previous number, it indicates that the attack initiative has changed hands. The photographs appearing in the Engagement sections are keyed to these numbers. Numbers within parentheses, as below, refer to line drawings in which white identifies Uke and black, Tori.

♦ OPENING

Tori takes his position with Uke on his right; approximately 18 feet separates them from each other and that distance is centered on the center of the *kamiza*. Both Tori and Uke stand erect, heels together, composed and quietly alert, facing the *kamiza*, at their salutation positions. Fig. (1), p. 156.

The practice begins with Tori and Uke simultaneously executing the standing salutation (*ritsurei*) toward the *kamiza*. Fig. (2). They pause momentarily after coming back to the erect posture. Fig. (3).

They then simultaneously turn in place, coming around to face each other in the same erect standing posture, heels together, looking directly at each other with composure and quiet alertness. Figs. (3), (4). They pause momentarily.

Then simultaneously they assume the kneeling-sitting posture (*seiza*). Figs. (5)-(7). They pause once again momentarily, keeping composure, quiet alertness, and visual contact.

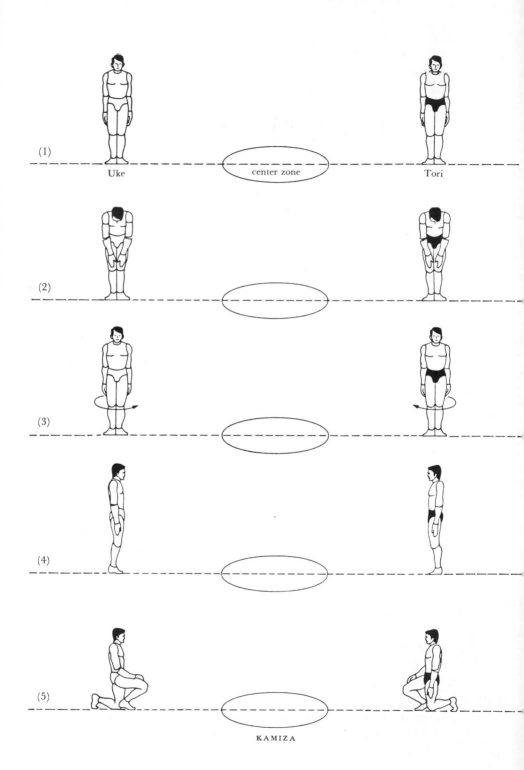

(1) Uke   center zone   Tori

(2)

(3)

(4)

(5)

KAMIZA

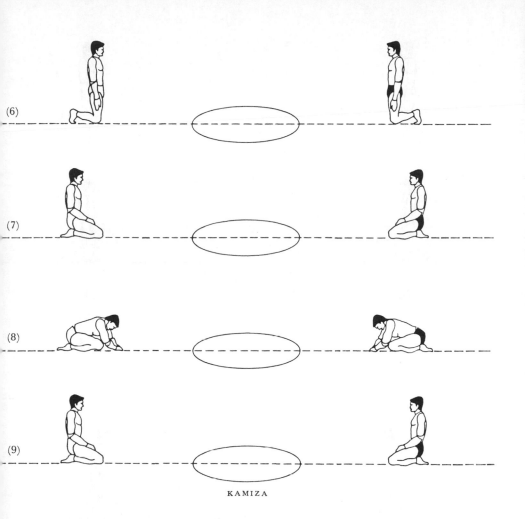

(6)

(7)

(8)

(9)

KAMIZA

They execute the sitting salutation (*zarei*) together. Fig. (8). Likewise together, they reassume the kneeling-sitting posture. Fig. (9). There is another momentary pause with composure, quiet alertness, and visual contact.

Then they rise simultaneously, coming to an erect posture once again, heels together, keeping visual contact all the way. Figs. (10)-(12). They pause once again momentarily with composure and quiet alertness, maintaining visual contact.

They then simultaneously advance one step, beginning with their left feet, and come to *shizenhontai*. These are their engagement positions. Figs. (13), (14). Another momentary pause, and they are ready for actual engagement in the techniques of this kata.

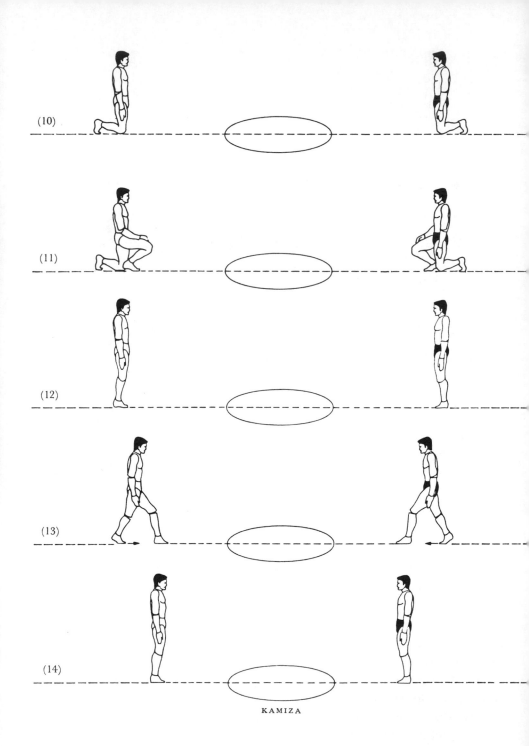

(10)

(11)

(12)

(13)

(14)

KAMIZA

UKI-OTOSHI

◆ **ABOUT THIS TECHNIQUE**

This throw, the floating drop, is classified as a hand technique (*te waza*). It exemplifies the beauty and dynamic precision of the forces which can unbalance an opponent and cause his body to trace a long arc in the air as he is snapped forward, off his feet, by the downward drawing power of the thrower's body transmitted through the arms. Distinctly *go no sen*, this technique was well chosen as the kata leadoff in that it most graphically demonstrates the essence of all throwing actions, that is, the breaking of an imposed rhythm of stepping with an unexpected change in body position to produce the throw. This technique remains unchanged from the form finally adopted by the founder, and must not be confused with similar earlier jujutsu forms which bring the thrower at almost right angles to the direction of movement and require him to use "circular steering" arm action to complete the throw.

◆ **TECHNIQUE SUMMARY**

Uke faces Tori at the near position with intent to attack. Uke steps unhesitatingly forward, gripping Tori in *shizentai* in order to push Tori and unbalance him backward. Uke continues his attack initiative for two steps in *tsugi ashi*, with Tori yielding to his push while gripping and retreating in *shizentai* by *tsugi ashi* and pulling Uke forward in an unsuccessful attempt to unbalance him. Suddenly, during the third step of Uke's attack, Tori steals the attack initiative by breaking the rhythm. Using a long backward step and a sudden sinking of his body onto his rearmost leg's knee, Tori reinforces the stepping action with a diagonally downward, straight pull of his hands to his rear to unbalance and throw Uke forward in a big arc.

◆ **TECHNIQUE KEY POINTS**

○ UKE ○

1. Keeps his weight on the forward part of his advanced foot, not on the outer edge, at takeoff.

● TORI ●

1. Throws with the drawing power of his whole body, timing the snap pull of both hands with the lowering of his body;

1

2

(UKE)

2 . Takes off from his advanced foot, his body not bent forward at the hips, placing the takeoff foot inside (alongside) Tori's lead foot (the foot of his raised knee).

3. Feels as though he is being thrown from his advanced shoulder, face up; is unbalanced forward.

4. Makes his body turn in a big arc, head over heels, past the kneeling side of Tori's body; does not spill around the side. His body actually moves forward and comes to rest facing in the direction of original movement.

(TORI)

his in-side hand pulls diagonally downward to his belt knot as his outside hand-pulls diagonally downward to his hip bone on that side; makes no wheeling action with his hands. Unbalances Uke forward.

2. Keeps erect and balanced in kneeling-throwing position, chest up, abdominal region thrust forward. The angle formed by the shin and thigh of his leg with raised knee approximates 120 degrees; the sole of the foot is firmly on the mat. His head remains facing the direction from which Uke came, and he does not attempt visual contact with Uke in flight or at *ukemi* (Fig. 1).

3. Braces with his rearmost leg, kneeling, with instep off the mat; this leg is placed at no more than 45 degrees to the axis of movement (Fig. 2).

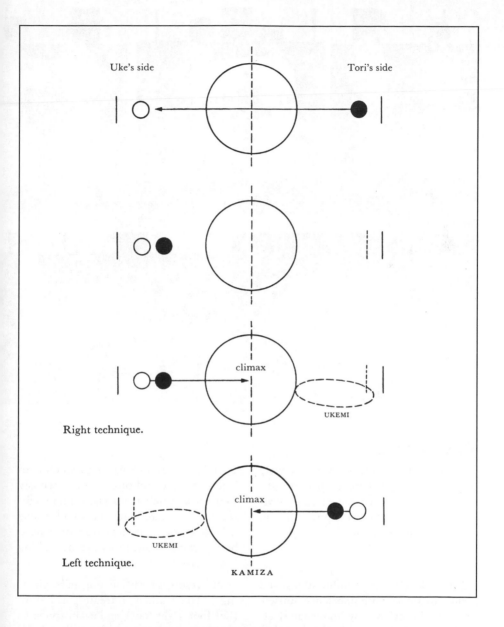

Uke's side

Tori's side

Right technique.

climax

UKEMI

Left technique.

climax

UKEMI

KAMIZA

◆ PREPARATION FOR ENGAGEMENT

After opening the kata, Tori and Uke, from standing in *shizenhontai* at their respective engagement positions, come forward along, the longitudinal axis by *ayumi ashi*, beginning with their left feet, moving simultaneously to a position on Uke's side of the center zone. Stopping to face each other at an engagement distance of about 2 feet (near position), they pause momentarily with composure and quiet alertness, making visual contact.

Engagement distance.   1

♦ ENGAGEMENT

1. UKE: Attacks Tori by simultaneously stepping, taking a standard grip in right *shizentai*, and advancing one step by *tsugi ashi* (right foot, left foot) to push Tori and unbalance him backward.

TORI: Preserves his balance by yielding to Uke's advance and push, simultaneously stepping and taking a standard grip in right *shizentai* as he retreats one step by *tsugi ashi* (left foot, right foot) in an attempt to break Uke's balance forward by pulling him horizontally.

2. UKE: Having failed in his attack, and being threatened with unbalance himself, preserves his balance by immediately attacking similarly again (right foot, left foot).

TORI: Preserves his balance again by yielding to Uke's attack, retreating as before (left foot, right foot), and again trying to unbalance Uke forward by pulling horizontally.

UKE: Having twice failed in his attacks and once again being threatened with unbalance, attempts to preserve his balance by immediately attacking similarly once again, but only succeeds in moving his right foot forward.

2 → 3 →

→

UKE: Unprepared for this unexpected change in the stepping-and-pulling pattern, is thrown forward in a big arc beyond Tori's left side. Executes *ukemi*, beating with his left arm, as his body comes to rest on the left side of his back, his head near Tori's left leg, the *kamiza* to his right, in an area outside the center zone, slightly off the longitudinal axis on the *kamiza* side, near Tori's salutation position.

3. TORI: Preserves his balance once again by yielding to Uke's pushing attack, but having twice failed to break Uke's balance, changes the pattern to foil Uke and takes the attack initiative. Instead of taking a normal-length step in *tsugi ashi*, takes his left foot a double-length step backward without really stepping, going directly onto his left knee, which is placed on a line straight back from his right heel; the toes of his left foot are flexed, with their sole surfaces resting on the mat, the heel pointing upward. His left leg is placed at 30-45 degrees to the axis of movement. Throws Uke by a strong, diagonally downward, straight snap pull of both hands, working simultaneously. Retains his left-hand grip on Uke's right sleeve; his right hand is placed nearby on that sleeve as Uke turns over and settles into *ukemi*. Exhibits *zanshin*.

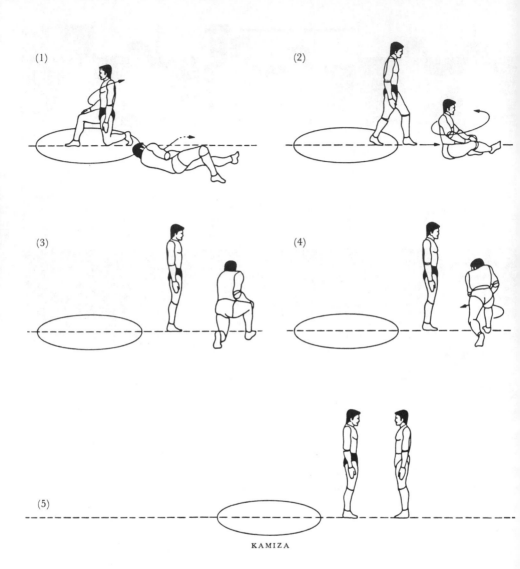

(1)

(2)

(3)

(4)

(5)

KAMIZA

◆ RISING AND FACING

After completion of Uke's *ukemi* from the right technique (in which Tori's left knee is down), Tori, the *kamiza* at his left, releases his grip and rises in place, turning naturally to his left (into the *kamiza*), adjusting by coming forward to his approximate original engagement position to wait in *shizenhontai* facing Uke. Uke, who has simultaneously sat up, folded his left leg, and risen onto his left knee, stands and moves forward a bit, turning naturally (his back to the *kamiza*) to his left to face Tori; Uke adjusts to an engagement distance of about 2 feet (near position), standing in *shizenhontai*. Figs. (1)-(5). They pause momentarily with composure and quiet alertness, making visual contact.

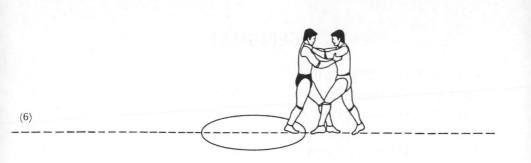

(6)

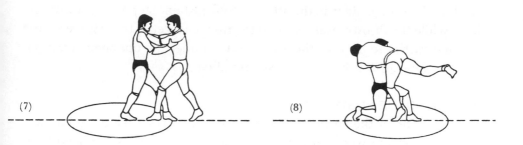

(7)

(8)

(9)

KAMIZA

◆ COMPLETION

Together, Tori and Uke perform *uki-otoshi* in left *shizentai* (in which Tori kneels onto his right knee), beginning at Tori's approximate original engagement position and moving back in the opposite direction to that just used for the right technique, along the longitudinal axis. Uke's *ukemi* (he beats with the right arm) brings him to rest just outside the center zone on his own side, but off the longitudinal axis on the *kamiza* side, the *kamiza* to his left. Tori exhibits *zanshin* and, after a short pause, releases his grip on Uke. Figs. (6)-(9).

SEOI-NAGE

◆ **ABOUT THIS TECHNIQUE**

This throw, the shoulder throw, is classified as a hand technique (*te waza*). It is of the one-arm (*ippon*) type, which displays the powerful effect made possible by unbalancing and levering an opponent's body high up and over the back-and-shoulder region of the thrower. Strictly *go no sen*, this technique is the first of four in this kata in which the attacking opponent strikes a blow at the thrower to clearly mark the self-defense value inherent in the kata. In the founder's original form, the attacker took just one step forward with the blow while the thrower was required to grip the jacket of the attacker at the shoulder with the hand of the arm inserted under the opponent's armpit. Both of these aspects have now been modified.

◆ **TECHNIQUE SUMMARY**

Uke faces Tori at the far position with intent to attack. Uke unhesitatingly takes two steps forward with alternate feet in *ayumi ashi*, striking with his bottom fist straight down from overhead at the top of Tori's head in order to knock Tori backward and down. Tori foils Uke by stepping forward one step to meet the attack, deflecting the intended blow, and blends with Uke's body by pivoting and backing quickly in front of him; Uke's blow misses the intended target and he collides with Tori more quickly than anticipated, unable to stop his forward momentum. Tori takes advantage of these forces by clamping Uke tightly to his upper back by pulling Uke forward to unbalance him, and then throws Uke forward over his shoulder by continued pulling and springing Uke upward with his legs.

◆ **TECHNIQUE KEY POINTS**

○ UKE ○

1. Makes his stepping movement forward, straight at, not across, Tori's front.

2. Strikes with his bottom fist straight down at the front top of Tori's head; times his fist's arrival with the placement of his advancing foot on the mat. Is unbalanced to that front corner.

● TORI ●

1. His parry does not stop Uke's striking arm, but deflects it a bit outward and upward along the course of its motion and into the coming throw; keeps the fingers of his parry hand splayed at initial contact; turns his hand, palm toward Uke's arm, slipping that hand slightly downward to grip at Uke's elbow (jacket or arm).

1   2

(UKE)

3. At the strike, holds his body straight, but fully commits his weight to the forward portion of his advanced foot (his front corner).

4. Keeps the throw from slipping or being off the longitudinal axis by executing the closed-gate effect (see p. 106).

5. Keeps legs naturally together as he rises over Tori; feels as if he is being thrown from his advanced shoulder. His body comes to rest facing in the direction of original movement.

(TORI)

2. Simultaneously places his pivotal foot with the forward portion touching the mat, heel off the mat, toes pointing in the direction of the coming throw; uses for the pivot the foot on the side opposite his parry arm.

3. Pivots back into Uke to bring his belt line lower than Uke's, concentrating on his hip-turning action, but tries to touch his far shoulder blade to Uke's chest on the far side for tight contact; holds his body erect at contact. Positions his feet inside Uke's with his toes pointing approximately in the same direction as Uke's movement. Unbalances Uke to the front corner (Fig. 1).

4. On his pivot, hooks the arm he thrusts under Uke's armpit upward to permit high placement of that hand; need not grip, but just press against Uke's shoulder and arm (Fig. 2).

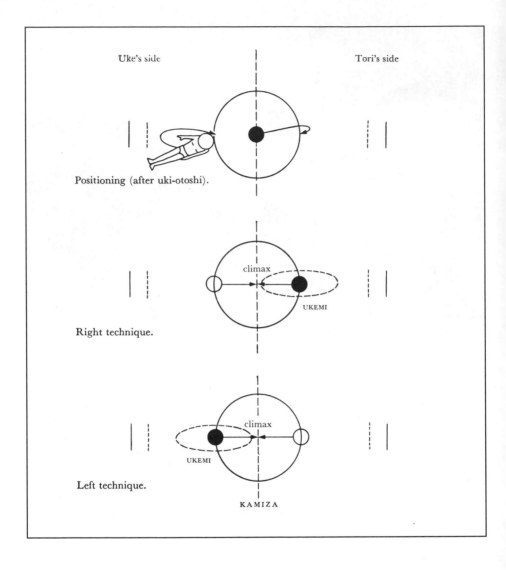

Uke's side

Tori's side

Positioning (after uki-otoshi).

Right technique.

climax

UKEMI

Left technique.

climax

UKEMI

KAMIZA

◆ PREPARATION FOR ENGAGEMENT

Completing the left *uki-otoshi* (with Tori's right knee down), Tori, the *kamiza* at his right, rises and moves a bit forward, turning naturally to his right (into the *kamiza*) and adjusts approximately to his edge of the center zone to wait in *shizenhontai* facing Uke. Uke has simultaneously sat up, folded his right leg, and risen onto his right knee to turn naturally (his back to the *kamiza*) to his right as he stands up to face Tori; Uke adjusts to an engagement distance of about 6 feet (far position), standing in *shizenhontai*. They pause momentarily with composure and quiet alertness, making visual contact.

Engagement distance. ⟶ 1

2

◆ ENGAGEMENT

1. UKE: Threatens Tori by advancing his left foot far forward, simultaneously raising his right arm so as to bring it upward from the right back corner with his bottom fist directly overhead, facing Tori.

2. UKE: Attacks Tori by advancing his right foot and simultaneously bringing his right bottom fist straight down from overhead in an attempt to hit Tori on the top of his head and knock him backward and down.

TORI: Remains motionless, but quietly alert.

3. TORI: Blends with Uke's attack by advancing his right foot to a position just inside but ahead of Uke's right foot; meets Uke approximately in the center of the center zone. Simultaneously parries Uke's attacking arm by bringing his outer left-wrist edge against the inside of Uke's attacking right arm at a point just above the elbow. Yields to Uke's forward momentum by changing his parry action to a grip at Uke's middle right sleeve; unbalances Uke

3

UKE: Loses his balance forward by being unprepared for this sudden collision with Tori; executes the closed-gate effect and is thrown forward over Tori's right shoulder and back. Executes *ukemi*, beating with his left arm, as his body comes to rest, head at Tori's feet, on the left side of his back, the *kamiza* to his right, along the longitudinal axis of movement in an area just on the edge of the center zone on Tori's side.

(TORI)

to the right front corner as he pivots on the ball of his right foot, with knee slightly bent, and brings his left foot around behind him in a short arc to a position in line with his other foot, just inside and ahead of Uke's left foot. At the same time, thrusts his right arm under Uke's right armpit, bending his right arm to enable him to contact Uke's *judogi* near the right shoulder; uses a forceful squeezing action of his bent right arm against Uke's trapped right arm. Clamps Uke tightly to his upper back and throws him forward over his shoulder by straightening his legs with a snap, bending forward, and continued forceful pulling downward and inward with both hands. Retains his left-hand grip on Uke's right sleeve; places his right hand nearby as Uke goes into *ukemi*. Exhibits *zanshin*.

(1)

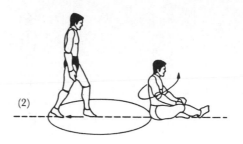

(2)

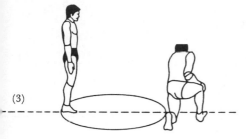

(3)

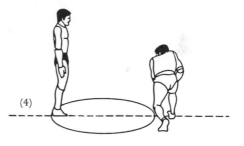

(4)

(5)

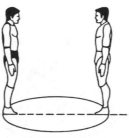

KAMIZA

◆ RISING AND FACING

After completion of Uke's *ukemi* from the right technique (over Tori's right shoulder), Tori, the *kamiza* at his right, releases his grip and backs up slightly to Uke's edge of the center zone, to wait in *shizenhontai* facing Uke. Uke has simultaneously sat up, folded his left leg, and risen onto his left knee to turn naturally (his back to *kamiza*) to his left as he stands up to face Tori; Uke adjusts to an engagement distance of about 6 feet (far position), standing in *shizenhontai*. Figs. (1)-(5). They pause momentarily with composure and quiet alertness, making visual contact.

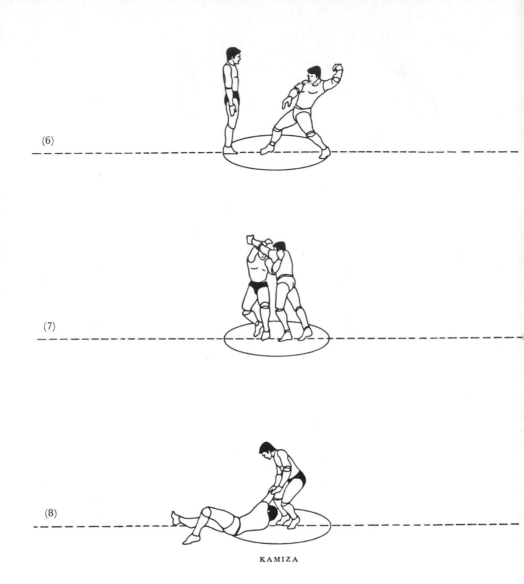

(6)

(7)

(8)

KAMIZA

♦ COMPLETION
Together, Tori and Uke perform the left *seoi-nage* (over Tori's left shoulder), each moving from opposite edges of the center zone into collision at the center along the longitudinal axis just used for the right technique, but throwing and falling in the opposite direction. Uke's *ukemi* (he beats with the right arm) brings him to rest just on the edge of the center zone on his side, the *kamiza* on his left, along the longitudinal axis. Tori exhibits *Zanshin* and, after a short pause, releases his grip on Uke. Figs. (6)-(8).

KATA-GURUMA

◆ **ABOUT THIS TECHNIQUE**

This throw, the shoulder wheel, is classified as a hand technique (*te waza*). It can produce a fall from the highest position possible by a throwing technique. It traces a large wheeling action by which an opponent can be unbalanced, lifted, and shouldered high in the air before being thrown. *Go no sen* in nature, this technique was the founder's final choice as a replacement for the technique of *sukui-nage*, the "scooping throw," which was originally in this kata. The early form of *kata-guruma* required the thrower to slide his trailing foot out on the third step and then slide it back in again as he lifted the opponent; also required was a short sliding step by the thrower's outside foot as he threw the opponent. Neither of these actions is practiced in the modern form.

◆ **TECHNIQUE SUMMARY**

Uke faces Tori at the near position with intent to attack. Uke steps forward carefully, gripping Tori in *shizentai* in order to push Tori and unbalance him backward, but takes care not to be overthrown himself by bracing slightly with his advancing leg. Uke continues his attack initiative for two steps in *tsugi ashi*, with Tori yielding to the push by gripping and retreating in *shizentai* by *tsugi ashi* and pulling. Uke forward in an unsuccessful attempt to unbalance him. Tori steals the attack initiative suddenly on the third step by breaking the stepping pattern with a long step backward and a ducking-under action, reinforced by a continued pull which unbalances Uke forward across Tori's shoulders; Tori throws Uke by shouldering him, standing erect, and then bringing him abruptly to the mat.

1

◆ **TECHNIQUE KEY POINTS**

○ UKE ○

1. Keeps his weight on the forward part of his advanced foot, not on the outer edge, on his first step, making a light bracing action by slightly bending the knee to avoid being thrown forward. Is unbalanced forward later.

● TORI ●

1. Changes grips during his second step to pull Uke forward and upward or "float" Uke off his bracing leg action, as well as to protect his neck during the coming throw (Fig. 1).

2   3

(UKE)

2. Tilts forward onto Tori with some stiffness in his body on his third step.

3. Keeps the throw from slipping off by executing the closed-gate effect, dropping his grip on Tori's sleeve, and placing that hand, with palm flat and fingers pointing downward, firmly against Tori's lower back to stabilize himself.

4. Slightly separates his legs by raising the one which is not grasped by Tori and holds his body with enough stiffness to form a T with Tori as he is shouldered; feels as if he is being lifted and thrown from his hips. His body comes to rest facing in the direction of original movement.

(TORI)

2. Keeps his pulling hand exerting a slight pressure upward on his third step, as he ducks under Uke; leaves his trailing foot (that nearer Uke) in place as a platform foot when he ducks under Uke; takes his lead foot (the one away from Uke) well back to reinforce his pull and to lower his hips. Unbalances Uke forward.

3. Places the side of his neck under Uke's center of gravity, below Uke's belt line, by squatting down deep, not by bending forward from the hips. His upper body is held quite erect (Fig. 2).

4. Lifts from the back of his neck by a driving action of his hip and near leg under Uke as his advanced foot (that farther from Uke) slides in toward the platform foot (the one nearer Uke); his pulling hand changes to a circular downward pull which brings the elbow down and in toward his hip. Stands fully erect before throwing, but does not stop the rhythm of the throw; bends his knees as he throws; keeps his feet in place (Fig. 3).

◆ **PREPARATION FOR ENGAGEMENT**

Completing the left *seoi-nage* (over Tori's left shoulder), Tori, the *kamiza* at his left, adjusts by coming forward to a position on Uke's side of the center zone (from which he began *uki-otoshi*), to wait in *shizenhontai* facing Uke. Uke has simultaneously sat up, folded his right leg, and risen onto his right knee to stand, and moves a bit forward, turning naturally to his right (his

❌ *Wrong.* ❌ *Wrong.*

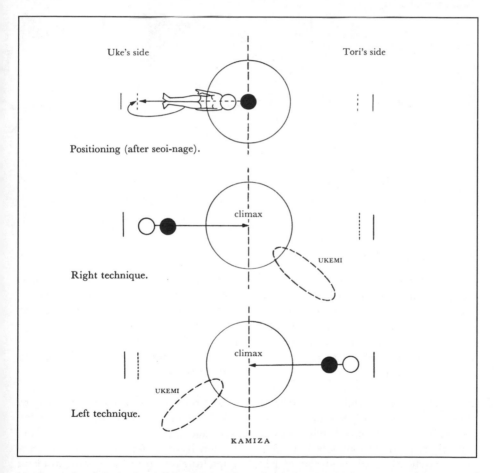

Uke's side Tori's side

Positioning (after seoi-nage).

climax

UKEMI

Right technique.

climax

UKEMI

Left technique.

KAMIZA

back to the *kamiza*) to face Tori; Uke adjusts to an engagement distance of about 2 feet (near position), standing in *shizenhontai*. They pause momentarily with composure and quiet alertness, making visual contact.

Engagement distance.   1

2   3

◆ ENGAGEMENT

1. UKE: Attacks Tori by simultaneously stepping, taking a standard grip in right *shizentai*, and advancing one step by *tsugi ashi* (right foot, left foot), to push Tori and unbalance him backward; keeps his advancing leg slightly bent as he makes a light bracing action.

TORI: Preserves his balance by yielding to Uke's advance and push, simultaneously stepping and taking a standard grip in right *shizentai* as he retreats one step by *tsugi ashi* (left foot, right foot) in an attempt to break Uke's balance forward, by pulling him horizontally.

2. UKE: Having failed in his attack and being threatened with unbalance himself, preserves his balance by immediately attacking similarly again (right foot, left foot), continuing to slightly bend his advancing right knee and bracing back lightly.

TORI: Preserves his balance by yielding to Uke's attack as before, but changes his left-hand grip during his retreat by taking his left hand under Uke's right arm; regrips, little fingers upward, at the inside of Uke's middle sleeve. Attempts to unbalance Uke forward by pulling a bit upward.

UKE: Having failed twice in his attacks, and once again being threatened with unbalance, attempts to preserve his balance by immediately attacking similarly once again, but only succeeds in moving his right leg forward.

UKE: Unprepared for this sudden lowering action, loses his balance forward, while pressing his right lower pelvic region against the right side of Tori's neck. Executes the closed-gate effect.

UKE: Rides up on Tori's shoulders and is thrown forward to his right front. Executes *ukemi*, beating with his left arm, as his body comes to rest with his head at Tori's left foot, on the left side of his back, the *kamiza* on the right, in an area slightly off the longitudinal axis on the *kamiza* side, near Tori's original engagement position (where Tori stood in *shizentai* to begin kata action).

3. TORI: Preserves his balance by once again yielding to Uke's attack, but having twice failed to break Uke's balance, changes the stepping pattern to foil Uke. Instead of taking a normal-length step in *tsugi ashi*, slides his left foot a double-length step backward, leaving his right foot in place, and drops into a deep squat. His left hand continues to pull a bit upward and, as Uke tips forward, he applies the right side of his neck to Uke's upper right-thigh region where it joins the lower abdomen; dropping his right grip, thrusts his right arm between Uke's legs, far enough to permit him to bend the arm and cup Uke's outer-and-rear right thigh. Hugs Uke's thigh tightly to him, or may grip Uke's trouser leg. Sliding his left foot inward, stands up in *shizenhontai* while maintaining a strong pulling action with his left hand, now a circular motion in toward his left side. Uke is borne aloft, riding across his upper back and both shoulders. Throws Uke in the direction the toes of his left foot are pointing, by bending a bit forward and dropping his head to unload Uke diagonally in that direction; pulls in with his left hand and pushes up and over with his right hand. Retains his left-hand grip on Uke's right sleeve; his right hand is placed nearby as Uke settles into *ukemi*. Exhibits *zanshin*.

(1)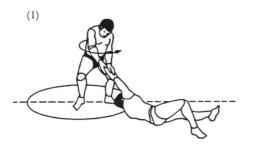

(2)

(3)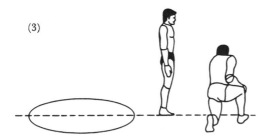

(4)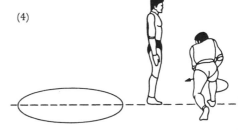

(5)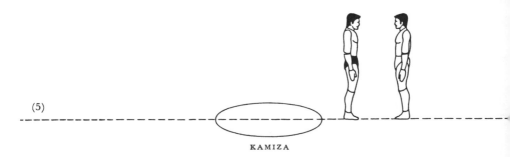

KAMIZA

◆ RISING AND FACING

After completion of Uke's *ukemi* from the right technique (in which Tori attacks Uke's right leg), Tori, the *kamiza* to his front, releases his grip and turns naturally to his left, moving forward to approximately his engagement position to wait facing Uke in *shizenhontai*. Uke, who has simultaneously sat up, folded his left leg, and risen onto his left knee, stands and moves forward a bit, turning naturally (his back to the *kamiza*) to his left to face Tori; Uke adjusts to an engagement distance of about 2 feet (near position), standing in *shizenhontai*. Figs. (1)-(5). They pause momentarily with composure and quiet alertness, making visual contact.

◆ COMPLETION

Together, Tori and Uke perform *kata-guruma* in left *shizentai* (in which Tori attacks Uke's left leg), beginning at Tori's approximate engagement position and moving back in the opposite direction to that just used for the right

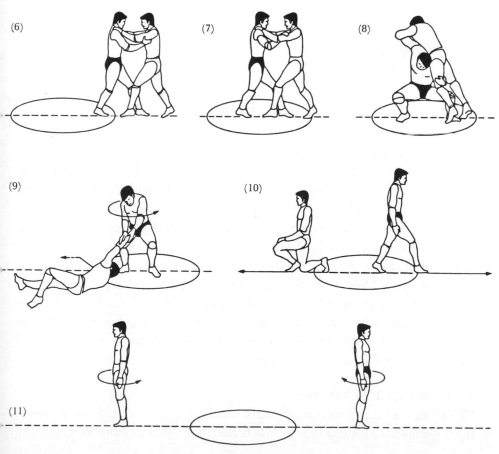

(6) (7) (8) (9) (10) (11)

KAMIZA

technique, along the longitudinal axis. Uke's *ukemi* (he beats with his right arm) brings him to rest just outside the center zone on his own side, the *kamiza* on his left, but off the longitudinal axis on the *kamiza* side and near his own engagement position. Tori exhibits *zanshin* and, after a short pause, releases his grip on Uke. With the *kamiza* to his front, Tori turns naturally to his left (away from Uke) and walks quietly, directly along the longitudinal axis, to his engagement position, adjusting his *judogi* unobtrusively as he walks. Arriving there, he stands momentarily facing away from Uke in *shizenhontai*; simultaneously, Uke has risen from his *ukemi* by folding his right leg and kneeling on his right knee to stand up, and has walked straight ahead, quietly, to his engagement position along the longitudinal axis. He adjusts his *judogi* unobtrusively as he walks, arriving about the same time as Tori does at his respective position, to stand momentarily facing outward, also in *shizenhontai*. They turn in place (toward the *kamiza*) to simultaneously face each other in *shizenhontai* and thereby end the *te waza* category. Figs. (6)-(11).

KOSHI WAZA

UKI-GOSHI

◆ ABOUT THIS TECHNIQUE

This throw, the floating loin, is classified as a hip-loin technique (*koshi waza*). It constitutes a monument to the pet throw of the founder of Judo, who considered it exemplary of the half-hip type of throwing action by which an opponent can be slung around and out, away from the thrower's hip. Reminiscent of the old *yoroi kumi-uchi*, by which armor-clad warriors grappled in battlefield combat, this technique is *go no sen* in nature and the second of four in which a blow is struck at the thrower by the attacking opponent; it further serves to point out the combative essence of this kata. The technique in its early form had the striking attacker take one step forward with the blow, which was aimed at the thrower's temple. Both these original aspects have been modified and are no longer standard.

◆ TECHNIQUE SUMMARY

Uke faces Tori at the far position with intent to attack while both are moving. Uke takes two steps forward with alternate feet in *ayumi ashi*, keeping his weight centered between his feet, striking with his bottom fist straight down from overhead at the top of Tori's head in order to knock Tori backward and down. Tori foils Uke by closing quickly, avoiding the blow and blending with Uke's body by a pivotal action at Uke's front corner (on the striking-arm side), clamping Uke tightly to his side by pulling him forward and to Uke's front corner to unbalance him, and then with a half-hip action throwing Uke forward, around, and out by continued pulling and a twist of his upper body and hips.

◆ TECHNIQUE KEY POINTS

○ UKE ○

1. Makes his stepping movement forward, straight at, not across, Tori's front.

2. Strikes with his bottom fist straight down at the front top of Tori's head; times his fist's arrival with his advancing foot's placement on the mat.

3. At the strike, holds his body erect with stiffness, keeping his weight centered between his feet.

4. Allows his striking arm to pass over Tori's shoulder, behind the neck; his other arm is "fed" into Tori's cup grip by executing the closed-gate effect without pressing that hand onto Tori's buttock.

5. Comes up tightly against Tori's side and is raked into unbalance diagonally forward (toward Tori's far hip) before being thrown; feels as if he is being slung around Tori's hip, not lifted up and over, but revolving around his own outside leg (that farther away from Tori) as an axis. His body comes to rest facing in the original direction of movement.

● TORI ●

1. Leads off with left-hip contact by moving in fast, obliquely, to Uke; performs the second technique with his right hip.

2. Steps in on the forward part of his pivotal foot, heel free of the mat, toes pointing in the direction of the coming throw.

3. Pivots enough to permit only a half-hip contact; the point of his hip is placed just on or just beyond Uke's belt knot. Must execute *tsukuri* before Uke softens his body (Fig. 1).

4. At the pivot, his encircling arm reaches along the belt line as far through as possible; tries to contact Uke's far side, pressing with the flat palm (its power in the little finger), not gripping, on Uke's hip bone (Figs. 2, 3).

5. On pivoting, his body is erect and has the feeling of leaning backward with a dropped contact shoulder, chest up; his pivotal foot comes around parallel to Uke's foot while his outside foot points a bit outward. Turns his face away for protection, in the direction of the coming throw (Figs. 4, 5).

6. At completely fitted position, feels as though Uke will slip off; leans out over his own outside foot, keeping Uke in tight contact with his side by hugging Uke to him. Unbalances Uke to the front and to his front corner (Fig. 1, p. 182).

1

❌ *Wrong.*

2

❌ *Wrong.*

3

❌ *Wrong.*

4

❌ *Wrong.*

5

❌ *Wrong.*

(TORI)

7. Slings Uke around his hip with upper-body-and-hip action; does not spring Uke upward. Harmonizes his body twist and arm actions, which are parallel to the mat in the direction of effort.

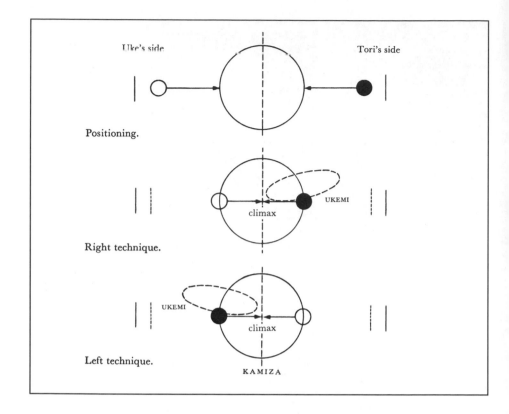

Uke's side   Tori's side

Positioning.

UKEMI

climax

Right technique.

UKEMI

climax

Left technique.

KAMIZA

◆ PREPARATION FOR ENGAGEMENT

Standing at their engagement positions, Uke and Tori pause momentarily with composure and quiet alertness, making visual contact. Then in *ayumi ashi*, beginning with their left feet, they come forward along the longitudinal axis toward the center zone. They arrive simultaneously at their respective edges of the center zone, and without stopping they engage.

◆ ENGAGEMENT

1. UKE: Threatens Tori by advancing his left foot far forward, simultaneously raising his right arm so as to bring it upward from the right back corner with his bottom fist directly overhead, while facing Tori.

2. UKE: Attacks Tori by advancing his right foot and simultaneously bringing his right bottom fist straight down from overhead in an attempt to hit Tori on the top of his head and knock him backward and down.

TORI: Closes quickly (left foot, right foot).

3. TORI: Blends with Uke's attack so that the blow passes over his left shoulder and behind him, by quickly taking a short oblique step with his left foot to place it just inside but ahead of Uke's left foot; meets Uke in the approximate center of the center zone. Simultaneously, encircles Uke's waist along Uke's belt line with his left arm, keeping erect with chest high, and

Engagement distance. 1

2   3   ⟶

(UKE)

UKE: Unprepared for this sudden collision with Tori, loses his balance forward and is drawn up onto his toes tightly against Tori. His unbalance is accentuated somewhat to his right front corner and he executes the closed-gate effect, leaving his left arm free: reaches with it naturally a bit forward on the left side of Tori as if to grab Tori to steady himself.

(TORI)

passing his left shoulder under Uke's right armpit; pivots on the ball of his left foot and brings his right foot behind him in a wide arc so that this foot comes to rest outside and ahead of Uke's right foot, toes pointing well outward. As he pivots, clamps Uke tightly to his left side, his left hip centering on Uke's midsection, by a combined left-arm hugging action and his right hand's cup grip on Uke's left arm at outer middle sleeve just above the elbow, pulling that arm high across his chest. Severely unbalances Uke by leaning over his right knee in the direction his toes are

(UKE)

UKE: Is thrown forward around Tori's left hip. Executes *ukemi*, beating with his right arm as he comes to rest on the right side of his back, head at Tori's feet, the *kamiza* on his right, along the longitudinal axis of movement in an area just within the center zone on Tori's side.

(TORI)

pointing; his left leg straightens without stiffness. Throws Uke forward by a quick twist of his body to the right as he straightens his right leg. Retains his right-hand contact (may now grip) with Uke's sleeve; places his left hand nearby as Uke settles into *ukemi*. Exhibits *zanshin*.

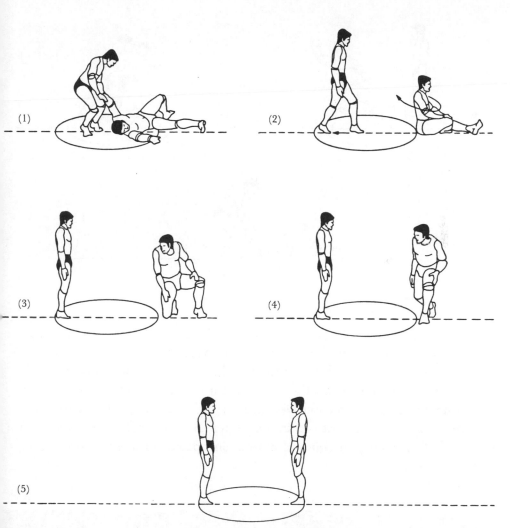

(1)

(2)

(3)

(4)

(5)

KAMIZA

◆ RISING AND FACING

After completion of Uke's *ukemi* from the left technique (around Tori's left half-hip), Tori, the *kamiza* at his right, releases his grip and backs up slightly to Uke's edge of the center zone, to wait in *shizenhontai* facing Uke. Uke has simultaneously sat up, folded his right leg, and risen onto his right knee to turn naturally to his right (into the *kamiza*) as he stands up to face Tori; Uke adjusts to an engagement distance of about 6 feet (far position), standing in *shizenhontai*. Figs. (1)-(5). They pause momentarily with composure and quiet alertness, making visual contact.

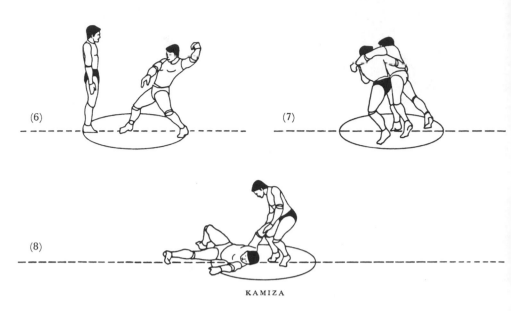

(6)   (7)

(8)

KAMIZA

◆ COMPLETION

Together, from a standing position, Tori and Uke begin *uki-goshi* on the right side (around Tori's right half-hip), each moving from each other's edge of the center zone into collision in the middle, the throw and fall being made along the longitudinal axis they have just used for the left technique, only now in the opposite direction. Uke's *ukemi* (he beats with the left arm) brings him to rest in an area just within the center zone on his side, the *kamiza* on his left. Tori exhibits *zanshin* and, after a short pause, releases his grip on Uke. Figs. (6)-(8).

1 Preparing for half-hip throwing action.   ☒ *Wrong.*   ☒ *Wrong.*

HARAI-GOSHI

◆ ABOUT THIS TECHNIQUE

This throw, the sweeping loin, is classified as a hip-loin technique (*koshi waza*). It evolved from the half-hip throwing action characteristic of the preceding *uki-goshi*, with the added feature of a rear brushing action of one leg to assist in overturning the opponent by springing him upward and over from an unbalanced state in which he is tightly pinned against the thrower's side. As *go no sen*, this technique in its original form required the thrower to take a normal third step with both feet in turn and to throw by jumping "back in under" the opponent, moving the platform foot into position beside the opponent's trailing foot and sweeping upward with the attacking leg. This action has been modified in the present-day form. Contrary to popular opinion, Jigoro Kano did not invent or design this throw, but merely adapted it to Judo from jujutsu and *sumo*, which had been using it for centuries.

◆ TECHNIQUE SUMMARY

Uke faces Tori at the near position with intent to attack. Uke steps forward, gripping Tori in *shizentai* in order to push Tori and unbalance him backward. Uke's attack initiative continues for one step in *tsugi ashi* with Tori yielding to the push while gripping and retreating in *tsugi ashi*, pulling Uke forward in an unsuccessful attempt to unbalance him. On the second step by Uke in *tsugi ashi*, Tori shifts his assist-hand grip, startles Uke into stiffness, and begins to take the attack initiative. Suddenly on the third step, with Uke attempting to attack in *tsugi ashi*, Tori steals the attack initiative from Uke completely by breaking the pattern of stepping. Using a short backward step, Tori pivots in front of Uke and draws hi m tightly to his side, unbalancing Uke forward and to the front corner, to throw Uke by a half-hip action produced by the combined effects of the pull of his hands and the upward springing and twisting of his hips, assisted by the backward-and-upward brushing action of his free leg against Uke's pinned advanced leg.

◆ TECHNIQUE KEY POINTS

○ UKE ○

1. On the first step, keeps his weight on the forward part of his advanced foot, not on the outer edge; holds his body pliable without stiffness.

● TORI ●

1. Changes his hand grip at the beginning of his second step to float Uke and stiffen him preparatory to a half-hip throwing action (Fig. 1, p. 188).

(UKE)

2. As Tori floats him by the change of grip on the second step, tries to keep erect and in so doing stiffens his body; is becoming a bit defensive at this point.

3. Completes his third step but makes it only a very short one as he is drawn tightly up against Tori's side and half-hip; executes the closed-gate effect when his advancing foot is pinned by his shifting weight, and is unable to advance a full-length step.

4. Keeps his body straight, with stiffness, as he is unbalanced and raked forward to his front corner (over his advanced foot) and twisted slightly onto Tori; feels as if he is being thrown from his midsection. Turns over in midair with some remaining stiffness; his body comes to rest facing in the direction of original movement.

(TORI)

2. His assist hand does not grip the upper back of Uke's *judogi*; pulls with that hand in an upward scooping action with the power concentrated in the little finger; must harmonize his other hand's pulling action, and the combined pulls must further harmonize with his stepping; unbalances Uke to the front corner.

3. His third step is diagonally back behind the heel of his trailing foot onto the forward portion, not the whole sole; to make a platform leg, the knee must be slightly bent to provide spring action for the coming throw.

4. Pivotal action must bring the platform foot to point in the same direction as the axis of movement or even slightly outward, not in toward Uke, in order to preserve balance; the platform leg must be fully weighted (Fig. 2).

5. Pulls Uke forward and upward and rakes him into slow-action tight contact with his side and half-hip. His body forms approximate right angles with Uke's body. Places his hip on or just behind Uke's belt knot; throws without overbending forward, in a positive twisting half-hip action, reinforced by a circular pulling action of his hands and assisted by the sweeping action of his free leg backward and upward approximately to the horizontal, against Uke's pinned advanced leg. His sweeping leg must be kept straight, toes pointed, and contact Uke's advanced leg below the knee; his platform foot may pivot a bit outward (Fig. 3).

◆ PREPARATION FOR ENGAGEMENT

Completing the right *uki-goshi* (around Tori's right half-hip), Tori, the *kamiza* at his left, adjusts by coming forward to a position on Uke's side of the center zone (the place from where he began *uki-otoshi*), to wait in *shizenhontai* facing Uke. Uke has simultaneously sat up, folded his left leg, and risen onto his left knee to stand and move a bit forward, turning naturally to his left (into the *kamiza*) to face Tori; Uke adjusts to an engagement distance of about 2 feet (near position), standing in *shizenhontai*. They pause momentarily with composure and quiet alertness, making visual contact.

2   3

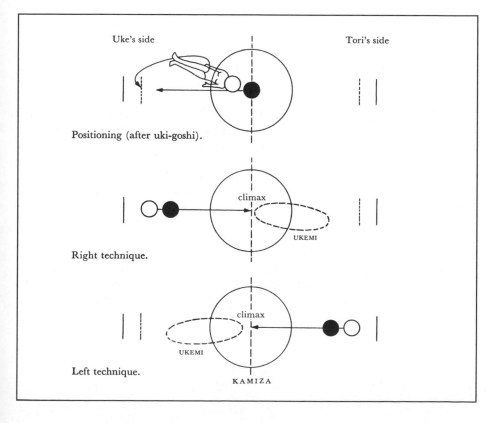

Uke's side   Tori's side

Positioning (after uki-goshi).

climax

UKEMI

Right technique.

climax

UKEMI

Left technique.

KAMIZA

Engagement distance.   *1*

◆ ENGAGEMENT

1. UKE: Attacks Tori by simultaneously stepping, taking a standard grip in right *shizentai*, and advancing one step by *tsugi ashi* (right foot, left foot) to push Tori and unbalance him backward; is cautious in his push, keeping his body erect without stiffness.

2. UKE: Having failed in his attack, and being threatened with unbalance himself, preserves his balance by immediately attacking similarly again (right foot, left foot).

UKE: Having failed twice in his attacks and once again being threatened with unbalance, attempts to preserve his balance by immediately attacking with his body, now held somewhat stiffly erect, but does not succeed in taking a complete full-length step forward with his right foot.

TORI: Preserves his balance by yielding to Uke's advance and push, simultaneously stepping and taking a standard grip in right *shizentai* as he retreats one step by *tsugi ashi* (left foot, right foot) in an attempt to break Uke's balance forward by pulling him horizontally.

TORI: Preserves his balance again by yielding to Uke's attack, but feeling the cautious pliancy in Uke, changes his right-hand grip at the moment of his retreat, taking his right hand under Uke's left armpit and pressing the flat palm high on Uke's left shoulder blade, and attempts to unbalance Uke forward by pulling forward and a bit upward with both hands.

3. TORI: Having twice failed to break Uke's balance, changes the stepping pattern to foil Uke. Instead of taking a normal-length

2

3

(UKE)

UKE: Unprepared for the sudden change in the stepping pattern, loses his balance forward and to his right front corner as he is brought tightly up against Tori's right side, with Tori's half-hip in the center of his midsection. Has his weight pinned onto his short-stepped advanced right foot and keeps his body straight with stiffness. Executes the closed-gate effect.

(TORI)

step in *tsugi ashi*, slides his left foot in a short arc behind his right heel so that his toes point in the direction of the axis of movement; simultaneously pivots on the ball of the left foot and twists his body halfway around to the left; severely unbalances Uke to the right front corner by pulling with both hands so that Uke is brought up onto his right side, his half-hip centering on Uke's midsection.

(UKE)

UKE: Is thrown forward by being sprung up and swept upward head over heels by Tori's right half-hip and upper thigh action. Executes *ukemi*, beating with his left arm as he comes to rest on the left side of his back, his head at Tori's feet, the *kamiza* on his right, in an area slightly off the longitudinal axis on the *kamiza* side, near Tori's edge of the center zone.

(TORI)

Throws Uke in a big arc forward by the combined actions of his hands pulling Uke forward and upward, then down and around; his right rear thigh sweeps back against Uke's weighted right leg. As Uke's body leaves the mat he twists his body to the left, sweeping and springing upward by straightening his left (platform) leg. Retains his left-hand grip on Uke's right sleeve; places his right hand nearby as Uke settles into *ukemi*. Exhibits *zanshin*.

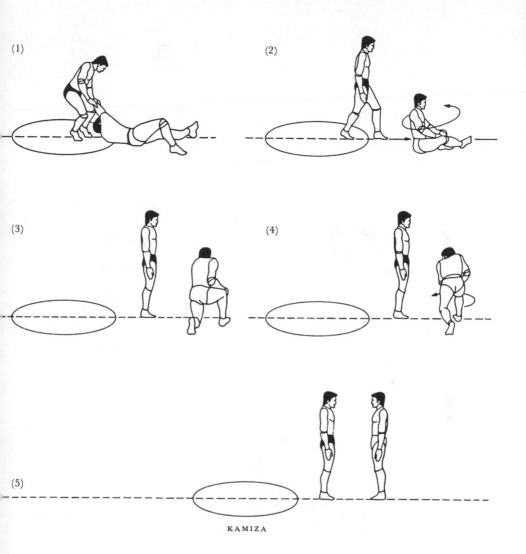

(1)

(2)

(3)

(4)

(5)

KAMIZA

◆ RISING AND FACING

After completion of Uke's *ukemi* from the right technique (over Tori's right half-hip), Tori, the *kamiza* at his right, releases his grip and comes directly forward along the longitudinal axis, adjusting to his approximate original engagement position to wait in *shizenhontai*, facing Uke. Uke who has simultaneously sat up, folded his left leg, and risen onto his left knee, stands and moves forward a bit, turning naturally (his back to the *kamiza*) to his left to face Tori; Uke adjusts to an engagement distance of about 2 feet (near position), standing in *shizenhontai*. Figs. (1)-(5). They pause momentarily with composure and quiet alertness, making visual contact.

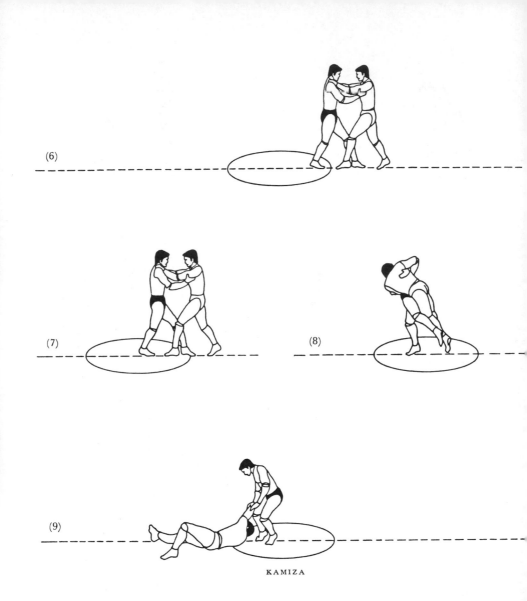

(6)

(7)

(8)

(9)

KAMIZA

◆ COMPLETION

Together, Tori and Uke perform *harai-goshi* in left *shizentai* (over Tori's left half-hip), beginning at Tori's approximate engagement position and moving back in the opposite direction to that just used for the right technique Uke's *ukemi* (he beats with the right arm) brings him to rest in an area near his edge of the center zone, with the *kamiza* on his left, but off the longitudinal axis on the *kamiza* side. Tori exhibits *zanshin* and, after a short pause, releases his grip on Uke. Figs. (6)-(9).

TSURIKOMI-GOSHI

◆ ABOUT THIS TECHNIQUE

This throw, the lift-pull loin, is classified as a hip-loin technique (*koshi waza*). It clearly demonstrates the principles by which an opponent's defensive hardness of body may be used against him in *go no sen* fashion. It is a powerful decoy action caused by the sudden, direct, and unexpected lowering of the thrower's center of gravity, which lures and brings the stiff opponent straight over like a stick, end over end, in the air; it is the result of the opponent's reaction to an *anticipated* throw which never comes. Originally, this technique was designed by the founder to operate as an opponent's reaction to an *attempted* throw. It required the attacker and thrower to take a full third step, with each foot in turn; the thrower pivoted in front of the attacker and attempted a high-placed full-hip throw. As the opponent braced backward to foil the attempt, the thrower used that body rigidity to slide his body downward (much like a train guided by tracks) to a new low position with hips against the attacker's thighs, and to throw the attacker with a second full-hip technique. The modern-day form is a direct entry-and-throw technique.

◆ TECHNIQUE SUMMARY

Uke faces Tori at the near position with intent to attack. Uke steps forward, gripping Tori in *shizentai* in order to push Tori and unbalance him backward. Uke continues his attack initiative for two steps in *tsugi ashi*, with Tori yielding to his push by modified gripping and retreating in *shizentai* by *tsugi ashi*, pulling Uke forward in an unsuccessful attempt to unbalance him. Suddenly, during the third step, Tori steals the attack initiative from Uke by breaking the pattern of stepping. Using a pivotal action in front of Uke, Tori clamps Uke tightly to his side to unbalance him and throws Uke forward by placing his loins directly down deeply against Uke's thighs, and springing Uke up and over by straightening his legs and pulling circularly with his hands.

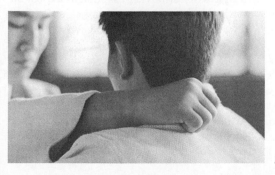

1

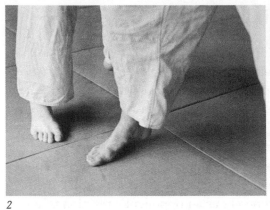

2

✗ *Wrong.*

◆ TECHNIQUE KEY POINTS

○ UKE ○

1. Takes a standard grip on engagement with Tori.

2. Keeps his weight centered between his feet, and his body pliable on engagement; stiffens his body on the second step when he feels the strong, high grip of Tori's assist-arm hand.

3. Takes his third step with his advancing foot only to be unbalanced forward and upward tightly against the side of Tori's back and full loins; executes the closed-gate effect, making sure to release his grip on Tori's sleeve and to place that hand on Tori's back; braces hard backward to avoid an anticipated hip throw which would bring him forward and over. Does not get his trailing foot (now advancing) solidly weighted (Fig. 6).

4. Gets thrown with his body stiff in a backward bracing action against an anticipated throw which never comes; does not lose this stiffness in the air, but comes over like a rigid stick. Feels as if he is being thrown from just below his midsection. His body comes to rest facing in the direction of movement.

● TORI ●

1. Takes a modified grip on engagement with Uke; his assist-arm hand grips Uke's collar in back of Uke's ear (Fig. 1).

2. The pivotal foot carries his weight on its forward part, not on the whole sole, and is placed with the toes pointing in the direction of the coming throw. This foot must not be placed too far ahead of Uke's advanced foot (Fig. 2).

3. Pivots and simultaneously quickly drops directly into a low position without sliding downward against Uke.

4. His pulling arm pulls outward (over Uke's advanced foot) at first, to keep Uke from weighting his trailing foot; then it pulls high to bring Uke's arm tightly across Tori's chest under his chin. Uke is unbalanced forward and to his front corner, over his advanced foot (Fig. 3). His assist arm is kept as straight as possible with the forearm against the side of Uke's chest as the throw is made; the wrist must not be "goosenecked" (Figs. 4-6).

5. His weight is on the forward part of both feet as he throws; does not merely pull Uke over His jutting hip, but springs Uke upward by leg power, which is harmonized with the arm-and-hand pulling-and-lifting actions. Holds his upper body quite erect while throwing from a crouch; throws with one motion.

3

4

5

6

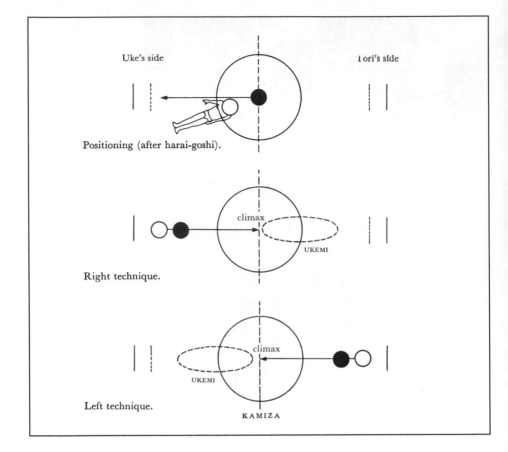

Positioning (after harai-goshi).

Right technique.

UKEMI

Left technique.

UKEMI

KAMIZA

◆ PREPARATION FOR ENGAGEMENT

Completing the left *harai-goshi* (over Tori's left half-hip), Tori, the *kamiza* at his left, adjusts by coming forward to a position on Uke's side of the center zone (the place from which he began *uki-otoshi*), to wait in *shizenhontai* facing Uke. Uke has simultaneously sat up, folded his right leg, and risen oijto his right knee to stand, and moves forward a bit, turning naturally to his right (away from the *kamiza*) to face Tori; Uke adjusts to an engagement distance of about 2 feet (near position), standing in *shizenhontai*. They pause momentarily with composure and quiet alertness, making visual contact.

◆ ENGAGEMENT

1. UKE: Attacks Tori by simultaneously stepping, taking a standard grip in right *shizentai*, and advancing one step by *tsugi ashi* (right foot, left foot) to push Tori and unbalance him backward.

TORI: Preserves his balance by yielding to Uke's advance and push, simultaneously stepping and taking a modified grip in right shizentai(his right hand takes Uke's collar behind the ear) as he retreats one

Engagement distance.   1

2

(UKE)

UKE: Having failed in his attack, and being threatened with unbalance himself, preserves his balance by immediately attacking similarly once again (right foot, left foot), responding to Tori's high right-hand grip with some body stiffness.

(TORI)

step by *tsugi ashi* (left foot, right foot) in an attempt to break Uke's balance forward through horizontal pulling.

TORI: Preserves his balance by again yielding to Uke's attack as before, but feeling the stiffness in Uke's body, pulls more strongly in a horizontal direction as he retreats to get Uke to stiffen still more, in another attempt to break Uke's balance forward.

3

(UKE)

UKE: Having failed twice in his attacks and once again being threatened with unbalance, attempts to preserve his balance by immediately attacking in a similar manner once more, as he keeps erect with more stiffness anticipatory of a high hip throw, and just manages to move his right foot forward.

(TORI)

TORI: Having twice failed to break Uke's balance, changes the stepping pattern to foil Uke. Instead of taking a normal-length step in *tsugi ashi*, takes his left foot back (less than he normally would in stepping) slightly on a diagonal, to his right rear; slides his right foot to the inside but ahead of Uke's right foot, then quickly pivots his body around to the left by weighting his right foot and sliding his left foot around behind him in a normal-sized arc so that this foot comes to rest inside, but ahead of, Uke's now advancing left foot. Simultaneously pulls Uke forward, lifting up with his right hand as he pulls forward and

(UKE)

UKE: Loses his balance forward and up-ward, his weight shifting primarily onto his advanced right foot; is brought tightly up against the lower right side of Tori's back and buttocks. Performs the closed-gate effect and continues to keep erect by bracing hard backward. Is thrown forward, head over heels, over Tori's right full hip. Executes *ukemi*, beating with his left arm, as he comes to rest on the left side of his back, with his head at Tori's left foot, the *kamiza* on his right, in an area slightly off the longitudinal axis on the *kamiza* side near Tori's edge of the center zone.

(TORI)

a bit outward with his left hand to severe-ly unbalance Uke over the right foot, and brings him directly onto the lower right side of his back. As Uke comes into close contact with him, places his loins across Uke's lower thighs and applies his buttocks tightly up against Uke. Throws Uke for-ward over his jutting right loin in a single motion, by combining a circular forward and down-and-around pull of both hands with the straightening of both legs with a snap. Uke is sprung up and over; Tori re-tains his left-hand grip on Uke's right sleeve and places his right hand nearby as Uke settles into *ukemi*. Exhibits *zanshin*.

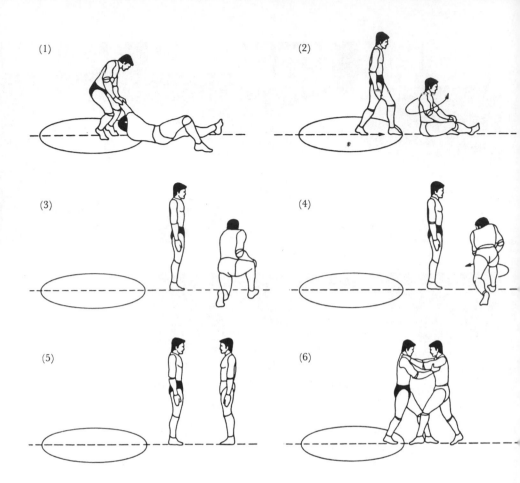

◆ RISING AND FACING

After completion of Uke's *ukemi* from the right technique (over Tori's right full hip), Tori, the *kamiza* at his right, releases his grip and comes directly forward along the longitudinal axis, adjusting to approximately his original engagement position to wait in *shizenhontai*, facing Uke. Uke, who has simultaneously sat up, folded his left leg, and risen onto his left knee, stands and moves forward a bit, turning naturally (his back to *kamiza*) to his left to face Tori; Uke adjusts to an engagement distance of about 2 feet (near position), standing in *shizenhontai*. Figs. (1)-(5). They pause momentarily with composure and quiet alertness, making visual contact.

◆ COMPLETION

Together, Tori and Uke perform *tsurikomi-goshi* in left *shizentai* (over Tori's left full hip), beginning at Tori's approximate engagement position and moving back in the opposite direction to that they have just used for the right

(7)

(8)

(9)

(10)

(11)

KAMIZA

technique, along the longitudinal axis. Uke's *ukemi* (he beats with the right arm) brings him to rest in an area near his edge of the center zone, with the *kamiza* on his left, but slightly off the longitudinal axis on the *kamiza* side. Tori exhibits *zanshin* and, after a short pause, releases his grip on Uke. With the *kamiza* on his left, Tori turns naturally to his left (away from Uke) and walks quietly, directly along the longitudinal axis, to his engagement position, adjusting his *judogi* unobtrusively as he walks. Arriving at his engagement position, he stands momentarily facing away from Uke in *shizenhontai*; simultaneously, Uke has risen from his *ukemi* by sitting up, folding his right leg, and kneeling onto his right knee to stand up, and has walked straight ahead, quietly, to his engagement position along the longitudinal axis. He adjusts *his judogi* unobtrusively as he walks, arriving about the same time as Tori does at his engagement position, to stand momentarily facing outward, also in *shizenhontai*. They turn in place (toward the *kamiza*) to simultaneously face each other in *shizenhontai*, thereby ending the *koshi waza* category. Figs. (6)–(11).

OKURI-ASHI-HARAI

♦ **ABOUT THIS TECHNIQUE**

This throw, the accompanying foot sweep, is classified as a foot-leg technique (*ashi waza*). It is characterized by light action, which requires the thrower to utilize a minimum of effort to unbalance and throw an opponent by sweeping, or "accompanying," both his feet out from under him together. Originally designed by the founder to demonstrate the factors involved in *go no sen* by which the thrower recovers a distinctly lost attack initiative, today's version is an example of what may better be regarded as nearer to *sen*. In the old form, it was the attacking opponent who initiated the movement, pulling the thrower with him, only to be caught up with and thrown down. In the modern-day form, however, the thrower obtains the attack initiative from the start and never loses it.

♦ **TECHNIQUE SUMMARY**

Uke faces Tori at the closed position with intent to attack, but never really gets started. As Uke grips Tori with the idea of moving Tori sideways (out of *shizenhontai*) to unbalance and topple him, Tori steals the attack initiative by gripping Uke similarly before Uke can tighten his grip and move. Tori moves sideways, push-pulling Uke along with him for two steps in *tsugi ashi*, and then on the third step throw's Uke in the direction of movement by sweeping Uke's feet together and out from under him.

♦ **TECHNIQUE KEY POINTS**

○ UKE ○

1. Attempts to grip Tori in *shizenhontai* at a standstill; catches his grip as he is moved by Tori.

2. Moves directly sideways, keeping his feet in line as he goes; has the feeling of being pushed a bit ahead of Tori's parallel movement.

3. Has his trailing foot swept into his lead foot, ankle into ankle, as both feet are brought together and carried out beyond him and upward in the direction of his movement; feels as if he is being thrown from his ankles. Is

● TORI ●

1. As Uke attempts to cinch his grip, takes the attack initiative without a lag between gripping and sideward movement; beats Uke to a fixed grip by a fraction of a second (Fig. 1).

2. Pushes Uke into movement primarily with a sleeve grip coordinated with his lead step. The sleeve grip is taken on the trailing side of Uke; push action is timed with the closing-up motion of the trailing leg. Moves along the lateral axis (Fig. 2).

3. His rhythm of movement begins with a normal stepping tempo but picks up speed as it progresses; allows himself to fall a bit behind

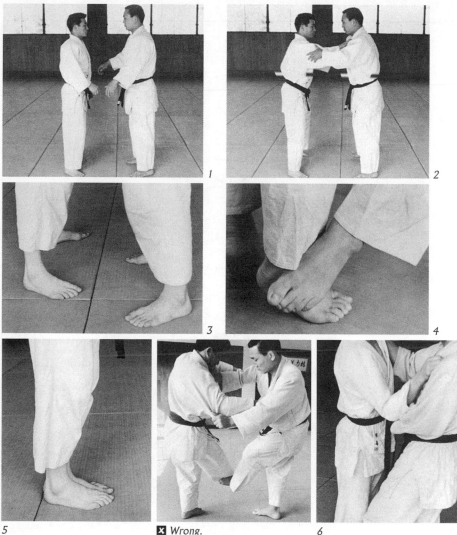

1

2

3

4

5

❌ *Wrong.*

6

(UKE)

unbalanced sideways.

4. In the first (right) technique, moves and falls away from the *kamiza* along the lateral axis. His body comes to rest facing the direction of his movement. In the returning (left) technique, moves and falls toward the *kamiza* along the lateral axis. Executes *ukemi* facing in the direction of his movement.

(TORI)

Uke. Makes his last step (with the lead foot) larger than the others (Fig. 3).

4. Applies a sweep against the trailing ankle of Uke and sends that ankle crashing into Uke's lead ankle; sweeps with the power of his whole body, allowing his midsection to drive forward under Uke. His sweeping foot is directed into contact with Uke's ankle so that his sole is used; his little toe brushes lightly over the mat surface. Does not kick abruptly nor use his inner foot edge as the sweeping surface; unbalances Uke sideways (Figs. 4-6).

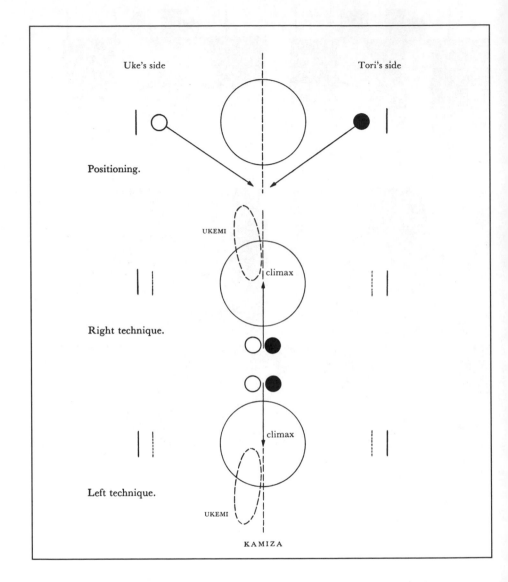

Uke's side   Tori's side

Positioning.

UKEMI

climax

Right technique.

climax

Left technique.

UKEMI

KAMIZA

♦ **PREPARATION FOR ENGAGEMENT**

Standing at their engagement positions, Uke and Tori pause momentarily with composure and quiet alertness, making visual contact. Then in *ayumi ashi*, beginning with their left feet, they come forward at a slight diagonal (toward the *kamiza*) so that they arrive simultaneously on the lateral axis (outside the center zone) to face each other at an engagement distance of about 1 foot (closed position), and stand in *shizenhontai*. They pause momentarily with composure and quiet alertness, making visual contact.

Engagement distance.

1   2

♦ ENGAGEMENT

UKE: Has it in mind to attack Tori by taking a right standard grip in *shizenhontai*, and to pull Tori to his left in *tsugi ashi* (left foot, right foot) to unbalance and topple him sideways, but only succeeds in reaching for his grip and catching it without tightening it.

UKE: With his grip now secure, loses the attack initiative, and being threatened with unbalance himself, yields to Tori's push-pull by maintaining *shizenhontai* and moving directly to his left in *tsugi ashi* (left foot, right foot) in an attempt to keep his balance.

1. TORI: Takes the attack initiative by quickly gripping in a right standard manner while in *shizenhontai*, and simultaneously moving directly to his right one gliding step in *tsugi ashi* (right foot, left foot), push-pulling Uke a bit ahead in an attempt to unbalance Uke sideways.

2. TORI: Having failed to unbalance Uke sideways, tries again by moving similarly but somewhat faster, while push-pulling to his right, increasing the force of his push-pull and the speed of his stepping.

→ 3

UKE: Unable to gain the attack initiative, and once again being threatened with unbalance, yields to Tori's push-pull by maintaining *shizenhontai* and moving directly to his left side in *tsugi ashi* (left foot, right foot) in an attempt to keep his balance.

UKE: Loses his balance as both feet are brought together hard, and comes off his feet in the direction of movement, with feet riding upward and out. Levels off and begins to twist a bit to his left as he executes *ukemi* by relaxing his left-hand grip and beating the mat with his left arm. Comes to rest on the left side of his back, head near Tori's right foot, the *kamiza* behind him, in an area slightly off the lateral axis, away from the *kamiza* on his side.

3. TORI: Having twice failed to unbalance Uke, takes a bigger step with his right foot, increasing the speed of that step and increasing the force of his push-pull to keep Uke a bit ahead of him. Simultaneously with the shift of his weight onto his right foot, applies the sole of his left foot, with ankle flexed to permit this action, to the outer right ankle of Uke, and sweeps Uke's right foot directly into his left foot; his hands push-pull, and hook circularly upward to unbalance Uke and float him with the force of the sweep. Throws Uke sideways in the direction of movement by the combined use of his hands and left foot. Retains his left-hand grip on Uke's right sleeve; places his right hand nearby as Uke levels off and settles into *ukemi*. Exhibits *zanshin*.

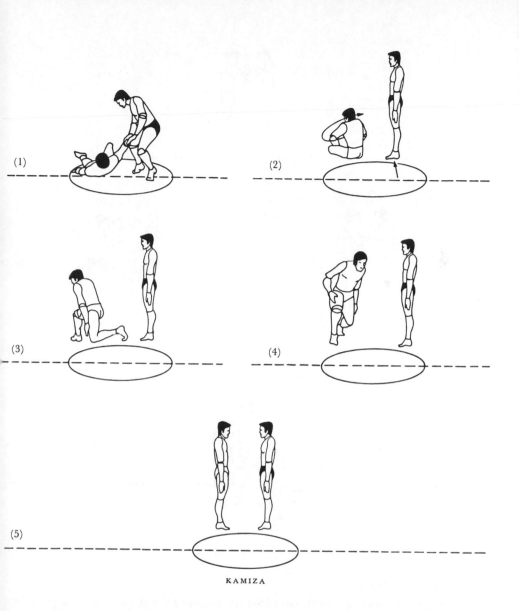

(1)

(2)

(3)

(4)

(5)

KAMIZA

◆ RISING AND FACING

After completion of Uke's *ukemi* from the right technique (in which Tori's left foot sweeps), Tori, the *kamiza* on his left, releases his grip to adjust to his right and waits for Uke in *shizenhontai*. Uke sits up, folds his left leg, and kneels onto his left knee to turn naturally to his left (toward the *kamiza*) as he stands to face Tori; Uke adjusts to an engagement distance of about 1 foot (closed position), standing in *shizenhontai*. Figs. (1)-(5). They pause momentarily with composure and quiet alertness, making visual contact.

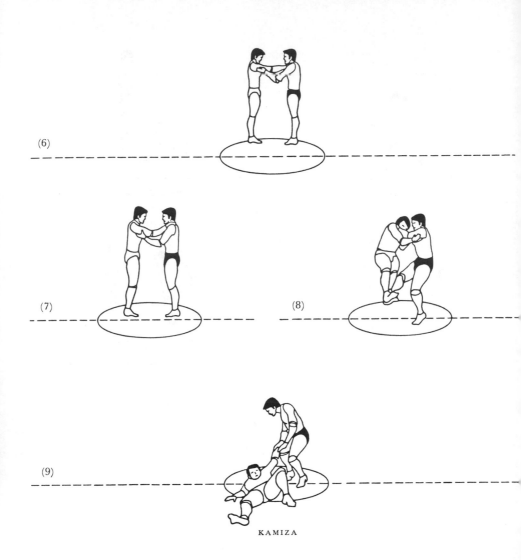

(6)

(7)

(8)

(9)

KAMIZA

◆ COMPLETION

Together, Tori and Uke perform *okuri-ashi-harai* by left standard gripping in *shizenhontai* (in which Tori's right foot sweeps), beginning where Tori completed the right technique (with a slight adjustment to Tori's right) and moving back along the lateral axis in the opposite direction to that just used for the right technique (toward the *kamiza*). Uke's *ukemi* (he beats with the right arm) brings him to rest in an area just outside the center zone (on the *kamiza* side), on his side of the lateral axis but slightly off it, with the *kamiza* at his feet. Tori exhibits *zanshin* and, after a short pause, releases his grip on Uke. Figs. (6)-(9).

SASAE-TSURIKOMI-ASHI

◆ ABOUT THIS TECHNIQUE

This throw, the blocking lift-pull foot, is classified as a foot-leg technique (*ashi waza*). It is an example of the method of unbalancing and throwing an opponent through an interrupted pattern of stepping, by checking the movement of his lower body as the speed of his upper body is accelerated and drawn forward into a big arc through the air. Originally designed by the founder to be performed on the thrower's short third step, which required the thrower to make an extremely fast weight shift and blocking placement to catch the attacker before he could follow into a third step, this throw in today's version is executed in fewer steps as a reminder that throws can be effected without establishing an extended pattern of rhythm. Like the original, the modern-day throw is an example of go *no sen*.

◆ TECHNIQUE SUMMARY

Uke faces Tori at the near position with intent to attack. Uke steps forward, gripping Tori in *shizentai* in order to push Tori and unbalance him backward. Uke continues his attack initiative for two steps in *tsugi ashi*, with Tori yielding to his push by gripping and retreating in *shizentai* by *tsugi ashi* and pulling Uke forward in an unsuccessful attempt to unbalance him. Tori suddenly steals the attack initiative from Uke at the end of the second step by breaking the rhythm of his stepping. Instead of taking a normal third step, Tori does not stop his advanced foot, but slides it back smoothly in a curve to his rear corner and uses it as a platform foot, while his other foot moves directly to quickly block Uke's advancing foot. Tori throws Uke by pulling Uke into unbalance forward in a large arc.

◆ TECHNIQUE KEY POINTS

○ UKE ○	● TORI ●
1. The unexpected stepping pattern by Tori causes him to stiffen his body.	1. After his completed second step, his trailing foot (near Uke) is made a weighted platform foot by his taking a smooth, sliding, unbroken step circularly along the mat to a new position diagonally back in his rear corner (at 45 degrees to the longitudinal axis); does not slide that foot directly to the side (at 90 degrees to the longitudinal axis).
2. Takes off from an advanced foot which is trying to move forward into its third step; his weight is placed on the forward part of that foot, not on the outer edge. Is	2. The toes of his platform foot must be turned

1

2

✗ *Wrong.*   **✗** *Wrong.*

(UKE)

unbalanced forward and feels stretched out.

3. Keeps his body straight by not bending at the hips; makes his body turn in a big arc, head over heels, beyond Tori (as in *uki-otoshi*). Does not spill around the side; feels as if he is being thrown from the advanced shoulder. His body actually moves forward and comes to rest facing in the direction of original movement.

(TORI)

inward enough to permit his body to turn naturally with the motion of the coming throw; shifts his weight over that foot and keeps it on the forward part, not the whole sole. Unbalances Uke forward (Figs. 1, 2).

3. His blocking foot must be placed against Uke's advanced leg quickly, almost as soon as his own right (platform) foot is weighted on the mat; it is placed with the sole surface touching Uke's advanced leg just above the instep; the blocking leg is firm without extreme rigidity and straight so that the knee does not buckle or the foot fall away during the early part of the throw. The contact point on Uke's advanced leg may be above the ankle if necessary (Fig. 1).

4. Opens his body with the motion of the throw, coming around to follow Uke's trajectory 180 degrees if necessary; his pulling arm pulls horizontally until his body leans backward away from Uke, then changes to a sharp, circular, downward pull. Does not buckle at the midsection, but pushes his abdominal region forward so as to keep his body in a straight line from head to the toes of his blocking foot.

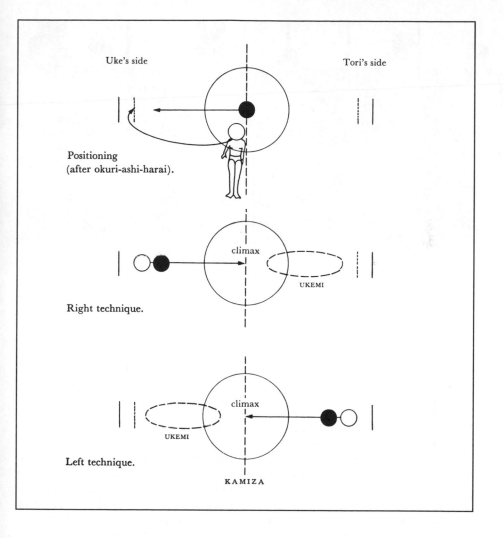

Positioning
(after okuri-ashi-harai).

Right technique.

Left technique.

KAMIZA

◆ PREPARATION FOR ENGAGEMENT

Completing the left *okuri-ashi-harai* (Tori's right-foot sweep), Tori, the *kamiza* at his left, moves forward onto the longitudinal axis and adjusts to a position on Uke's side of the center zone (where he began *uki-otoshi*), to wait in *shizenhontai* as Uke moves in from his left. Uke has simultaneously sat up, folded his right leg, and risen onto his right knee to turn naturally to his right (away from the *kamiza*) as he stands and moves diagonally toward his engagement position on the longitudinal axis. He turns naturally to his right to face Tori in *shizenhontai*; Uke adjusts to an engagement distance of about 2 feet (near position). They pause momentarily with composure and quiet alertness, making visual contact.

Engagement distance.　*1*　→

◆ ENGAGEMENT

1. UKE: Attacks Tori by simultaneously stepping, taking a standard grip in right *shizentai*, and advancing one step by *tsugi ashi* (right foot, left foot) to push Tori and unbalance him backward.

2. UKE: Having failed in his attack, and being threatened with unbalance himself, preserves his balance by immediately attacking similarly again (right foot, left foot).

UKE: Having twice failed in his attacks, is startled and unprepared for this unexpected change in Tori's stepping pattern, and being threatened with unbalance himself, seeks to preserve his balance by immediately attempting to attack similarly once again in *tsugi ashi* (right foot, left foot), but does not succeed in getting his right foot started (his trailing left foot is just settling onto the mat) when he is unbalanced forward.

TORI: Preserves his balance by yielding to Uke's advance and push, simultaneously stepping and taking a standard grip in right *shizentai* as he retreats one step by *tsugi ashi* (left foot, right foot) in an attempt to break Uke's balance forward by pulling him horizontally.

TORI: Preserves balance again by yielding to Uke's attack as before, retreating by *tsugi ashi* (left foot, right foot) and again trying to unbalance Uke forward by pulling horizontally.

3. TORI: Takes the attack initiative by changing the pattern of stepping to foil Uke. Does not halt his trailing right foot, but carries it diagonally backward and out to his right rear corner, turning the toes inward; shifts his weight onto that foot, keeping the knee slightly bent as he continues the horizontal pull on Uke with both hands, unbalancing him forward.

2 → 3 →

(UKE)

UKE: Is thrown forward in a big arc to his front, beyond Tori. Executes *ukemi*, beating with his left arm as he comes to rest on the left side of his back, his head at Tori's left foot as Tori turns to follow the motion of the throw, the *kamiza* on his right, along the longitudinal axis near Tori's engagement position.

(TORI)

Applies the sole of his left foot firmly against the outside and front of Uke's right ankle, blocking it securely as he turns his body sharply to his left; reinforces the blocking action by continuing a strong pull horizontally on Uke's upper body with both hands. Throws Uke by the combined action of his pulling, blocking, and body twist into his left rear corner. Retains his left-hand grip on Uke's right sleeve; his right hand is placed nearby as Uke settles into *ukemi*. Exhibits *zanshin*.

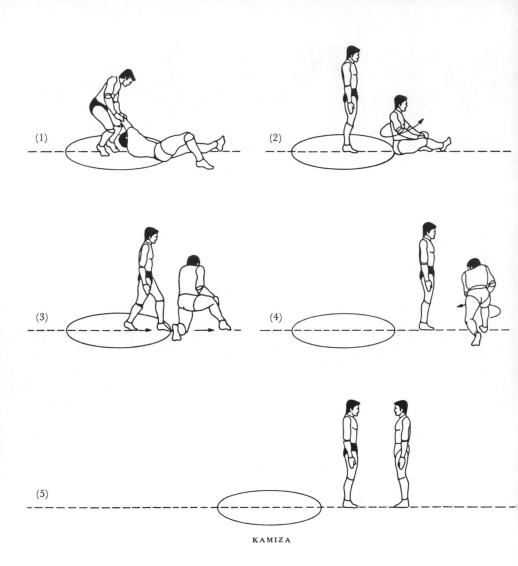

(1)

(2)

(3)

(4)

(5)

KAMIZA

◆ RISING AND FACING

After completion of Uke's *ukemi* from the right technique (in which Tori blocks with his left foot), Tori, the *kamiza* on his right, releases his grip and adjusts by coming forward along the longitudinal axis to his approximate engagement position to wait in *shizenhontai* facing Uke. Uke has simultaneously sat up, folded his left leg, and risen onto his left knee to stand. Uke then moves forward a bit, turning naturally (his back to *kamiza*) to his left to face Tori; Uke adjusts to an engagement distance of about 2 feet (near position), standing in *shizenhontai*. Figs. (1)-(5). They pause momentarily with composure and quiet alertness, making visual contact.

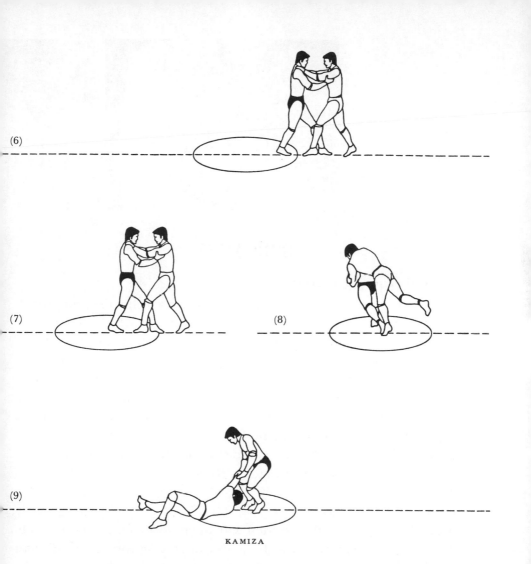

(6)

(7)

(8)

(9)

KAMIZA

♦ **COMPLETION**

Together, Tori and Uke perform *sasae-tsurikomi-ashi* in left *shizentai* (in which Tori blocks with his right foot), beginning at Tori's approximate engagement position and moving back in the opposite direction to that just used for the right technique, along the longitudinal axis. Uke's *ukemi* (he beats with the right arm) brings him to rest outside the center zone on his own side, along the longitudinal axis, the *kamiza* on his left. Tori exhibits *zan-shin* and, after a short pause, releases his grip on Uke. Figs. (6)-(9).

1

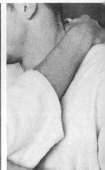

❌ *Wrong.*

UCHI-MATA

◆ ABOUT THIS TECHNIQUE

This throw, the inner thigh, is classified as a foot-leg technique (*ashi waza*). It demonstrates the efficient use of centrifugal force, by which an opponent can be placed on the outer perimeter of a rotary movement, unbalanced, and thrown by sweeping him up off his feet by a leg action directed upward between his thighs. Today's version, which like the original may be regarded as an example of quasi-*sen*, differs little from the early form designed by the founder. The original design was more graphically defensive on the part of the opponent, who was thrown out of movement in a defensive stance (*jig-otai*), and also permitted the thrower to grip somewhat higher on his opponent's lapel, a bit below the ear as in *tsurikomi-goshi*.

◆ TECHNIQUE SUMMARY

Uke faces Tori at the semifar position with intent to attack, but never really gets started. As Uke grips Tori with the idea of moving Tori out of *shizentai* to unbalance and topple him, Tori steals the attack initiative by gripping Uke similarly before Uke can tighten his grip and move. Tori advances and swings Uke circularly around behind him for two steps by *tsugi ashi* with Uke becoming defensively straddle legged. Tori unbalances Uke and throws him up and over on the third step by sweeping the back of his thigh upward between Uke's widespread legs.

◆ TECHNIQUE KEY POINTS

<table>
<tr><td align="center">○ UKE ○</td><td align="center">● TORI ●</td></tr>
<tr><td>1. Attempts to grip Tori in *shizentai* at a standstill; catches his grip as he is moved by Tori.</td><td>1. Takes a standard grip; does not place his assist-arm hand up high on Uke's collar (Fig. 1).</td></tr>
</table>

2

2. Moves circularly around as he is pulled in behind Tori, with Tori quartering into him; has the feeling of being pulled around and is purely defensive.

3. His balance worsens on each step. (This can be likened to standing a Japanese oilpaper umbrella on its butt end and suddenly rotating it so that it unfurls.) Takes bigger steps than Tori and braces lightly in defense. Is unbalanced forward.

4. Is thrown just as he is about to weight his advancing foot at the third step; releases his grip on Tori's sleeve and executes the closed-gate effect, but bends forward and widens his stance; feels as if he is being thrown from the advancing leg (Fig. 2).

5. Is carried upward and turned over. His body comes to rest facing his engagement position in the first (right) technique, which pulls him clockwise; the second technique pulls him counterclockwise and brings his body to rest facing Tori's engagement position. If his body comes to rest in any other direction, Tori's technique is weak. Must not simply revolve around Tori's attacking leg and drop straight down to the mat.

2. His circular movement is smoothly performed without halting or gaps in its flow, but should allow a slight feeling of pulsation; each step turns about a half circle. Too small a stepping pattern will make the unbalancing weak. Brings Uke around a point in front of him (creating this new center point with each revolution), not around a center point between them.

3. Pulls Uke more strongly on each step. (This can be likened to holding a cord to which a small weight has been attached at the end, then beginning to rotate one's body in a circle with a moving center; a progressive speed increase straightens the cord, tightens it, and causes the weight to rise from the ground and trace a circular orbit around the body.) Unbalances Uke forward.

4. His lapel-grip hand works harder to pull Uke; the elbow may be lifted a bit to accommodate this.

5. Throws with almost a full step, wide forward on the third step, rather than backing his platform foot under Uke; his sweeping leg, held straight, rises about to the horizontal as it cuts upward, back into Uke's rear corner in the direction of movement (Fig. 2).

6. His platform foot carries his body weight on its forward part, not on the whole sole.

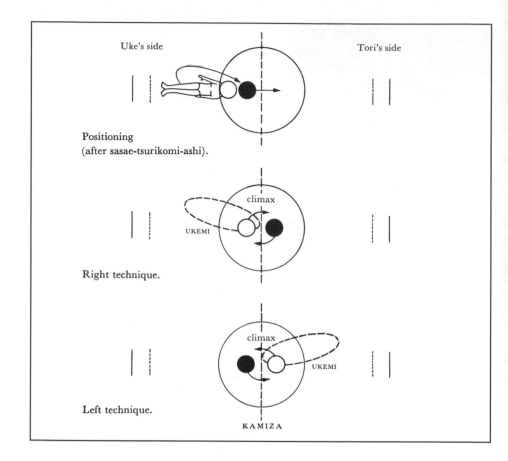

Uke's side   Tori's side

Positioning
(after **sasae-tsurikomi-ashi**).

climax

UKEMI

Right technique.

climax

UKEMI

Left technique.

KAMIZA

◆ PREPARATION FOR ENGAGEMENT

Completing the left *sasae-tsurikomi-ashi* (in which Tori blocks with his right foot), Tori, the *kamiza* to his left, adjusts by backing up a bit to his side but within the center zone to wait in *shizenhontai* facing Uke. Uke has simultaneously sat up, folded his right leg, and risen onto his right knee to turn naturally (his back to the *kamiza*) to his right to stand to face Tori; Uke moves forward along the longitudinal axis to the center zone and adjusts to an engagement distance of about 3 feet (semifar position) to stand in *shizenhontai*. They pause momentarily with composure and quiet alertness, making visual contact.

◆ ENGAGEMENT

UKE: Attacks Advances his right foot half a step forward to take a standard grip in right *shizentai*, and has it in mind to attack Tori by moving him to unbalance and topple him, but never gets started.

1. TORI: Takes the attack initiative by simultaneously advancing his right foot half a step forward and taking a standard grip on Uke in right *shizentai*, and before Uke can launch his attack, advances his left foot

Engagement distance.

1

(UKE)

UKE: Unprepared for this unexpected, sudden movement by Tori, is swung circularly around in *tsugi ashi* (left foot, right foot) and comes up nearer Tori's right hip. Being threatened with unbalance, attempts to get the attack initiative by widening his stance for stability as he comes around, lagging a bit behind.

UKE: TORI swung around in *tsugi ashi* once again (left foot, right foot), and is purely defensive now as his balance worsens; widens his stance as he steps, still lagging behind, but bends forward somewhat more, in an attempt to slow the rotary action.

(TORI)

circularly forward a full step to his left front corner, then withdraws his right foot circularly to follow in *tsugi ashi* fashion. Simultaneously with the circular stepping, swings Uke around behind him to his right rear corner by giving a strong horizontal pull with his right hand in an attempt to unbalance Uke forward.

2. TORI: Having failed to unbalance Uke, repeats his movement to continue his attack initiative as before, moving circularly in *tsugi ashi* (left foot, right foot) around a new center point he selects at his left front. He increases the power of his horizontal pulling with his right hand, thus

2

3

(UKE)

(TORI)

bringing Uke around further behind him
so that he now quarters into Uke.

UKE: Is swung around Tori again in *tsugi
ashi* (left foot, right foot). Loses his balance for-ward and is brought up against
Tori just as he is coming onto his advancing left foot; is on his toes, raked forward,
and feels as if he were floating as his right
foot slides across the mat and into the air
in the direction of his movement.

3. TORI: Feeling Uke's balance collapse,
widens the advancing step of his left foot
out a bit, off its circular path, and increases the power of his pull on Uke as both
hands hook Uke into tight contact with
his lower right side. Keeping his weight
on his left leg, knee slightly bent, sweeps
his right leg

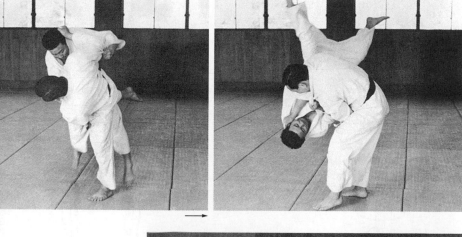

(UKE)

UKE: Rides up and over Tori's upward sweeping, extended right leg and twists to his left as he turns head over heels in mid-air and executes *ukemi*, beating with his left arm. Comes to rest on the left side of his back, head to the inside of Tori's left foot, the *kamiza* at his left, in an area slightly off of the longitudinal axis and close to the *kamiza*, but inside the center zone.

(TORI)

backward and up against Uke's inner left thigh just as Uke begins to weight that leg. Throws Uke upward and over his extended right leg, making contact with the rear portion of his right thigh on Uke's inner left thigh, by the downward pulling actions of his arms and the upward sweep of his right leg, reinforced by the springing action of his left (platform) leg. Retains his left-hand grip on Uke's right sleeve; places his right hand nearby as Uke settles into *ukemi*. Is now standing approximately where he began the technique. Exhibits *zanshin*.

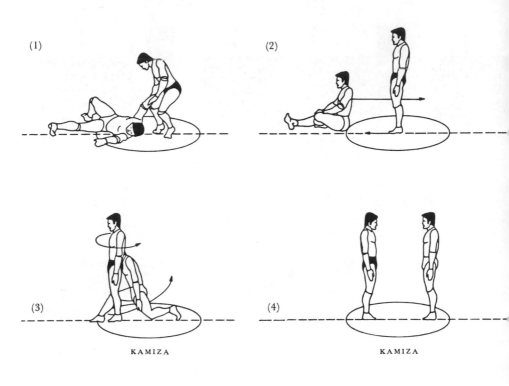

(1)　　　　　　　　　　(2)

(3)　　　　　　　　　　(4)

KAMIZA　　　　　　　　KAMIZA

◆ RISING AND FACING

After completion of Uke's *ukemi* from the right technique (in which Tori's right leg sweeps upward), Tori, the *kamiza* on his left, releases his grip and moves a bit forward to Uke's side of the center zone but stays within the center zone, then turns naturally to his left (into the *kamiza*) to stand in *shizenhontai* facing his engagement position. Uke, who has simultaneously sat up, folded his left leg, and kneeled onto his left knee, rises by backing up (the *kamiza* at his left) along the longitudinal axis to Tori's side of the center zone, but within the center zone. Uke faces Tori and adjusts to an engagement distance of about 3 feet (semifar position). Figs. (1)-(4). They pause momentarily with composure and quiet alertness, making visual contact.

◆ COMPLETION

Together, Tori and Uke perform *uchi-mata* in left *shizentai* (in which Tori's left leg sweeps upward), beginning at the approximate center of the center zone and rotating in the opposite direction to that used for the right technique. Uke's *ukemi* (he beats with the right arm) brings him to rest in an area slightly off the longitudinal axis but close to the *kamiza* and within the center zone, with the *kamiza* on his right. Tori exhibits *zanshin* and, after a short pause, releases his grip on Uke. With the *kamiza* on his right, Tori walks

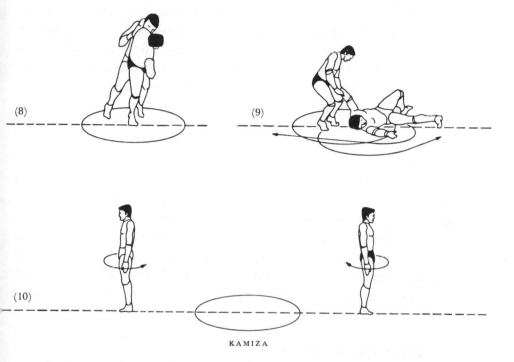

quietly along the longitudinal axis to his engagement position, adjusting his *judogi* unobtrusively as he walks. Arriving at his engagement position he stands momentarily facing away from Uke in *shizenontai*; simultaneously, Uke has risen from his *ukemi* by folding his right leg and kneeling onto his right knee to turn naturally (into the *kamiza*) to his right and stand up, and has walked straight ahead, quietly, to his engagement position along the longitudinal axis. He adjusts his *judogi* unobtrusively as he walks, arriving about the same time as Tori does at his engagement position, to stand momentarily facing outward, also in *shizenhontai*. They turn in place (toward the *kamiza*) to face each other in *shizenhontai*, thereby ending the *ashi waza* category. Figs. (5)–(10).

TOMOE-NAGE

◆ **ABOUT THIS TECHNIQUE**

This throw, the whirl throw, is classified as a back sacrifice technique (*ma sutemi waza*). It is a fine classical example of *hando no kuzushi* (unbalancing by reaction). In this technique, the thrower first pushes and moves his opponent backward in order to provoke a forward pushing response by the opponent, at which moment the opponent is flung forward in a high semicircular pattern over and behind the recumbent thrower, who has "sacrificed" himself or "thrown himself away" from a standing posture. Today's version, which involves elements of both quasi-*sen* and *go no sen*, remains relatively unchanged from its original form except that a definite number of steps replace the earlier unspecified stepping, which was prolonged until Uke reacted.

◆ **TECHNIQUE SUMMARY**

Uke faces Tori at the semifar position with intent to attack, but never really gets started. As Uke advances and grips Tori in *shizentai* with the idea of moving Tori to unbalance and topple him, Tori steals the attack initiative by advancing and gripping similarly in *shizentai*, simultaneously pushing Uke backward three steps in *ayumi ashi*. Feeling backward unbalance, Uke resists Tori by pushing forward; Tori takes advantage of this sought-for reaction by accelerating Uke into forward unbalance in the direction of his push and, dropping to the mat at Uke's feet, places a foot in Uke's midsection to throw Uke head over heels behind him.

◆ **TECHNIQUE KEY POINTS**

○ UKE ○

1. His first step after *shizentai* is a half step backward, starting with his *retreated* foot; thereafter takes full steps.

2. Is definitely pushed backward by Tori; is semiunbalanced backward and purely defensive.

● TORI ●

1. His first step after *shizentai* is a half step forward, starting with his *advanced* foot; thereafter takes full steps.

2. Controls Uke as he pushes Uke backward; is trying to obtain a forward pushing reaction from Uke, not trying to throw Uke backward. Is careful not to float his body as he pushes; bends his knees slightly to stay down.

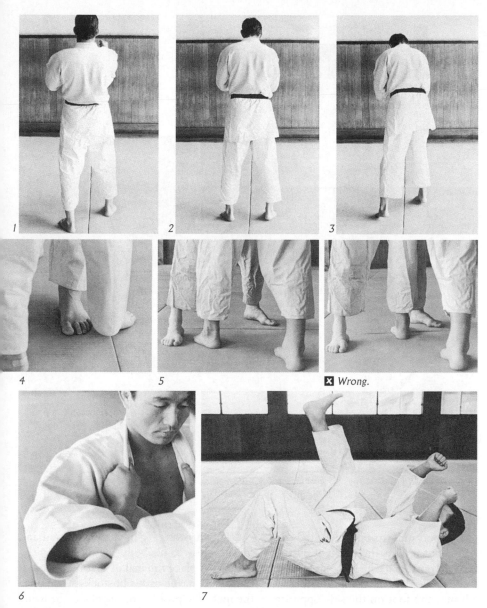

X Wrong.

(UKE)

3. Recovers his balance after the third step, pushing back against Tori with his upper body only; his feet remain in a *shizentai* identical to starting *shizentai* (Fig. 1). Moves his trailing foot into line with his advanced foot (Fig. 2). Loses his balance forward.

(TORI)

3. Blends Uke's forward pushing reaction with the entry step of his trailing leg, its foot being placed on the mat alongside and inside of Uke's advanced foot (Figs. 4, 5). As that foot enters, changes his hand grip from Uke's sleeve to Uke's front lapel (Fig. 6); simultaneously drops to the mat, quickly sitting near his platform-foot heel (Fig. 7).

8 (second view)

❌ Wrong.

(UKE)

4. Expert judoists take off with both feet about in line, their weight on the forward portion of the feet, not leaning to one side; less skilled judoists may advance the foot on the side opposite Tori's attacking leg a short step to a position next to Tori's buttocks, in order to assist the takeoff. Feels as if he is being thrown from his midsection in a long, looping arc forward (Fig. 3).

5. Must come to his feet and remain motionless in place; the lack of wavering or bouncing forward to gain balance demonstrates full control of his body.

(TORI)

4. His throwing leg must be well bent and tucked close to his body as he drops to the mat; must place the ball of that foot just below Uke's navel, as his buttocks settle onto the mat. The pushing thrust of the throwing leg must not come too early; waits until Uke unbalances forward over him. His body must double and rock back, combining the push and thrust of the leg with the arm pull, which is circularly upward, then in a short curve downward with the hands coming in to the chest. The platform leg remains fixed with knee upright, the ball of the foot on the mat, for stability (Fig. 8).

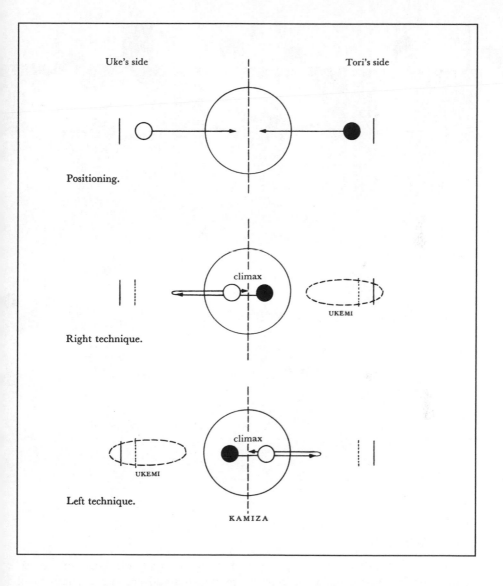

Uke's side   Tori's side

Positioning.

climax

UKEMI

Right technique.

climax

UKEMI

Left technique.

KAMIZA

◆ PREPARATION FOR ENGAGEMENT

Standing at their engagement positions, Uke and Tori pause momentarily with composure and quiet alertness, making visual contact. Then in *ayumi ashi*, beginning with their left feet, they come forward along the longitudinal axis toward the center zone. Arriving simultaneously inside the center zone, they face each other at an engagement distance of about 3 feet (semifar position), and stand in *shizenhontai* a bit on Tori's side. They pause momentarily with composure and quiet alertness, making visual contact.

Engagement distance. 1

◆ ENGAGEMENT

UKE: Advances his right foot half a step forward to take a standard grip on Tori in right *shizentai*, and has it in mind to attack Tori by moving and toppling him, but never gets started.

1. TORI: Takes the attack initiative by simultaneously advancing his right foot half a step forward and taking a standard grip on Uke in right *shizentai*; before Uke can launch his attack, advances three steps by *ayumi ashi* (right foot, left foot, right foot), pushing and attempting to unbalance Uke backward.

UKE: Unprepared for this unexpected movement by Tori, yields to Tori's push by taking three steps backward in *ayumi ashi* (left foot, right foot, left foot); is purely defensive. Threatened with unbalance backward on the third step and standing in right *shizentai*, begins to resist Tori by pushing back against him; recovers his balance momentarily.

UKE: His pushing reaction forward is accentuated by Tori's pull and he begins to lose balance forward; in an attempt to preserve his balance, moves his left foot forward and succeeds in bringing it level with his right foot.

UKE: Is doubled over on top of Tori as his balance is destroyed. Is supported by Tori's right foot in his midsection; begins to ride up and over. Turns over, head down and legs high up in the air, and is propelled forward, over behind Tori in a semicircular trajectory. Executes *ukemi* over his right shoulder (*zempo kaiten*), beating with his left arm. Comes to rest in a standing position, *shizen-hontai*, on the longitudinal axis or slightly on the *kamiza* side, with the *kamiza* on his right, at a spot near Tori's engagement position, facing outward (away from Tori).

2. TORI: As Uke pushes back, slides his left foot deep between Uke's feet, and at the same time releases his left-hand grip on Uke's right sleeve and transfers that grip to Uke's right lapel; breaks Uke's balance straight forward with a circular upward pull of both hands.

3. TORI: Bends his left knee and sits down quickly onto the mat, using the left leg as a platform. Simultaneously bends his right knee and tucks it close to his chest; flexing his right ankle upward, places the upper portion of the sole on the center of Uke's lower abdomen. Continuing his pull, throws Uke forward by the combined action of his pulling and the momentum of his falling body, followed by the pushing thrust of his bent right leg; straightens that leg as Uke comes forward and rises above him. His left leg braces, with the ball of the foot on the mat, to aid in bridging upward with his body (buttocks off the mat) to reinforce the throw. Removes both hands from Uke's lapels allowing a free fall, and extends both arms in the direction of Uke's motion as Uke turns over into *ukemi*, then snaps them to his chest. Exhibits *zanshin*.

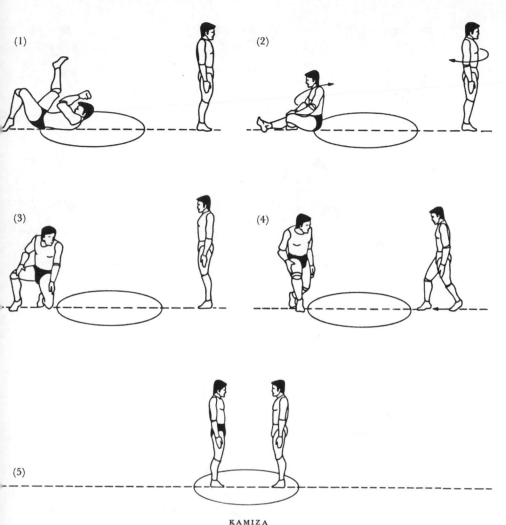

(1) (2) (3) (4) (5)

KAMIZA

◆ RISING AND FACING

After completion of Uke's *ukemi* from the right technique (in which Tori's right leg attacks), Tori, the *kamiza* at his left, sits up, folds his left leg, kneels onto his left knee, rises, and turns naturally to his left (into the *kamiza*), adjusting to a position within the center zone on Uke's side to wait facing Uke in *shizenhontai*. Uke, standing at Tori's engagement position, turns naturally to his right (into the *kamiza*) to face Tori and walks quietly along the longitudinal axis to adjust to an engagement distance of about 3 feet (semifar position), standing in *shizenhontai*. Figs. (1)-(5). They pause momentarily, keeping composure and quiet alertness, making visual contact.

(6) (7) (8) (9) (10) (11) (12) (13)

KAMIZA

◆ COMPLETION

Together, Tori and Uke perform *tomoe-nage* in left *shizentai* (in which Tori's left leg attacks), beginning within but a bit on Uke's side of the center zone, the throw and the fall being made along the longitudinal axis in the opposite direction to that just used for the right technique. Uke's *ukemi* (he beats with the right arm) brings him to rest standing in *shizenhontai* in an area along the longitudinal axis near his engagement position, the *kamiza* on his left, facing outward (away from Tori). Tori exhibits *zanshin*. Figs. (6)-(13).

URA-NAGE

♦ ABOUT THIS TECHNIQUE

This throw, the rear throw, is classified as a back sacrifice technique (*ma sutemi waza*). It demonstrates the powerful countering effect made possible by unbalancing an attacking opponent by scooping him up off his feet and launching him over the thrower's shoulder and behind the thrower, who has "sacrificed" or thrown himself to the ground. This *go no sen* technique is the third of four in which a blow is struck at the thrower, and forcefully shows the combative value intended in this kata. The founder's original version of this technique required the thrower to get further behind the opponent on his entry step, with the arm encircling the opponent's waist inserted so deep that the hand could be placed on the far side of the opponent's abdomen. Today's version has modified this entry by requiring the thrower to position himself somewhat more frontally to his opponent.

♦ TECHNIQUE SUMMARY

Uke faces Tori at the far position with intent to attack. Uke takes two careful steps forward with alternate feet in *ayumi ashi*, striking with his bottom fist straight down from overhead at the top of Tori's head in order to knock Tori down on the spot. Tori foils Uke by stepping forward to meet the attack, ducking under the blow, and blending with Uke's body to unbalance Uke forward by crouching low at Uke's advanced front corner; hugging Uke tightly to himself, he throws Uke forward by heaving him over his shoulder as he straightens up and falls straight to the mat on his back.

♦ TECHNIQUE KEY POINTS

○ UKE ○

1. Makes a stepping movement forward, straight at, not across, Tori's front.

2. Strikes with his bottom fist straight down at the front top of Tori's head; times his fist's arrival with his advancing foot's placement on the mat. Sinks his weight down as he strikes, by slightly bending his knees, to drive Tori into the ground like a post and avoid being thrown over (Fig. 1).

● TORI ●

1. Takes a deep step forward with the leg on the same side as Uke's attacking blow, stepping outside of Uke's advancing leg (that on the side of the striking arm) so that Uke quarters into him; lowers his body simultaneously with the stepping, thus simplifying the dodging of Uke's blow, and gets his center of gravity well below that of Uke (Fig. 2). The arm on the side of his advanced leg reaches well around the rear of Uke's body; the other hand presses hard up into Uke's lower abdomen (Figs. 3, 4).

1 2 3

(UKE)

3. His blow passes behind Tori, his arm not stopping at head level but continuing its downward swing over Tori's shoulder where it is stopped by the shoulder. The underside of his upper striking arm drops well over Tori's shoulder and presses down hard against it. Must get this arm out as a lead arm in *ukemi*. Is unbalanced forward.

4. His fall is high and hard; must not flinch, try to hang back, jump ahead of the throw, or hang on. Must remain on the mat in *ukemi*; feels as if he is thrown from the loins.

5. After *ukemi*, rises instantly with Tori to begin the left technique without the pause usually taken between other techniques; adjustment to the proper engagement distance (far position) must be made quickly. His body comes to rest facing in the direction of movement.

(TORI)

2. Comes up under Uke to face him out of quartering position by moving his trailing foot between Uke's legs; this action must bring his weight fully onto his heels as he hugs Uke tightly, without gripping, to the front of his body. If he releases his hands from Uke at this point, he should topple backward.

3. His throwing action has its source of power in the legs, which drive hard to straighten ánd snap his midsection forward, under and up against Uke, scooping him up as if uprooting a tree. Straddles Uke's advanced leg. Avoids just collapsing to the mat by not buckling at his hips; must lay well back as he falls flat on his back and concentrates on unbalancing Uke forward and throwing Uke straight behind and clear of him. Does not interfere with Uke's forward motion. Bridges his buttocks off mat (Figs. 5, 6).

4. Rises instantly after completing the throw and is prepared for Uke's second attack on the other side (in which Uke's left arm attacks), without taking the usual pause while standing and facing Uke.

4

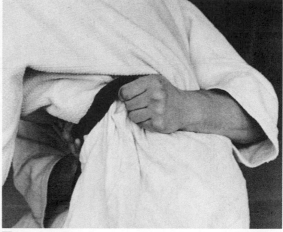

❌ *Wrong.*

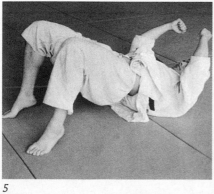

5

❌ *Wrong.*

6

❌ *Wrong.*

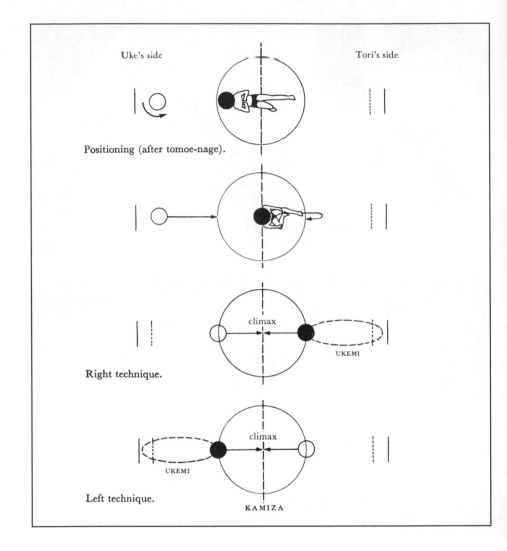

Positioning (after tomoe-nage).

Uke's side

Tori's side

climax

UKEMI

Right technique.

climax

UKEMI

Left technique.

KAMIZA

♦ **PREPARATION FOR ENGAGEMENT**

Completing the left *tomoe-nage* (in which Tori's left foot attacks), Tori, the *kamiza* at his right, quickly rises (after *zanshin*) in place at a point near the center of the center zone by sitting up, folding his right leg, and kneeling onto his right knee to move a bit forward along the longitudinal axis to a point on his edge of the center zone, there turning naturally to his right (into the *kamiza*) to face Uke in *shizenhontai*. Uke, standing in *shizenhontai* at a point near his engagement position, turns naturally to his left (into the *kamiza*) to face Tori and quickly adjusts to an engagement distance of about 6 feet (far position), standing in *shizenhontai*. They make visual contact and engage immediately.

Engagement distance.   *1*

2   *3*   →

◆ ENGAGEMENT

1. UKE: Threatens Tori by advancing his left foot far forward, simultaneously raising his right arm so as to bring it upward from the right back corner with his bottom fist directly overhead, facing Tori.

2. UKE: Attacks Tori by advancing his right foot and simultaneously bringing his right bottom fist straight down from overhead in an attempt to hit Tori on top of his head and knock him down on the spot.

UKE: His blow passes over Tori's left shoulder and his body rides up frontally onto Tori, his weight a bit dropped to avoid being thrown over. Keeps his upper body erect.

TORI: Remains motionless but quietly alert.

3. TORI: Blends with Uke's attack by advancing his left foot a deep step, well along the outside of Uke, the toes of that foot pointing behind Uke; meets Uke approximately in the center of the center zone. Simultaneously lowers his body into a deep squat position by bending his knees. At the same moment, slips his left arm along Uke's belt line, around behind Uke, reaching around to the far left side of Uke, and presses his left palm against Uke's left side below the hip bone. Hugs Uke tightly to him with this left arm, then quickly arc-steps his right foot between Uke's legs to a position near and parallel to Uke's right foot, by leaving his left foot in place and pivoting while crouching low to face frontally

(UKE)

(TORI)

UKE: Loses his balance forward as his right side is hugged into tight contact with Tori, and his striking arm drops well over Tori's left shoulder, behind Tori.

UKE: Is taken off his feet high into the air behind Tori, by being flung over Tori's left shoulder. Executes *ukemi* by getting his right arm free and going over his right shoulder (*zempo kaiten*) to beat with his left arm, as he comes to rest on the left side of his back, head to head with Tori, along the longitudinal axis, the *kamiza* at his right, at a point near Tori's salutation position.

into Uke; simultaneously applies the palm of his right hand, with fingers together and pointing straight upward, firmly against Uke's lower abdomen below the belt knot. Unbalances Uke forward. Throws Uke clear over his left shoulder by the combined upward action of his straightening legs and the momentum of his body bending backward as he falls straight on his back to the mat; his arms have heaved upward and over his left shoulder in the direction of Uke's flight. Removes both his arms from Uke, allowing Uke a free fall, extending them in the direction of Uke's motion as Uke settles into *ukemi*. Bridges his buttocks off the mat by using both feet, with the balls of the feet on the mat, as platform feet to reinforce the throw. Exhibits *zanshin*, but more briefly than usual.

◆ RISING AND FACING

After completion of Uke's *ukemi* from the right technique (over Tori's left shoulder), Tori, the *kamiza* at his left, sits up instantly, folds his left leg, kneels onto his left knee, and turns naturally to his left (into the *kamiza*) to quickly stand and face Uke in *shizenhontai*, adjusting his position to the approximate edge of Uke's side of the center zone. Uke rises together with Tori by sitting, folding his left leg, kneeling onto his left knee, and turning naturally to his left (his back to *kamiza*), then rises by taking a big step toward the center as he moves to face Tori; Uke quickly adjusts to an engagement distance of about 6 feet (far position), standing in *shizenhontai*. Figs. (1)-(4). Without pause, but keeping composure and quiet alertness and making visual contact, they continue.

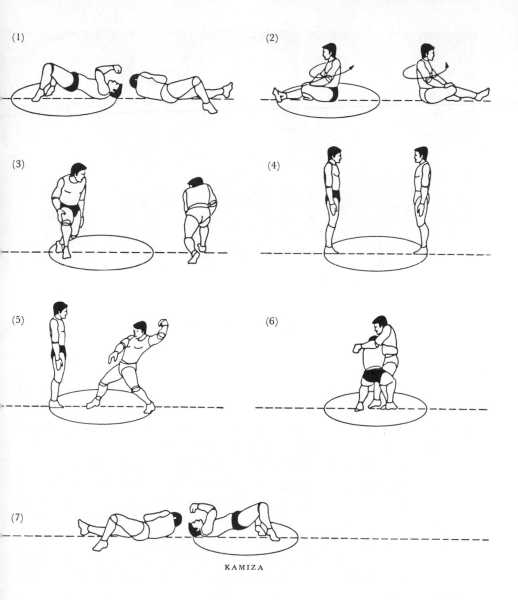

(1)

(2)

(3)

(4)

(5)

(6)

(7)

KAMIZA

◆ COMPLETION

Together, Tori and Uke perform left *ura-nage* (over Tori's right shoulder), beginning from opposite edges of the center zone and moving into collision at the approximate center of the center zone to throw and fall back along the longitudinal axis in the opposite direction to that just used for the right technique. Uke's *ukemi* (he beats with the right arm) brings him to rest outside of the center zone, along the longitudinal axis on his own side, the *kamiza* on his left, near his salutation position, facing outward (away from Tori). Tori exhibits *zanshin*. Figs. (5)-(7). The normal rhythm of the kata is restored here.

1   *2*   *3*

SUMI-GAESHI

◆ ABOUT THIS TECHNIQUE

This throw, the corner overturning, is classified as a back sacrifice technique (*ma sutemi waza*). It stands as a classic example of the use of resistance in Judo to overcome, unbalance, and throw an opponent by the use of the circular drawing power of the thrower's body, aided by one leg acting as the radius of the low arc that the opponent's body will trace as he is flung forward, over and behind the reclining thrower. Like its original form, it involves elements of both quasi-*sen* and *go no sen*. The original form was less efficient in that it required the thrower to slide his platform foot to a position behind the foot of his attacking leg before it was lifted. This tended to seat the thrower too far from the opponent, weakening the lifting action of the attacking leg, which could be placed anywhere along the opponent's back thigh. The stepping action of the platform foot has been efficiently modified in today's style.

◆ TECHNIQUE SUMMARY

Uke faces Tori at the semifar position with intent to attack, but never really gets started. Uke advances and grips Tori by hand pressure alone in a modified *jigotai* with the idea of pulling Tori forward to unbalance and topple him, but Tori steals the attack initiative by advancing and gripping similarly in a modified *jigotai*, simultaneously resisting and counterpulling Uke forward in one arc step. Feeling himself unbalanced forward, Uke resists Tori by straightening up; Tori takes advantage of Uke's floated posture and drops

4

5

❌ Wrong.

6 7

straight on his back to the mat at Uke's feet to throw Uke forward in a low arc, over and behind him, by the momentum of his falling body aided by the lifting action of one of his feet, which is behind Uke's knee.

◆ TECHNIQUE KEY POINTS

○ UKE ○

1. Is pulled against his resistance by Tori; is purely defensive, but recovers his balance at the end of his first step, straightening up to do so. Has a floating feeling at this point. Moves his trailing foot forward into line with his advanced foot (Figs. 1-3).

● TORI ●

1. His arc step to the rear must be wide and long enough to overcome Uke's drag resistance; pulls with his *whole* body. The hand which presses against Uke's shoulder blade, from under Uke's armpit, scoops upward with strength in the little finger; the other hand pulls only a little without gripping Uke's sleeve (Figs. 6, 7).

8

❌ *Wrong.*

8 (second view, detail)

(UKE)

2. Takes off as both feet come approximately into line, with weight on the forward portion of the feet, not leaning to one side in anticipation of the coming throw. Is unbalanced forward (Figs. 4, 5).

3. Gets his arm loose from under Tori's armpit to use as the lead arm for his forward rolling *ukemi* (Fig. 9).

4. Is thrown forward in a low arc; may elect to stay down on the mat in *ukemi* or come to a balanced position

(TORI)

2. At the end of the first arc step, allows Uke to straighten up and recover his balance; must not overpower Uke.

3. Uses both hands to float Uke as Uke straightens himself up, by pulling and scooping upward with the power of both palms (especially the little fingers), direct to Uke's front.

4. His second step is not complete and must be taken by bringing together the heels of both feet, with weight on the heels; if the moving foot is carried behind the other foot (soon to be used to attack Uke's trailing leg), the reclining

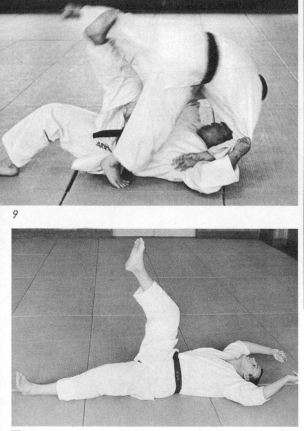

9

10

❌ *Wrong.*

(UKE)

on his feet, depending upon the force of the throw; feels as if he is being thrown from his trailing knee, directly forward. His body moves forward and comes to rest facing in the direction of original movement.

(TORI)

position will be too far from Uke to throw him efficiently (Fig. 8).

5. Unbalances Uke forward and throws from flat on his back; must not tip Uke to either side. Throws without any delay from the moment of sinking to the mat. Does not grip Uke's *judogi* at the shoulder blade with his hand; may grip Uke's sleeve, if inexperienced, to accelerate and guide Uke. Takes care not to trap Uke's lead arm (the arm under his armpit). (Fig. 9). On throwing, bridges his buttocks off mat and keeps his chin tucked in to his chest. Ensures that his throwing leg's knee is bent; the ankle is locked with the toes pointed away from the shin. The platform leg is fixed on the mat for stability (Fig. 10).

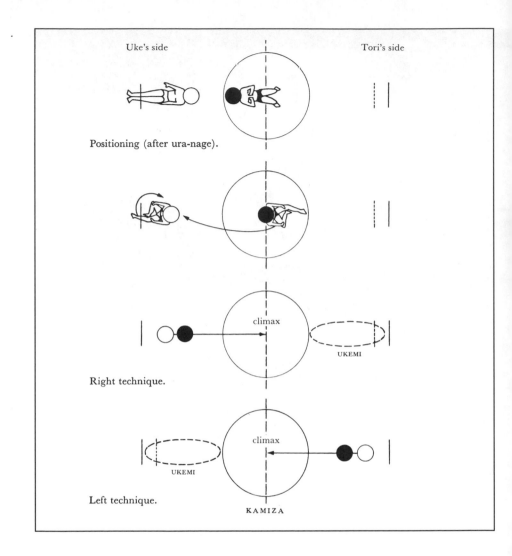

Positioning (after ura-nage).

climax

UKEMI

Right technique.

climax

UKEMI

Left technique.

KAMIZA

♦ **PREPARATION FOR ENGAGEMENT**

Completing the left *ura-nage* (over Tori's right shoulder), Tori, the *kamiza* at his right, sits up, folds his right leg, kneels onto his right knee to turn naturally to his right (into the *kamiza*) to stand, and comes forward along the longitudinal axis to adjust to a position on Uke's side of the center zone (from which he began *uki-otoshi*) to wait facing Uke in *shizenhontai*. Uke has simultaneously sat up, folded his right leg, and kneeled onto his right knee to turn naturally to his right (his back to *kamiza*) as he stands to face Tori; Uke adjusts to an engagement distance of about 3 feet (semifar position), standing in *shizenhontai*. They pause momentarily with composure and quiet alertness, making visual contact.

Engagement distance.   1

2

◆ ENGAGEMENT

UKE: Advances his right foot a full step forward to engage Tori in a modified right *jigotai* and attempts to attack Tori by pulling him forward to unbalance and topple him, but never gets started with more than his pulling.

UKE: Yields to the arc step and counter-pull of Tori's resistance by moving his left foot forward in a similar arc step. Being threatened with unbalance, becomes purely defensive and seeks to preserve his balance by straightening up from the modified *jigotai* to center his weight more evenly.

1. TORI: Takes the attack initiative by similarly advancing and engaging Uke in a modified right *jigotai*, and simultaneously, before Uke can do more than pull, resists Uke's pull and overpowers it by taking a deep, wide arc step back with his right foot, floating Uke a bit upward with his right hand under Uke's armpit in an attempt to unbalance Uke.

2. TORI: Yields to Uke's straightening-up effort and aids it by using both hands to float Uke farther upward and unbalance him directly forward; immediately begins to slide his left foot diagonally straight back, heel first, toward his right foot, so that his left heel is positioned near or a bit ahead of his right heel, on the inside of his right foot. His feet form approximately a 45-degree angle, with heels together.

3

(UKE)

UKE: Seeks to improve his balance still more by sliding his right foot diagonally forward to his right front, but only succeeds in getting it approximately in line with his left foot.

UKE: Is doubled over on top of Tori as his balance is destroyed. Begins to ride up and over. Turns over, head down, legs up in the air, past the left side of Tori's head, and is propelled forward, over behind Tori, in a low arc. Executes *ukemi* over his right shoulder (*zempo kaiten*), beating with his left arm, and comes to a standing position, or remains lying on the longitudinal axis or slightly on the *kamiza* side, at a spot near Tori's salutation position, with the *kamiza* on his right, facing outward (away from Tori), on the left side of his back.

(TORI)

3. TORI: Sinks rapidly to the mat, sitting near his left heel, and simultaneously throws himself straight backward as he applies the instep of his right foot to the rear left thigh of Uke at a point just behind the knee. Unbalances Uke forward and throws Uke straight forward, head over heels, in a low arc behind him by the combined pulling of both arms, the momentum of his falling body, and the upward springing action of his right leg in the direction of Uke's movement. His left leg braces, with the ball of the foot on the mat, to reinforce the throw. Removes both hands from Uke, allowing Uke a free fall, and extends both arms in the direction of Uke's motion as Uke turns over into *ukemi*. Bridges his buttocks off the mat. Exhibits *zanshin*.

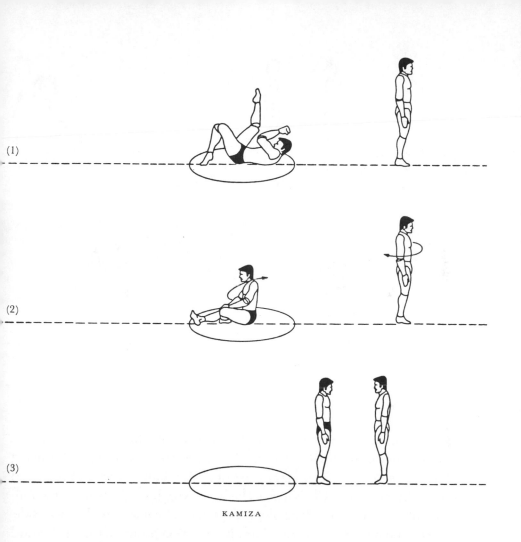

(1)

(2)

(3)

KAMIZA

◆ RISING AND FACING

After completion of Uke's *ukemi* from the right technique (in which Tori's right leg attacks), Tori, the *kamiza* at his left, sits up, folds his left leg, kneels onto his left knee, rises and turns naturally to his left (into the *kamiza*) to stand and move along the longitudinal axis to his approximate engagement position, then waits facing Uke in *shizenhontai*. Uke, if electing to remain on the mat in *ukemi*, has simultaneously sat up, folded his left leg, and risen onto his left knee; he then turns naturally to his left (his back to the *kamiza*) to stand and face Tori. If Uke comes to his feet in *ukemi* he turns naturally to his right (toward the *kamiza*) to stand and face Tori. In either case, Uke adjusts to an engagement distance of about 3 feet (semifar position), standing in *shizenhontai*. Figs. (1)-(3). They pause momentarily with composure and quiet alertness, making visual contact.

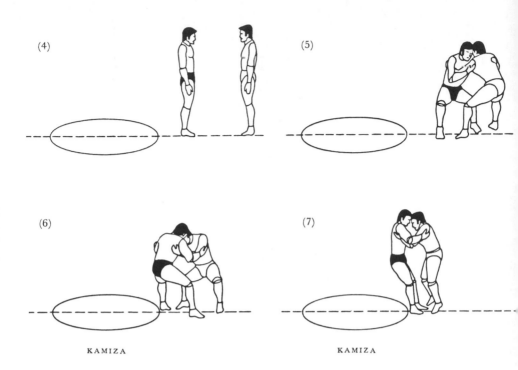

(4) (5) (6) (7)

KAMIZA

KAMIZA

◆ COMPLETION

Together, Tori and Uke perform left *sumi-gaeshi* (in which Tori's left leg attacks), beginning at Tori's approximate engagement position and moving back along the longitudinal axis in the opposite direction to that just used for the right technique. Uke's *ukemi* (he beats with his right arm) brings him to rest outside the center zone along the longitudinal axis, on his own side, the *kamiza* on his left, in an area near his salutation position, facing outward (away from Tori). Tori exhibits *zanshin* and, after a short pause, with the *kamiza* to his right, sits up, folds his right leg, kneels onto his right knee, and rises to walk quietly and directly along the longitudinal axis to his engagement position, adjusting his *judogi* unobtrusively as he walks. Arriving at his engagement position he stands momentarily facing away from Uke in *shizenhontai*. Simultaneously, Uke, if remaining on the mat in *ukemi*, has risen by folding his right leg and kneeling onto his right knee to stand up; otherwise he is already standing. In either case he adjusts to his engagement position, quietly and unobtrusively fixing *his judogi* and arriving about the same time as Tori does at his position, to stand momentarily facing outward, also in *shizenhontai*. They turn in place (toward the *kamiza*) to face each other in *shizenhontai*, thereby ending the *ma sutemi waza* category. Figs. (4)-(12).

(8)

(9)

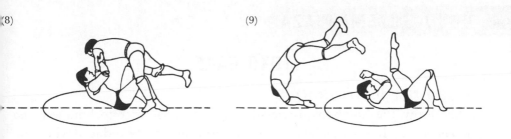

(10)

(11)

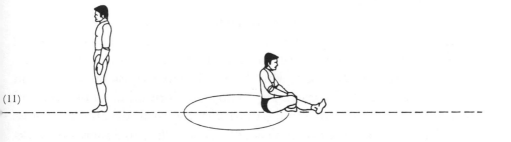

(12)

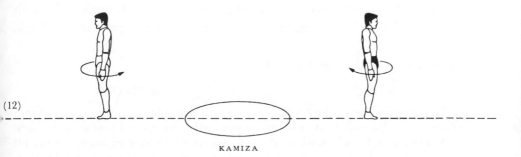

KAMIZA

YOKO-GAKE

◆ ABOUT THIS TECHNIQUE

This throw, the side hook, is classified as a side sacrifice technique (*yoko sutemi waza*). It gives evidence of the devastating effect produced when the entire weight of the body is used in thrust fashion to unbalance and throw an opponent by cutting his feet out from under him with the combined forces of the thrower's arc pull and falling body. The founder's early form required the thrower to take a full third step with his retreating foot and then, without drawing in his trailing foot, execute the throw with the re-treated foot; this positioned him directly in front of the opponent and re-sulted in a very brutal, pulled-out fall. Today's stepping action for the thrower has been modified for efficiency and brings him closer, in this ex-ample of *go no sen*, to the opponent.

◆ TECHNIQUE SUMMARY

Uke faces Tori at the near position with intent to attack. Uke steps unhesitat-ingly forward, gripping Tori in *shizentai* in order to push Tori and unbalance him backward without overbalancing himself. Uke continues his attack initia-tive for two steps by *tsugi ashi*, with Tori yielding to his push by gripping and retreating in *shizentai* by *tsugi ashi*, pulling Uke forward in an unsuccessful attempt to unbalance him. On the third step, Tori steals the attack initiative from Uke by a prolonged twisting action against Uke and a short step back-ward; then, suddenly falling to the mat on his side under Uke, he thrusts his foot against Uke's advanced foot, cutting that foot out from under Uke with the whole weight of his falling body, and throws Uke abruptly onto his back.

◆ TECHNIQUE KEY POINTS

○ UKE ○

1. On the second step, holds his body erect and braces backward somewhat as he is twisted, with his advanced shoul-der inward; his body must not be bent forward, but kept stretched out (Fig. 1). Is unbalanced to his front corner.

● TORI ●

1. His arm actions during his second step must make Uke stiffen himself; his final arm action rakes Uke forward, rotating him a bit onto the outer edge of his advanced foot on the third step (Figs. 1, 2).

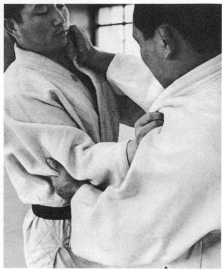

1

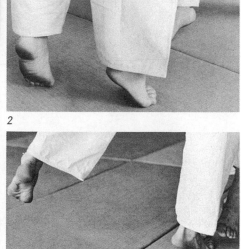

3

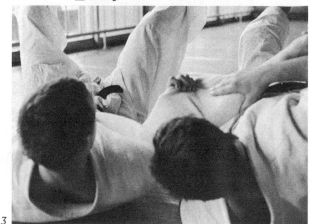

❌ Wrong.

(UKE)

2. Just prior to the throw, his weight is on his advanced foot's outer edge (little toe), not the forward portion, and his body begins to revolve on his advanced leg, without his trailing leg being raised in the air (Fig. 2).

3. The true fall is hard and abrupt; it can be dangerous. He must land flat on his back at impact with his legs rising; feels as if he is being thrown from his advanced ankle, and both legs are taken out from underneath him.

(TORI)

2. His throwing action must not be hurried; Uke must be fully unbalanced and well rotated onto the outer edge of his advanced foot (little toe) before placing the *sutemi*.

3. Throws by the momentum of his falling body without undue buckling at his hips and attempts to swing under Uke; uses his body like a curved stick, thrusting against Uke's legs. His buttocks contact the mat approximately where Uke's attacking advanced foot was momentarily before it was cut away. The sweeping thrust of his attacking leg and the

4

4 (second view)

(UKE)

4. His lower body is thrust out to his opposite rear corner as his upper body is pulled down; his body moves backward a bit. Faces in the same direction as Tori and is approximately parallel to the longitudinal axis.

(TORI)

arc pull of his hand on Uke's sleeve are blended with the force of the fall; falls onto his side, thrusting his attacking leg through and across Uke, pushing Uke's advanced foot ahead of it. Bridges his buttocks off the mat on his stable platform foot; holds his chin tucked into his chest. Must push up on Uke's sleeve at *ukemi* (Figs. 3, 4).

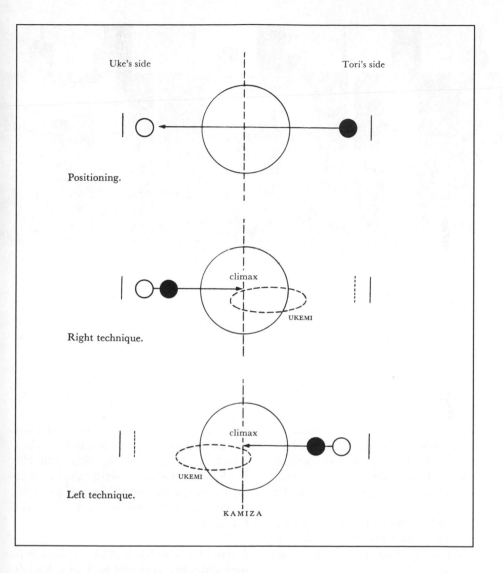

Positioning.

Right technique.

Left technique.

Uke's side

Tori's side

climax

UKEMI

climax

UKEMI

KAMIZA

◆ PREPARATION FOR ENGAGEMENT

Standing at their respective engagement positions, Tori and Uke pause momentarily with composure and quiet alertness, making visual contact. Then in *ayumi ashi*, beginning with their left feet, they come forward along the longitudinal axis to a position on Uke's side of the center zone (from which they began *uki-otoshi*). Stopping to face each other at an engagement distance of about 2 feet (near position), they pause momentarily with composure and quiet alertness, making visual contact.

Engagement distance.   *1*

◆ ENGAGEMENT

1. UKE: Attacks Tori by simultaneously stepping, taking a standard grip in right *shizentai*, and advancing one step by *tsugi ashi* (right foot, left foot) to push Tori and unbalance him backward, taking care not to overpush.

2. UKE: Having failed in his attack and being threatened with unbalance himself, preserves his balance by immediately attacking similarly once again (right foot, left foot), hanging back a bit.

UKE: Stiffens his body a bit as his body is twisted, with his right shoulder inward and his body beginning to slant forward.

UKE: Having twice failed in his attacks and once again being threatened with unbalance, attempts to preserve his balance by immediately attacking similarly again, bracing lightly backward, but succeeds only in bringing his right foot forward; his right foot moves slightly inward off its normal track, as his weight comes onto that foot.

TORI: Preserves his balance by yielding to Uke's advance and push, simultaneously stepping and taking a standard grip in right *shizentai* as he retreats one step by *tsugi ashi* (left foot, right foot) in an attempt to break Uke's balance forward, by pulling him horizontally.

TORI: Preserves his balance again by yielding to Uke's attack as before, but feeling Uke's hesitancy, changes his horizontal pull. His left hand push-pulls inward against Uke's right elbow, as his right hand pushes across Uke to the right while pulling as if to meet his other hand.

3. tori: Moves his left foot back a short step, then slides his right foot back near his left foot and further unbalances Uke forward and to the right front, twisting Uke inward still more. Quickly shifting his weight onto his slightly advanced right foot, throws himself onto his left side on the mat; simultaneously sweeps the sole of his left foot against the outer front of Uke's right ankle. As he falls to the mat, his body swings under Uke, thrusting its full weight and force along the length of his attacking left leg, into Uke.

2

3

(UKE)

UKE: His trailing left foot slides up in *tsugi ashi*, and his body twists with the right shoulder far inward and rotates counterclockwise on the right foot; his weight is placed on the outer edge of his advanced right foot, the left foot trailing tiptoe on the mat, with his body straight; is unbalanced to his right front.

(TORI)

Throws Uke suddenly on the spot by cutting out Uke's advanced right leg by the combined sweeping thrust of his falling body and the inward-and-upward, scooping arc pull of his left hand. Retains his left-hand grip on Uke's right sleeve; his right hand is placed on that sleeve nearby as Uke settles into *ukemi*. Grips the mat firmly with the ball of the right foot as he bridges his buttocks off the mat; his attacking left leg is firmly and well out-stretched off the mat. Exhibits *zanshin*.

(UKE)

UKE: With his right foot cut out from under him, falls heavily downward onto the flat of his back on the mat, both legs rising (not too bent) into the air. Executes *ukemi*, beating with his left arm, as he comes to rest parallel to the longitudinal axis, the *kamiza* on his left, in an area slightly off the longitudinal axis on the *kamiza* side, near the center of the center zone.

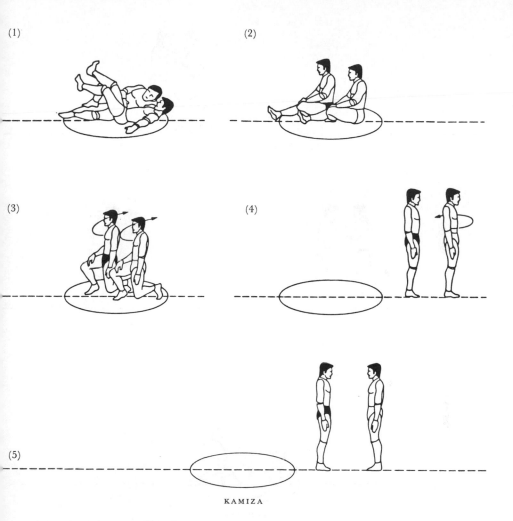

(1)

(2)

(3)

(4)

(5)

KAMIZA

◆ RISING AND FACING

After completion of Uke's *ukemi* from the right technique (in which Tori's left foot attacks), Tori, the *kamiza* at his left, releases his grip, sits up, folds his left leg, and kneels onto his left knee to rise in place and turn naturally to his left (into the *kamiza*). He then moves quietly along the longitudinal axis to his approximate engagement position and waits facing Uke in *shizenhontai*. Simultaneously, Uke sits up, the *kamiza* at his left, folds his left leg, kneels onto his left knee, and turns naturally to his left (into the *kamiza*) to move obliquely but directly to Tori's approximate engagement position, there to turn naturally to his left (his back to *kamiza*) to face Tori. Uke adjusts to an engagement distance of approximately 2 feet (near position) to stand in *shizenhontai*. Figs. (1)-(5). They pause momentarily with composure and quiet alertness, making visual contact.

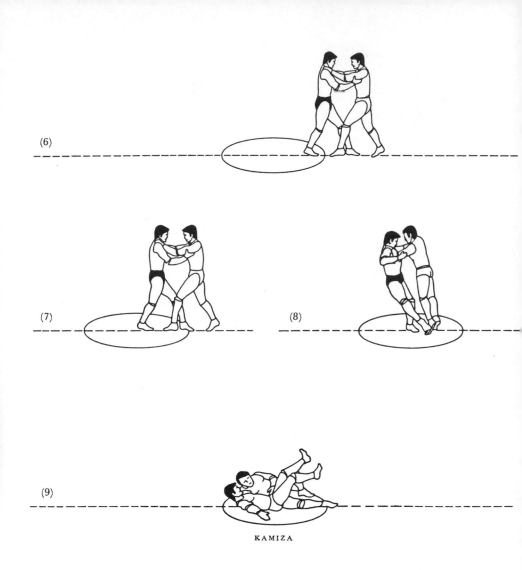

(6)

(7)

(8)

(9)

KAMIZA

◆ COMPLETION

Together, Tori and Uke perform left *yoko-gake* (in which Tori's right foot attacks), beginning at Tori's approximate engagement position and moving back with the throw and fall along the longitudinal axis in the opposite direction to that just used for the right technique. Uke's *ukemi* (he beats with the right arm) brings him to rest inside the center zone, slightly off the longitudinal axis but parallel to it, on the *kamiza* side, the *kamiza* on his right; he falls parallel to Tori (facing the same direction). Tori exhibits *zanshin* and, after a short pause, releases his grip on Uke. Figs. (6)-(9).

YOKO-GURUMA

◆ **ABOUT THIS TECHNIQUE**

This throw, the side wheel, is classified as a side sacrifice technique (*yoko sutemi waza*). It is the fourth and last in which a blow is struck at the thrower, reminding us of the combative essence of kata. It is the only technique in the modern-day kata in which the thrower makes use of the opponent's reaction to an *attempted* throw; it is therefore the best example of *go no sen*. The opponent, who has foiled the thrower's first attempt at unbalancing and throwing, is, by his own defense, unbalanced and thrown in a new direction in a very low arc, by the thrower's sacrifice of his standing posture in order to slide deeply under the opponent's center of gravity. In the founder's original design this technique stood with *tsurikomi-goshi* as an example of the thrower's gaining the attack initiative, losing it, and then regaining it. The early form of this throw differed from that of today with respect to the final throwing position of the thrower. The leg inserted between the opponent's legs was held straight and off the mat; the outside leg was the source of stability, and was held bent. Today's version permits bending the inside leg for stability and straightening the outside leg to make the thrower's twist to that side more efficient.

◆ **TECHNIQUE SUMMARY**

Uke faces Tori at the far position with intent to attack. Uke steps forward with two alternate steps in *ayumi ashi*, being careful to keep his feet wide apart along the axis of movement to avoid being thrown in that direction. He strikes with his bottom fist straight down from overhead at the top of Tori's head in order to knock Tori backward and down. Tori foils Uke by taking one step forward to meet the attack, ducking under the blow, and blending with Uke's body in an attempt to unbalance and throw him by *ura-nage*. Uke foils this attempt by bending forward at right angles to the attempted throw and forces Tori's head down. Tori takes advantage of Uke's reaction to the attempted throw by launching a counterattack in the form of a wheeling action; Tori slides his inside leg between Uke's widespread legs, as he deliberately falls to the mat on his side and slings the unbalanced Uke over him in the direction of Uke's bent body.

1   ❌ *Wrong.*   2

◆ TECHNIQUE KEY POINTS

○ UKE ○

1. Makes his stepping movement forward, straight at, not across, Tori's front.

2. Strikes with his bottom fist straight down at the front top of Tori's head; times his fist's arrival with his advancing foot's placement on the mat. Uses his body as in *ura-nage*, but does not allow his trailing foot to slide up in line with his advanced foot; keeps his feet well apart. Avoids overly frontal contact with Tori and positions his body at about right angles to the longitudinal axis to check his unbalance in that direction (Fig· 1).

3. Foils Tori's *ura-nage* attempt by his stance and by bracing back with his advanced foot. Bends forward at approximate right angles to Tori and the longitudinal axis, simultaneously using his striking arm (which now encircles Tori's neck) to press against Tori's neck and bend Tori over in the same direction he is bending. With Tori so bent, *ura-nage* is impossible. The bending action

● TORI ●

1. Enters into collision with Uke just as he did for *ura-nage*, making actual effort to achieve that throw. The effort is difficult due to Uke's quartering stance, which brings must come with the *ura-nage* attempt; premature bending is meaningless (Fig. 2). Uke to approximate right angles to the attempted throw. Uke's widely separated feet make Tori feel as if he has run into an object immovable by *ura-nage* (Fig. 2).

2. Does not impede Uke's bending actions which are forcing his neck downward, nor initiate the bend himself, but keeps trying to throw by *ura-nage* until he is interrupted by Uke's actions. Takes advantage of this new self-imposed unbalance of Uke (Fig. 2).

3. Must slide his leg deeply through and between Uke's legs and get his head well down as he falls on his side; keeps hugging Uke tightly to keep both bodies in contact as he falls. If his arm encircling Uke's waist is allowed to slip, a true throwing action is impossible. That hand must press Uke's far hipbone firmly (Fig. 3).

3   ☒ *Wrong.*   ☒ *Wrong.*

4   ☒ *Wrong.*

(UKE)

4. Is thrown in an abrupt low arc downward; feels as if he is being thrown from his loins as he is unbalanced forward, at right angles to longitudinal axis (Fig. 3). Feels a positive rotation of his body outward, before going into his *ukemi*. May elect to stay down on the mat in *ukemi* or come to his feet in a balanced position, depending upon the force of the throw. His body actually moves forward very little during its turn in midair, and comes to rest facing in the direction of his bending action.

(TORI)

4. Makes a big twist onto his side, stabilizing the action with his platform foot, with knee bent, using the leg which he slides or thrusts between Uke's legs. Must avoid just collapsing to the mat by not buckling at the hips. Must truly sacrifice himself without reserve.

5. Concentrates on unbalancing Uke forward (in the direction of Uke's bending) and on throwing Uke by imparting a strong rotary outward action to him, by the pull of the arm encircling Uke's waist. Pitches Uke over his far shoulder. Bridges his buttocks off the mat, using the leg inserted between Uke's as a platform, with knee bent, the ball of that foot firmly on the mat. Keeps his chin tucked tightly against his chest (Fig. 4).

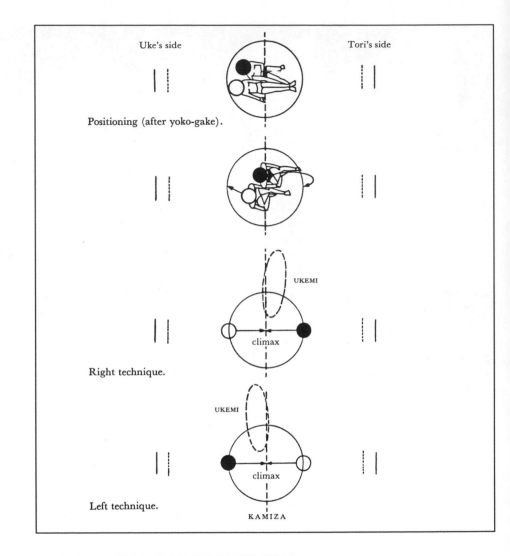

Uke's side   Tori's side

Positioning (after yoko-gake).

UKEMI

climax

Right technique.

UKEMI

climax

Left technique.

KAMIZA

◆ PREPARATION FOR ENGAGEMENT

Completing the left *yoko-gake* (in which Tori's right foot attacks), Tori, the *kamiza* at his right, sits up, folds his right leg, kneels onto his right knee to stand, and moves a bit forward along the longitudinal axis to turn naturally to his right (toward the *kamiza*), then adjust to his edge of the center zone and wait facing Uke in *shizenhontai*. Simultaneously Uke sits up, the *kamiza* at his right, folds his right leg, kneels onto his right knee to stand up, and adjusts to his edge of the center zone by backing up; Uke faces Tori at an engagement distance of about 6 feet (far position), standing in *shizenhontai*. They pause momentarily with composure and quiet alertness, making visual contact.

Engagement distance.   1

2

◆ ENGAGEMENT

1. UKE: Threatens Tori by advancing his left foot far forward, simultaneously raising his right arm so as to bring it upward from the right back corner with his bottom fist directly overhead, facing Tori.

UKE: Attacks Tori by advancing his right foot and simultaneously bringing his right bottom fist straight down from overhead in an attempt to hit Tori on the top of his head and knock him backward and down.

TORI: Remains motionless but quietly alert.

2. TORI: Blends with Uke's attack by advancing his left foot a deep step; meets Uke approximately in the center of the center zone, with his left foot well along the outside of Uke, the toes of that foot pointing behind Uke. Simultaneously lowers his body into a deep squat position by bending his knees. At the same time, slips his left arm along Uke's belt line, reaching around to the far left side of Uke, and presses his left palm against Uke's left side below the hipbone. Hugs Uke tightly to him with this left arm, then quickly attempts *ura-nage* by arc-stepping his right foot between Uke's legs to a position near and parallel to Uke's right foot, leaving his left foot in place and pivoting,

3

4 →

UKE: His blow passes over Tori's left shoulder; sensing a balance problem, keeps very erect and allows his left foot to trail rather than bringing it up in line with his right foot; avoids facing frontally into Tori.

3. UKE: Avoids being thrown by *ura-nage* by forcefully bending his upper body forward (at approximate right angles to the longitudinal axis) and encircles Tori's neck with his striking right arm to force Tori's head down; bends forward at about right angles to Tori's attempted throw, clamping Tori to his right front.

UKE: His body loses balance forward; is rotated outward to his right, abruptly pulled down, and turned head over heels by Tori's falling body. Is flung over Tori's left shoulder in an abrupt, low arc. Executes *ukemi* by getting his right arm free and going over his right shoulder (*zempo kaiten*), beating with his left arm, as he comes to a standing position or remains lying on the left side of his back, head to head with Tori, along the lateral axis (or a line a maximum of 45 degrees off the lateral axis), away from the *kamiza*, which is behind him.

while crouching low, to face frontally into Uke; simultaneously applies the palm of his right hand, with fingers together and pointing straight upward, firmly against Uke's lower abdomen below the belt knot. Tries to unbalance Uke forward (along the longitudinal axis), and to throw Uke over his left shoulder.

4. TORI: Without resisting Uke's force pressing downward against his neck, quickly drops under Uke's center of gravity by sliding his right leg deep between Uke's legs, and lies back and falls by twisting onto his left side; simultaneously uses his left arm to hug and pull Uke into him, also imparting a rotation outward (to his left) to Uke's body as he brings Uke into unbalance forward in the direction of Uke's forward bend. His right hand pushes upward. Throws Uke in a low arc over his left shoulder by the combined rotary pull-push of his hands and the momentum of his falling body joined to the force of Uke's forward bending action. Removes both arms from Uke, allowing Uke a free fall, but extends his arms in the direction of Uke's motion as Uke turns over and settles into *ukemi*. Bridges his buttocks off the mat by using his right foot, with the ball of that foot firmly on the mat, as a platform foot to reinforce the throw. Exhibits *zanshin*.

(1)

(2)

(3)

KAMIZA

(4)

KAMIZA

◆ RISING AND FACING

After completion of Uke's *ukemi* from the right technique (in which Tori falls on his left side), Tori, the *kamiza* at his feet, sits up, folds his left leg, kneels onto his left knee, and turns naturally to his left (into the *kamiza*) to stand up, backing up a bit to adjust to Uke's edge of the center zone and wait for Uke in *shizenhontai*. Uke, who has simultaneously sat up, folded his left leg, and risen onto his left knee, turns naturally to his left (toward the *kamiza*) to stand and moves obliquely but directly to Tori's edge of the center zone on the longitudinal axis. He adjusts to an engagement distance of about 6 feet (far position), standing facing Tori in *shizenhontai*. Figs. (1)-(5). They pause momentarily with composure and quiet alertness, making visual contact.

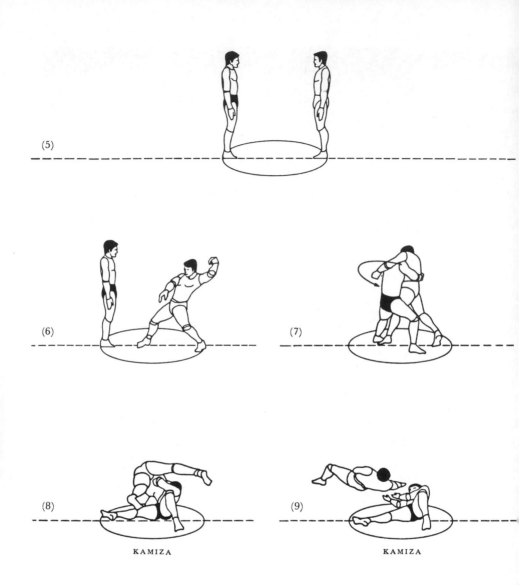

(5)

(6)

(7)

(8)

KAMIZA

(9)

KAMIZA

◆ COMPLETION

Together, Tori and Uke perform left *yoko-guruma* (in which Tori falls on his right side), beginning from opposite edges of the center zone, moving into collision at the approximate center of the center zone, and throwing and falling along the lateral axis (or a line at least 45 degrees off the longitudinal axis), away from the *kamiza* side, on Uke's side. Uke's *ukemi* (he beats with the right arm) brings him to rest on the right side of his back (or standing in *shizenhontai*), facing outward (away from Tori). Tori exhibits *zanshin*. Figs. (6)-(9).

UKI-WAZA

◆ ABOUT THIS TECHNIQUE

This throw, the floating technique, is classified as a side sacrifice technique (*yoko sutemi waza*). It is an excellent example of quas-*sen*, though it contains elements of *go no sen*. The drawing-power principle of the body is graphically illustrated here, as in the opening technique of this kata, *uki-otoshi*, but here the opponent is unbalanced and flung far forward in a long, low, looping arc by the thrower's body, which is sacrificed to the mat on its side. It is a classical example of the use of resistance in Judo and its present-day form differs little from that designed by the founder, but centers on a less-prolonged circular swinging action imparted to the opponent, more floating action, and more direct sacrificing of the thrower's body to the mat.

◆ TECHNIQUE SUMMARY

Uke faces Tori at the semifar position with intent to attack, but never really gets started. Uke advances and grips Tori by hand pressure in a modified *jigotai* with the idea of pulling Tori forward to unbalance and topple him, but Tori steals the attack initiative by advancing and gripping similarly in a modified *jigotai*, simultaneously resisting and counterpulling Uke forward in one arc step. Feeling himself unbalanced forward, Uke resists Tori by straightening up; Tori takes advantage of Uke's floated posture by dropping straight to the mat on his side at Uke's feet, to throw Uke forward in a long, low, looping arc, over and diagonally away from him, in a slinging action caused by the momentum of his drawing and falling body as Uke steps forward to gain his balance.

◆ TECHNIQUE KEY POINTS

○ UKE ○

1. Is pulled against his resistance by Tori; is purely defensive, but recovers his balance at the end of his first step, straightening up to do so. Has a floating feeling at this point.

2. Gets his arm loose from under Tori's armpit to use as a lead arm for his forward rolling *ukemi*.

3. Takes off with his lead foot fully advanced (on the side of Tori's extended leg), with weight on its forward portion. Is unbalanced to his front corner (Figs. 1-4).

● TORI ●

1. His arc step to the rear must be a long one to overcome Uke's dragging resistance; pulls with his whole body. His hand pressing against Uke's shoulder blade from under Uke's armpit scoops upward with strength concentrated in the little finger. The other hand pulls only a little at this stage.

2. At the end of his first arc step, must allow Uke to straighten up and recover his balance; must not overpower him, and does not stop his own action.

1   2   3

(UKE)

4. Is thrown forward beyond Tori's far shoulder (on the side of his lead arm for *ukemi*) in a long, low, looping arc; may elect to stay down on the mat or come to a balanced position on his feet, depending upon the force of the throw; feels as if he is being thrown from his lead shoulder, diagonally outward. His body moves far forward and comes to rest facing approximately 45 degrees off the direction of original movement.

(TORI)

3. Uses both hands to float Uke as Uke straightens up, by pulling upward, scooping with the power of both palms (especially the little fingers), directly to Uke's front corner, in the direction of the coming throw.

4. Takes no second step, but moves directly without a lag into his sacrifice to the mat; extends his leg powerfully with no intention to block or trip Uke's advanced leg, but to supply drawing power from his falling body to throw Uke. Is on his heels as he sacrifices (Fig. 4).

5. Throws while on the side of his back; must not be flat on the mat. Does not fall onto the longitudinal axis, but diagonally away from it. Does not grip with his hand on Uke's shoulder blade; may grip with his hand on Uke's sleeve, if inexperienced, to accelerate and guide Uke into *ukemi*. Takes care not to trap Uke's lead arm (the arm under his armpit) (Fig. 4). His extended leg is held straight; his platform leg fixed on the mat for stability (Fig. 5).

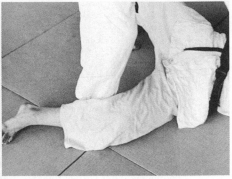

X *Wrong.*

4

5

◆ **PREPARATION FOR ENGAGEMENT**

Completing the left *yoko-guruma* (in which Tori falls on his right side), Tori, the *kamiza* at his feet, sits up, folds his right leg, kneels onto his right knee, stands, and moves along the longitudinal axis to adjust to Uke's approximate engagement position (from which he began *uki-otoshi*) and wait for Uke in *shizenhontai*. Uke has simultaneously sat up, folded his right leg, and kneeled onto his right knee to rise and turn naturally to his right (into the *kamiza*)— if he has come to his feet in *ukemi*, he merely turns naturally to his left—and moves obliquely but directly to his own approximate engagement position, there to turn naturally to his left (into the *kamiza*) to face Tori in *shizenhontai*. Uke adjusts to an engagement distance of about 3 feet (semifar position). They pause momentarily with composure and quiet alertness, making visual contact. (See p. 275.)

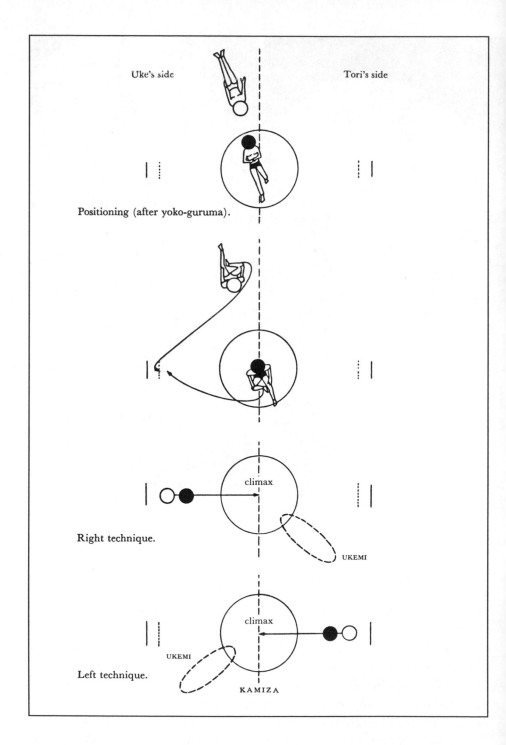

Uke's side   Tori's side

Positioning (after yoko-guruma).

Right technique.

UKEMI

climax

Left technique.

UKEMI

KAMIZA

Engagement distance.   *1*

2

◆ ENGAGEMENT

UKE: Advances his right foot a full step forward to engage Tori in a modified right *jigotai* and attempts to attack Tori by pulling him forward to unbalance and topple him, but never gets started with more than his pulling.

UKE: Yields to the arc step and counterpull of Tori's resistance by moving his left foot forward in a similar arc step. Being threatened with unbalance, becomes purely defensive and seeks to preserve his balance by straightening up from the modified *jigotai* to center his weight more evenly. Seeks to improve his balance by stepping diagonally forward with his right foot and succeeds in getting it halfway along.

1. TORI: Takes the attack initiative by similarly advancing and engaging Uke in the same modified right *jigotai*, and simultaneously, before Uke can do more than pull, resists Uke's pull and overpowers it by taking a deep, wide arc step back with his right foot, floating Uke a bit upward with his right hand under Uke's armpit in an attempt to unbalance him.

2. TORI: Yields to Uke's straightening up and aids it by using both hands to float Uke farther upward and unbalance him directly forward; immediately begins to slide his left leg into an extended position, wide to his left rear corner.

3

(UKE)

UKE: Steps fully onto his right foot in a diagonal step to his right front, but his balance is destroyed in that direction by the abrupt falling action of Tori and he shoots out in a long, looping arc, over and beyond Tori. Executes *ukemi* over his right shoulder *(zempo kaiten)* by getting his right arm free and beating with his left arm as he comes to a standing position or remains lying on the left side of his back, head to head with Tori, with the *kamiza* at the right, along a line diagonally away from the longitudinal axis and toward the *kamiza* on Tori's side.

(TORI)

3. TORI: Brushing the outer edge of his left foot over the mat surface, throws himself on the left side of his back, unbalancing Uke and throwing him to the right front corner by the combined drawing power of his falling body (which is wide off the longitudinal axis to his left), and the slinging action of his hands which operate to project Uke beyond his left shoulder. Bridges up onto his left shoulder in the direction of Uke's movement, bracing with both feet on the mat. Removes both hands from Uke, allowing Uke a free fall, but extends his arms in the direction of Uke's motion as Uke turns over and goes into *ukemi*, then snaps them in toward his body. Exhibits *zanshin*.

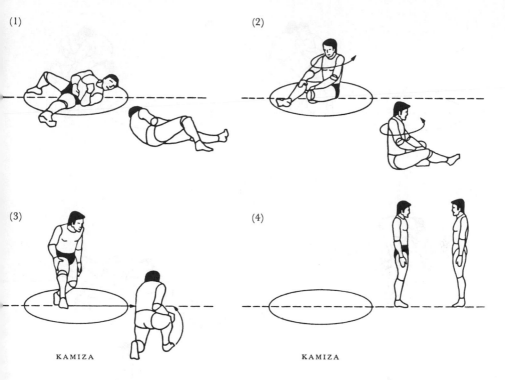

(1)   (2)   (3)   (4)

KAMIZA   KAMIZA

◆ RISING AND FACING

After completion of Uke's *ukemi* from the right technique (in which Tori falls on his left side), Tori, the *kamiza* at his left, sits up, folds his left leg, kneels onto his left knee, and turns naturally to his left (into the *kamiza*) to stand facing Uke; Tori adjusts to his approximate engagement position by moving quietly, obliquely but directly, to stand there in *shizenhontai*. Uke has simultaneously sat up, folded his left leg, and kneeled onto his left knee to stand and turn naturally a bit to his left (his back to *kamiza*)—if standing in *shizenhontai* from *ukemi*, he turns identically—and moves obliquely but directly to Tori's approximate engagement position, there to turn naturally again to his left (his back to the *kamiza*) to face Tori in *shizenhontai*. Uke adjusts to an engagement distance of about 3 feet (semifar position), facing Tori. Figs. (1)-(4). They pause momentarily with composure and quiet alertness, making visual contact.

◆ COMPLETION

Together, Tori and Uke perform left *uki-waza* (in which Tori falls on his right side), beginning at Tori's approximate engagement position and throwing and falling back along a line diagonally away from the longitudinal axis, toward the *kamiza*, on Uke's side. Uke's *ukemi* (he beats with his right arm)

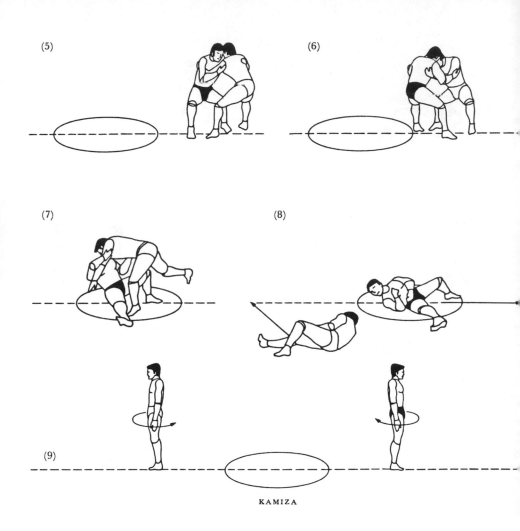

(5)

(6)

(7)

(8)

(9)

KAMIZA

brings him to rest on the right side of his back (or standing in *shizenhontai*), facing outward (away from Tori). Tori exhibits *zanshin*, and, after a pause, with the *kamiza* to his right, sits up, folds his right leg, and kneels onto his right knee to rise and walk quietly, obliquely but directly, to his approximate engagement position on the longitudinal axis, adjusting his *judogi* unobtrusively as he walks. Arriving at his engagement position he stands momentarily facing away from Uke in *shizenhontai*. Simultaneously Uke has risen from *ukemi* by folding his right leg and kneeling onto his right knee to rise (unless he is already standing in *shizenhontai* from *ukemi*) and walk quietly, obliquely but directly, to his approximate engagement position on the longitudinal axis, adjusting his *judogi* unobtrusively as he walks. Arriving about the same time as Tori does at his position, he stands momentarily facing outward also in shizenhontai. They turn in place (toward the *kamiza*) to face each other

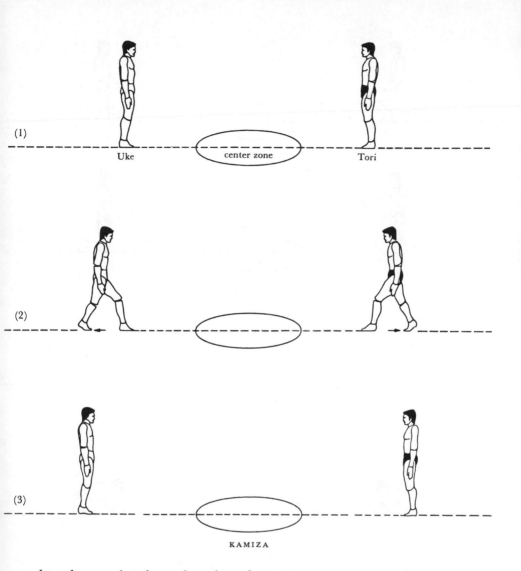

(1) Uke   center zone   Tori

(2)

(3)

KAMIZA

in *shizenhontai*, thereby ending the *yoko sutemi waza* category, the last category of techniques in this kata. Figs. (5)-(9).

◆ CLOSING

Standing facing each other in *shizenhontai*, Tori and Uke pause momentarily with composure and quiet alertness at their respective engagement positions. Fig. (1).

Simultaneously they take one step backward, beginning with their right feet, bringing their heels together. They pause in this position with composure and quiet alertness, maintaining visual contact, at their respective salutation positions. Figs. (2), (3).

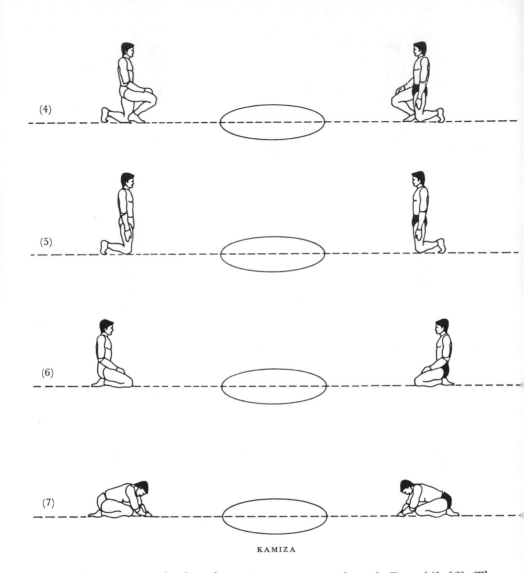

(4)

(5)

(6)

(7)

KAMIZA

They assume the kneeling-sitting posture (*seiza*). Figs. (4)-(6). They pause once again momentarily, keeping composure, quiet alertness, and visual contact.

They execute the sitting salutation (*zarei*) together. Fig. (7). Together they return to the kneeling-sitting position. Fig. (8). There is another momentary pause with composure, quiet alertness, and visual contact.

They rise in place together, coming to an erect position once again, heels together, keeping visual contact all the time. Figs. (9)-(11). They pause once again momentarily with composure and quiet alertness, maintaining visual contact.

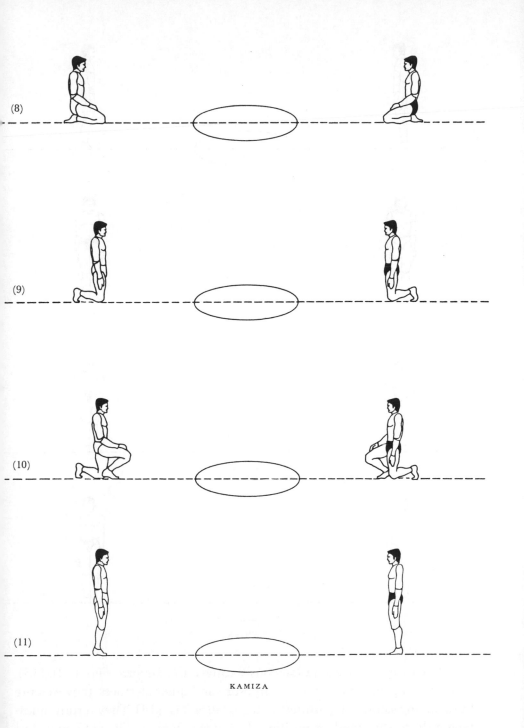

(8)

(9)

(10)

(11)

KAMIZA

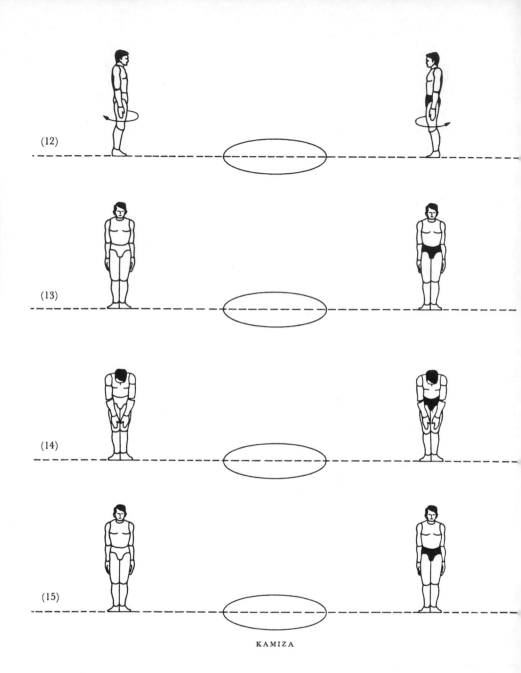

(12)

(13)

(14)

(15)

KAMIZA

They turn in place simultaneously to face the *kamiza*. Figs. (12), (13). After pausing once more with composure and quiet alertness, they execute the standing salutation (*ritsurei*) to the *kamiza*. Fig. (14). They return simultaneously to the standing position, facing the *kamiza*, Fig. (15), and thus complete this kata.

CHAPTER 9
Katame No Kata

Perfection is a trifle dull.
—W. SOMERSET MAUGHAM

The Engagement section under each technique in this chapter has been somewhat arbitrarily divided into three stages, numbered 1 to 3 in bold face, to indicate who has the attack initiative at all points. The numbers appear in Uke's column or Tori's, depending on who then has the attack initiative. When a number appears in a different column from the previous number, it indicates that the attack initiative has changed hands. The photographs appearing in the Engagement sections are keyed to these numbers. Numbers within parentheses, as below, refer to line drawings in which black identifies Tori and white identifies Uke.

Note in the Engagement sections that Tori takes the left column and Uke the right, because Tori is initiating most of the action. Under Suggested Escape Actions and Suggested Control Actions, however, the pattern is reversed. Uke takes the left column and Tori the right, because Uke is initiating the action and Tori is responding.

◆ OPENING
Tori and Uke stand erect, with heels together, composed and quietly alert, facing the *kamiza*. Tori takes his position with Uke on his right; approximately 18 feet separates them from each other and that distance is centered on the center of the *kamiza*. These are their salutation positions (See Fig. (1), p. 284).

The practice begins with Tori and Uke simultaneously executing the standing salutation (*ritsurei*) toward the *kamiza*. Fig. (2). They pause momentarily after coming back to the erect position. Fig. (3).

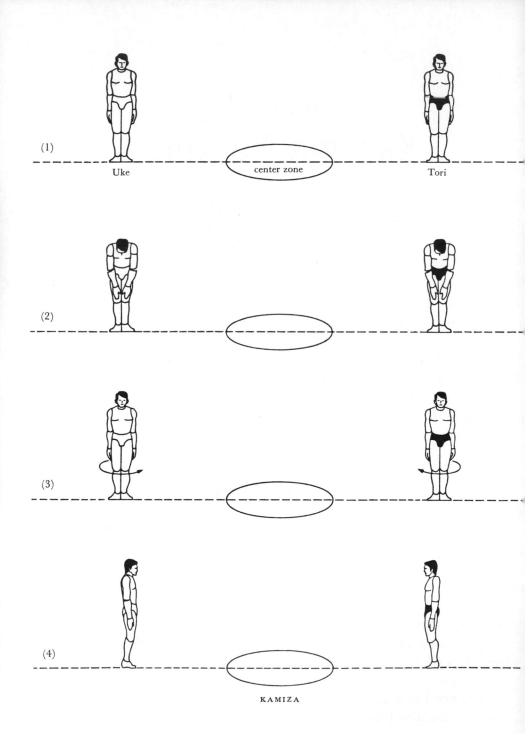

(1) Uke   center zone   Tori

(2)

(3)

(4)

KAMIZA

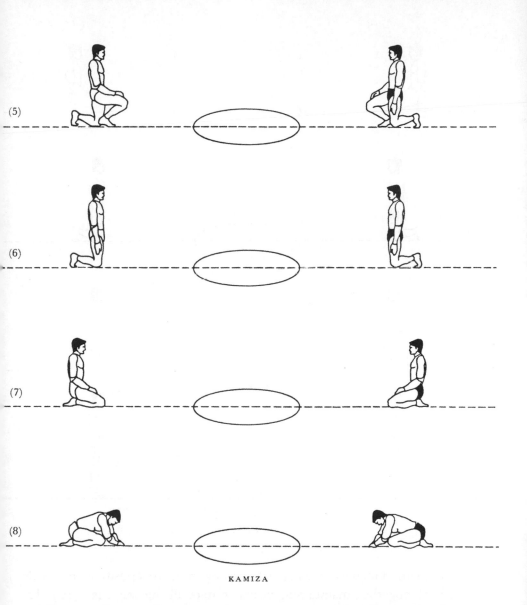

(5)

(6)

(7)

(8)

KAMIZA

They simultaneously turn in place, coming around to face each other in the same erect standing posture, heels together, looking directly at each other with composure and quiet alertness. Fig. (4). They pause momentarily.

Simultaneously, they assume the kneeling-sitting posture (*seiza*). Figs. (5)-(7). Pausing momentarily once again, they maintain composure, quiet alertness, and visual contact.

They execute the sitting salutation (*zarei*) together. Fig. (8). Together, they return to the kneeling-sitting position. Fig. (9). There is another momentary pause with composure, quiet alertness, and visual contact.

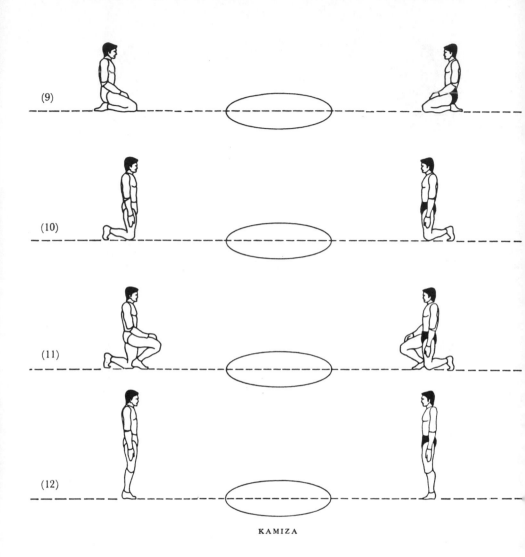

(9)

(10)

(11)

(12)

KAMIZA

They simultaneously rise in place, coming to an erect position once again, with heels together, maintaining visual contact all the way. Figs. (10)-(12). They pause once again momentarily with composure, quiet alertness, and visual contact.

Simultaneously they advance one step, beginning with their left feet, and come to *shizenhontai* at their respective engagement positions. Figs. (13), (14). Another momentary pause, and they simultaneously position themselves in *kyoshi* (open). Figs. (15), (16).

As Tori remains motionless in *kyoshi* (open), Uke advances one step by *tsugi ashi* in *kyoshi* (closed), then returns to *kyoshi* (open), all the while keep-

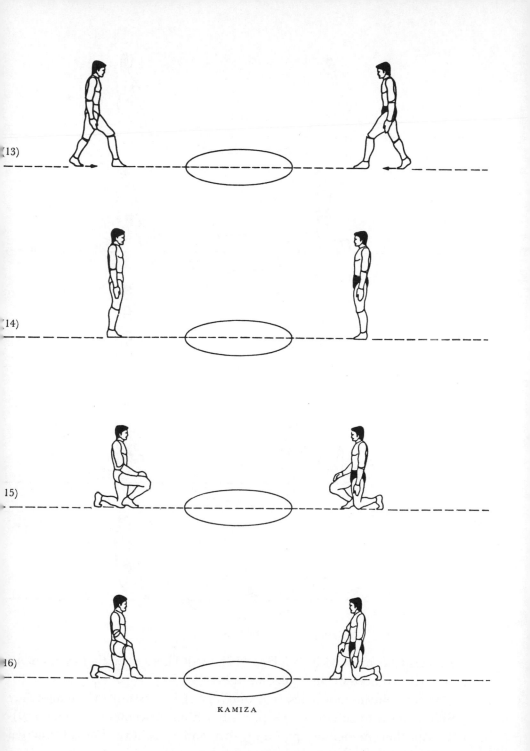

(13)

(14)

15)

16)

KAMIZA

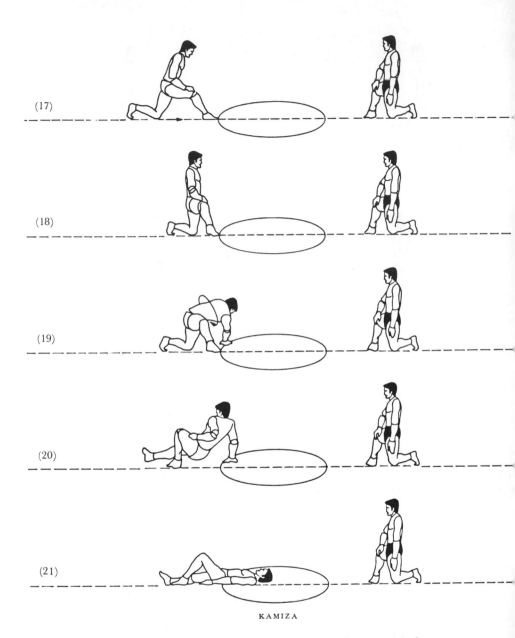

ing up visual contact with Tori. Figs. (17), (18). There is another momentary pause with composure and quiet alertness.

As Tori remains motionless in *kyoshi* (open), Uke assumes the lying-ready position on the longitudinal axis, partially within the center zone. Figs. (19)-(21). Another momentary pause by Tori, and all is in readiness for actual engagement in the first technique of this kata.

KUZURE KESA-GATAME

◆ **ABOUT THIS TECHNIQUE**

This immobilization, the irregular scarf hold, is classified as a holding technique (*osae-komi waza*). It gets its name from the judoist's application of his body pressure along a diagonal line across his opponent's body, which is somewhat similar to the positioning of the Buddhist priest's surplice or vestment stole, looped and hanging from one shoulder. This technique is executed in the variation form, *kuzure kesa-gatame*, not the fundamental form, *hon kesa-gatame*. It was chosen by the founder because it permits the holder greater mobility. It remains unchanged from its early form.

◆ **PREPARATION FOR ENGAGEMENT**

While Uke settles onto his back in the lying-ready position, Tori is at his engagement position in *kyoshi* (open) on the longitudinal axis, facing the reclining Uke; Tori slides his right foot inward a bit and stands up in *shizenhontai*. Pivoting in place 45 degrees to his right (away from the *kamiza*), Tori steps off with his left foot and walks diagonally to the far position (about 5 feet from Uke's right side) on the lateral axis, and turns to his left (toward the *kamiza*) to stand facing Uke in *shizenhontai*. Immediately, but unhurriedly, he lowers himself and assumes *kyoshi* (open), then pauses momentarily with composure and quiet alertness, making visual contact with a point beyond Uke's body (on the *kamiza* side). Tori advances two steps by *tsugi ashi* in *kyoshi* (closed) to the near position (about 1½ feet from Uke's right side) on the lateral axis and once there again assumes *kyoshi* (open) as he maintains composure and quiet alertness. Figs. (1)-(8). Tori shifts his gaze to Uke's face.

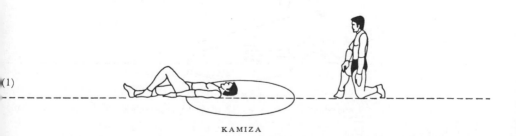

(1)

KAMIZA

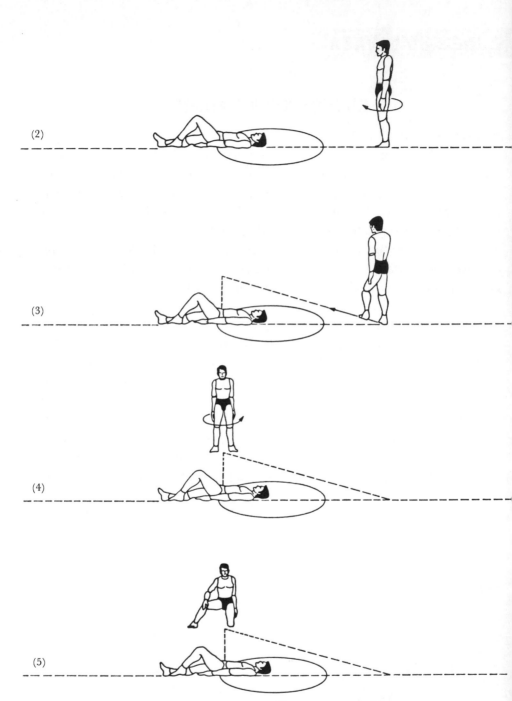

(2)

(3)

(4)

(5)

KAMIZA

(6)

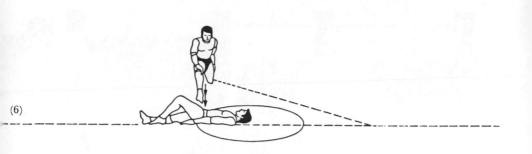

(7)

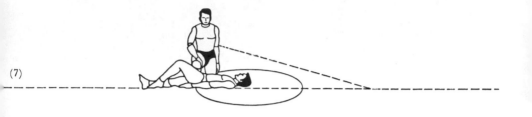

(8)

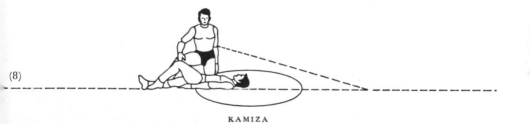

KAMIZA

Near position.

Engagement distance.   *1*

◆ ENGAGEMENT

1. TORI: Takes a short entry step (right foot, left knee slides up) and picks up Uke's right arm with both hands; his left hand, palm up, cups Uke's arm from underneath just above the elbow as his right hand, palm down, grasps Uke's arm near the wrist. Lifting Uke's right arm, feeds it under his own left armpit.

2. TORI: Moves his own right hand as he clamps Uke's right arm under his left armpit and kneels on his right knee near Uke's right armpit. Slipping his right arm across the far left side of Uke, passes it through under Uke's left armpit so that his right forearm comes to rest on the mat; supports his body on that arm and the left foot as he settles down onto the mat on his right buttock, sitting by Uke's right side; simultaneously slides his right knee under Uke's right armpit. Spreads his legs wide, his bent right leg forward so that it rests on its outer surface, while his left leg, a bit bent at the knee, is placed to the rear with its inner surface on the mat. Applies the right side of his chest against the front of Uke's chest by positioning his head above Uke's left chest area.

1. TORI: Takes the attack initiative by similarly advancing and engaging Uke in the same modified right *jigotai*, and simultaneously, before Uke can do more than pull, resists Uke's pull and overpowers it by taking a deep, wide arc step back with his right foot, floating Uke a bit upward with his right hand under Uke's armpit in an attempt to unbalance him.

2. TORI: Yields to Uke's straightening up and aids it by using both hands to float Uke farther upward and unbalance him directly forward; immediately begins to slide his left leg into an extended position, wide to his left rear corner.

UKE: Remains motionless in the lying-ready position, maintaining his position, yielding to Tori's efforts to take his right arm.

2

3

3. TORI: Signals that his hold is on by tightening his whole body, bringing the palm of his right hand flat against the underside of Uke's left shoulder as Tori twists to his left, pulling Uke's upper body obliquely upward so that the right side of Uke's chest presses tightly against his right chest.

TORI: Controls Uke's attempts to escape, varying his position as required, but without changing his technique.

TORI: Relaxes his tight control actions, but maintains the *kesa-gatame* form, adjusting to the initial starting position if necessary.

UKE: Remains motionless in the lying-ready position, yielding to Tori's efforts to place the form of the hold, as he gathers his energy and takes a deep breath.

UKE: At Tori's "on" signal, immediately attempts three distinctly different escape measures of his own choice. Being unsuccessful in his attempts to escape, gives the *mairi* signal and ceases all escape actions.

(a)

(a¹)

(b)

(b¹)

(c)

(c¹)

1

UKE'S SUGGESTED ESCAPE ACTIONS

1. Brings both feet well under his body, his weight resting on the forward portions, and bridges his midsection strongly upward with a snap in an attempt to dislodge Tori; assists this action with both arms (Fig. a, p. 294).

2. Takes advantage of Tori's temporary floated position by using *taisabaki* to twist to his right, trying to get well under Tori; may also attempt to put his right knee between Tori and himself to create a space and loosen the hold; withdraws his right arm by pulling his right shoulder under himself (Fig. b).

3. Uses his inward twist (into Tori) to try and get his left arm far around behind Tori to grip Tori's belt near the left-hip area; with a strong bridging action onto his left shoulder, attempts to pull and boost Tori obliquely across his upper body, over his left shoulder, aiding this action with both arms pulling around in the direction of the bridge (Fig. c).

TORI'S SUGGESTED CONTROL ACTIONS

1. Neutralizes Uke's bridging action by checking his body motion forward, bracing with his right arm, the hand flat on the mat near Uke's left shoulder, and his left leg which is moved forward, the foot firmly on the mat (Fig. a¹).

2. Stops Uke's turning action by increasing his pull on Uke's right sleeve (pulls his left shoulder back); drives his right knee tightly under Uke's right shoulder and pries up against Uke's shoulder with that leg. Repositions his left leg to a widespread rear position (Fig. b¹).

3. Stops Uke's bridging action and overturning attempt by placing his right palm flat on the mat, a bit away from Uke's left shoulder, using the whole arm as a wedge stop, stiffening it against the motion of Uke's attempt; raises his upper body a bit to separate himself from Uke's body (Fig. c¹).

◆ TECHNIQUE KEY POINTS

● TORI ●

Hold with the power of your whole body, which is kept unified by tensing your midsection; do not use your arms alone to control Uke. Your legs are your base of power; keep them widespread, more than 90 degrees apart, for

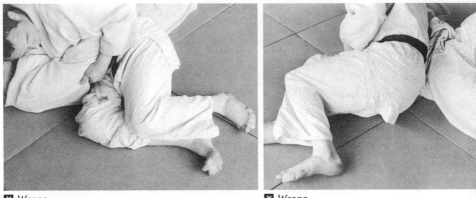

| ❌ Wrong. | ❌ Wrong. |

stability (Fig. 1). If your legs simply lie loosely on the mat, you cannot "dig in" or brace your body effectively. Also, Uke may be able to sit you up to your left rear corner if you narrow the spread of your legs.

Seek to keep your butt down, with your right side close up against Uke's right side at a point just above his right hip; do not let a gap develop between yourself and Uke at this point of contact. Position your head above his chest,"-floating" it to change its position as needed for good balance. Your legs may change position, but they must be kept widespread at all time. Keep your right elbow clamped in against Uke's far left side to prevent his drifting to his left; trap Uke's right arm tightly under your left arm by clamping your armpit down hard on Uke's arm just where his wrist meets his hand, so he can't easily withdraw that arm. Your left hand, gripping Uke's right sleeve, is secondary to this clamping action. If Uke attacks your left arm with *kansetsu waza*, increase the downward clamping pressure, and if necessary bring your left leg forward so that the inner side of your thigh (near the knee) presses inward against your left arm.

Focus your body power diagonally downward against Uke's upper body. Have the feeling of "cutting" into Uke from his right side, diagonally across his body toward his left shoulder. Do this by twisting your body a bit to the left; pull your left arm and shoulder back as you let your chest rise as if you were drawing an arrow on that side. Do not just drape your body over Uke's like a "wet noodle."

○ UKE ○

Move with the power of your whole body, not isolated parts, when you try to escape; move into a determined weakness in Tori's technique, but not by wild thrashing actions.

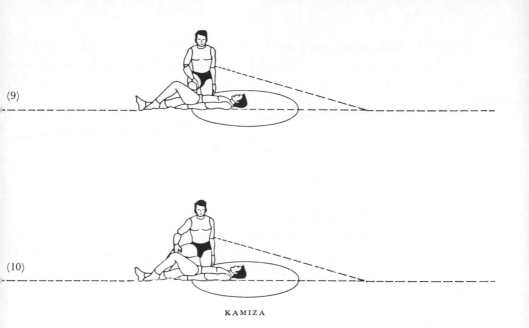

(9)

(10)

KAMIZA

Seek to destroy Tori's base of power, that is, the position (angle) of his legs. Make him lose his widespread leg position by attacking his rearmost leg with either of your legs; also wiggle a good deal and use big body-turning actions. As his legs come together, either create a space between yourself and him (so that you may sit up and topple him backward, or bring your right leg up under him and twist to withdraw your right shoulder under your body and thus free your trapped right arm), or get close to him, hugging him into your lap, to bridge up onto your left shoulder and thus turn him over. Smaller actions such as trying to "grapevine" his leg to stalemate the hold or *kansetsu waza* attacks against his left arm are legitimate, but these minor body actions should not be the focus of your escape measures.

♦ **COMPLETION**

Upon Uke's *mairi* signal, Tori immediately, but unhurriedly, assumes *kyoshi* (open) at the near position (about 1½ feet from Uke's right side) on the lateral axis. Tori does this by reversing the movements he made to get into the technique, in a natural way; he slides his right palm out from under Uke's left armpit and presses his palm onto the mat at Uke's left side. Using that hand as a support point, he comes up onto his left knee in the right kneeling *shizentai*, still maintaining his left-hand cupping action on Uke's right arm; Tori slips Uke's right arm from under his left armpit and, placing his right hand on Uke's right arm near the wrist, palm downward, replaces Uke's arm on the mat alongside Uke. Holding himself erect, Tori moves back the short distance he took for his entry step by sliding his left knee back, then his right foot. Tori assumes *kyoshi* (open) and pauses momentarily, with composure and quiet alertness, keeping visual contact with Uke's body. He is now ready for the next technique. Figs. (9), (10).

KATA-GATAME

◆ ABOUT THIS TECHNIQUE

This immobilization, the shoulder hold, is classified as a holding technique (*osae-komi waza*). It gets its name from the very powerful effect achieved by the judoist's taking the hold as he applies his body pressure diagonally forward and downward, pinning his opponent's arm and head together in a vice-like action and completely immobilizing the shoulder area. Today's form remains identical to the original one.

◆ PREPARATION FOR ENGAGEMENT

With Uke in the lying-ready position on the longitudinal axis, Tori, in *kyoshi* (open) on the lateral axis at the near position (about 1½ feet from Uke's right side), keeps composure and quiet alertness as he shifts his gaze to make visual contact with Uke's face.

◆ ENGAGEMENT

1. TORI: Takes a short entry step (right foot, left knee slides up) and picks up Uke's right arm with both hands; his left hand, palm down, grasps Uke's right arm from the top just above the elbow, as his right hand, palm up, grasps Uke's arm near the wrist. Lifting Uke's right arm, places it along the right side of Uke's head; simultaneously kneels on his right knee up against Uke's right armpit, bringing his right leg parallel to Uke's body with the right foot resting on the sole surfaces of the toes.

2. TORI: Kneeling by Uke's right side on both knees, continues to press Uke's right arm against the right side of Uke's head, leaning diagonally forward and downward toward Uke's left shoulder. Removes his right hand from Uke's arm and slides it in a short circular route over the top of Uke's left arm (to block any lifting of that arm), and then around and under Uke's neck from Uke's far left side;

UKE: Remains motionless in the lying-ready position, maintaining his position, yielding to Tori's efforts to take his right arm.

Engagement.

1

2

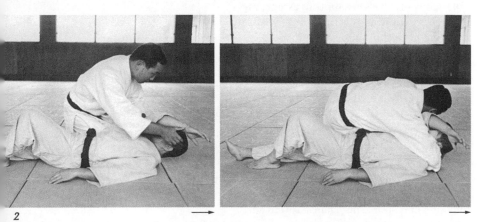

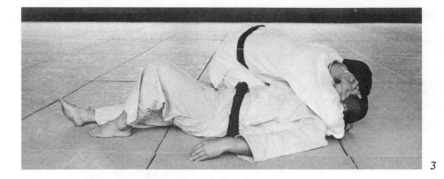

3

(TORI)

simultaneously stretches out his left leg directly to his left side. Lowering his body, comes
tightly up against Uke's upper right arm, trapping Uke's arm between the right side of his
head and neck and the right side of Uke's
head. As his head and neck and body press into
Uke, slides his left hand out from pressing
against Uke's right arm, and clasps his own
right hand firmly with his left so that the right
is palm down and the left palm up; the palms
form right angles. Stretches his extended left
leg fully, positioning the sole flat on the mat
at a point in line with Uke's shoulders.

    3. TORI: Signals that the hold is on by tight-
ening his whole body as he drives his weight
forward and diagonally downward toward the
mat in a direction directly through Uke's right
shoulder.

TORI: Controls Uke's attempts to escape, varying his position as required, but without
changing his technique.

TORI: Relaxes his tight control action, but
maintains the *kata-gatame* form, adjusting to
the initial starting position if necessary.

UKE: Remains motionless in the lying-ready position, yielding to Tori's
efforts to place the form of the hold
as he gathers his energy and takes a
deep breath.

UKE: At Tori's "on" signal, immediately attempts three distinctly different escape measures of his own
choice. Being unsuccessful in his
attempt to escape, gives the *mairi*
signal and ceases all escape actions.

UKE'S SUGGESTED ESCAPE ACTIONS

    1. Attempts to neutralize or break Tori's
immobilizing pressure against his right-
arm-and-head region by placing the palm
of his free left hand against the palm (or
fist) of his trapped right hand and forcefully pressing both arms against Tori in an
attempt to create counterpressure and a
space between himself and Tori (Fig. a).

TORI'S SUGGESTED CONTROL ACTIONS

    1. Lunges more forcefully in the diagonal-
ly downward direction by driving hard off
solidly placed feet; squeezes Uke's neck
with his encircling right arm (Fig. a).

(a)

(b)

(c)

(UKE)

2. Tries to take advantage of any gap created between Tori and himself by twisting hard to his right, into Tori; attempts to loosen Tori's position and reduce its effect by inserting his right (or left) knee between Tori and himself and thrusting Tori away (Fig. b).

3. By swinging both his legs up and over, tries to turn a backward somersault over his own left shoulder and over the back of Tori's encircling right arm; may use his own left hand to push his hips up and over (Fig. c).

(TORI)

2. Closes any gap between Uke and himself by moving his body toward Uke and also by sliding his right leg tightly up against Uke's right side (parallel to Uke's body); may increase the squeezing action of his encircling right arm (Fig. b).

3. Concentrates his body forces so as to put more diagonally downward pressure onto Uke's right shoulder; pulls Uke into himself with his encircling right arm (Fig. c).

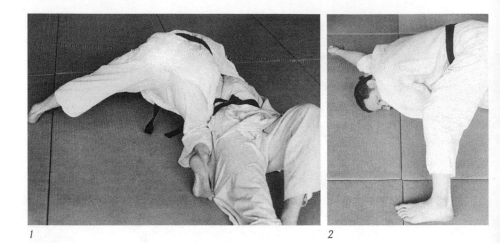

1

2

● TORI ●

Hold with the power of your whole body, which is kept unified by tensing your midsection; do not use only your arms to control Uke. Your legs are your base of power; keep them widespread, the right knee, right foot, and left foot forming a tripod, for stability. Your left leg must be fully stretched out, as it serves as a brace for your body, with the full sole of that foot firmly on the mat (which is turned parallel to Uke, as in Fig. 1).

Seek to keep your butt down low, though it is necessarily in a relatively raised position (body jackknifed, butt high); your left leg's position controls the height of your butt, so keep your base as wide as you can by adjusting that leg. Your left leg must be positioned straight in line with Uke's shoulders (Fig. 2). Your bent right leg wedges up against Uke's right side with that foot resting on the sole surfaces of the toes, not with the instep resting on the mat (Fig. 1). While your left leg remains straight, your right leg may change position by moving so that only your right knee wedges up against Uke's right side just above his hip. You may even sit down on the mat as if in *kesa-gatame* position, but this form is weaker than the kneeling type, as it releases a lot of your forward and diagonally downward pressure against Uke. It is also essential to note that the original placement of Uke's right arm is alongside his head, pressing into his ear, not merely folded across his face. Figures 3-6 show how to hold, pick up, and position Uke's arm across his eyes or higher; a lower position is incorrect and weakens your immobilization. Always keep his right arm trapped in the correct position with your head low, face turned a bit to your left so that the right side of the back of your head presses hard against Uke's trapped

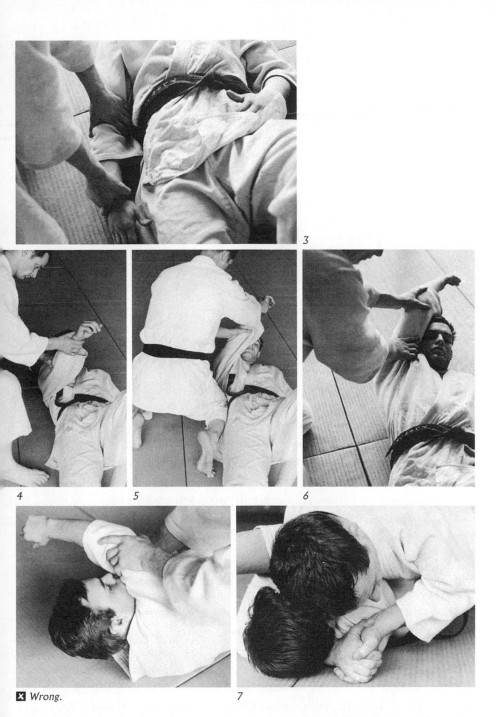

X *Wrong.*   7

arm; the crook of your right arm contains his neck-and-head region from the other (far) side and serves to block his head motion more than squeezing his neck with your right arm. Clasp your hands at right angles (Fig. 7).

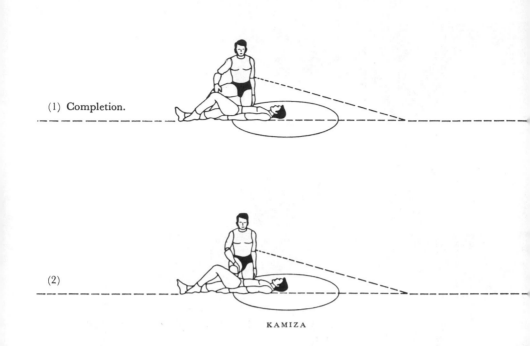

(1) Completion.

(2)

KAMIZA

Focus your body power diagonally forward and downward against his body in a direction running through his right shoulder into his left on the mat; use the right side of the back of your head and neck, as well as your right shoulder, as contact points. Have the feeling of launching your body toward your right front corner as if you wanted to stake Uke to the mat at his right shoulder. Do this by driving hard off solidly placed legs. Do not just kneel next to Uke and rely upon squeezing his neck with your arms.

○ UKE ○

Move with the power of your whole body, not isolated parts, when you try to escape. However, move carefully as you can be injured in your neck-and-spine region or choked into unconsciousness if you jump too quickly into an escape action. "Feel it out" as you move in any direction, but when you finally move into a determined weakness of Tori, do so with your whole body power.

Seek to destroy Tori's base of power, that is, the position of his legs. Make him lose his low position by twisting and squirming. As his left leg bends and moves inward, his butt will be raised; then try to push him away from tight contact up against you so that you can better loosen your trapped right arm. You may then either turn in under him or somersault back over his right arm.

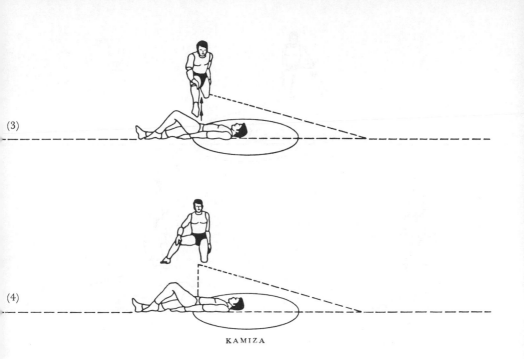

(3)

(4)

KAMIZA

◆ COMPLETION

Upon Uke's *mairi* signal, Tori immediately but unhurriedly assumes *kyoshi* (open) at the near position (about 1½ feet from Uke's right side) on the lateral axis. Tori does this by reversing the movements he made to get into the technique, in a natural way; he relaxes his right-head-and-neck-region pressure on Uke's right arm, and places his left hand, palm down, on Uke's right arm above the elbow as he slides his extended left leg inward so as to kneel onto that knee. Simultaneously he extricates his right arm from around and under Uke's neck to right his body as he places his right hand, palm up, under Uke's right arm near the wrist. He returns Uke's right arm to alongside Uke's body, on the mat, turning his body a bit to the right and raising his right knee to come to the right kneeling *shizentai*, to create the space to do so. Holding himself erect, Tori moves back the short distance he took for his entry step by sliding his left knee back, then his right foot.

Tori assumes *kyoshi* (open) and pauses momentarily, with composure and quiet alertness, keeping visual contact with Uke's body, then moves backward two steps by *tsugi ashi* in *kyoshi* (closed) to the far position (about 5 feet from the right side of Uke's body) on the lateral axis and once again assumes *kyoshi* (open); once again he pauses momentarily with composure and quiet alertness, making visual contact with a point beyond Uke's body (on the *kamiza* side). Figs. (1)-(4). He is now ready for the next technique.

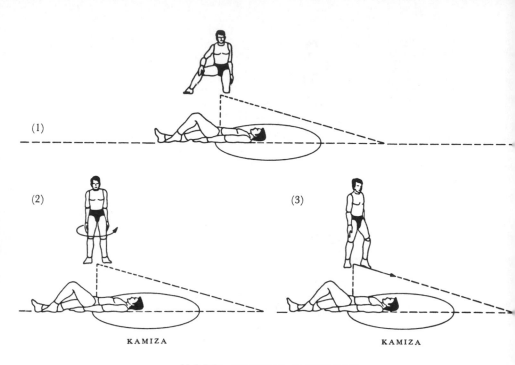

(1)

(2)

(3)

KAMIZA

KAMIZA

KAMI-SHIHO-GATAME

◆ ABOUT THIS TECHNIQUE

This immobilization, the upper holding of the four corners, is classified as a holding technique (*osae-komi waza*). It gets its name from the judoist's use of his body position atop his opponent's head-and-shoulder region to control four points on the opponent's upper body. This technique is the same as that adopted by the founder.

◆ PREPARATION FOR ENGAGEMENT

With Uke in the lying-ready position on the longitudinal axis, Tori, in *kyoshi* (open) on the lateral axis at the far position (about 5 feet from the right side of Uke), keeps composure, quiet alertness, and visual contact with a point beyond Uke (on the *kamiza* side) as he slides his right foot inward a bit and stands up in *shizenhontai*. Pivoting in place 45 degrees to his left (toward his side of the kata area), Tori steps off with his left foot and walks diagonally to the far position (about 5 feet directly behind Uke) on the longitudinal axis, then turns to his right (into the *kamiza*) to stand facing Uke in *shizen-hontai*. Immediately, but unhurriedly, Tori lowers himself and assumes *kyoshi* (open), then pauses momentarily, making visual contact with a point beyond Uke's feet. Tori advances two steps by *tsugi ashi* in *kyoshi* (closed) to the near position (about 1½ feet behind Uke) on the longitudinal axis and once more

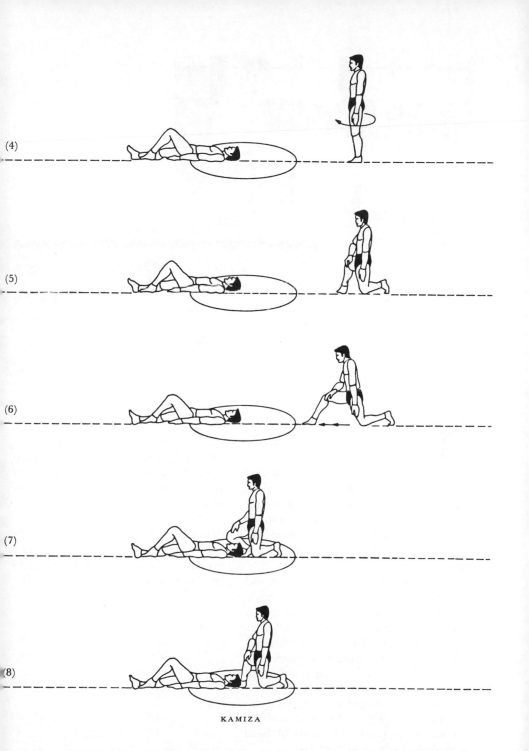

(4)

(5)

(6)

(7)

(8)

KAMIZA

assumes *kyoshi* (open) with composure and quiet alertness as he makes visual contact with Uke's body. Figs. (1)-(8).

Engagement.

1

◆ ENGAGEMENT

1. TORI: Takes a short entry step (right foot, left knee slides up) and then, bending forward, lowers his upper body as he begins to reach forward with both hands, knuckles up, under Uke's arms; simultaneously with his lowering and reaching, kneels onto his right knee, placing both knees in line, spread apart, with his feet resting on the sole surfaces of the toes.

2. TORI: Continues to reach forward and takes Uke's belt with both hands, gripping at Uke's hip regions; flattens out his feet so as to bring his insteps onto the mat. Makes chest contact with Uke's upper body and pulls it tight by lowering his buttocks and bringing both knees, in line, to positions on either side of Uke's head. Clamping his elbows tightly inward and spreading his knees a bit for stability, turns his head to either the right or left, placing the side of his head on the upper midsection of Uke.

UKE: Remains motionless in the lying-ready position, but turns his head to either the right or left as he yields to Tori's efforts to gather in both of his arms.

UKE: Remaining motionless in the lying-ready position, yields to Tori's efforts to place the form of the hold, as he gathers his energy and takes a deep breath.

2

3

(TORI)

3. TORI: Signals that the hold is on, tightening his whole body, as he compresses Uke with his weight bearing diagonally downward against Uke's head and chest regions toward Uke's belt.

TORI: Controls Uke's attempts to escape, varying his position as required by extending or bracing with his leg or legs, but without changing his technique.

TORI: Relaxes his tight control actions but maintains the *kami-shiho-gatame* form, adjusting to the initial starting position if necessary.

UKE: At Tori's "on" signal, immediately attempts three distinctly different escape measures of his own choice. Being unsuccessful in his attempts to escape, gives the *mairi* signal and ceases all escape actions.

UKE'S SUGGESTED ESCAPE ACTIONS

1. Attempts to turn over under Tori and come onto all fours by running either arm up under Tori's chin and pressing upward, twisting forcefully in the direction that hand is pointing (Fig. a).

2. Tries to take advantage of Tori's elevated position by pressing both hands against Tori's shoulders and shoving Tori back as he works his body downward, away from Tori; then doubles his body up, bringing his legs over the upper back of Tori in an attempt to hook them under Tori's thighs and pull himself out of Tori's grip (Fig. b).

3. Tries to turn Tori over and counter-hold him, taking advantage of Tori's momentary narrowness of base in a kneeling position, by bridging his body forcefully upward and turning over either to the right or left (Figs, c, c¹).

TORI'S SUGGESTED CONTROL ACTIONS

1. Slips his head to the side away from Uke's turning attempt, jackknifing his body, buttocks upward, as he stretches both legs outward, feet firmly on the mat, and spreads them wide to apply downward pressure against Uke's turning action, on the high side (Fig. a).

2. Immediately drops his hips to the mat, drawing up his knees tightly alongside of Uke's head, keeping his insteps resting close to the mat, as he tightens his grips on Uke's belt and pulls Uke in under him, then fixes him by clamping his elbows tightly inward; may narrow the position of his knees a bit so as to offer a smaller target to Uke's feet (Fig. b).

3. Widens his knee positions and arches his back by holding his head high as he forces his abdominal region forward and down into Uke. May stretch his legs wide as above, or may sit in *kesa-gatame* fashion on the side to which Uke is turning (Figs, c, c¹).

(a)

(b)

(c)

(c¹)

1

❌ *Wrong.*

◆ TECHNIQUE KEY POINTS

● TORI ●

Hold with the power of your whole body, which is kept unified by tensing your midsection; do not use only your arms to control Uke. Your legs are your base of power, even when folded and tucked under you, so spread your knees wide for stability; and it is best to keep your insteps on the mat rather than coming up onto the sole surfaces of your toes. By this method you will keep your butt low while you are in the kneeling position (Fig. 1).

Seek to keep your butt down when kneeling, your back flat or somewhat arched, and your head up, rather than humping over your opponent; smother Uke's head-and-upper-chest region with your midsection and chest. Your legs may change position to brace as Uke tries various escapes. In the leg changes, it is best to come up onto the sole surfaces of your toes, especially when you stretch your leg (or legs) or jackknife your body, butt high. Position yourself directly behind Uke, in line with his body, but avoid forming a straight line with either side of your body (Figs. 2, 3). This would provide an "axle" upon which you would rotate easily as Uke attempts to turn you over; always avoid straight lines by body positioning. Clamp your elbows hard inward, tightly against Uke's arms as you retain your grip on his belt.

Focus your body power diagonally forward and downward against his head and extreme-upper-body-and-chest region; do not get down deep into his lap. Have the feeling of riding up against him with your chest or abdominal region, your chest held high as if you were riding the crest of a wave up onto a beach by body surfing. Concentrate on staking his shoulders to the mat. Do this by pulling on his belt with both hands and bridging him up against you, driving your body forward off braced legs. Don't just lie flat on top of Uke, parallel to the mat; hunker your butt down and keep your head a bit higher than your tail. Occasionally you may need to use one side of your

2   3

❌ *Wrong.*

head or your chin to aid you in wedging down into him.

○ UKE ○

Move with the power of your whole body, not isolated parts, when you try to escape; move into a determined weakness in Tori's technique.

Seek to destroy Tori's base of power, that is, the position of his legs. Make him lose his widespread position of knees or feet by moving your body to the right or left so as to form a straight line along one of his sides; twist hard from a strongly based bridge into that straight side to turn him over. By driving one or both arms up under his chin and forcing him back and upward, you may loosen his hold enough to enable you to twist onto your face and free yourself. Sometimes by this arm action you can get him to change position from directly behind you to off to one side or the other, which, if you persist in your twisting, may free you.

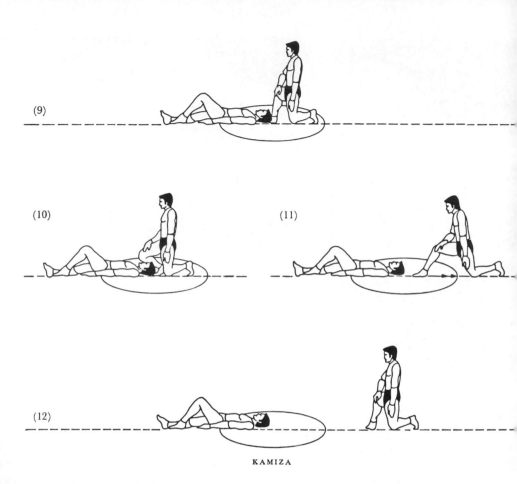

(9)

(10) (11)

(12)

KAMIZA

♦ COMPLETION

Upon Uke's *mairi* signal, Tori immediately but unhurriedly assumes *kyoshi* (open) at the near position (about 1½ feet directly behind Uke) on the longitudinal axis; Uke is in the lying-ready position. Tori does this by reversing the movements he made to get into the technique, in a natural way; he relaxes his body pressure against Uke and slides both of his knees back a bit, relaxing his two-hand grip on Uke's belt. Then he raises his upper body from Uke, simultaneously bringing both feet onto the sole surfaces of their toes. Raising his right knee, Tori takes the kneeling *shizentai*. Holding himself erect, Tori moves back the short distance he took for his entry step by sliding his left knee back, then his right foot.

Tori assumes *kyoshi* (open) and pauses momentarily, with composure and quiet alertness, keeping visual contact with Uke's body, then moves backward two steps by *tsugi ashi* in *kyoshi* (closed) to the far position (about 5 feet directly behind Uke, who is in the lying-ready position) on the longitudinal axis, and once again assumes *kyoshi* (open). Once again he pauses momentarily with composure and quiet alertness, making visual contact with a point beyond Uke's feet. Figs. (9)-(12). He is now ready for the next technique.

YOKO-SHIHO-GATAME

♦ **ABOUT THIS TECHNIQUE**
This immobilization, the side holding of the four quarters, is classified as a holding technique (*osae-komi waza*). It is named from the way the judoist positions his body alongside his opponent and controls four points on the opponent's upper body. This is the classical style of side holding and it remains unchanged from the form adopted by the founder.

♦ **PREPARATION FOR ENGAGEMENT**
With Uke in the lying-ready position on the longitudinal axis, Tori, in *kyoshi* (open) on the longitudinal axis at the far position (about 5 feet directly behind Uke) facing Uke's reclining body, slides his right foot inward a bit and stands up in *shizenhontai*. Pivoting in place 45 degrees to his right (away from the *kamiza*), Tori steps off with his left foot and walks diagonally to the far position (about 5 feet from Uke's right side) on the lateral axis, and turns to his left (toward the *kamiza*) to stand facing Uke in *shizenhontai*. Immediately but unhurriedly, he lowers himself and assumes *kyoshi* (open), then pauses momentarily with composure and quiet alertness, making visual contact with a point just beyond Uke's reclining body (on the *kamiza* side). Tori advances two steps

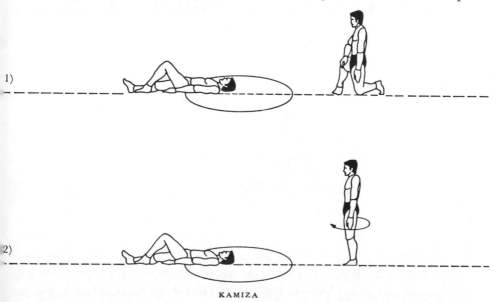

1)

2)

KAMIZA

(3)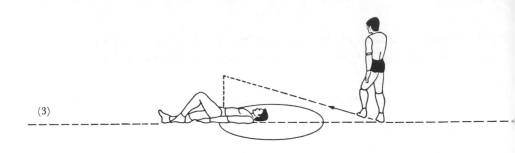

(4)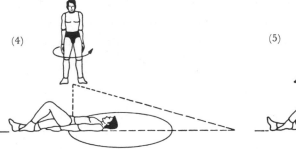

(5)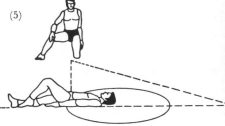

(6)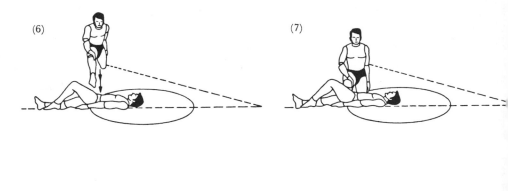

(7)

(8)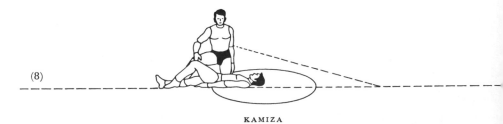

KAMIZA

by *tsugi ashi* in *kyoshi* (closed) to the near position (about 1½ feet from Uke's right side) on the lateral axis and once again assumes *kyoshi* (open), keeping composure and quiet alertness. Figs. (1)-(8). Tori shifts his gaze to Uke's face.

Engagement.

1   2   ⟶

◆ ENGAGEMENT

1. TORI: Takes a short entry step (right foot, left knee slides up) and picks up Uke's right arm with both hands; his left hand, palm up, cups Uke's arm from underneath just above the elbow as his right hand, palm down, grasps Uke's arm near the wrist. Lifting Uke's right arm, places it on the mat alongside his own left leg so that the arm is approximately at right angles to Uke.

2. TORI: Removing both of his hands from Uke's right arm, kneels on his right knee up against Uke's right hip, then slides his left knee up against Uke's body. Flattening out his feet so that his insteps rest on the mat, bends his upper body forward and grasps Uke's belt with his left hand, fingers underneath and palm up; simultaneously runs his right arm between Uke's legs near the groin. With his left hand, feeds Uke's belt into his righthand and cinches that grip,

UKE: Remains motionless in the lying-ready position, maintaining his position, yielding to Tori's efforts to take his right arm.

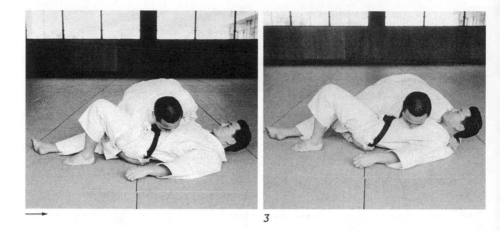

3

(TORI)

palm upward, by pulling downward on Uke's belt. Lowering his chest to the middle right side of Uke's chest, scoops up Uke's free right arm with his left hand and clamps that arm under his left armpit, then runs his left arm under Uke's neck far enough to grasp Uke's upper left lapel in his left hand, thumb inside. Positions his head so he looks straight ahead, with his chin in contact with Uke's midsection.

3. TORI: Signals that the hold is on by tightening his whole body as he pulls Uke into him with both arms, wedging his right knee tightly into Uke's right hip. Brings his body pressure to bear diagonally downward into the right side of Uke's chest.

TORI: Controls Uke's attempts to escape, varying his position as required by extending or bracing his left leg, but without changing his technique.

TORI: Relaxes his tight control actions, but maintains the *yoko-shiho-gatame* form, adjusting to initial starting position if necessary while in that form.

UKE: Remaining motionless in the lying-ready position, yields to Tori's efforts to place the form of the hold, as he gathers his energy and takes a deep breath.

UKE: At Tori's "on" signal, immediately attempts three distinctly different escape measures of his own choice. Being unsuccessful in his attempt to escape, gives the *mairi* signal and ceases all escape actions.

(a)

(a¹)

(a²)

(a³)

UKE'S SUGGESTED ESCAPE ACTIONS

1. Attempts *kansetsu waza* on Tori's left elbow by cupping Tori's elbow in his right palm and using the flat of his left hand to push the left side of Tori's head downward toward his feet, thus stretching out Tori's left arm; may use his left leg, swung up over the left side of Tori's neck, to assist. May also use his left hand on Tori's left elbow to reinforce the *kansetsu waza*, passing it over from the top, placing it on the back of his right hand, and pulling inward (Figs. a-a³).

TORI'S SUGGESTED CONTROL ACTIONS

1. Neutralizes Uke's *kansetsu waza* attempts on his left elbow by clamping the elbow downward and tilting his body onto his left hip; turns his head to the right. May find it necessary to extend his right leg to accommodate the body tilt; this reduced control of Uke's hips must be compensated for by stronger right-hand action on Uke's belt. Changes that pull to a pressing action (Fig. a-a³).

(b)

(c)

(UKE)

2. Takes advantage of Tori's reduced control of his hips by wriggling and turning his body sharply to his right and trying to withdraw his right shoulder under him, as he works to wedge his right knee between Tori and himself in an effort to loosen Tori's holding pressure (Figs. b-b^2).

3. Grips the back, of Tori's belt in the middle with his left hand and tries to turn Tori over by a strong bridging action across his left shoulder, boosting upward and twisting to his left onto his left shoulder, with his midsection heaving in that direction from platform feet firmly on the mat, well under his body; may use his right arm to push upward (Figs. c, c^1).

(TORI)

2. Stops Uke's inward turning action by sitting on his left hip; slides his left leg through underneath him so he sits facing Uke's feet, in a body position like that of *ushiro-gesa-gatame*. May also sit to face Uke as in *kesa-gatame*. Stops Uke's head from turning inward by increasing shoulder pressure (Figs. b-b^2).

3. Controls Uke's head-turning action by shoulder pressure and extends his left leg to counterbalance Uke's efforts; arches his back, trying to hold his head up high. Pulls strongly inward with his right hand gripping Uke's belt (Figs. c, c^1).

(b¹)

(b²)

(c¹)

◆ TECHNIQUE KEY POINTS

● TORI ●

Hold with the power of your whole body, which is kept unified by tensing your midsection; do not use your arms alone to control Uke. Your legs are your base of power; keep your knees widespread for stability. Your legs must dig in to brace your body; do not let them simply lie loosely upon the mat, even when they are folded and tucked under you. It is best to keep your insteps on the mat when both your legs are folded and tucked under you, with left and right knees wedged tightly up against Uke's right armpit and hip, respectively.

Seek to keep your butt down and your back flat instead of humped over when you take the starting position with both legs folded and tucked under you. Note that your right knee must be on Uke's belt line or above it (toward his head), never below it, or you will give him a chance to escape (Fig. 1). Prevent Uke's hip region from moving to either side by lifting upward with the combined efforts of your right hand on his belt and your right knee wedg-

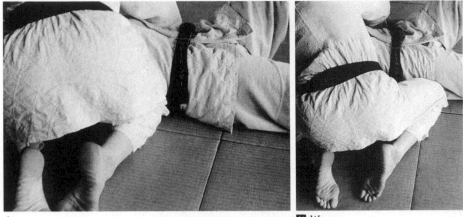

1   ❌ *Wrong.*

ing ever more tightly against his right hip; sometimes a straight inward pull
or a direct pushing action with your right hand stabbing into the mat is effective. Your legs may change position, but as long as you position yourself
with your midsection downward, your right knee must be kept in tight contact
with Uke's right hip. When you change leg position, it is best to put the whole
sole of your left leg flat on the mat and rise onto the sole surfaces of the toes
of your right foot; you may also sit on your left or right hip and spread your
legs much as if in *kesa-gatame* body form. Control Uke's upper body regions
by the pulling-and-squeezing action of your left shoulder and arm against the
right side of Uke's neck (Fig. 2). Be sure to scoop up Uke's right arm with
your left arm *before* you run your left arm under his neck for that control;
leaving his right arm out puts him well on his way to escape (Figs. 3, 4).

Focus your body power forward into the right side of Uke's chest, favoring the area above his belt line; about two-thirds of your body power should
be directed into his head and upper chest regions as shown (p. 322). The
correct right-knee position, mentioned earlier, will ensure this balance for
you; without it, a good Uke can escape. Have the feeling that you are rolling
a log with your chest, Uke being that log; don't just lie flat on top of Uke,
trying to press him straight down into the mat, and don't just drape yourself
over him as shown. You may also think of your body-power application as
similar to a wedge driven under one side of a ship while it is in drydock, to
keep it from rolling to that side. Tip your whole body a bit toward Uke's head
as if to stake his right shoulder to the mat; do not be centered too deep toward
his feet. Your head may aid you to hold him; if Uke pushes against your head,
it is best to place the left side of your face against his midsection, ear down.

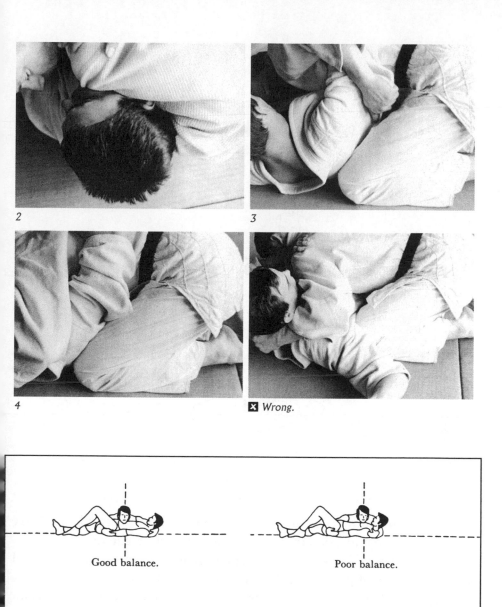

2

3

4

 Wrong.

Good balance.

Poor balance.

Good balance.

Poor balance.

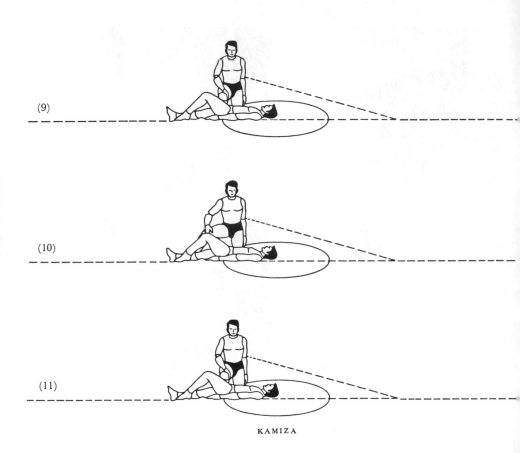

(9)

(10)

(11)

KAMIZA

○ UKE ○

Move with the power of your whole body, not isolated parts, when you try to escape; move into a determined weakness in Tori's technique.

Seek to loosen Tori's squeezing action against your neck and head, and destroy his base of power, that is, his leg position. Try to create a space between your right side and Tori's wedging right knee; then twist and turn onto your right side and get your right knee or leg under him and catch his right leg. By pushing with your right arm against his left leg, you may also get him to narrow his leg position, which will raise his butt; grip his belt in the middle of his back with your left hand and try to bridge him up and over your left shoulder.

◆ COMPLETION

Upon Uke's *mairi* signal, Tori immediately but unhurriedly assumes *kyoshi* (open) at the near position (about 1½ feet from Uke's right side) on the

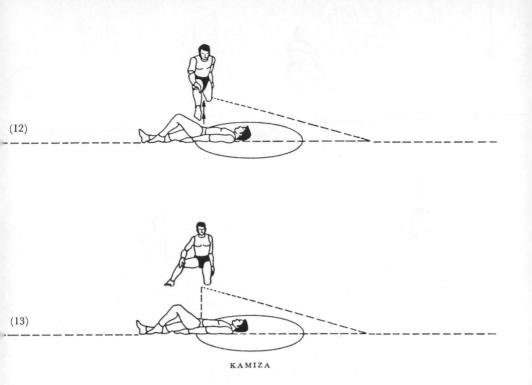

(12)

(13)

KAMIZA

lateral axis. Tori does this by (12) reversing the movements he made to get into the technique, in a natural way; he relaxes his left-shoulder-and-arm pressure by withdrawing his left arm from under Uke's neck, simultaneously relaxing his right-hand grip on Uke's belt. Tori raises his upper body and grasps Uke's right arm with his right hand, palm down, near Uke's wrist, and with his left hand, palm upward, just above the elbow; he simultaneously comes up onto the sole surfaces of the toes of both feet. Tori moves Uke's right arm to its starting position alongside Uke on the mat, raising his right knee to come into the right kneeling *shizentai*, to create the space to do so. Holding himself erect, Tori moves back the short distance he took for his entry step by sliding his left knee back, then his right foot.

Tori assumes *kyoshi* (open) and pauses momentarily with composure and quiet alertness, keeping visual contact with Uke's body, then moves backward two steps by *tsugi ashi* in *kyoshi* (closed) to the far position (about 5 feet from the right side of Uke's body) on the lateral axis and once again assumes *kyoshi* (open); once more he pauses momentarily with composure and quiet alertness, making visual contact with a point beyond Uke's body (on the *kamiza* side). Figs. (9)-(13). He is now ready for the next technique.

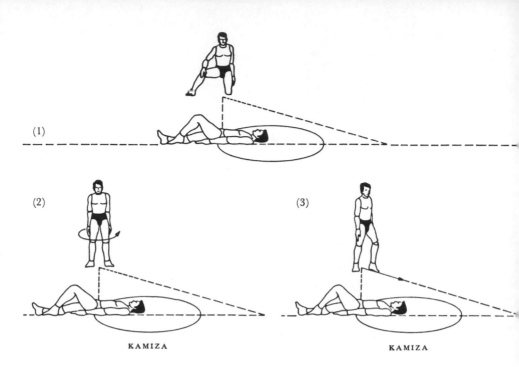

(1)

(2)

KAMIZA

(3)

KAMIZA

KUZURE KAMI-SHIHO-GATAME

◆ ABOUT THIS TECHNIQUE

This immobilization, the irregular upper holding of the four quarters, is classified as a holding technique (*osae-komi waza*). It gets its name from the way the judoist doing the holding modifies his body position (atop his opponent's head and controlling four points on the opponent's upper body) from that of the basic *kami-shiho-gatame* to produce a more powerful effect. This technique remains the same as the founder's original.

◆ PREPARATION FOR ENGAGEMENT

With Uke in the lying-ready position on the longitudinal axis, Tori, in *kyoshi* (open) on the lateral axis at the far position (about 5 feet from the right side of Uke), keeps composure, quiet alertness, and visual contact with a point beyond Uke (on the *kamiza* side) as he slides his right foot inward a bit and stands up in *shizenhontai*. Pivoting in place 45 degrees to his left (toward his side of the kata area), Tori steps off with his left foot and walks diagonally to the far position (about 5 feet directly behind Uke) on the longitudinal axis, and turns to his right (into the *kamiza*) to stand facing Uke in *shizenhontai*. Immediately, but unhurriedly, Tori lowers himself and assumes the *kyoshi* (open), then pauses momentarily, making visual contact with a point beyond Uke's feet. Tori advances two steps by *tsugi ashi in kyoshi* (closed) to

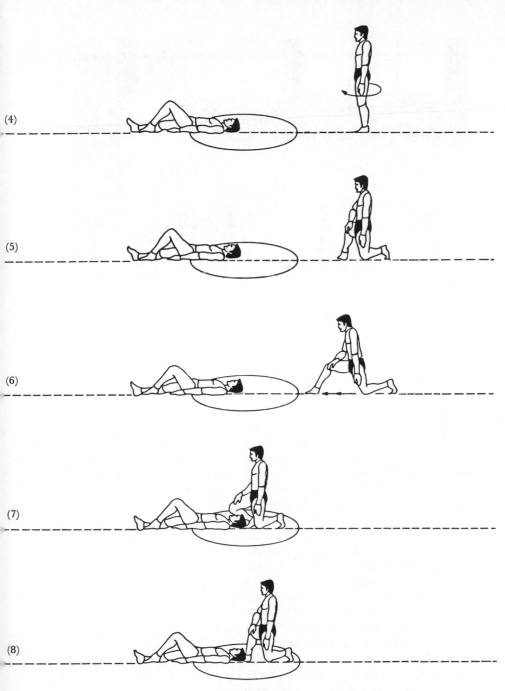

(4)

(5)

(6)

(7)

(8)

KAMIZA

the near position (about 1½ feet behind Uke) on the longitudinal axis and once again assumes *kyoshi* (open) with composure and quiet alertness as he makes visual contact with Uke's body. Figs. (1)-(8).

Engagement.

◆ ENGAGEMENT

1. TORI: Takes a short entry step (right foot, left knee slides up) and then kneels on his right knee, keeping his right foot in place (this action turns his body a bit to his left and places him at about 45 degrees to Uke). Keeping both of his feet resting on the sole surfaces of the toes, bends his upper body forward and reaches forward with both arms, left hand (palm up) under his right hand (palm down), toward Uke's right arm.

2. TORI: Continues to reach forward and takes Uke's right arm with his left hand cupping Uke's outer upper arm above the elbow, thumb in, and his right hand grasping Uke's arm below the elbow from the top, thumb out. Lifts Uke's right arm and feeds it under his own right armpit by cradling it in his left hand, palm up, as he relaxes his right-hand grip and runs his right arm deep under Uke's arm; simultaneously flattens out both of his feet so that their insteps rest on the mat. He grips the back of Uke's collar in his right hand, fingers inside, knuckles resting on the mat; then runs his left arm under Uke's left shoulder and arm along the left side of Uke and grips Uke's belt at the side.

UKE: Remains motionless in the lying-ready position, maintaining his position but yielding to Tori's efforts to take his right arm.

UKE: Remains motionless in the lying-ready position, but yields to Tori's efforts to place the form of the hold, as he gathers his energy and takes a deep breath.

1

2   3

3. TORI: Signals that the hold is on by tightening his whole body, clamping both elbows inward as he pulls with both arms, compressing Uke with his weight bearing diagonally downward into Uke's right-shoulder-and-chest region.

TORI: Controls Uke's attempts to escape, varying his position as required by extending or bracing with his leg or legs, but without changing his technique.

TORI: Relaxes his tight control actions, but maintains the *kuzure kami-shiho-gatame* form, adjusting to starting position if necessary while in that form.

UKE: At Tori's "on" signal, immediately attempts three distinctly different escape measures of his own choice. Being unsuccessful in his attempts to escape, gives the *mairi* signal and ceases all escape actions.

(a)

UKE'S SUGGESTED ESCAPE ACTIONS

1. Attempts to slide his body downward (away from Tori) and turn to his right in an effort to pull his right arm out of Tori's clamping action; does so by a forceful bridging action and twist to his right as he pushes his left forearm up under the right side of Tori's neck and pushes Tori's right thigh with his right hand in an effort to dislodge Tori upward and to Tori's left (Figs. a-a²).

2. Takes advantage of Tori's balance weakness to the left rear by seizing Tori's belt with both hands and trying to turn him over to the left rear by a forceful swinging, twisting, and bridging action of his body in that direction. May reinforce that action by a lifting-and-pulling action of his right hand which is gripping Tori's right trouser leg (Figs. b, bi).

3. Attempts to take advantage of Tori's high jackknifed position by turning a somersault over Tori's back and trying to catch his feet under Tori's thighs; from this anchored position, may extricate himself by a forceful pullover of his body (Figs. c, c¹).

TORI'S SUGGESTED CONTROL ACTIONS

1. Clamps his elbows more tightly inward as he sits on his left hip in *ushiro-ge-sa-gatame* fashion; the force of his body shift is directed against Uke's right shoulder and head, and flattens Uke to the mat. Braces strongly from widespread legs placed firmly on the mat and launches his body into Uke's right shoulder (Figs. a¹, a²).

2. Checks Uke's turning actions to the left by immediately raising his hips a bit and withdrawing his left leg so as to come more to a stomach-down position; spreads both legs wide and braces from feet firmly placed on the mat, soles down. Lunges forward and diagonally downward into Uke (Figs. b, b¹).

3. Drops his full weight onto Uke, leaving his high position and sagging to the mat at his midsection. Stretches out both legs to maximum width and arches his back, with head held high (Figs. c, c¹).

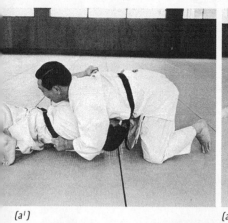

(a¹)   (a²)

(b)   (b¹)

(c)   (c¹)

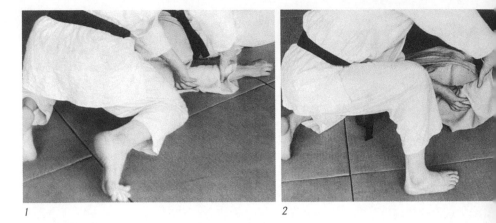

1   2

◆ TECHNIQUE KEY POINTS

● TORI ●

Hold with the power of your whole body, which is kept unified by tensing your midsection; do not let your arms do all the work to control Uke. Your legs are your base of power, even when they are folded and tucked under you. Spread your knees wide for stability, and keep your insteps on the mat (Fig. 4) rather than coming up onto the sole surfaces of your toes when your legs are tucked up underneath you. If your legs simply lie loosely on the mat you will be unable to dig in or brace your body.

Seek to keep your butt down when your legs are folded and tucked under you; hunker down. Keep your back flat or arch it a bit by holding your head up high; do not hump over Uke. Your legs may change position, with one or both stretching out at a time; if you stretch out only one leg, the other, the bent one, must be braced off its foot which is placed on the sole surfaces of its toes. You may jackknife your body, butt high, if you stretch out your legs and spread them wide; brace against the mat with the soles of your feet. The angle which you form with Uke as you position yourself to immobilize him is very important; keep it more or less the same as when first taking this technique. Notice in Figures 1 and 2 that you may pick up Uke's right arm from either a right-knee-down or a right-knee-raised position. Thread Uke's right arm under your right armpit, clamping it tightly with your right arm to trap it there; grip the back of Uke's lapel with your right hand (Fig. 3). This permits maximum clamping action of your right arm. That clamping action must be reinforced, initially, by contact between your right elbow and your right thigh, when your legs are tucked up underneath you (Fig. 4). Keep your left elbow clamped tightly inward against his neck, not just lying loosely against his outer left arm or shoulder; there must be no gap between your arm and his neck (Fig. 5).

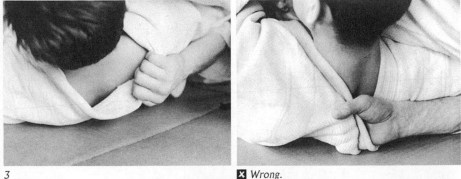

3

X *Wrong.*

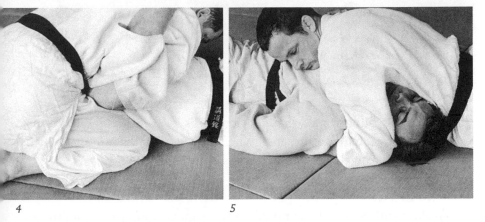

4   5

Focus your body power forward and diagonally downward into Uke's right-shoulder-and-neck region, that V-shaped area which lies between the right side of his head and his trapped right arm. Get the feeling of rolling a log with your chest by pushing with your whole body, from your legs; don't just lie there flat on top of Uke, hugging him and trying to press him straight down into the mat. Let your chest rise and your head come up as you sag your midsection onto the mat; if you jackknife your buttocks upward, drive hard off your legs, again as if rolling a log with your chest. Clamp your elbows hard inward as if you were trying to make them meet.

○ UKE ○

Move with the power of your whole body, not isolated parts, when you try to escape; move into a determined weakness in Tori's technique.

Seek to destroy Tori's base of power: his leg positions. Begin by trying to loosen Tori's left-arm pressure against your neck and head so that you can move, swing, and twist your body more easily; if Tori keeps up this pressure, you cannot move effectively. Once you get moving, move strongly, so that Tori narrows his leg position and raises his butt; thus you may be able to rock

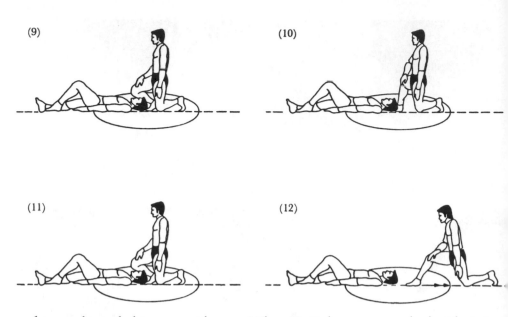

(9)　(10)　(11)　(12)

him and topple him over sideways. When Tori's legs are stretched wide, it is worth trying to catch one and grapevine it if you can; this is most easily accomplished on your right side, against his right leg.

◆ COMPLETION

Upon Uke's *mairi* signal, Tori immediately assumes *kyoshi* (open) unhurriedly at the near position (about 1½ feet directly behind Uke) on the longitudinal axis; Uke is in the lying-ready position. Tori does this by reversing the movements he made to get into the technique, in a natural way; he relaxes his body pressure against Uke and slides both of his knees back a bit, then relaxes his left-hand grip on Uke's belt. Tori raises his upper body, placing his left hand, palm up, on Uke's right arm at a point above the elbow; he relaxes his right-hand grip on Uke's back collar and places his right hand, palm down, on Uke's right arm below the elbow to return Uke's right arm to the mat alongside Uke, simultaneously bringing both feet onto the sole surfaces of their toes. Raising his right knee, Tori takes the kneeling *shizentai*. Holding himself erect, Tori moves back the short distance he took for his entry step, by sliding his left knee back, then his right foot.

Tori assumes *kyoshi* (open) and pauses momentarily with composure and quiet alertness, keeping visual contact with Uke's body, then moves backward two steps by *tsugi ashi* in *kyoshi* (closed) to the far position (about 5 feet directly behind Uke) on the longitudinal axis and once again assumes *kyoshi* (open). As Tori is moving backward to the far position, Uke sits up (sitting-ready position) and then assumes *kyoshi* (open), facing Tori just as Tori

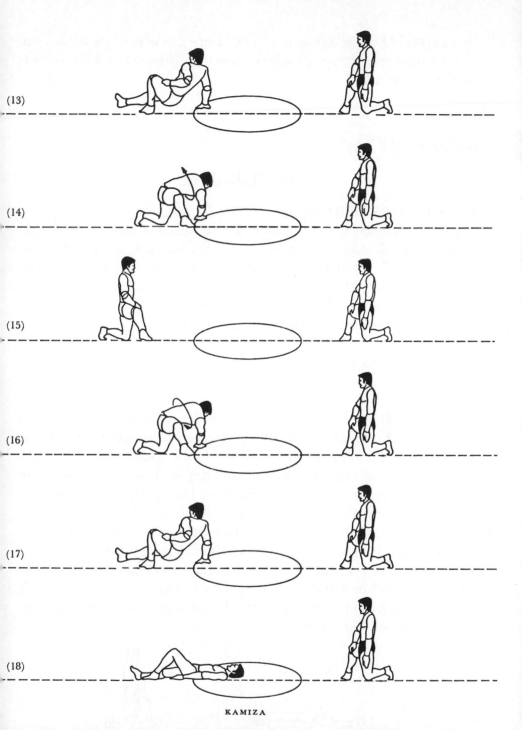

(13)

(14)

(15)

(16)

(17)

(18)

KAMIZA

comes into his *kyoshi* (open). Together they pause, adjusting *their judogi* as they keep composure and quiet alertness and maintain visual contact, to end the category of holding techniques. Upon completion of costume adjustment, Uke again assumes the lying-ready position, Figs. (9)–(18); and Tori is ready for the next technique.

SHIME WAZA

KATA-JUJI-JIME

◆ ABOUT THIS TECHNIQUE
This immobilization, the half-cross choke, is classified as a choking technique (*shime waza*). Its name comes from the way the judoist applying it grips and chokes with his two hands held quite differently. The choke is thus composed of two asymmetrical "halves" which, as the arms cross each other, form the sign of a cross or the Japanese ideogram ✝ *ju*, meaning the number "ten." The technique remains unchanged from that adopted by the founder.

◆ PREPARATION FOR ENGAGEMENT
As Uke settles onto his back in the lying-ready position, Tori is at the far position (about 5 feet directly behind Uke) on the longitudinal axis in *kyoshi* (open) facing the now reclining Uke; Tori slides his right foot inward a bit and stands up in *shizenhontai*. Pivoting in place 45 degrees to his right (away from the *kamiza*), Tori steps off with his left foot and walks diagonally to the far position (about 5 feet from Uke's right side) on the lateral axis, and turns to his left (toward the *kamiza*) to stand facing Uke in *shizenhontai*. Immediately, but unhurriedly, he lowers himself and assumes *kyoshi* (open), then pauses momentarily, making visual contact with a point beyond Uke's body (on the *kamiza* side), with composure and quiet alertness. Tori advances two steps by *tsugi ashi* in *kyoshi* (closed) to the near position (about 1½ feet from Uke's right side) on the lateral axis and once there again assumes *kyoshi* (open), keeping composure and quiet alertness. Figs. (1)–(7). Tori makes visual contact with Uke's face.

(1)

KAMIZA

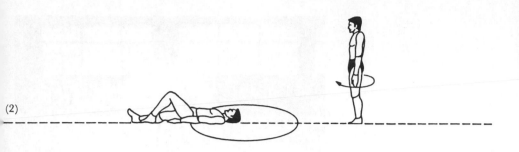

(2)

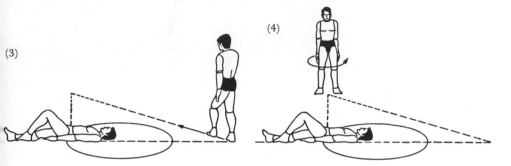

(3)

(4)

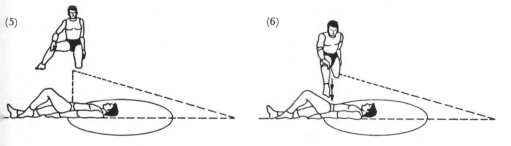

(5)

(6)

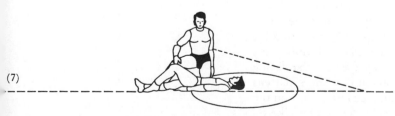

(7)

KAMIZA

Engagement.

◆ ENGAGEMENT

1. TORI: Takes a short entry step (right foot, left knee slides up) and picks up Uke's right arm with both hands; his left hand, palm up, cups Uke's arm from underneath just above the elbow, as his right hand, palm down, grasps Uke's arm near the wrist. Lifting Uke's right arm, places it on the mat alongside his left leg so that the arm is approximately at right angles to Uke; simultaneously moves his left knee up against Uke's right side. Keeping his right hand on Uke's wrist to prevent Uke from using that arm, releases his left-hand grip on Uke's arm and reaches across to the far left side of Uke, grasping Uke's upper left lapel deep under the ear, fingers inside, with the reverse grip.

2. TORI: Removing his right hand from Uke's right wrist, reaches across Uke's body and inserts his fingers between Uke's left side and his left arm near the wrist; simultaneously brushes Uke's arm a bit outward (away from Uke) as he moves his right leg across to kneel astride Uke, facing him. As he settles onto his knees, flattens out his feet so that the insteps rest on the mat, and wedges his feet under Uke on both sides, clamping them there tightly to restrict Uke's movement; simultaneously continues the motion of his right hand

UKE: Remains motionless in the lying-ready position, maintaining his position, yielding to Tori's efforts to take his right arm and left lapel.

UKE: Remains motionless in the lying-ready position, yielding to Tori's efforts to place the form of the choke, as he gathers his energy and takes a deep breath.

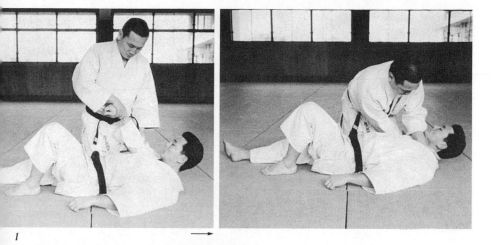

1

2

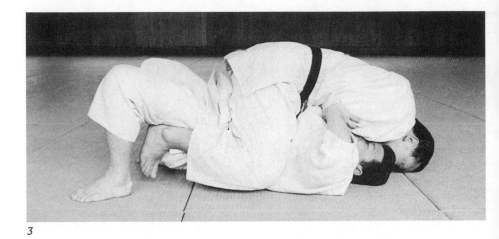

3

Uke's arm outward) around in a circular route over Uke's head, in order to take a grip on Uke's right lapel, deep under Uke's right ear, thumb inside, with the normal grip.

3. TORI: Signals that the choke is on, applying choke pressure by pulling with his left hand and twisting the palm upward to force the bony inner (thumb-side) edge of his wrist (radius) onto the left side of Uke's neck, as he presses the right outer (little-finger side) edge of his right wrist (ulnar) downward against the right front of Uke's neck; simultaneously bends forward, dropping his body well over Uke to add its weight to his choking efforts, positioning his head near or on the mat at the left side of Uke's head.

TORI: Relaxes his tight control actions and choke pressure, but maintains the form of the *kata-juji-jime*, adjusting to initial starting position if necessary while in that form.

UKE: At Tori's "on" signal, immediately attempts to neutralize or escape from Tori's choke by at least one method and possibly more. Being unsuccessful in his attempt to neutralize or escape the choke, gives the mairi signal and ceases all escape actions.

UKE'S SUGGESTED ESCAPE ACTIONS

1. Attempts to neutralize Tori's choke by pressing both of his hands upward and inward hard against Tori's elbows, trying to keep them from spreading; may prop both of his elbows against the mat directly under Tori's elbows to aid his neutralization attempt (Fig. a).

TORI'S SUGGESTED CONTROL ACTIONS

1. Pulls both hands into his abdominal region, spreading his elbows forcefully as he bends well forward (to his right) over Uke's head; his feet are well anchored under Uke's body and his abdominal region thrusts forward (Fig. a).

(a)

(b)

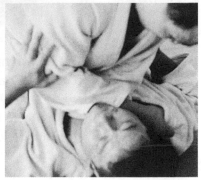

(c)

(UKE)

2. Attempts to bridge and dislodge Tori from astride him and to turn Tori over as he neutralizes the choke, by a strong upward heaving of his midsection; this action is made possible by firmly placing his feet on the mat, well under him. (Fig. b).

3. Attempts to break the cross-choking action by pushing upward over his head with his left hand against Tori's uppermost (right) elbow; his right hand pushes Tori's left elbow inward. Tries to remove his neck from the cross-choke if space is created by this action (Fig. c).

(TORI)

2. Clamps both feet tighter under Uke's buttocks, hooking his heels and pulling harder upward with the heel on the side that Uke is lifting. This action tends to neutralize Uke's lift (Fig. b).

3. Clamps his right elbow downward and spreads it more forcefully as he drives his weight somewhat more to the right side (Fig. c).

♦ **TECHNIQUE KEY POINTS**

● **TORI** ●

Hold with the power of your whole body, which is kept unified by tensing your midsection as you choke. Do not rely solely upon the choke action of

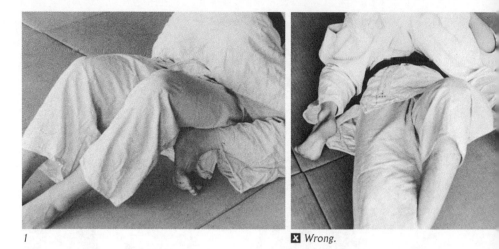

1
❌ Wrong.

your arms to control Uke: you must be able to immobilize him before you can apply effective choking. Your legs are your base of power; keep them hooked tightly under Uke's body at the backs of his thighs or under his buttocks (Fig. 1). If they simply lie tucked under you or loosely at Uke's sides you cannot effectively control Uke and therefore you will be unable to choke him as he struggles to escape.

Seek to take the proper grips preparatory to taking the choke. After releasing your right hand from Uke's right arm and before moving astride him, you may use your right hand to pull Uke's left lapel downward through your gripping left hand to remove any slack. Then use your right hand to brush Uke's left arm away from his body so that your right knee will have a place on the mat next to his body when you come astride him (Figs. 2-5). Your right hand, thumb down and inside Uke's lapel, grips deeper back on Uke's neck than does your left hand; your right arm crosses over your left. But you must use more than just arms and hands to create choking forces. Launch your body well forward, out over Uke, and if you attempt to touch your head to the mat a bit to your right (by the left side of Uke's head) the choke will be strongest. Your legs must not unhook from tight contact with Uke; pull hard upward with both your heels underneath Uke's thighs or buttocks, but harder on the side Uke is raising most. Do not let him fool you by suddenly rocking to the opposite side. Do not simply hunch over Uke; if your feet are firmly hooked under him you can actually launch your body, with your abdominal region thrusting hard forward into Uke's upper body.

Focus your body power well forward, diagonally downward into his neck region by tensing your midsection as you thrust it forward; do not lie loosely, face to face with Uke, or resting on your knees and head. Make Uke's neck

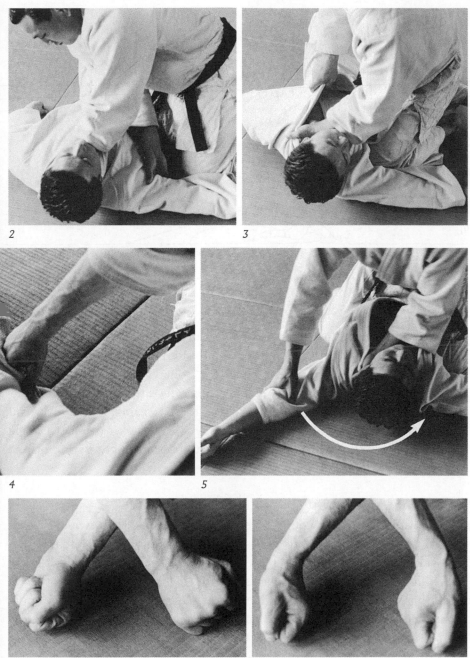

2

3

4

5

6   ☒ *Wrong.*

the target for as much of your body pressure as possible. Pull both of your hands in toward your midsection as you spread your elbows to choke; actually lift Uke's head up a bit as you apply the action. Your right wrist's outer

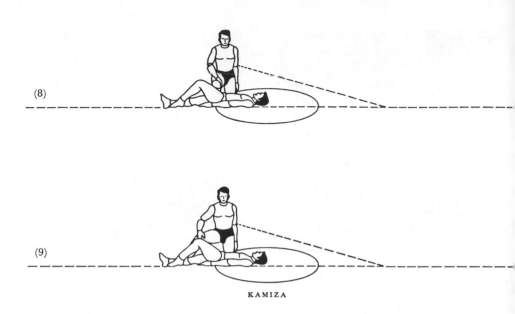

KAMIZA

area (little-finger side) is the "cutting edge" of this choke; it must be placed so as to "cut" against the right side of Uke's neck, not just frontally onto his windpipe. Your left wrist's inner area (thumb side) presses tightly up against the left side of Uke's neck; avoid making a "collar" which fits comfortably around Uke's neck and has little real choking effect; that is, do not let your hands slip so that the backs of your wrists lie flat against Uke's neck. You should have the feeling of squeezing Uke's whole neck as if you had a single cord around it and were slipping the cord tighter and tighter; do not just compress his windpipe (Fig. 6, p. 343).

○ UKE ○

Move with the power of your whole body, not isolated parts, when you try to escape; move carefully into a determined weakness in Tori's technique.

Seek to make Tori lose his tight contact with one or both of his heels, which should be up against the backs of your thighs or buttocks; if he fails to make this contact, or if you dislodge it, you can easily rock him and tumble him over by bridging and twisting hard as you raise your buttocks off the mat on the side of this loose foot contact, and then suddenly turning your body toward the opposite side. Bridge and turn toward the foot of Tori which is making tighter contact and combine this action with the pushing of both of your arms against his elbows. You may also stop him from coming forward over you by placing the flat palm or heel of your hand (or hands) directly on his midsection and resisting his forward motion.

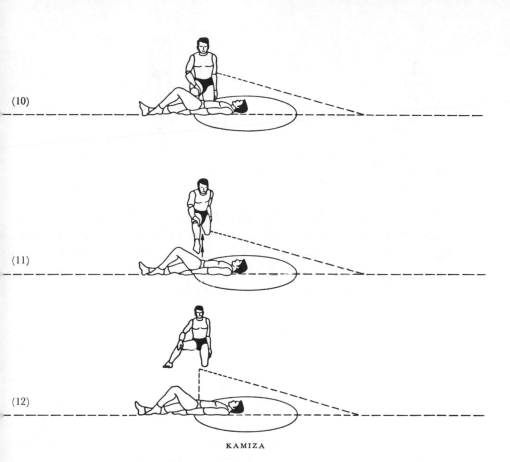

(10)

(11)

(12)

KAMIZA

◆ COMPLETION

Upon Uke's *mairi* signal, Tori immediately but unhurriedly assumes *kyoshi* (open) at the near position (about 1½ feet from Uke's right side) on the lateral axis. Tori does this by reversing the movements he made to get into the technique, in a natural way. He relaxes his uppermost (right-hand) grip and pivots on his left knee to dismount from Uke. At the same time he uses his right hand to brush Uke's left arm to a position on the mat alongside Uke's left side. With his right knee raised, he slides his left knee a bit away from Uke, relaxes his left-hand grip on Uke's left lapel, and places both hands on Uke's right arm; his left hand, palm up, cups under that arm above the elbow while his right hand grips from the top near Uke's wrist, to move Uke's right arm back alongside his body on the mat in the space created by what is now his right kneeling *shizentai*. Holding himself erect, Tori moves back the short distance he took for his entry step by sliding his left knee back, then his right foot.

Tori assumes *kyoshi* (open) and pauses momentarily with composure and quiet alertness, keeping visual contact with Uke's body, then moves backward

(1)　　　　　　　　　　　　　　(2)

two steps by *tsugi ashi* in *kyoshi* (closed) to the far position (about 5 feet from the right side of Uke's body) on the lateral axis and once again assumes *kyoshi* (open). He pauses momentarily with composure and quiet alertness, making visual contact with a point beyond Uke's body (on the *kamiza* side). Figs. (8)-(12). He is now ready for the next technique.

HADAKA-JIME

◆ ABOUT THIS TECHNIQUE
This immobilization, the naked choke, is classified as a choking technique (*shime waza*). Its name is derived from the fact that the judoist securing it does not rely on gripping his or his opponent's *judogi*, but chokes with the constricting effect caused by the leverage of his own entangled arms. The present-day form is similar to that adopted by the founder.

◆ PREPARATION FOR ENGAGEMENT
With Uke in the lying-ready position on the longitudinal axis, Tori, in *kyoshi* (open) on the lateral axis at the far position (about 5 feet from Uke's right side), keeps composure, quiet alertness, and visual contact with a point beyond Uke (on the *kamiza* side) as he slides his right foot inward a bit and stands up in *shizenhontai*. Simultaneously, Uke sits up to the sitting-ready position, folding his left leg with the outer thigh surface resting on the mat and the sole near the inside of his right leg above the knee joint, and places his hands, palms down, naturally on his knees. Pivoting in place 45 degrees to his left (toward his side of the kata area), Tori steps off with his left foot and walks diagonally to the far position (about 5 feet directly behind Uke, now at a *new* point to compensate for Uke's sitting action) on the longitudinal axis, and turns to his right (into the *kamiza*) to stand facing Uke. Immediately, but unhurriedly, he lowers himself and assumes *kyoshi* (open), then pauses momentarily making visual contact with a point beyond Tori's

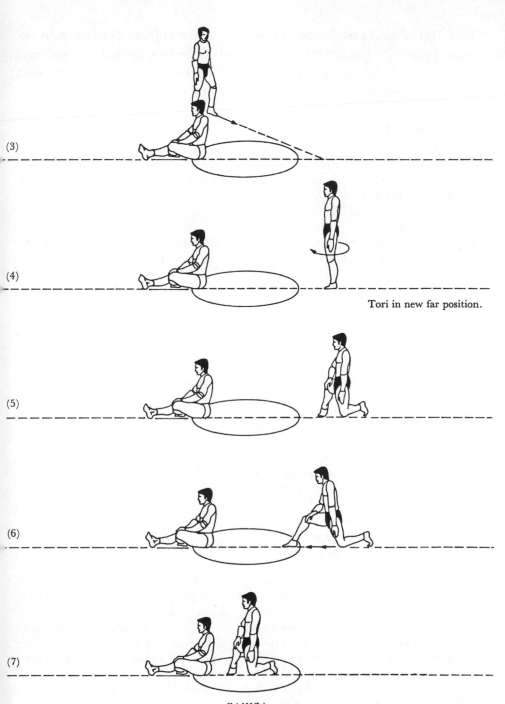

(3)

(4) Tori in new far position.

(5)

(6)

(7)

KAMIZA

feet. Tori advances two steps by *tsugi ashi* in *kyoshi* (closed) to the near position (about 1½ feet directly behind Uke) on the longitudinal axis, and once again assumes *kyoshi* (open). Figs. (1)-(7). He makes visual contact with Uke's body and maintains composure and quiet alertness.

◆ ENGAGEMENT

1. Takes a short entry step (right foot, left knee slides up), passes his right arm, bent at the elbow, over Uke's right shoulder, and brings the inside edge of his wrist (radius) against the left side of Uke's neck, palm down; simultaneously positions his left hand, palm up, over Uke's left shoulder.

UKE: Remains motionless in sitting-ready position, maintaining his position, yielding to Tori's efforts to encircle his neck.

2. Clasping his right hand over his left with palms together, bends his upper body forward a bit and positions his own head so as to press its right side against the left side of Uke's head (more or less ear to ear).

UKE: Remains motionless in the sitting-ready position, yielding to Tori's efforts to encircle his neck and place the form of the choke, as he takes a deep breath.

3. TORI: Signals that the choke is on by moving back a short distance directly to the rear by sliding his left knee back, then his right foot, bringing Uke, who is in tight contact, along with him; Uke is unbalanced and cannot resist the choke well. Simultaneously applies choke pressure against both sides of Uke's neck; the inner edge of his right wrist and forearm cuts into the left side of Uke's neck as he pulls his right arm in toward his own shoulder and at the same time presses the right side of his head inward against the left side of Uke's head, to drive the right side of Uke's neck into immobilization against his upper right arm.

UKE: Reaches up with both hands to grip Tori's upper right sleeve (much as he would for *ippon seoi-nage*), as he takes a deep breath.

TORI: Controls Uke's attempts to neutralize or escape, clamping his choke tighter.

UKE: At Tori's "on" signal, immediately attempts to neutralize or escape from Tori's choke by at least one method and possibly more. Being unsuccessful in his attempt to neutralize or escape, gives the *mairi* signal and ceases all escape actions.

TORI: Relaxes his tight control actions and choke pressure, but maintains the form of the *hadaka-jime* as he returns Uke to balance in the sitting-ready position by stepping forward the same short distance he withdrew to choke Uke, with his right foot, and then sliding his left knee up a bit.

Engagement.

1

2

3

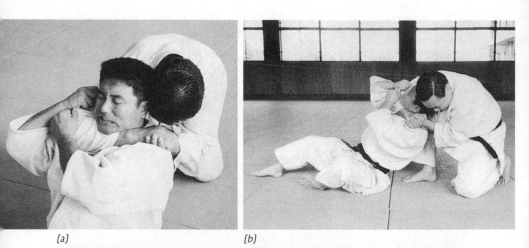

(a)   (b)

(c)

UKE'S SUGGESTED ESCAPE ACTIONS

1. Attempts to neutralize Tori's choke by pulling downward with both hands on Tori's outer upper-right sleeve (Fig. a).

2. Attempts to break the choke by pulling Tori's right arm upward and over his head as he ducks out under that arm; uses both hands to pull (Fig. b).

3. Attempts to turn around inside the choke by pulling with both hands on Tori's outer upper-right sleeve and by twisting his body to the right (Fig. c).

TORI'S SUGGESTED CONTROL ACTIONS

1. Tightens his choking action by squeezing and brings Uke further off-balance, straight backward, to weaken Uke's pulling actions (Fig. a).

2. Clamps down on his right elbow and drives his head more tightly against the left side of Uke's head (Fig. b).

3. Tightens the choking action by squeezing and uses his upraised right leg to check Uke's twist to the right by inward pressure of the right knee against Uke's body (Fig. c).

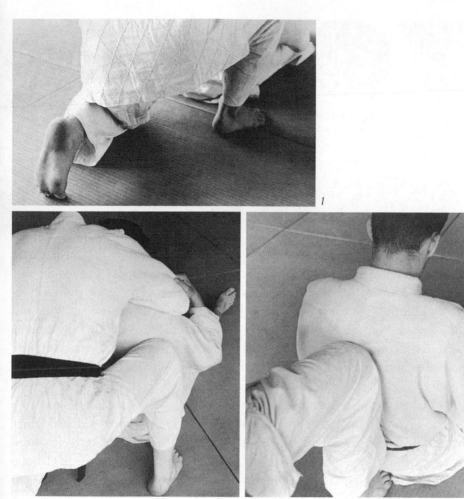

2

X *Wrong.*

◆ TECHNIQUE KEY POINTS

● TORI ●

Hold with the power of your whole body, which is kept unified by tensing your midsection as you choke. Do not rely solely upon the choke action of your arms to control Uke. Your legs are your base of power; keep them solidly placed in the kneeling *shizentai*; do not try to choke while in *kyoshi* (either open or closed). Your left foot rests on the sole surfaces of its toes; do not place your instep flat on the mat or you will have little stability, especially when Uke struggles to escape (Fig. 1). Your upraised right knee must not be used as a support in the middle of Uke's back, but is positioned a bit to Uke's right to keep him from turning that way (Fig. 2). (See Tori's control, Fig. c, p. 334.)

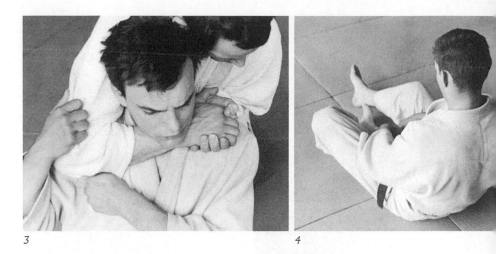

3   4

Seek to leave as little space as possible between the inner surface of your right arm and the right side of Uke's neck. The crook of your right elbow should point more or less forward, in front of Uke's right shoulder; it should not be positioned on top of Uke's right shoulder (Fig. 3). Pull Uke straight backward to unbalance him. Do this by your stepping movement; don't just rock your body backward with your feet in place. Bring Uke back onto his tailbone (Fig. 4). Place the right side of your head flush up against the left side of Uke's head so that you are ear to ear.

Focus your body power with a squeezing action into both sides of Uke's trapped neck; use your right arm and the right side of your head to effect the squeeze while Uke is off-balance backward. Think of your right arm as a huge nutcracker, with Uke's neck as the nut. If you have positioned your right arm correctly, you will be able to bring the inner edge of your right wrist against the left front of Uke's neck, where pressure will shut off the blood flow in his jugular vein; on the right side of Uke's neck, your upper right arm similarly affects his carotid artery. Do not merely crush his Adam's apple. The right side of your head must be pressed tightly up against the left side of Uke's head to push him deeper into the choke. Do not pry Uke's neck forward with the top of your right shoulder as you choke, nor should you push the top of your head behind Uke's neck to effect the choke. These actions can cause dangerous pressures against the spine. Keep your head-to-head position with Uke as you choke; straightening up your body weakens the choke.

○ UKE ○

Move with the power of your whole body, not isolated parts, when you try to escape. However, be careful and move slowly as you can be injured in the neck

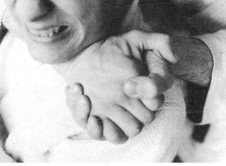

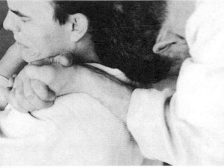

❌ *Wrong.*

❌ *Wrong.*

❌ *Wrong.*

❌ *Wrong.*

❌ *Wrong.*

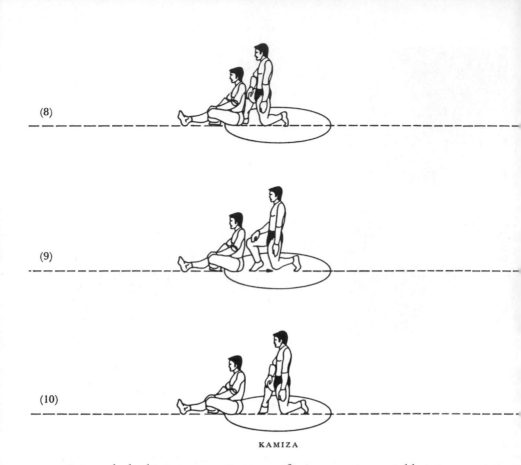

(8)

(9)

(10)

KAMIZA

region or choked into unconsciousness if you move too quickly into an escape action. Feel it out as you move in any direction, but once you finally move into a determined weakness of Tori, do so with the power of your whole body.

Seek to sit forward into a normal balanced position; do this by sliding your buttocks backward under Tori as you pull with both hands on his outer upper-right sleeve (as if for *ippon seoi-nage*) to neutralize the choke; use both hands. Escape is difficult and you may have to settle for neutralization at best. Give the *mairi* signal with either foot.

◆ COMPLETION

Upon Uke's *mairi* signal, Tori immediately but unhurriedly assumes *kyoshi* (open) at the near position (about 1½ feet directly behind Uke's sitting body) on the longitudinal axis. Tori does this by reversing the movements he made to get into the technique, in a natural way; he unclasps his hands and removes his right arm from around Uke's neck, and from the right kneeling *shizentai* moves back the short distance he took to enter into this technique by sliding his left knee back, then his right foot. Tori assumes *kyoshi* (open) and pauses

momentarily with composure and quiet alertness, maintaining visual contact with Uke's body. Figs. (8)-(10). He is now ready for the next technique.

OKURI-ERI-JIME

◆ **ABOUT THIS TECHNIQUE**
This immobilization, the sliding lapel choke, is classified as a choking technique (*shime waza*). It is so named because the judoist applying it uses both of his opponent's lapels, pulling them in different directions to achieve constricting pressure against the opponent's neck. This form is identical to that adopted by the founder.

◆ **PREPARATION FOR ENGAGEMENT**
With Uke in the sitting-ready position on the longitudinal axis, Tori, in *kyoshi* (open) on the same axis at the near position (about 1½ feet directly behind Uke), facing Uke, maintains composure, quiet alertness, and visual contact with Uke's sitting body. Fig. (1).

◆ **ENGAGEMENT**
1. TORI: Takes a short entry step (right foot, left knee slides up), slips his left hand under Uke's left armpit, and grasps the front of Uke's left lapel at breast level with his left hand. While pulling Uke's front left lapel downward, simultaneously runs his bent right arm over Uke's right shoulder, palm down, and across Uke's throat to grip Uke's upper left lapel as deep as possible with a normal grip, thumb inside, bringing the inside edge of his wrist (radius) against the left back of Uke's neck.

UKE: Remains motionless in the sitting-ready position, maintaining his position, yielding to Tori's efforts to encircle his neck and grasp his lapels.

2. Changes his left-hand grip on Uke's front left lapel to a grip on Uke's front right lapel at breast level. Bends his upper body a bit forward and positions his head

UKE: Remains motionless in the sitting-ready position, yielding to Tori's efforts to encircle his neck and place the form of the choke, as he gathers his energy and takes a deep breath.

Engagement.

(TORI)

so as to press its right side against the left side of Uke's head; the front of his right shoulder is up against the back of Uke's neck

3. Signals that the choke is on by moving back the short distance he covered in his entry step, sliding his left knee back, then his right foot, bringing Uke, who is in tight contact, with him; Uke is unbalanced and cannot resist the choke well. Simultaneously applies choke pressure against both sides of Uke's neck by bringing his inner right-wrist bone (radius) across the left side and front of Uke's neck; his left hand pulls Uke's front right lapel downward and a bit inward. His right hand pulls around in front of Uke's neck as if to pull over Uke's right shoulder. His grips remain fixed on Uke's lapels. Simultaneously with these hand actions, presses the right side of his head forward and to his right so as to drive Uke's neck forward and to the right, into the choking right arm and against Uke's own right lapel, into immobilization.

TORI: Controls Uke's attempts to neutralize or escape by clamping his choke tighter.

UKE: Reaches up with both hands to grip Tori's upper right sleeve (much as for *ippon seoi-nage*).

1

2

3

TORI: Relaxes his tight control actions and the choke pressure, but maintains the form of the *okuri-eri-jime* as he returns Uke to balance in the sitting-ready position by stepping forward the same short distance he withdrew to choke Uke, with his right foot, and then sliding his left knee up a bit.

UKE: At Tori's "on" signal, immediately attempts to neutralize or escape Tori's choke by at least one method and possibly more. Being unsuccessful in his attempt to neutralize or escape, gives the *mairi* signal and ceases all escape actions.

UKE'S SUGGESTED ESCAPE ACTIONS

1. Attempts to neutralize Tori's choke by pulling downward with both hands on Tori's outer upper-right sleeve. May also fight to return to a seated balance, shifting his hips under and nearer to Tori; may detach one arm to assist in this shift of body (Fig. a).

TORI'S SUGGESTED CONTROL ACTIONS

1. Tightens his choking action by sliding the gripped lapels simultaneously in opposite directions, and brings Uke further off-balance backward and a bit to the right to weaken Uke's pulling (Fig. a, p. 342).

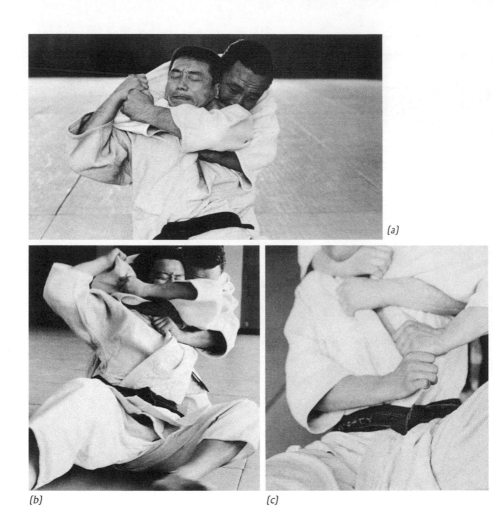

(a)

(b)

(c)

2. Attempts to turn around inside Tori's choke by pulling forward and upward with both hands on Tori's outer upper-right sleeve and twisting his body to the right or left as if to slip his head out from under Tori's right arm; may duck out from under (Fig. b).

3. Attempts to break the choke by pulling his own left lapel downward, gripping it with his left hand just below Tori's left hand; may maintain his right-hand grip on Tori's right sleeve, pulling downward, or use the right hand to aid the left (Fig. c).

2. Clamps down with his right elbow, increasing the pull of his right hand, and uses his upraised right leg to check Uke's turning action to the right with inward pressure against Uke's body (Fig. b).

3. Pulls harder with his right hand and clamps down on his right elbow, as he drives his head more tightly into the left side of Uke's head (Fig. c).

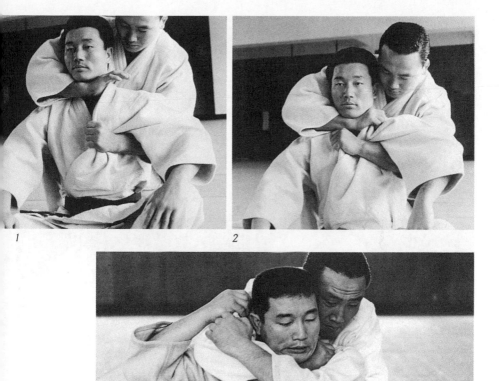

1   2

3

◆ TECHNIQUE KEY POINTS

● TORI ●

Hold with the power of your whole body, which is kept unified by tensing your midsection as you choke. Do not rely solely upon the choke action of your arms to control Uke. Your legs are your base of power; keep them solidly placed in kneeling *shizentai*. Do not try to choke while in *kyoshi* (either open or closed). Your left foot rests on the sole surfaces of its toes; do not place your instep flat on the mat or you will have little stability as Uke struggles to escape.

Seek to grip Uke's left lapel with your right hand as high up as possible, under his left ear; make this possible by pulling his left lapel downward and outward with your left hand, which has been inserted through and under his left armpit. Transfer your left hand to his right lapel by running your left arm below your right arm to grip his right lapel as high up as possible, just under

4

X Wrong.   **X** Wrong.

your right wrist and forearm (Figs. 1, 2). Place your right cheek flush against his left cheek (more or less ear to ear) (Fig. 3). An alternate head position permissible in this technique is to use the top of your head against the back of Uke's neck (Fig. 4). Pull Uke backward as you did for *hadaka-jime*, but also bring him very slightly to your right rear corner as you choke him; move your body backward by stepping, not just rocking back with your feet in place. Balance him on his tailbone, for in this position he is very weak and cannot resist the choke. Your upraised right knee must not be used as a support in the middle of his back, but is positioned toward his right shoulder to keep him from turning outward (right) and out of your choke, as in *hadaka-jime*.

Focus your body power with a shearing action into his neck. Pull your right hand with a twisting action (the thumb moves downward) around to your right as if you wanted to bring your right hand across the top of Uke's

(2)   (3)

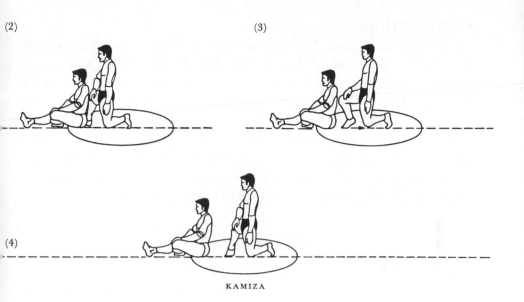

(4)

KAMIZA

right shoulder; do not raise your right elbow as you do this. Your right hand, firmly anchored on Uke's upper left lapel, provides the cutting action as the inner wrist edge cuts back into the left front of Uke's neck, while your left hand pulls Uke's right lapel tightly against the right side of his neck to constrict it. Keep Uke's head immobilized as you choke with the combined pressures from your right shoulder and the right side of your head, which may also push him more deeply into your choke. Have the feeling of squeezing Uke's whole neck as if you had a single cord around it and were drawing it tighter; do not just cut against his windpipe. Do not lose your bent posture; straightening up to make this choke weakens it considerably. Overbalancing Uke backward can also weaken the choke.

○ UKE ○

Move with the power of your whole body, not isolated parts, when you try to escape. Move against a determined weakness in Tori's technique; don't just thrash wildly about.

Seek to sit forward to a normally balanced position; do this by sliding your buttocks backward under and near Tori. You may detach one hand to aid you in this, using it as a prop on the mat; the other hand must continue to pull down against Tori's sleeve in a neutralization attempt. Do not just sit with your arms idle as Tori chokes you. Escape is very difficult and you may have to settle for neutralization. Give the *mairi* signal with either foot.

◆ COMPLETION

Upon Uke's *mairi* signal, Tori immediately but unhurriedly assumes *kyoshi* (open) at the near position (about 1½ feet directly behind Uke's sitting body) on the longitudinal axis. Tori does this by reversing the movements he made to get into the technique, in a natural way; he releases Uke's lapels, removes his arms from Uke, and, from the right kneeling *shizentai*, moves back the short distance he covered to enter into this technique, by sliding his left knee back, then his right foot. Tori assumes *kyoshi* (open) and pauses momentarily with composure and quiet alertness, maintaining visual contact with Uke's body. Figs. (2)-(4). He is now ready for the next technique.

KATAHA-JIME

◆ ABOUT THIS TECHNIQUE

This immobilization, the single-wing choke, is classified as a choking technique (*shime waza*). Its name comes from the way the judoist applying it uses the combination of a grip on one of his opponent's lapels and the leverage of one of his arms against one of his opponent's to create constricting pressure, in an action resembling a wing effect. This technique remains essentially as adopted by the founder.

◆ PREPARATION FOR ENGAGEMENT

With Uke in the sitting-ready position on the longitudinal axis, Tori, in *kyoshi* (open) on the same axis at the near position (about 1½ feet directly behind Uke), facing Uke, maintains composure and quiet alertness, continuing visual contact with Uke's sitting body.

◆ ENGAGEMENT

1. TORI: Takes a short entry step (right foot, left knee slides up), and slips his left hand under Uke's left armpit to grasp Uke's front left lapel at breast level with his left hand. While pulling Uke's front left lapel downward, simultaneously runs his bent right arm over Uke's right shoulder, palm down, across Uke's throat, and grips Uke's upper left lapel as deep as possible with a normal grip, thumb inside, to bring the inside wrist edge (radius) against the left back of Uke's neck.

UKE: Remains motionless in the sitting-ready position, maintaining his position, but yielding to Tori's efforts to encircle his neck and take his lapel.

Engagement.   1

2   →

→

(TORI)

2. TORI: Relaxes his left-hand grip on Uke's front left lapel and, turning that palm downward, slides the back of that hand along the underside of Uke's left arm, taking that arm outward to the left and then raising it as he pulls it backward. As Uke's left arm comes just above shoulder height, brings his left hand in and runs it, screw fashion, behind Uke's neck so that the back of his hand contacts the back of Uke's neck; thrusts that hand well under his own right arm. Simultaneously straightens up his body.

3. TORI: Signals that the choke is on by moving back the short distance he covered in his entry step, sliding his left knee back, then his right foot, bringing Uke, who is in tight contact, with him. His right foot slides

UKE: Remains motionless in the sitting-ready position, yielding to Tori's efforts to encircle his neck, raise his arm, and place the form of the choke, as he gathers his energy and takes a deep breath.

UKE: At Tori's "on" signal, reaches up with his right arm and grasps his own left wrist with his right hand.

3

(TORI)

a bit to his right rear corner; Uke is unbalanced backward and to his right rear corner, and cannot resist the choke well. Simultaneously applies choke pressure against both sides of Uke's neck by bringing his inner right-wrist bone (radius) across the left side and front of Uke's neck, pulling around in front of Uke's neck as if to pull his hand over Uke's right shoulder. His right-hand grip remains fixed on Uke's left lapel. His left arm and hand drive Uke's head forward into the choking lapel and immobilize Uke's head.

TORI: Controls Uke's attempts to neutralize or escape by clamping his choke tighter.

TORI: Relaxes his tight control actions and the choke pressure, but maintains the form of the *kataha-jime* as he returns Uke to balance in the sitting-ready position by stepping forward the same short distance he withdrew to choke Uke, with his right foot, and then sliding his left knee up a bit.

UKE: Immediately attempts to neutralize or escape from Tori's choke by at least one method and possibly more. Being unsuccessful in his attempt to neutralize or escape, gives the *mairi* signal and ceases all escape actions.

UKE'S SUGGESTED ESCAPE ACTIONS

1. Attempts to neutralize Tori's choke by grasping his own left wrist with his right hand to force his left arm down like a lever, to break the leverage of the choke. Does not fight to stay in balance (Fig. a).

2. Grabs his own left lapel below Tori's right hand in an attempt to pull that lapel out of Tori's hand and thus break the choke or neutralize the pressure (Fig. b).

TORI'S SUGGESTED CONTROL ACTIONS

1. Increases choke pressure by keeping his left arm screwed deep behind Uke's neck, pressing the back of his left hand tightly against Uke's neck for a firm anchor effect (Fig. a).

2. Increases his pull on Uke's left lapel with his right hand and increases his unbalancing of Uke to the right rear corner (Fig. b).

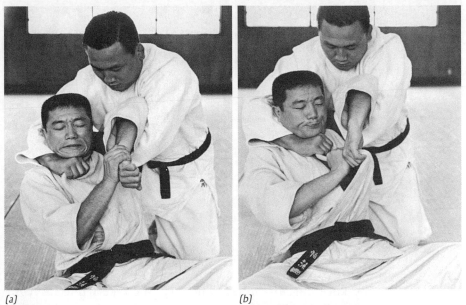

(a)   (b)

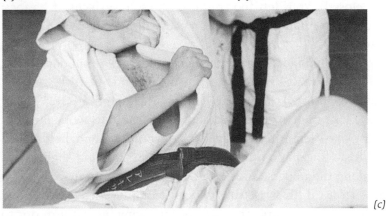

(c)

3. Attempts to take advantage of Tori's loosened right-hand grip on his left lapel by moving his buttocks out away from Tori, overbalancing himself backward into Tori, and ducking out from under Tori's right arm (Fig. c).

3. Restores Uke to a more forward position and clamps his right elbow down forcefully as he increases the pull and the thrust pressure of his right and his left arms, respectively (Fig. c).

◆ TECHNIQUE KEY POINTS

● TORI ●

Hold with the power of your whole body, which is kept unified by tensing your midsection as you choke. Do not rely solely upon the choke action of your arms to control Uke. Your legs are your base of power; keep them sol-

1   2

idly placed in the kneeling *shizentai*. Do not try to choke while in *kyoshi* (either open or closed). Your left foot rests on the sole surfaces of its toes; do not place your instep flat on the mat or you will have little stability as Uke struggles to escape.

Seek to grip Uke's left lapel with your right hand, high up under his ear; make this possible by pulling his left lapel downward and out with your left hand, which has been inserted through and under his left armpit (Fig. 1). Your left arm, in lifting Uke's left arm upward and out to the side, works in a circular fashion. Lift Uke's left arm with the back of your left hand, held flexed upward at the wrist (fingers pointing outward to your left and slightly upward). Slide it along the underside of Uke's left arm to a point well below Uke's left elbow (toward his wrist) to achieve strong leverage; do not just come up under or near his armpit (Fig. 2). As you swing his left arm out to the side and bring it upward, pull it back a bit, and then take it right up as you screw the back of your left hand, palm turned inward (facing you) with the fingers extended and together, up over Uke's left shoulder; the back of your left hand goes against the back of Uke's head and neck. Thrust your left arm well through and pass your left hand *under* your right arm (Figs. 3, 4). Your body must not be hunched over (as it was for *hadaka-jime* and *okuri-eri-jime*), but held upright (Fig. 3). Pull Uke backward and considerably over to your right rear corner as you move his left arm upward to choke him; move by stepping backward to do this, not by rocking back and to your right with your feet in place. Unbalance him in that manner and pull him close up against you so that he lies against your front lower body and inner right thigh. Your upraised right leg must not be used as a support in the middle of his back,

3

❌ Wrong.

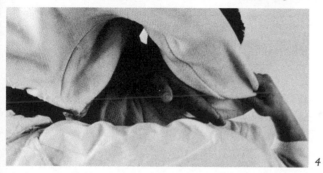

4

but rather slides backward and somewhat wide to your right rear corner to allow Uke to drop into this area. Balance Uke on his tailbone, for in this position he is very weak and cannot resist the choke. Do not overbalance him; support him with your body to keep him from turning out of your choke.

Focus your whole body power with a shearing action into his neck. Pull your right hand with a twisting action (the thumb moves downward) around to your right as if you wanted to bring your right hand across the top of Uke's right shoulder; do not raise your right elbow as you do this. Your right hand, firmly anchored on Uke's upper left lapel, provides the cutting action as the inner wrist edge cuts back into the left front of Uke's neck, while your left arm fixes against the back of his head-and-neck region. Your left arm does not primarily push forward and drive Uke's head into your cutting right-hand action, but plays a fixation or immobilization role. Have the feeling of squeezing Uke's whole neck as if you had a single cord around it and were drawing it tighter; do not just cut against his windpipe. Overbalancing Uke sideways and backward will weaken the choke.

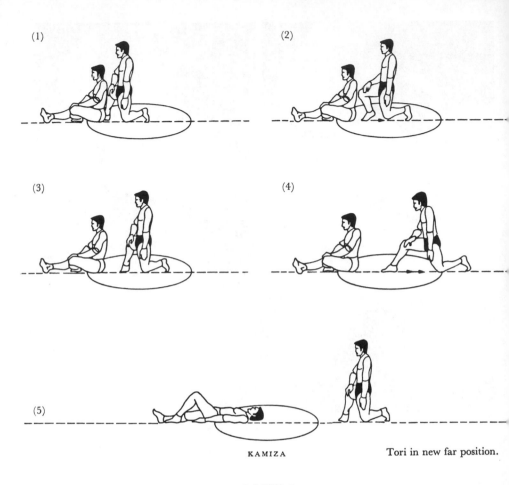

(1) (2) (3) (4) (5)

KAMIZA   Tori in new far position.

○ UKE ○

Move with the power of your whole body, not isolated parts, when you try to escape. Move against a determined weakness in Tori's technique; don't just thrash wildly about.

Seek to sit back and overbalance yourself, driving off well-placed feet. If you can loosen Tori's stability in his right kneeling *shizentai* you have a chance to duck out under his right arm and escape the choke, or at least neutralize it. Do not sit with your arms idle. Escape is difficult and you may have to settle for neutralization.

◆ COMPLETION

Upon Uke's *mairi* signal, Tori immediately but unhurriedly assumes *kyoshi* (open) at the near position (about 1½ feet directly behind Uke's sitting body) on the longitudinal axis. Tori does this by reversing the movements he made to get into the technique, in a natural way; he releases Uke's lapel, removes

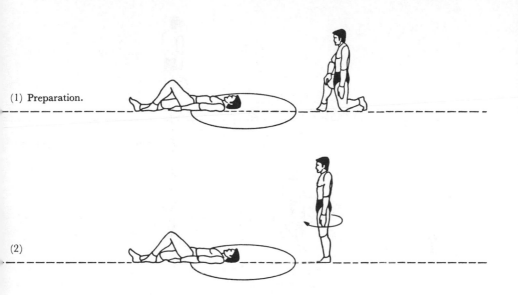

(1) Preparation.

(2)

his arms from Uke, and, from the right kneeling *shizentai*, moves back the short distance he covered to enter into this technique by sliding his left knee back, then his right foot. Tori assumes *kyoshi* (open) and pauses momentarily with composure and quiet alertness, maintaining visual contact with Uke's body, then moves back two steps by *tsugi ashi* in *kyoshi* (closed) to the far position (about 5 feet directly behind the sitting Uke) on the longitudinal axis and once again assumes *kyoshi* (open); once again he pauses momentarily with composure and quiet alertness, making visual contact with a point beyond Uke's body, which now assumes the lying-ready position. Figs. (1)-(5). He is now ready for the next technique.

GYAKU-JUJI-JIME

♦ **ABOUT THIS TECHNIQUE**
This immobilization, the reverse cross choke, is classified as a choking technique (*shime waza*). Its name comes from the way the judoist applying it grips with both hands reversed so that his arms form a cross or the Japanese ideogram 十 *ju*, meaning the number "ten." Today's form is a modification of the original, in which the right hand went under the left.

♦ **PREPARATION FOR ENGAGEMENT**
As Uke settles into the lying-ready position on the longitudinal axis, Tori, in *kyoshi* (open) on the same axis at the far position (about 5 feet directly behind the sitting Uke) facing Uke's body, slides his right foot inward a bit and

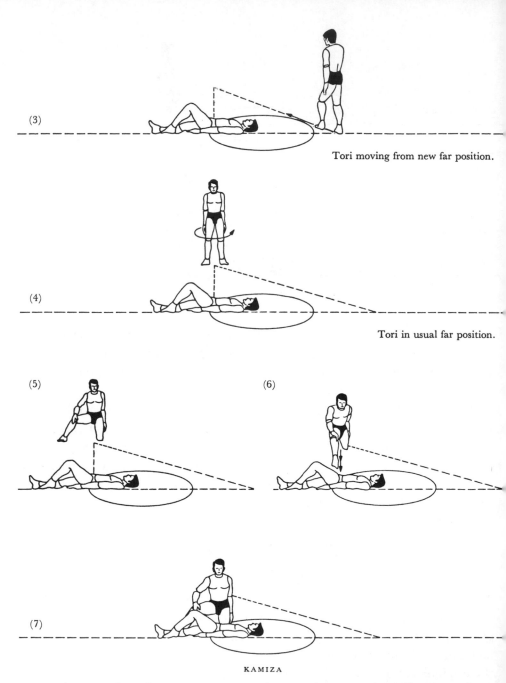

(3)

Tori moving from new far position.

(4)

Tori in usual far position.

(5) (6)

(7)

KAMIZA

stands up in *shizenhontai*. Pivoting in place 45 degrees to his right (away from the *kamiza*), Tori steps off with his left foot and walks diagonally to the far position (about 5 feet from Uke's right side) on the lateral axis, and turns to his left (toward the *kamiza*) to stand facing Uke in *shizenhontai*. Immediately, but unhurriedly, he lowers himself and assumes *kyoshi* (open), then paus-

Engagement.

1   2   →

es momentarily with composure and quiet alertness, making visual contact with a point just beyond Uke's reclining body (on the *kamiza* side). Tori advances two steps by *tsugi ashi* in *kyoshi* (closed) to the near position (about 1½ feet from Uke's right side) on the lateral axis and once again assumes *kyoshi* (open), maintaining composure and quiet alertness. Figs. (l)-(7). He makes visual contact with Uke's face.

◆ ENGAGEMENT

1. TORI: Takes a short entry step (right foot, left knee slides up) and picks up Uke's right arm with both hands; his left hand, palm up, cups Uke's arm from underneath just above the elbow, as his right hand, palm down, grasps Uke's arm near the wrist. Lifting Uke's right arm, places it on the mat alongside his left leg so that the arm is at approximate right angles to Uke; simultaneously moves his left knee up against Uke's right side. Keeping his righthand on Uke's wrist to prevent Uke from using that arm, relaxes his left-hand grip on Uke's right

UKE: Remains motionless in the lying-ready position, maintaining his position, but yields to Tori's efforts to take his right arm and left lapel.

(TORI)

arm and reaches across to the far left side of Uke, grasping Uke's upper left lapel deep under the ear, fingers inside, with the reverse grip.

2. TORI: Relaxing his right-hand grip on Uke's right wrist, reaches across Uke's body and inserts his fingers between Uke's left side and his left arm near the wrist; simultaneously brushes Uke's arm a bit outward (away from him) as he moves his right leg across to kneel, straddling and facing Uke. As he settles onto his knees, flattens out his feet so that the insteps rest on the mat, clamping them tightly there to restrict Uke's movement; simultaneously reaches with his right hand directly across Uke's upper body (not circularly around the top of Uke's head as in the *kata-jvji-jime*) and takes a reverse grip on Uke's upper right lapel, deep under Uke's right ear, with thumb outside and fingers inside.

3. TORI: Signals that the choke is on, applying choking pressure by pulling with both hands; turns both wrists inward, bringing the bony inside edges of both wrists (radii) against the sides and front of Uke's neck, as he pulls and squeezes with both hands. Simultaneously bends forward, dropping his body well over Uke to add his body weight to his choking efforts, positioning his head near or on the mat at the left side of Uke's head, but in so doing loosens his right-foot contact with Uke's left thigh or buttock.

UKE: Remains motionless in the lying-ready position, yielding to Tori's efforts to place the form of the choke, as he gathers his energy and takes a deep breath.

UKE: At Tori's "on" signal, immediately attempts to neutralize or escape from Tori's choke by pushing on Tori's elbows; hid left hand pushes upward on Tori's right elbow, while his right hand pushes inward on Tori's left elbow, as he attempts to lessen the constriction action and possibly duck out from the choke; simultaneously takes advantage of Tori's loosened control of his left thigh or buttock by bridging upward and rotating his body to his right. Spills

3 ⟶

TORI: Loses control of Uke and is unable to successfully choke in his straddle position; is then toppled to his left, onto the mat. Takes advantage of Uke's force, which is rolling him to the mat, by yielding and blending with it, and positioning himself on the left side of his back; engages Uke's body with his legs to restrict its movement; reapplies choking pressure by continued pulling and squeezing with both hands, spreading his elbows as he draws Uke's neck into his midsection to control Uke's final attempts at neutralization or escape.

TORI: Relaxes his tight control actions and choke pressure, but maintains the form of the *gyaku-juji-jime*, adjusting to initial starting position by rolling back together while in that form.

(UKE)

Tori out of his top position onto the mat by driving off his left leg, which is firmly placed on the mat, and twisting to his right in harmony with the upward push of his left arm against the choke.

UKE: Unable to regain his balance, is trapped between Tori's legs and is unsuccessful in further attempts to neutralize or escape from the choke. Gives the *mairi* signal and ceases all escape actions.

UKE: Yields to and assists Tori's actions to restore the starting position.

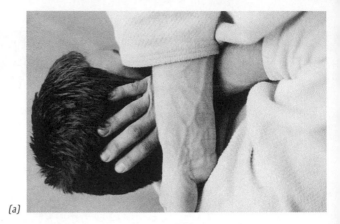

[a]

UKE'S SUGGESTED ESCAPE ACTIONS

Two escape actions (neutralization pressure and the dislodging of Tori) are built-in aspects of the technique already described. Another action is given for additional study and practice.

1. Attempts to neutralize the choke by twisting his body a bit to the left as he pushes his left hand upward, hard against Tori's right elbow; simultaneously inserts his right hand under Tori's right forearm and places the hand, palm open, flat against the right side or back of his own face and neck to relieve the choke pressure; dislodges Tori while retaining this neutralization (Fig. a).

TORI'S SUGGESTED CONTROL ACTIONS

Two control actions (increased forward leaning and blending with Uke's turnover action) are built-in aspects of the technique already described. Another action is given for additional study and practice.

1. As Uke twists to his left (Tori's right), clamps his left heel tighter under Uke's right thigh or buttock and pulls upward against Uke with that heel to impede the twist; drops his body well forward, positioning his head on the left side of Uke's head, and presses tightly up against it to thwart Uke's insertion of the right hand (Fig. a).

◆ TECHNIQUE KEY POINTS

● TORI ●

Hold with the power of your whole body, which is kept unified by tensing your midsection as you choke. Do not rely solely upon the choke action of your arms to control Uke; you must be able to immobilize Uke before you can apply effective choking. Your legs are your base of power and are primarily responsible for controlling Uke. In this technique we are reminded of the importance of the legs inasmuch as it is an exercise in what a temporary loss of Tori's leg control can do for Uke's escape actions. Deliberately lessen the clamping and pulling-up effect of your right heel under Uke's left thigh or buttock; you may even let your right foot rest idly on the mat alongside Uke as you apply the choke action (Fig. 1). Uke will be able to turn you over to his right because of the weak action of your right leg.

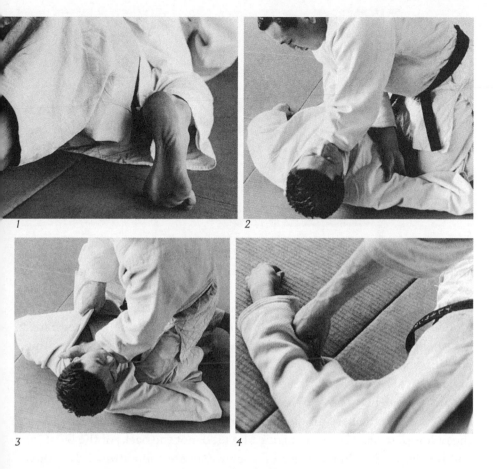

1

2

3

4

Seek to take the proper grips preparatory to taking the choke. After releasing Uke's right arm from your right hand, but before you come astride him, you may use your right hand to pull Uke's left lapel downward through your gripping left hand to remove any slack in the lapel. Then use your right hand to brush Uke's left arm away from his body so that your right knee will have a place to rest on the mat next to his body when you come astride him (this procedure is identical to that in *kata-juji-jime*). (Figs. 2-4). Both hands must be inserted deep on Uke's lapels, well back on his neck, gripping symmetrically with thumbs up; your right arm passes over your left (Fig. 5). (Notice here that the right-hand action for taking the grip differs from that of *kata-juji-jime* in that you reach directly across Uke's body to take the lapel). But you must use more than arms and hands to create choking forces. Launch your body well forward, out over Uke; if you attempt to touch your head to the mat a bit to your right (alongside the left side of Uke's head), the choke will be strongest. Uke is trying to neutralize your choke by pressing upward

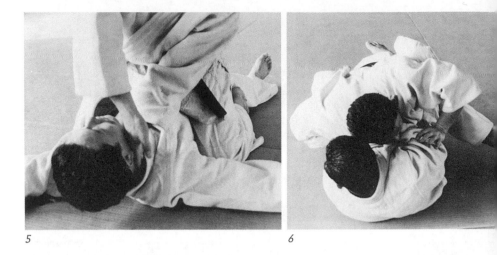

5   6

and over to his right with his left hand against your right elbow (while simultaneously pressing inward against your left elbow with his right hand), and takes advantage of your failure to use your right leg to control him; Uke turns you over onto the mat to your left. Blend with his action and reestablish control of him with your legs and feet, which grip and squeeze him, without crossing your legs. Do this from a position on the mat lying on the left side of your back, keeping your head off the mat (Fig. 6).

Focus your body power (initially, when astride Uke) as you did for *kata-juji-jime*. It is the hard, thin edges of your wrists which will do the choking; the radius portions of the wrists must be used, not the backs of the wrists and hands (Fig. 7). The inner edges of your wrists are the cutting edges of the choke, working symmetrically against the sides of Uke's neck; they are anchored on Uke's lapels, palms up, and both hands rotate inward (toward your thumbs) as you choke. Avoid making a collar which fits around Uke's neck and does little real choking; that is, do not let your hands slip so that the sides and backs of the wrists lie against Uke's neck. Once you are rolled onto the left side of your back (due to your lack of leg control over Uke), control Uke with your legs and choke him by pulling your hands in toward your midsection; bring Uke's head closer to your chest as you spread your elbows to complete the choke (Fig. 6).

○ UKE ○

Move with the power of your whole body, not isolated parts, when you are trying to escape; move into the prearranged weakness of Tori's technique—his lack of control against your left thigh or buttock with his right foot. Seek first to neutralize Tori's initial choking attempt as he sits astride you.

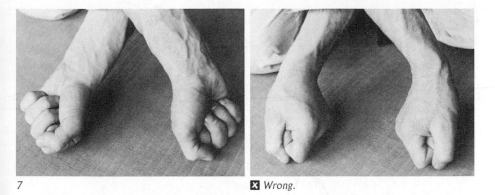

7   ❌ *Wrong.*

When you feel his right foot relax its pressure against your rear left thigh or buttock, roll him quickly to your right and tumble him to the mat; time this action with the pushing of your arms against his elbows. Try immediately to climb forward over Tori as you continue to neutralize his choke with both hands; push inward on his elbows. Try to get out from between his legs by moving to your right if you can.

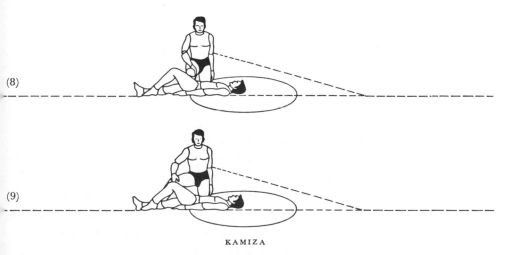

(8)

(9)

KAMIZA

◆ COMPLETION

Upon Uke's *mairi* signal, Tori and Uke cooperate in coming back to their initial starting positions with Tori astride Uke. Tori immediately but unhurriedly assumes *kyoshi* (open) at the near position (about 1½ feet from Uke's right side) on the lateral axis. Tori does this by reversing the movements he made to get into the technique, in a natural way; he relaxes his uppermost (right-hand) grip and pivots on his left knee to dismount from Uke. At the same time he uses his right hand to brush Uke's left arm to a position on the mat alongside Uke's left side. With his right knee raised, he slides his left knee a bit away

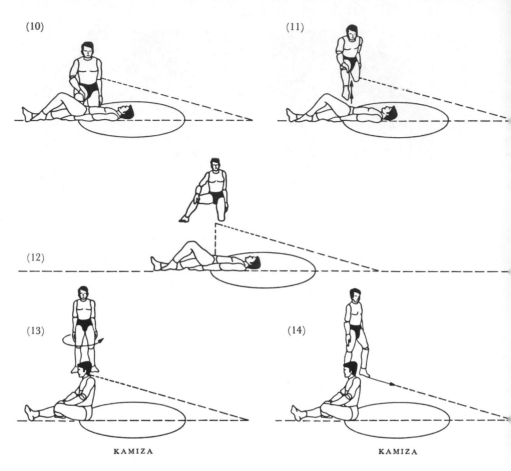

(10) (11) (12) (13) (14)

KAMIZA   KAMIZA

from Uke. He relaxes his left-hand grip on Uke's left lapel and places both hands on Uke's right arm, with left palm up, cupping under the arm above the elbow, and right hand gripping from the top near Uke's wrist, to move Uke's right arm back alongside his body on the mat in the space created by what is now his right kneeling *shizentai*. Holding himself erect, Tori moves back the short distance he took for his entry step by sliding his left knee back, then his right foot. Tori assumes *kyoshi* (open) and pauses momentarily, with composure and quiet alertness, keeping visual contact with Uke's body, then moves backward two steps by *tsugi ashi* in *kyoshi* (closed) to the far position (about 5 feet from the right side of Uke) on the lateral axis and once again assumes *kyoshi* (open); he pauses momentarily with composure and quiet alertness, making visual contact with a point beyond Uke's body (on the *kamiza* side). Tori slides his right foot inward a bit and stands up in *shizenhontai*; simultaneously Uke sits up, folding his left leg with the outer thigh surface resting on the mat, the sole near the inside of his right leg just above the knee joint. Tori pivots in place 45 degrees to his left (away from the *kamiza*) and steps off with his left

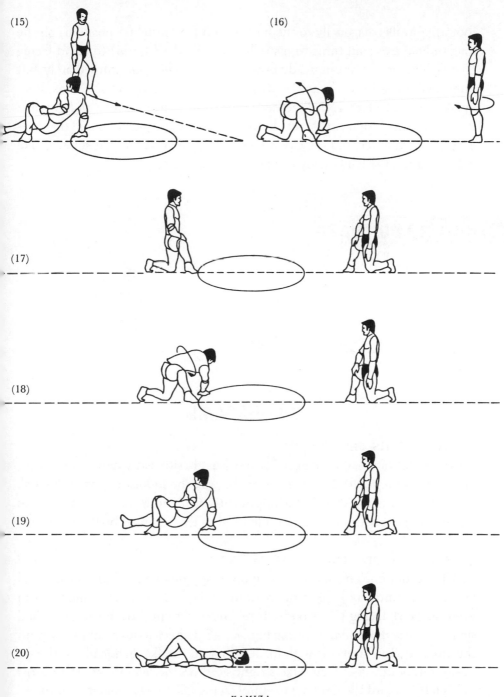

KAMIZA

foot as he walks diagonally to the far position (the usual far position) on the longitudinal axis, and turns to his right (toward the *kamiza*) to stand facing Uke (who is in the sitting-ready position) in *shizenhontai*. Immediately, but unhurriedly, Tori lowers himself and assumes *kyoshi* (open) just as Uke assumes *kyoshi* (open) to face Tori. Together they pause, adjusting their *judogi* while they maintain composure, quiet alertness, and visual contact, to end the category of choking techniques. Upon completion of costume adjustment, Uke again assumes the lying-ready position. Figs. (8)-(20).

KANSETSU WAZA

(1)

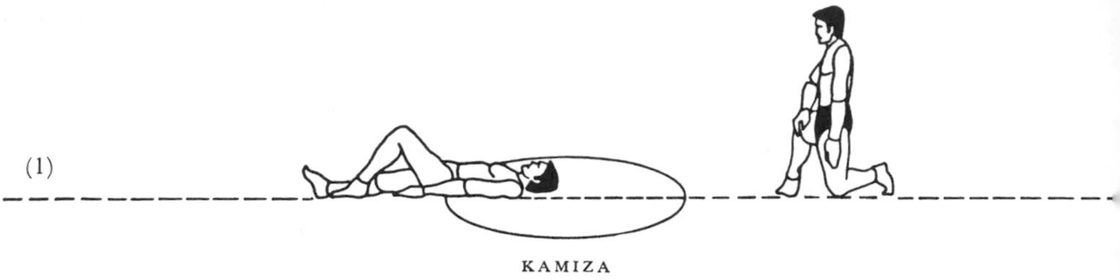

KAMIZA

UDE-GARAMI

◆ ABOUT THIS TECHNIQUE

This immobilization, the entangled armlock, is classified as a joint-locking technique (*kansetsu waza*). It is named for the way the judoist applying the lock threads his arms to entangle his opponent's arm and bring painful leverage against it. The modern-day form is identical to that adopted by the founder.

◆ PREPARATION FOR ENGAGEMENT

As Uke settles onto his back in the lying-ready position, Tori is at the usual far position (directly behind the reclining Uke) on the longitudinal axis in *kyoshi* (open), facing Uke's body; Tori slides his right foot inward a bit and stands up in *shizenhontai*. Pivoting in place 45 degrees to his right (away from the *kamiza*), Tori steps off with his left foot and walks diagonally to the far position (about 5 feet from Uke's right side) on the lateral axis, then turns to his left (toward the *kamiza*) to stand facing Uke in *shizenhontai*. Immediately, but unhurriedly, he lowers himself and assumes *kyoshi* (open), then pauses momentarily, making visual contact with a point beyond Uke's body (on the *kamiza* side), with composure and quiet alertness. Tori advances two

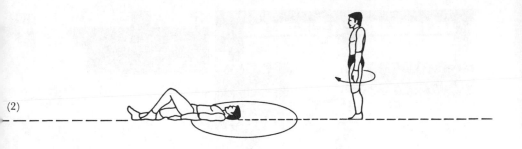

(2)

(3) 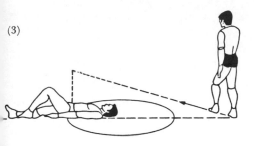 (4)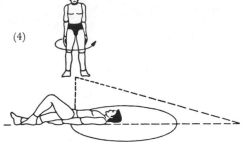

(5) (6)

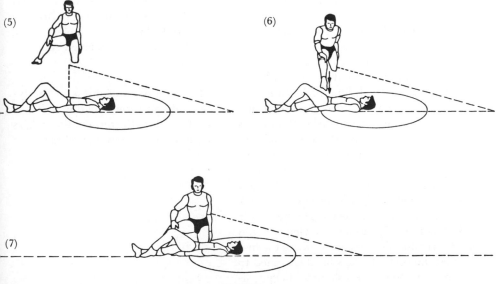

(7)

KAMIZA

steps by *tsugi ashi* in *kyoshi* (closed) to the near position (about 1½ feet from Uke's right side) on the lateral axis and once again assumes *kyoshi* (open), keeping composure and quiet alertness. Figs. (1)-(7). He makes visual contact with Uke's face.

Engagement.   1

♦ ENGAGEMENT

1. TORI: Takes a short entry step (right foot, left knee slides up) and picks up Uke's right arm with both hands; his left hand, palm up, cups Uke's arm from underneath just above the elbow, as his right hand, palm down, grasps Uke's arm near the wrist. Lifting Uke's right arm, places it on the mat alongside his own left leg so that the arm is at approximate right angles to Uke, bending forward to do so.

TORI: Removes both of his hands from Uke's right arm, and immediately attacks Uke's reaching left arm, sliding his left knee up against Uke's right side under the armpit, and bends his body forward as he kneels onto his right knee, wedging it tightly up against Uke's right hip; simultaneously deflects Uke's attacking left arm before it gets a chance to actually grip his right lapel. Grasps Uke's left wrist in his left hand, little finger up, the back of his hand facing him. Bending his body over Uke, falls forward, pushing Uke's left arm into a bent, right-angled position down to the mat so that the back of Uke's hand is pinned to the mat at about Uke's shoulder height; simultaneously drapes his body directly over Uke, pressing his chest to the right side of Uke's chest, and runs his free right arm under Uke's bent left arm from the elbow side, so that he is able to grasp his own left wrist with his right hand. His feet remain positioned on

UKE: Remains motionless in the lying-ready position, maintaining his position, but yields to Tori's efforts to take his right arm.

2. UKE: While Tori is occupied with placing his right arm on the mat and Tori's body is lowered, attempts to seize Tori's right lapel with his left hand, thumb inside, while making visual contact with Tori.

UKE: Remains motionless in the lying-ready position, yielding to Tori's efforts to place the form of the lock, as he gathers his energy and takes a deep breath.

2

3

(TORI)

the sole surfaces of the toes as he applies his body weight to Uke's upper body and pulls both of his hands inward a bit to bring Uke's trapped left arm to a slightly less than 90-degree bend at the elbow.

3. TORI: Signals that the lock is on by levering his right forearm upward against Uke's upper left arm above the elbow joint, as he pushes his left hand downward to keep the back of Uke's left hand on the mat; his body remains more or less horizontal and in contact with Uke.

TORI: Controls Uke's attempts to escape, keeping his posture as originally taken, without changing his technique, and obtains almost instant surrender by Uke.

TORI: Relaxes his tight control actions and the wrenching pressure of the lock, but maintains the form of the *ude-garami*, adjusting to starting position if necessary while in that form.

UKE: As he feels the wrenching pain set in, immediately attempts to neutralize or escape from the lock by at least one method or more. Being unsuccessful in his attempt to neutralize or escape from the lock, gives the *mairi* signal and ceases all escape actions.

(a)

(b)

(c)

UKE'S SUGGESTED ESCAPE ACTIONS

1. Attempts to bring his trapped left arm inward (and slip his elbow off Tori's right forearm) into his body. Bridges up onto his right shoulder in an attempt to neutralize the lock pressure and get onto his right side under Tori (Fig. a).

2. Attempts to twist his body to his left into the lock in an effort to neutralize it as he pulls his left elbow in close to his left side to lessen the angle (Fig. b).

3. Attempts to neutralize the pressure of the lock by bridging straight upward. Tries to bring his trapped left arm inward, close to his body (Fig. c).

TORI'S SUGGESTED CONTROL ACTIONS

1. Immobilizes Uke more securely by the combined wedging power of his left elbow against Uke's neck and the pressing of his left knee into Uke's right armpit. Pulls his right elbow in close to Uke's body to keep leverage above Uke's elbow joint.

2. Immobilizes Uke more securely by not allowing Uke's head to rotate to the left, using the combined pressure of his left elbow against Uke's neck and his left knee against Uke's right armpit. Also presses his chest more strongly against the right side of Uke's chest. Fixes Uke's trapped left wrist so as to keep the angle in that arm (Fig. b).

3. Increases his downward pressure against Uke's trapped upper left arm (Fig. c).

1

❌ Wrong.

2   3

◆ TECHNIQUE KEY POINTS

● TORI ●

Hold with the power of your whole body, which is kept unified by tensing your midsection as you apply the lock. Do not rely solely upon the lock action of your arms to control Uke; you should be able to completely control Uke without the pressure and pain caused by the lock. Your legs are your base of power; use your right knee as you did in the technique *oiyoko-shi-ho-gatame*, but notice that your left knee is used exactly as was warned against for that technique. Unlike *inyoko-shiho-gatame*, do not place your insteps flat on the mat; rather, rest your feet on the sole surfaces of your toes (Fig. 1). Leg changes are unnecessary.

Seek to intercept Uke's attacking left arm as it extends to grasp your right lapel; Uke attacks as you are placing his right arm on the mat (Figs. 2, 3). Deflect Uke's attacking left arm with your left arm; the outer edge of your hand contacts Uke's left arm at the underside of his middle forearm. Twist

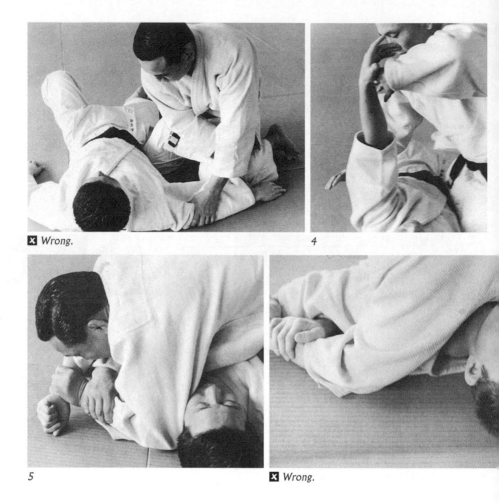

❌ *Wrong.*

4

5

❌ *Wrong.*

your left hand, palm downward, to sweep your left hand into full-palm contact with Uke's left wrist; grasp it firmly (Fig. 4). Fall forward quickly over Uke and insert your right arm under his left arm as you settle down over him. Control Uke's movement to his right (in toward you) by the wedging action of your knees up against his right side; if he bridges upward, use downward pressure from your body to negate it. Control his movement to his left (away from you) by the stopping action of your left elbow and the back of your upper left arm, which is clamped against the left side of his neck and head, preventing his face from turning to his left; if he can turn his head to his left he may escape (Fig. 5). Keep Uke's trapped left arm bent at about a 90-degree angle (forearm to upper arm), with the back of his left wrist and hand pressed down onto the mat about in line with his shoulders (Figs. 6, 7). You may grasp his left wrist with your left hand and your own left wrist with your right hand in a number of ways (Figs. 8-10).

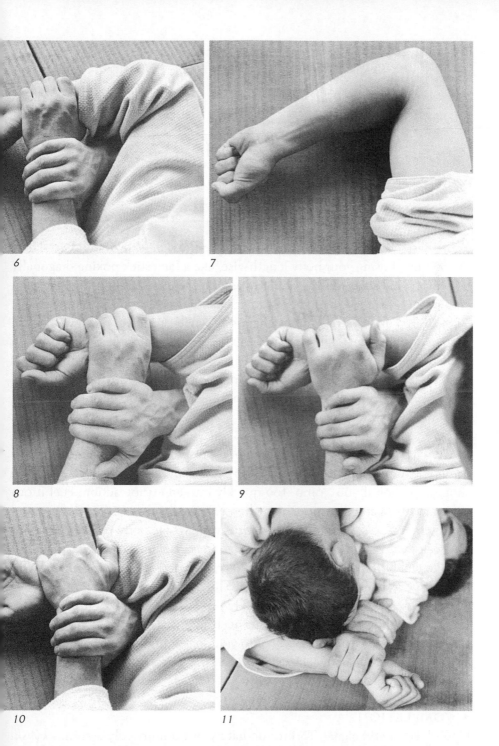

6

7

8

9

10

11

Focus your body power forward across the top of Uke, and down into his trapped left arm; your body lies over Uke, but not simply flat on top of him.

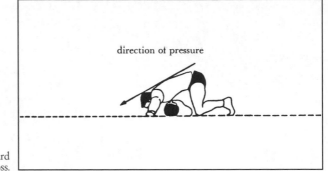

direction of pressure

Tori presses downward and across.

Your chest presses diagonally downward into the right side of his chest. Have the feeling of using your body lengthwise, like a long stick poking diagonally downward and across into his left arm as above; you may reinforce this action by pushing with the top of your head against the back of your right hand (Fig. 11, p. 387). Pull inward with both hands as you lever his trapped arm upward with your right arm, taking care not to lift your right shoulder in the process. Should you extend your left leg to aid in controlling Uke, it is best to tip your body a bit downward to your left by dropping your left hip, thereby cutting your weight into Uke from the top and bringing it to bear against his head.

○ UKE ○

Move with the power of your whole body, not isolated parts, when you try to escape. However, move carefully as you can injure your left elbow or shoulder region if you "jump" too quickly into an escape action. Feel it out as you move in any direction, but when you finally move into a determined weakness in Tori's technique, do so with your whole body power.

Seek to attack Tori's right lapel just as he is placing your right arm on the mat; he will have completed his short entry step and is in the kneeling *shizentai*, but has not yet released your arm. To lie there passively as he places your arm is to lose the opportunity. (Figs. 12, 13). Try to loosen Tori's left-arm clamping action against the left side of your neck and head, then turn your head to the left and try to twist your body onto your left shoulder as you pull your left arm in toward your body; perhaps you can use your right hand to aid in this action. Escape is very difficult and you may have to settle for neutralization.

◆ COMPLETION

Upon Uke's *mairi* signal, Tori immediately but unhurriedly assumes *kyoshi* (open) at the near position (about 1½ feet from Uke's right side) on the lateral axis. Tori does this by reversing the movements he made to get into

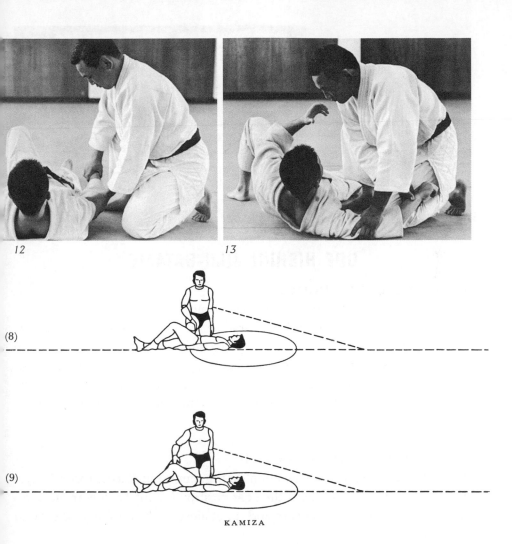

12 13

(8)

(9)

KAMIZA

this technique, in a natural way; he extricates his right arm from under Uke's bent left arm and also relaxes his left-hand grip on Uke's left wrist, sliding Uke's left arm by Uke's left side as he brings his upper body erect. Tori takes Uke's right arm with both hands, gripping it with his right hand, palm outward, near Uke's wrist and with his left hand, palm inward, just above the elbow; he raises his right knee to assume the right kneeling *shizentai* and places Uke's right arm alongside Uke's body on the mat in the space just created by the knee-raising action. Holding himself erect, Tori moves back the short distance he took for his entry step by sliding his left knee back, then his right foot. Tori assumes *kyoshi* (open) and pauses momentarily, with composure and quiet alertness, maintaining visual contact with Uke's body. Figs. (8), (9). He is now ready for the next technique.

Engagement.

UDE HISHIGI JUJI-GATAME

◆ ABOUT THIS TECHNIQUE

This immobilization, the arm-crush cross armlock, is classified as a joint-locking technique (*kansetsu waza*). For practical training purposes, its name is generally shortened to cross armlock (*juji-gatame*). It gets its name from the way the judoist applying it positions his body at right angles to his opponent's, the two bodies thus forming a cross or the Japanese ideogram 十 *ju*, meaning the number "ten." The technique is unchanged from that adopted by the founder.

◆ PREPARATION FOR ENGAGEMENT

With Uke in the lying-ready position on the longitudinal axis, Tori is in *kyoshi* (open) on the lateral axis at the near position (about 1½ feet from Uke's right side). He keeps composure and quiet alertness as he shifts his gaze to Uke's face.

◆ ENGAGEMENT

1. TORI: Takes a short entry step (right foot, left knee slides up) with intent to seize Uke's right arm, bending a bit forward to do this, but never gets past his entry step.

3. TORI: As Uke reaches for his upper left lapel, brings his body erect so that Uke misses his grasp; simultaneously catches Uke's right arm in both hands, gripping Uke's right wrist first with his right hand and then immediately with his left hand below his right, hands close together.

2. UKE: From the lying-ready position, reaches up with his right arm in an attempt to seize Tori's upper left lapel; makes visual contact with Tori but maintains his reclining body position.

UKE: Remains motionless in the lying-ready position, maintaining his position, but yields to Tori's efforts to take his right arm.

1

2

3 →

(TORI)

Stretches Uke's attacking right arm by pulling upward on it. Quickly moves his right foot into Uke's right armpit, wedging his instep tightly up against Uke; shifting his weight onto his right foot, sole flat on the mat, lifts his left knee off the mat and swings his left leg clockwise around Uke's head so as to bring his left foot to the left side of Uke's head, atop Uke's left shoulder. Keeping Uke's right arm fully stretched out upward, immediately sits back on the mat and rolls onto his back, taking care to sit close to Uke's right shoulder and to clamp his knees and thighs together, tightly trapping Uke's right arm as he rolls back, at right angles to Uke. Positions Uke's right arm with the little finger downward, next to his middle chest.

UKE: Remaining motionless in the lying-ready position, yields to Tori's efforts to place the form of the lock, as he gathers his energy and takes a deep breath.

(a)

TORI: Signals that the lock is on by pulling Uke's right hand to his chest and levering his abdominal region upward against Uke's right elbow by lifting his buttocks a bit off the mat; his whole body force is concentrated into Uke's right elbow joint.

TORI: Controls Uke's attempts to escape, keeping his right-angled position without changing his technique, and obtains almost instant surrender by Uke.

TORI: Relaxes his tight control actions and the wrenching pressure of the lock, but maintains the form of the *juji-gatame*, adjusting to starting position if necessary while in that form.

UKE: As he feels the wrenching pain set in, immediately attempts to neutralize or escape from the lock by at least one method and possibly more. Being unsuccessful in his attempt to neutralize or escape from the lock, gives the *mairi* signal and ceases all escape actions.

UKE'S SUGGESTED ESCAPE ACTIONS

1. Attempts to escape by drawing both feet under him and putting them firmly on the mat in order to bridge upward and, from that position, pulls (flexes) his trapped right arm as if to tear it from Tori's grips; twists his body to his right as he turns into Tori and tries to pull his right shoulder under him (Fig. a).
2. Tries to escape by slipping out from under Tori's controlling left leg, using his left hand to push-pull Tori's left leg out of position, then sitting up into the lock (Fig. b).
3. Attempts to escape by twisting his body to his left and coming up onto his knees to the outside of Tori's left leg (Fig. c).

TORI'S SUGGESTED CONTROL ACTIONS

1. Clamps his knees and thighs more tightly together and also wedges his right instep more tightly up under Uke's right armpit. Increases the downward leverage on Uke's trapped right arm by keeping Uke's little finger to his chest and arching his abdominal region upward against Uke's elbow (Fig. a).
2. Increases his clamping action inward, heel pulling hard against the left side of Uke's neck. At the same time increases the lock pressure by arching his abdominal region upward (Fig. b).
3. Increases the lock pressure on Uke's right elbow by pulling a bit to his right on Uke's trapped arm (Uke's little finger is turned to the right), and by more arching of his abdominal region upward (Fig. c).

(b)

(c)

1

◆ TECHNIQUE KEY POINTS

● TORI ●

Hold with the power of your whole body, which is kept unified by tensing your midsection as you apply the lock. Do not rely solely upon the lock action of your arms to control Uke; you should be able to control him without applying the joint-lock pressure. Your legs are your base of power; keep them in tight contact with Uke's body. If they simply lie loosely, you cannot control Uke properly and therefore cannot effectively lock his elbow.

Seek to intercept Uke's attacking (reaching) right arm as it comes straight up to grasp your upper left lapel; you must catch it before it does. Grasp with both hands (right hand slightly preceding left) at Uke's right wrist as you would take a right-handed grip on a baseball bat (right over left); do not grip his sleeve (Fig. 1). Stretch out Uke's arm even more than he intended by bringing your body erect simultaneously with the catch with both hands. Move into the lock by wedging your right instep tightly up under Uke's right armpit, toes turned inward; your left foot is still on the sole surfaces of its toes (Fig. 2). Move your left foot circularly around (not over) Uke's head as you sit down close to his right shoulder; your lower abdomen is a fulcrum

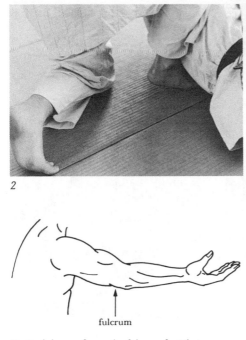

2

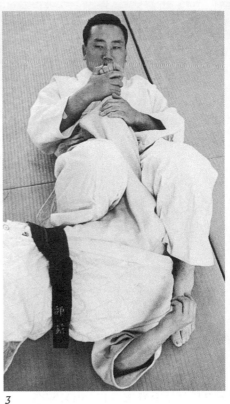

3

fulcrum

Tori's abdomen forms the fulcrum for Uke's arm.

placed above his elbow (Fig. 3). Clamp your left heel in against the left side of Uke's neck. Lie back into the lock and clamp your knees very tightly together; if they remain open, Uke can easily withdraw his right arm from your grip (Figs. 3-5). Pull his trapped right arm back with you and position it little finger downward, palm facing your right, the underside of his forearm tight to your abdominal region; try to bring his little finger to your chest (Fig. 6).

Focus your body power with a shearing action into his arm. Let the weight of your falling body pull Uke's arm into the lock; do not try to use arm power alone to force his arm into position. Have the combined feeling of wedging up under him with your right instep (to prevent him from turning to his right into you) and pulling with your left heel against the left side of his neck and head (to prevent him from turning to his left away from you); your feet must be somewhat pigeon-toed so that your knees may clamp hard together. Positioning your feet with toes pointing straight ahead makes it difficult to clamp . the knees together and thus offers Uke a fine avenue of escape. Complete the lock as you lie forming a curve (concave upward), with your chin in and head held off the mat. Raise your buttocks off the mat by bridging, enough

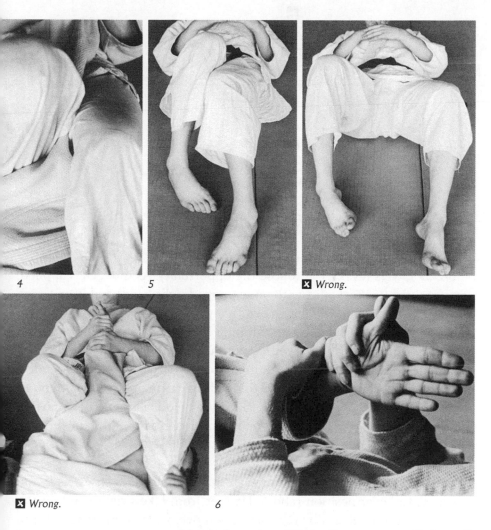

4   5   ❌ *Wrong.*

❌ *Wrong.*   6

to concentrate your upward body force into Uke's elbow joint; pull through his wrist toward yourself to increase the pressure.

○ UKE ○

Move with the power of your whole body, not isolated parts, when you try to escape. However, move very carefully as you can injure your right elbow or shoulder region if you jump too quickly into an escape action. Feel it out as you move in any direction, but when you finally do move, do so into a determined weakness in Tori's technique.

    Seek to attack Tori's upper left lapel just as he finishes his entry step and is reaching (or is about to reach) for your right arm from his kneeling *shizen-tai*; to lie there passively until he takes your arm, or to prematurely attack

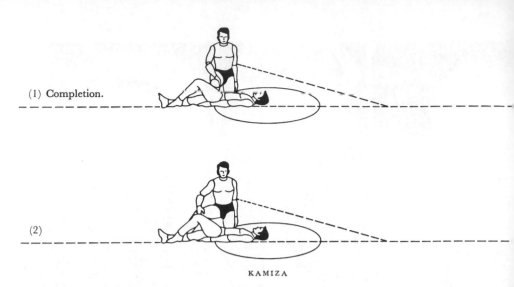

(1) **Completion.**

(2)

KAMIZA

before he lowers his body, is to lose the opportunity. As the lock is applied, flex your arm (making a fist with your trapped right hand) and keep trying to tear it from his grip. You may try to free yourself from his left-leg control action with your left hand by unclamping his knees or moving that leg, in which case you may withdraw your arm, sit up to turn into him, or twist onto your right side and out of the lock pressure. If you decide to go around to your left, keep flex tension in your trapped right arm and fist, but think of yourself as leaving your right arm in place and pivoting around it; do not try to tug it out of his grip. Escape and neutralization are very difficult.

◆ **COMPLETION**

Upon Uke's *mairi* signal, Tori immediately but unhurriedly assumes *kyoshi* (open) at the near position (about 1½ feet from Uke's right side) on the lateral axis. Tori does this by reversing the movements he made to get into this technique, in a natural way. He retains his hand grips on Uke's right arm. Tori sits up, positions the outer surface of his bent right leg on the mat and, leaning a bit to his right, swings his left leg around Uke's head and places it, bent, inner surface on the mat, at his left side. Tori then kneels on both knees, with feet resting on the sole surfaces of their toes, slides his left knee back a bit, and raises his right knee from the mat to assume the right kneeling *shizentai*. He places Uke's right arm on the mat alongside Uke, in the space just created by his knee-raising action. Holding himself erect, Tori moves back the short distance he took for his entry step by sliding his left knee back, then his right foot. Tori assumes *kyoshi* (open) and pauses momentarily, with composure and quiet alertness, maintaining visual contact with Uke's body. Figs. (1), (2). He is now ready for the next technique.

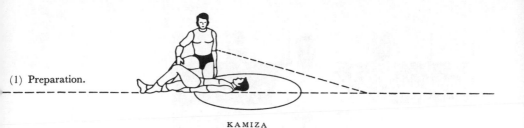

(1) Preparation.

KAMIZA

UDE HISHIGI UDE-GATAME

◆ ABOUT THIS TECHNIQUE

This immobilization, the arm-crush arm armlock, is classified as a joint-locking technique (*kansetsu waza*). For practical training purposes, its name is usually shortened to arm armlock (*ude-gatame*). It gets its name from the fact that, in the founder's original form (*ude hishigi zempaku-gatame*), the judoist applying the lock used his right forearm, not his hand, to achieve painful leverage against his opponent's trapped left arm; the lock was also applied after the opponent had taken his grip on the judoist's upper right lapel. Today's modern form is taken before the victim can grip and relies upon pressure transmitted through the hands, though the name implies otherwise.

◆ PREPARATION FOR ENGAGEMENT

With Uke in the lying-ready position on the longitudinal axis, Tori, in *kyoshi* (open) on the lateral axis at the near position (about 1½ feet from Uke's right side), maintains composure and quiet alertness. Fig. (1). He makes visual contact with Uke's face.

◆ ENGAGEMENT

1. TORI: Takes a short entry step (right foot, left knee slides up) and picks up Uke's right arm with both hands; his left hand, palm up, cups Uke's arm from underneath just above the elbow, as his right hand, palm down, grasps Uke's arm near the wrist. Lifting Uke's right arm and bending forward a bit, places the arm on the mat alongside his own left leg so that the arm is approximately at right angles to Uke.

3. TORI: Removes both of his hands from Uke's right arm, and immediately attacks Uke's reaching left arm by lowering his body still more so that Uke's hand over shoots its

UKE: Remains motionless in the lying-ready position, maintaining his position, but yields to Tori's efforts to take his right arm.

2. UKE: While Tori is occupied with placing his right arm on the mat and Tori's body is lowered, attempts to seize Tori's upper right lapel with his left hand, thumb inside, lifting the left side of his upper body slightly off the mat and turning a bit to his right to facilitate his reaching action; makes visual contact with Tori.

Engagement.

1

(TORI)

intended grip position on his upper right lapel; clamps Uke's left arm at the wrist between his right shoulder and the right side of
his neck and head by a shrugging, squeezing
action. Uke never gets his grip fixed. Immediately catches Uke's reaching left arm with
his right hand from the right, palm cupping
Uke's left arm just above the elbow joint
(toward Uke's shoulder), then quickly places
his left palm over his right hand and pulls
Uke's arm in toward him. Also wedges the
shin of his upright right leg tightly against the
front of Uke's midsection to keep Uke from
turning into him and relieving the coming
lock pressure.

(UKE)

UKE: Remaining motionless, somewhat
raised from the lying-ready position,
yields to Tori's efforts to place the form
of the lock, as he gathers his energy and
takes a deep breath.

2

3

TORI: Signals that the lock is on by moving his body slightly backward by *tsugi ashi* in the kneeling *shizentai*, maintaining the clamping action against Uke's trapped left wrist with his right shoulder and the right side of his neck and head: simultaneously pulls Uke's trapped arm in toward himself in an upward scooping motion as he twists his body a bit to his left, and draws up a bit more erect than he was at the catching of Uke's left arm.

TORI: Controls Uke's attempts to escape, keeping his posture and balance without changing his technique, and obtains almost instant surrender by Uke.

TORI: Relaxes his tight control actions and the wrenching pressure of the lock, but maintains the *ude-gatame* form, adjusting to starting position if necessary while in that form.

UKE: As he feels the wrenching pain set in, immediately attempts to neutralize or escape from the lock by at least one method and possibly more. Being unsuccessful in his attempts to neutralize or escape from the lock, gives the *mai-ri* signal and ceases all escape actions.

(a)

(b)

(c)

UKE'S SUGGESTED ESCAPE ACTIONS

1. Attempts to neutralize the lock pressure by turning into Tori and moving forward under him; loosens Tori's wedging right leg and may even try to bring his right leg up under Tori to hook and pull Tori into him (Fig. a).

2. Attempts to escape the lock by pushing his left arm upward and out of its trapped position by sitting up more, propping himself up on his right arm, and thrusting his trapped left arm over Tori's right shoulder (Fig. b).

3. Attempts to escape the lock by pulling his left arm downward and out of its trapped position by moving in closer under Tori and twisting to his left (Fig. c).

TORI'S SUGGESTED CONTROL ACTIONS

1. Wedges his right leg very tightly against Uke's right front, and increases the inward-and-upward scooping action of his hands as he augments his left turn (Fig. a).

2. Draws his body backward more by *tsugi ashi* in the kneeling *shizentai* to compensate for Uke's forward movement, but drives his right shin harder as a wedge into Uke's side to stop him (Fig. b).

3. Increases the inward-and-upward scooping action of his hands and turns more strongly to his left as he wedges his right shin more tightly against Uke (Fig. c).

Tori clamps Uke's wrist.

◆ TECHNIQUE KEY POINTS

● TORI ●

Hold with the power of your whole body, which is kept unified by tensing your midsection as you apply the lock. Do not rely solely upon the lock action of your arms to control Uke. Your legs are your base of power; keep them braced with your right foot wedging tightly against Uke's body; your left foot must always rest on the sole surfaces of its toes (Fig. 1). If your leg positions are bad you cannot control Uke's struggles due to your lack of mobility, and therefore you cannot effectively lock him.

Try to trap Uke's reaching left arm by clamping his wrist between your right shoulder and the right side of your neck and head; as he tries to grip, quickly lower your upper body more so that you can catch his wrist. Clamp

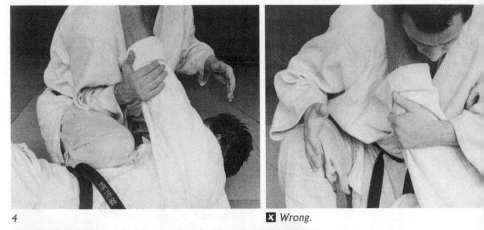

4

5

tightly; keep your chin tucked in (Figs. 2, 3). Simultaneously cup Uke's attacking arm just a bit above his elbow, with your right hand first, then rotate and pull it inward to your left; this "rolls" his arm and brings his elbow joint to its weakest position. You must master this circular action; without it, Uke can bend his arm and tear loose from your coming lock (Fig. 4). Your left hand, placed on top of your right or just below it, assists (Fig. 5). If you cup Uke's arm with your left hand first, he will be able to escape.

Focus your body power with a shearing action into his trapped left elbow. Pull with both of your hands, in concert with a step backward (*tsugi ashi*); twist to your left. Pull around and upward to your left, scooping inward (the power being transmitted through the outer edge of your right hand, which is just above Uke's left elbow), and bring your body a bit more erect as all this takes place. Have the combined feeling of pulling, straightening up, and wedging your right leg forward into Uke, as you clamp his wrist and twist a bit to your left (Fig. 6). Do not just pull inward with both hands, nor should you raise your chin during the lock. Your body must not hump over as you

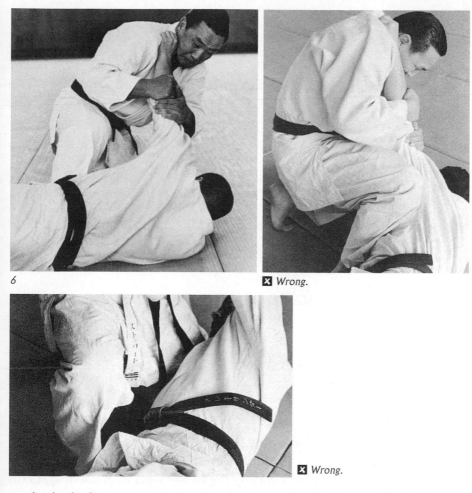

6

✗ *Wrong.*

✗ *Wrong.*

apply the lock pressure; sitting down on your left heel is equally bad. Don't lose the wedging power of your right shin against Uke's right side.

○ UKE ○

Move with the power of your whole body, not isolated parts, when you try to escape. However, move carefully as you can injure your left elbow if you jump too quickly into an escape action. Feel it out as you move in any direction, but when you finally move, do so into a determined weakness in Tori's technique.

Seek to seize Tori's upper right lapel just as he is placing your right arm on the mat from his kneeling *shizentai*; to lie there passively until he finishes placing your right arm, or to reach before he has taken it up in the first place, is to lose the opportunity. Quickly, as the lock comes on, crawl under Tori and raise your upper body to ease the pain somewhat. Try to dislodge Tori's wedging right leg, for this could lead to all sorts of opportunities to neutralize or escape.

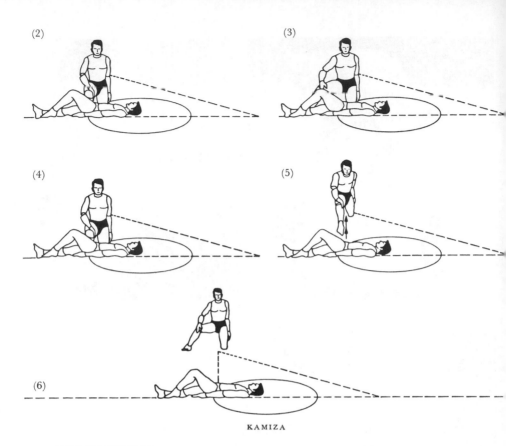

(2)

(3)

(4)

(5)

(6)

KAMIZA

◆ COMPLETION

Upon Uke's *mairi* signal, Tori immediately but unhurriedly assumes *kyoshi* (open) at the near position (about 1½ feet from Uke's right side) on the lateral axis. Tori does this by reversing the movements he made to get into this technique, in a natural way; he allows Uke to remove his formerly trapped left arm and return it to the mat alongside Uke, but then Tori picks up Uke's right arm, with Tori's left hand cupping the arm just above the elbow and his right hand on Uke's wrist from the top. Tori places Uke's right arm on the mat alongside Uke, while taking the right kneeling *shizentai* to create the space in which to do this. Holding himself erect, Tori moves back the short distance he took for his entry step by sliding his left knee back, then his right foot. Tori assumes *kyoshi* (open) and pauses momentarily, with composure and quiet alertness, keeping visual contact with Uke's body, then moves backward two steps by *tsugi ashi* in *kyoshi* (closed) to the far position (about 5 feet from the right side of Uke's body) on the lateral axis and once again assumes *kyoshi* (open); once again he pauses momentarily with composure and quiet alertness, making visual contact with a point beyond Uke's body (on the *kamiza* side). Figs. (2)-(6). He is now ready for the next technique.

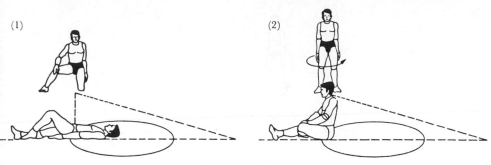

(1) Preparation.

(2) Usual far position.

UDE HISHIGI HIZA-GATAME

◆ ABOUT THIS TECHNIQUE

This immobilization, the arm-crush knee armlock, is classified as a joint-locking technique (*kansetsu waza*). For practical training purposes, its name is shortened to knee armlock (*hiza-gatame*). It gets its name from the way the judoist applying it uses the added weight and force of his body and leg transmitted through his knee to bring painful leverage against his opponent's trapped arm. The founder's original form required the lock to be applied from a left kneeling position, with the judoist gripping the sleeve of his opponent's trapped left arm and breaking the opponent's kneeling balance by pushing with his left foot against the right knee (which was on the mat). Today's modern form has modified these aspects.

◆ PREPARATION FOR ENGAGEMENT

With Uke in the lying-ready position on the longitudinal axis, Tori, in *kyoshi* (open) on the lateral axis at the far position (about 5 feet from Uke's right side), maintains composure, quiet alertness, and visual contact with a point beyond Uke (on the *kamiza* side) as he slides his right foot inward a bit and stands up in *shizenhontai*. Simultaneously Uke sits up to the sitting-ready position, folding his left leg so that its outer thigh surface rests on the mat, the sole near the inside of his right leg above the knee joint, and places his hands, palms down, naturally on his knees. Pivoting in place 45 degrees to his left (toward his side of the kata area), Tori steps off with his left foot and walks diagonally to the far position (about 5 feet directly behind Uke, now at a new point to compensate for Uke's sitting action) on the longitudinal axis, then turns to his right (into the *kamiza*) to stand facing Uke. Immediately, but unhurriedly, he lowers himself and assumes *kyoshi* (open), as Uke turns around to face Tori and also assumes *kyoshi* (open), at about the same time as Tori. They pause momentarily with composure and quiet alertness,

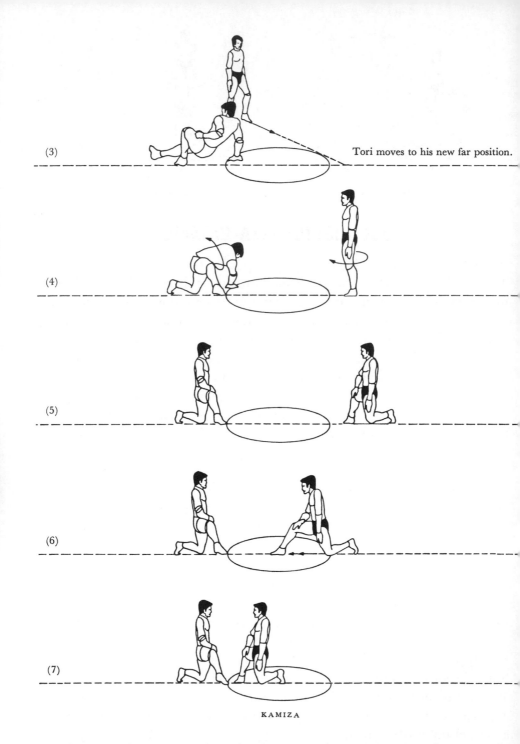

(3)   Tori moves to his new far position.

(4)

(5)

(6)

(7)

KAMIZA

making visual contact with each other. Tori advances two steps by *tsugi ashi* in *kyoshi* (closed) to the near position (about 1½ feet directly in front of

Engagement.

1

Uke), and once again assumes *kyoshi* (open), while they maintain composure, quiet alertness, and visual contact. Figs. (1)-(7).

◆ ENGAGEMENT

TORI: Duplicates Uke's reach for the standard grip as he moves a bit forward, into Uke, in the right kneeling *shizentai*; his right hand grips Uke's upper left lapel as his left hand grips Uke's outer right sleeve near the elbow. Grips just slightly ahead of Uke.

2. TORI: Relaxes his left-hand grip on Uke's right sleeve and passes his left arm under and inside Uke's right arm, so as to reach up and over, and gather it under his left arm. Clamps Uke's right wrist tightly under his armpit and cups a bit above Uke's right elbow with his open left palm.

1. UKE: Extends his arms to grip Tori in the right standard grip as he moves a bit forward into the right kneeling shizentai; his right hand grips Tori's upper left lapel as his left hand grips Tori's outer right sleeve near the elbow.

UKE: Obtains his grip.

2

(TORI)

TORI: Breaks Uke's balance forward by pulling Uke out over his left front corner (over his kneeling left knee). Immediately falls backward and to the mat into his right rear corner, onto the right side of his back; does so by moving his kneeling left leg so that the sole of that foot is firmly on the mat, near and inside of Uke's right foot, and using that new position as a platform foot from which to shift his weight. Simultaneously places the sole of his right foot firmly against Uke's upper left pelvis-and-thigh region (near the groin) from the front and, as he falls, pushes back a bit with that foot to keep Uke from coming forward. As he settles onto the right side of his back, maintains his two-handed grip as before the fall: his left arm clamps Uke's right wrist under his armpit and his left hand cups Uke just above the elbow as his

UKE: Remains motionless in the right kneeling *shizentai*, but yields to Tori's efforts to gather up his right arm; releases his right-hand grip on Tori's upper left lapel.

UKE: Loses his balance forward and is brought to the mat to his left front corner as he supports himself on his left forearm, his left knee, and the sole of his right foot; yields to Tori's efforts to place the form of the lock, as he gathers his energy and takes a deep breath.

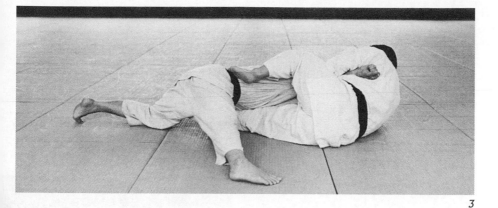

3

(TORI)

right hand grips Uke's upper left lapel. Swings his free left leg up so as to bring the inside portion of the thigh (near his knee) tightly against the back of his left hand; anchors his left foot on Uke's body near the belt line.

3. TORI: Signals that the lock is on by bringing pressure against Uke's trapped right elbow while he keeps Uke immobile. As he clamps Uke's trapped right arm under his armpit, pulls and twists his right hand inward as it grips high on Uke's left lapel; then, twisting his body more onto his right side (clockwise), pushes Uke backward at the front hip region with his right foot, while increasing the inward and lateral pressure with the squeezing action of his inner left thigh on the back of his left hand.

TORI: Controls Uke's attempts to escape, keeping his posture and balance without changing his technique, and obtains almost instant surrender by Uke.

TORI: Relaxes his tight control actions and the wrenching pressure of the lock, but maintains the *hiza-gatame* form, adjusting to starting position if necessary while in that form.

UKE: As he feels the wrenching pain set in, immediately attempts to neutralize or escape from the joint lock by at least one method and possibly more. Being unsuccessful in his attempts to neutralize or escape from the lock, gives the *mairi* signal and ceases all escape actions.

(a)

(b)   (c)

UKE'S SUGGESTED ESCAPE ACTIONS

1. Attempts to neutralize or escape from the joint lock by moving forward into Tori, thrusting his trapped right arm deeper under Tori's armpit; may take his blocked left leg back a bit and then try to disengage it from Tori's blocking right foot before coming forward (Fig. a).

2. Attempts to neutralize or escape from the joint lock by pushing Tori's blocking right foot to the mat with his left hand and then moving between Tori's legs (Fig. b).

3. Attempts to escape from the joint lock by turning to his left and withdrawing his trapped right arm from under Tori's left armpit (Fig. c).

TORI'S SUGGESTED CONTROL ACTIONS

1. Concentrates on blocking Uke from coming forward by stopping Uke's hips with his right foot. Keeps his blocking right foot high to avoid Uke's disengagement tactics and increases the pull with both hands to prevent Uke from moving backward for disengagement. Clamps his left arm down more tightly (Fig. a).

2. Keeps Uke in a state of unbalance just short of spilling onto the mat by pushing backward with his right foot high on Uke's upper thigh (Fig. b).

3. Strengthens his left-arm clamping action against Uke's trapped right arm; pulls hard and twists his right hand inward against Uke's neck to keep Uke from twisting to his left (Fig. c).

1

❌ *Wrong.*

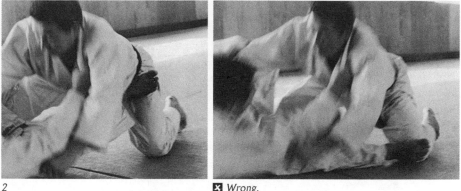

2

❌ *Wrong.*

◆ TECHNIQUE KEY POINTS

● TORI ●

Hold with the power of your whole body, which is kept unified by tensing your midsection as you apply the lock. Do not rely solely upon the lock action of your left arm against Uke's trapped right elbow. Your legs are your base of power; keep them in tight contact with Uke's body. If they simply lie loosely, you cannot control Uke properly, and therefore cannot choke him effectively.

Seek to gather up Uke's right arm under your left. Trap it securely by clamping down hard on Uke's wrist as in *kesa-gatame*. Cup Uke's right arm just above the elbow so that your fingers hook onto the bone prominences, to keep your grip from slipping; do not grip his sleeve, for if you do you will not know later where his elbow joint actually is, and thus it will be difficult to apply lock pressure quickly (Fig. 1). You must apply *kuzushi* against Uke; unbalance him well out over his kneeling left knee (his left front corner) before you sit back on the mat. Don't fall straight on your back; fall sideways and backward on the right side of your back from a deep crouching position using your left leg (fully bent) as a platform leg; continue pulling with both hands. Be very careful to place your blocking right foot properly; if it is placed

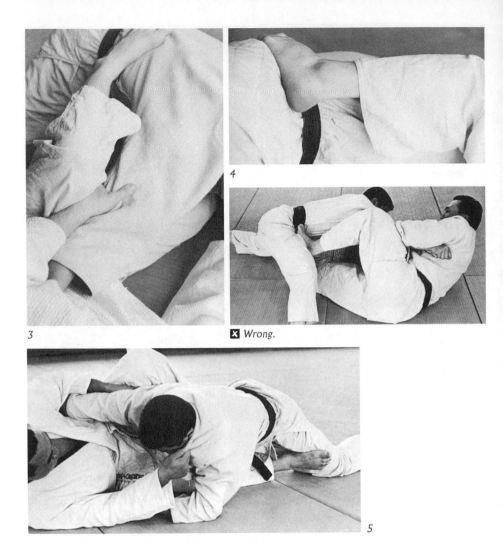

3

X *Wrong.*

4

5

too low—say, at Uke's knee—you will surely lose control of him (Fig. 2).

Focus your body power with a shearing action into Uke's trapped right arm at his elbow. Be sure to twist further onto your right side as you apply your inner left thigh (near your knee) to the back of your left hand, which now serves as a marker to instantly locate Uke's right elbow joint (Fig. 3). Continue the clamping action with your left arm. The placement of your left foot on the right side of Uke's back may vary somewhat depending on Uke's size, but generally you can anchor your foot on or near his belt line; do not put it on his raised right thigh (Fig. 4). The inward pulling twist of your right hand is vital and must be strong to keep Uke from going to his left; do not detach this hand or let it rest idly on his lapel (Fig. 5). Keep your body curved, with chin in and head off the mat.

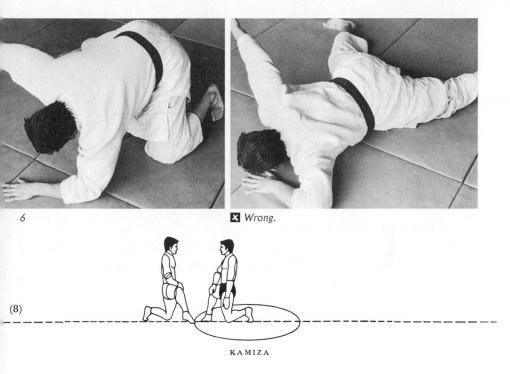

6   ☒ *Wrong.*

(8)

KAMIZA

○ UKE ○

Move with the power of your whole body, not isolated parts, when you try to escape. However, move carefully as you can injure your right elbow if you jump too quickly into an escape action. Feel it out as you move in any direction, but when you do move, do so into a determined weakness in Tori's technique.

Seek to fall to the mat and support yourself on your left forearm, left knee, and right foot; do not collapse face down on the mat, for there is little chance of escape from that awkward position (Fig. 6). Try to disengage from Tori's blocking right foot; you can then move forward or into him, or even pull away from him. Try also to slip away from the pressure of his right-hand grip on your left lapel; without control of your neck, he cannot stop you from turning to your left. Escape is very difficult.

♦ **COMPLETION**

Upon Uke's *mairi* signal, Tori immediately but unhurriedly assumes *kyoshi* (open) at the near position (about 1½ feet directly in front of Uke) on the longitudinal axis, fixing on Uke, who simultaneously assumes *kyoshi* (open) to face Tori. Tori and Uke do this naturally, by any convenient method. They pause momentarily, with composure and quiet alertness, maintaining visual contact. Fig. (8). They are now ready for the next technique.

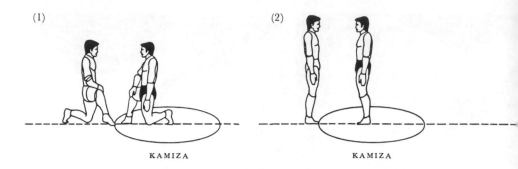

ASHI-GARAMI

◆ ABOUT THIS TECHNIQUE

This immobilization, the entangled leglock, is classified as a joint-locking technique (*kansetsu waza*). The name comes from the way the judoist applying it threads his leg so as to entangle and trap his opponent's leg and bring painful leverage against the knee joint. The founder's original form was a jujutsu "take down" which now is prohibited in the normal practice of modern Kodokan Judo, except in this kata.

◆ PREPARATION FOR ENGAGEMENT

Tori and Uke, in *kyoshi* (open), facing each other on the longitudinal axis at the near position (about 1½ feet apart), stand simultaneously by sliding their right feet inward and coming up into *shizenhontai;* they adjust to positions 3 feet apart (semifar position), with Tori in about the center of the center zone, and face each other maintaining composure, quiet alertness, and visual contact. Figs. (1), (2).

◆ ENGAGEMENT

TORI: Duplicates Uke's step (right foot), coming forward one-half step, and takes a standard grip in right *shizentai;* his right hand grips Uke's upper left lapel as his left grips Uke's outer right sleeve near the elbow. Grips just slightly ahead of Uke.

2. TORI: Unbalances Uke forward by quickly advancing his left foot deep between Uke's feet; without changing his grip, drops to the mat on his buttocks close to Uke's feet, simultaneously bending his right leg and placing the upper portion of the sole on Uke's central lower abdomen Attempts to bring Uke down and forward, over him..

1. Engages Tori by simultaneously stepping forward one-half step (right foot) and taking a standard grip in right *shizentai;* his right hand grips Tori's outer right sleeve near the elbow.

UKE: Obtains his grip.

UKE: Tori's dropping weight bends him severely forward so, being threatened with unbalance in that direction, quickly moves his right foot a bit forward to nullify Tori's takedown action; places his right foot fully on the mat near Tori's left armpit. Brac

Engagement.

1

2

→ 3

TORI: Yields to Uke's attempt to lift him up off the mat, but takes advantage of this force to slide deeper under Uke; pulls with both hands and swings his buttocks under Uke, allowing his left foot to come off the mat, and extends that leg deep between Uke's legs.

TORI: Shifts his right foot from Uke's mid-section to Uke's front-and-inner middle left thigh. Pushes Uke's left leg backward and out to Uke's left rear corner (in the direction of Uke's turn) and twists onto his right side. Uke's balance worsens, then Uke begins to fall to the mat. Continues the pushing action with his right foot but quickly coils his left leg up behind Uke's straightened right leg and passes it over from the outside, around and in front of Uke's right thigh. Continues this coiling action and thrusts the foot through and under Uke so that the instep is in contact with Uke's midsection.

3. TORI: Signals that the lock is on by pulling with both hands without relaxing his original grips, and brings pressure and leverage against Uke's trapped right knee joint by pushing with and straightening out both of his legs while he keeps Uke immobile.

TORI: Controls Uke's attempts to escape, keeping his posture and balance without

(UKE)

ing hard with both legs, resists the take-down attempt and tries to pull Tori up off the mat; pulls with both hands and attempts to straighten up his upper body.

UKE: Maintains his braced position with legs wide apart; is not perfectly erect. Keeping his feet in place, turns a bit to his left and leans to his left rear corner, thereby extending and straightening his right leg in an attempt to pull away from Tori; retains his hand grips.

UKE: Loses his balance forward as his left leg is driven out and back to his left rear corner. Falls to the mat to his left front corner and supports himself on his left forearm, left knee, and right foot; yields to Tori's efforts to place the form of the lock as he gathers his energy and takes a deep breath.

UKE: *As* he feels the wrenching pain set in, immediately attempts to neutralize or escape from the joint lock by at least one method and possibly more. Being unsuccessful in his attempts to neutralize or escape from the lock, gives the *mairi* signal and ceases all escape actions.

(a)

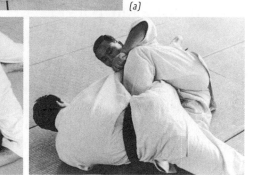

(b)   (c)

changing his technique and obtains almost instant surrender by Uke.

TORI: Relaxes his tight control action and the wrenching pressure of the lock, but maintains the *ashi-garami* form, adjusting to starting position if necessary while in that form.

UKE'S SUGGESTED ESCAPE ACTIONS

1. Attempts to escape from the lock pressure by turning to his left rear corner still more, and to bend his trapped right leg and withdraw it from entanglement by Tori, then stand up (Fig. a).

2. Attempts to dodge or avoid Tori's blocking right foot, which is breaking his balance; does this by using his left hand to push Tori's right leg loose and out of contact with his left thigh (Fig. b).

3. Falls to the mat face down and tries to escape from the lock pressure by dislodging Tori's blocking right foot and moving in closer to Tori (Fig. c).

TORI'S SUGGESTED CONTROL ACTIONS

1. Increases his pulling actions, especially with his right hand, to negate Uke's twist and backward movement; maintains pushing pressure with both legs to keep Uke unbalanced (Fig. a).

2. Keeps Uke unbalanced and well forward so that Uke cannot use his left hand to dislodge the blocking right foot; does this with his hand pull while not overpushing with his right foot (Fig. b).

3. Is careful not to lose his blocking right foot's contact with Uke's left thigh; twists further onto his right side to increase the lock pressure (Fig. c).

◆ TECHNIQUE KEY POINTS

● TORI ●

Hold with the power of your whole body, which is kept unified by tensing your midsection as you apply the lock. Do not rely solely upon your hands to control Uke. Your legs are your base of power; keep them both in proper contact with Uke's body. If they do not work together, or if your blocking right foot is loosely placed, you cannot control Uke properly and therefore cannot lock him effectively.

Seek to thoroughly understand the preliminaries to the lock itself. You are engaged with Uke in the standard grip from right *shizentai* and must try to break his balance forward; step deep between his legs with your left foot and pull with both hands as you sit down on the mat (Figs. 1, 2). You are *not* making an attempt at *tomoe-nage*; you are simply pulling Uke forward and down as you apply your body in what can be called a *tomoe* position. This is an old jujutsu take-down method which the founder of Judo preserved for the purposes of this kata. It must be an honest attempt to break Uke forward, not to throw him. Next, make good use of Uke's bracing action as he attempts to pick you up bodily off the mat; swing in under him, pendulum-like, as he lifts. Get your buttocks well under Uke to facilitate the left-leg coiling action that follows, making sure that your right foot remains in his midsection and that your left leg goes well through his legs (Figs. 2, 3). The order of action from here on is important: while on your back in a *tomoe* position, begin to lift your left leg behind and around from outside Uke's right leg. At the same time, remove your right foot from his midsection and thrust its sole against Uke's front-and-inner left thigh, about halfway up the thigh. Push out and back. Combined with your continued pulling actions, this will drop Uke forward onto the mat (Figs. 4, 5). As his balance crumbles and he falls forward, twist further onto your right side and simultaneously swing your left leg over his now straightened right leg, coiling it over and through so that your instep is wedged tightly against his midsection (Fig. 6). Do not lie on your back and attempt to coil your left leg. Notice also that you must time the coiling action to begin *slightly after* the

2

3

4

5

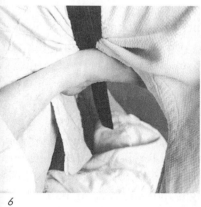

6

7

8   9   10

thrust of your right foot, when Uke is on his way to the mat; coiling before you break him to the mat, or after he has landed, increases the difficulty of this action. Lie curved, head up, chin in, as you apply the lock.

Focus your body power into Uke's trapped right knee by thrusting with both legs and pulling with both hands. Bring Uke to the mat so that he supports himself on his left forearm; your right foot keeps him from coming forward while your right hand keeps him from turning to his left (Fig. 7). If you overbalance Uke and he flattens out on the mat, you may lose the effect of your right foot.

○ UKE ○

Move with the power of your whole body, not isolated parts, when you are trying to escape. However, move carefully as you can injure your right knee and hip regions if you jump too quickly into an escape action. Feel it out as you move in any direction, but when you finally move, do so into a determined weakness in Tori's technique.

Seek to thoroughly understand the preliminaries to the lock itself. From your engagement in the standard grip in right *shizentai*, an action which you initiate, you immediately lose the attack initiative as Tori beats you to the grips. You must stop Tori from pulling you forward and down. Do this by resistance to his actions, stepping forward with your right foot and bracing hard off it. Then haul back, attempting to pick him up off the mat by pulling and straightening your body. As he swings deeper under you, turn to your left rear corner and bend away from Tori (without moving your feet) as if to walk away from him and out of the anticipated danger of the coming lock. Your actions here can be summarized as: step and brace; lift and pull; turn (Figs. 8-10). As you are broken forward to the mat, do not spill face down with body flat on the mat surface, but support yourself as you did for *hiza-gatame* on your left forearm, left knee, and right foot, sole on the mat. Once in the lock your best hope is to destroy the control exerted by Tori's blocking right foot and come forward, or to evade Tori's restrictive right-hand action so as to turn further to your left, bend your trapped right leg, and pull it out of the lock. Escape is difficult.

◆ COMPLETION

Upon Uke's *mairi* signal, Tori immediately but unhurriedly assumes *kyoshi* (open) at the semifar position (about 3 feet directly in front of Uke) on the longitudinal axis, fixing on Uke, who simultaneously assumes *kyoshi* (open)

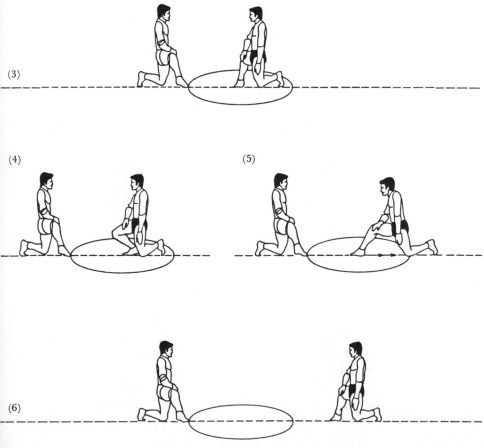

(3)

(4)   (5)

(6)

KAMIZA

and faces Tori. Tori and Uke do this naturally, by any convenient method, taking care that Tori stations himself at the center of the center zone. Uke holds fast; Tori retreats two steps by *tsugi ashi* in *kyoshi* (closed) to his approximate engagement position on the longitudinal axis and there once again assumes *kyoshi* (open). They pause momentarily with composure and quiet alertness, maintaining visual contact with each other, adjusting their *judogi*, to end the final category, the joint-locking techniques. Figs. (3)-(6). They are now ready to close the kata.

◆ CLOSING
Both Tori and Uke face each other in *kyoshi* (open) on the longitudinal axis, Tori positioned at his approximate engagement position and Uke approximately on his edge of the center zone. Fig. (1).

As Tori holds fast, Uke retreats one step by *tsugi ashi* in *kyoshi* (closed) and then once again assumes *kyoshi* (open), now positioned at his approximate engagement position. Figs. (2), (3). They pause momentarily with composure and quiet alertness, maintaining visual contact.

Tori and Uke stand up in *shizenhontai*, simultaneously and unhurriedly; they do this by sliding their right feet a bit inward and then standing. Fig. (4). They are careful to keep composure and quiet alertness as well as visual contact.

Standing in *shizenhontai* at their approximate engagement positions, Tori and Uke simultaneously take one step backward, beginning with their right

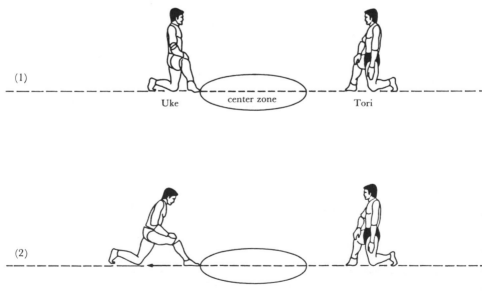

(1) Uke   center zone   Tori

(2) KAMIZA

feet, to bring them to their approximate salutation positions with heels together, toes pointing outward naturally. They pause momentarily in this position, with composure and quiet alertness, maintaining visual contact. Figs. (5), (6).

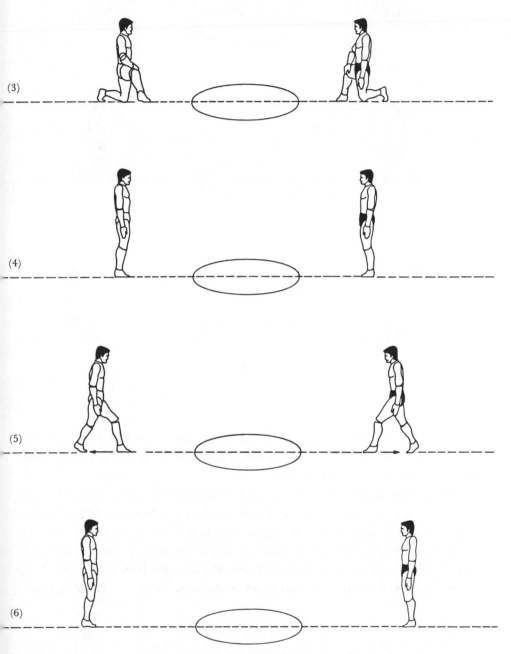

KAMIZA

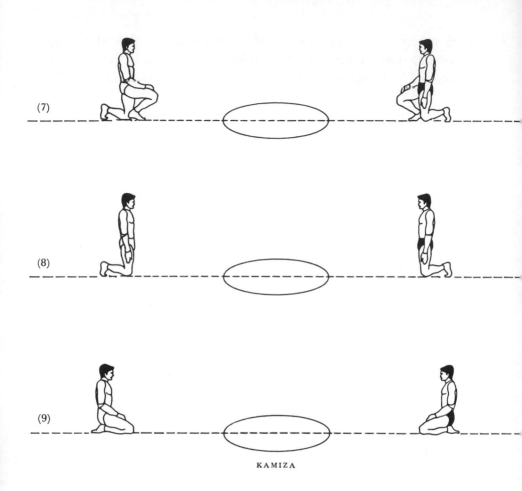

(7)

(8)

(9)

KAMIZA

They simultaneously kneel and assume the kneeling-sitting position (*seiza*). Figs. (7)-(9). They pause once more momentarily, maintaining composure, quiet alertness, and visual contact.

They execute the sitting salutation (*zarei*) together. Fig. (10). Then, simultaneously, they return to the kneeling-sitting position. Fig. (11). There is another momentary pause with composure, quiet alertness, and visual contact.

Simultaneously, they rise in place, coming to a standing position once again, with heels together, toes pointing outward naturally. Figs. (12)-(14). They pause again with composure and quiet alertness, maintaining visual contact.

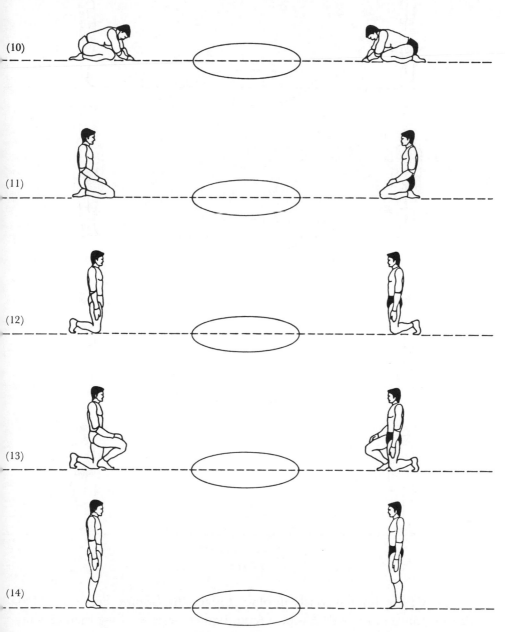

(10)

(11)

(12)

(13)

(14)

KAMIZA

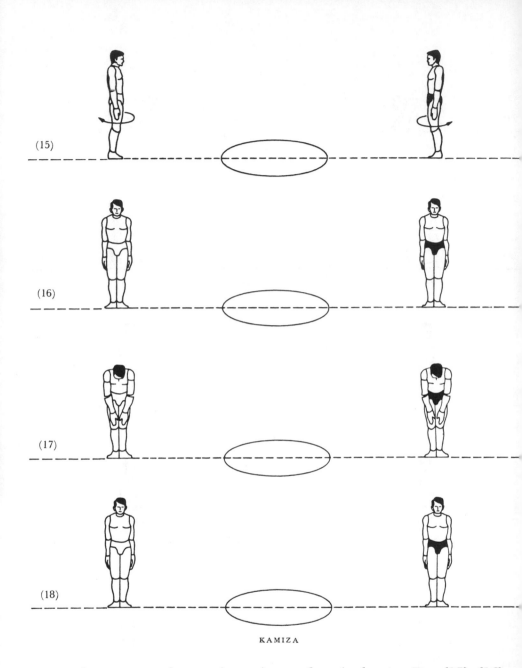

KAMIZA

They turn simultaneously in place to face the *kamiza*. Figs. (15), (16). Pausing, once more with composure and quiet alertness, they then execute the standing salutation (*ritsurei*) together, to the *kamiza*. Fig. (17). Simultaneously they return to the erect position, facing the *kamiza*. Fig. (18). Then they leave the practice area.

CHAPTER **10**

The Study and Practice of Kata

It's the singer, not the song.
—ANONYMOUS

Consider Kata a Training Method

If you lack enthusiasm for kata, and are disappointed to find that there are no books which contain enough information about it to pep up your practice and to make your study easier, then we trust that this is the book for which you have been searching. But as you read this book you must bear certain things in mind.

First, the Nage and Katame no Kata are the "grammar" for every judoist. How well you "spell" and "articulate" your Judo "language" (that is, the level of your skills) is in the main dependent upon your mastery of what is contained in this text. Kata was intended by Jigoro Kano as a medium for self-discovery and self-realization through Judo. He intended kata as the steering gear for the technical development of every judoist. But kata, as "grammar" or theoretical bases, must be joined to the practical side of training so that it may fulfill its intended purpose. To do this you must learn to take the ceremony out of kata.

It has been difficult, at best, for Western judoists to accept the study and practice of kata as a necessary element in their training programs. Significantly, kata is reputed to be generally useless for bringing a judoist to full technical maturity. This is a very serious error in thinking and it will continue to cost Western Judo valuable technical soundness until it is corrected. Kata can be understood and appreciated by all judoists, provided it is properly interpreted and meaningfully applied to their Judo training.

Most significant to you, for the purposes of this chapter, should be the knowledge that kata is intended to be a training method. All it accomplishes, or fails to accomplish, for you lies not in inherent aspects of kata, but in the way you learn to apply kata to your training. Remember that the basic values and benefits of these kata have been proved time and again by thousands of judoists before your time. You, the present-day user of kata, can derive similar benefits if you put kata to good use; add it to your *randori* as a useful supplement. To aid you in doing this, let us investigate when to study kata, how much practice is necessary, and the specific methods by which it can be made useful.

When to Begin Learning Kata

There is a time when you, the trainee, will be readier and abler to profit by kata instruction than any other. Readiness refers primarily to that level of maturity in your Judo experience which enables you to enter into kata study with meaning, interest, and a reasonable chance to achieve success. You are ready to profit by kata experience when you understand that what you are about to learn has a practical purpose. When to begin your study of kata, then, is not so much a matter of beginning at a certain age level or basic technical level, as a matter of wanting to study. If desire isn't there, no matter what your age or technical level, kata learning is not easily achieved.

Kata can be successfully learned at almost any early point in a judoist's career. It is more important to consider *ukemi* proficiency than Judo rank when it comes to deciding readiness for kata study. Insofar as you are concerned, however, the active practice of kata need not begin before you are *sankyu* (third-class Brown Belt). Of course, if you are studying Judo under a qualified instructor he will have very specific ideas about your study of kata and will indicate when he thinks you are ready for such study. However, when you are studying without qualified guidance, the *sankyu* level is a good choice for a start. Should you lack a nationally recognized Judo rank, you may base the starting point for your kata study upon your active Judo experience. If it has progressed along normal lines you may effectively begin kata at any time between your tenth and fourteenth months. If you practice almost daily, the earlier starting point will be appropriate, but if you practice only once or twice a week, the later starting point is better. These are approximate starting points only and can vary considerably from individual to individual.

How Much Kata Training?

Kata must be pursued as a serious study with sufficient practice during your entire Judo life. The intensity of application will vary in different stages of

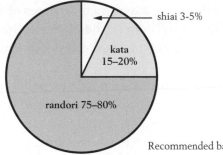

Recommended balance of randori, kata and shiai.

the judoist's technical development, and it is difficult to arrive at a single percentage of total training time to devote to kata which would be valid for all. However, some generalizations will help you in deciding just how much kata study and practice would be beneficial for you.

It is the consensus of Kodokan high-ranking instructors and teachers that the time period devoted to kata must lie between the periods allotted to *randori* and *shiai*. Priority should be given to *randori*; kata and *shiai* follow in importance. The chart above summarizes the recommended balance of these three major training methods.

Let us now see just how much actual time should be given to kata training. The table below summarizes this for you and gives you the approximate training time recommended for kata practice. This table is based on the number of days per week you train, and assuming that each training session in your *dojo* is about two hours long, you will be able to calculate the correct amount of time that should be devoted to kata. If your *dojo* training sessions are of less than two hours' duration, you will have to make some simple adjustments so that the table will be appropriate to your case.

RECOMMENDED TRAINING TIME FOR KATA

All Training		Kata		
days per week	hours per month	hours per month	hours per week	Study and Practice of Kata
7	56	11.2	2.8	Three or four 45- to 60-minute periods per week; on consecutive or spaced days
6	48	9.5	2.5	Three or four 40- to 50-minute periods per week; on consecutive or spaced days
5	40	8.0	2.0	Two or three 40- to 60-minute periods per week; on consecutive or spaced days
4	32	6.5	1.5	Two 45-minute periods per week; on consecutive or spaced days
3	24	4.8	1.2	Two 35-minute periods per week; on consecutive or spaced days
2	16	3.2	0.8	One 45-minute period per week; on your light-workout day
1	8	1.6	0.4	One 30-minute period per week; on your light-workout day

The chart and table are based on the actual training times of Japanese Judo champions over the last 35 years. There is, therefore, authenticity in these figures in that they have been instrumental in the development of highly skilled contest judoists.

The table cannot determine the needs of each judoist as he progresses through the various belt ranks, nor does it consider possible restrictions in training time. It must be used simply as a guide, with possible modifications as demanded by circumstance. We may add that several practice sessions spaced over a period of a few days produce better results than one unusually long session covering the same amount of time. Guided by intelligent regard for fullest Judo development, you can devise clever and practical schemes for training beneficially with kata. Here is an example:

Many Japanese champions were raised on a large share of kata practice on an almost daily basis during their high school and university days. This, however, was arranged so it never became boring or overly difficult; the time spent on such kata study was rationed to a few minutes each day. Knowing that a complete performance of either the Nage or Katame no Kata takes approximately seven minutes (considerably less if only one category is practiced), certain instructors required their student judoists to perform kata twice each training period. Early in the period, after warm-up and possibly *ukemi*, the trainees were paired off and performed kata for several minutes, each trainee taking only one role. Again, at the end of the day's heavy *randori* session, students were paired off and required to perform kata once again for several minutes, this time taking the opposite role. Carrying out this procedure almost daily, some days using Nage no Kata and other days Katame no Kata, students rapidly acquired an understanding of kata mechanics and eventually were able to further their development in a wide range of Judo techniques. None of the students saw these few minutes a day as a big chunk out of his valuable training time; in fact, many of those former students are now instructors and use a similar method with their own students.

How to Begin Learning Kata

The best way to begin kata is to study it, not to practice it. Don't go to your first kata lesson "cold." Before you begin that first lesson, you should have diligently studied the subject. Carefully memorize the names of all the techniques in the kata, their sequence, and the categories they represent. This information is invaluable and will lessen your mental burden when you begin actual practice; there are enough problems in learning kata without making any more. Knowing each technique in its right order, where to position yourself and what comes next, whether to stand close to your partner or apart from him, and whether to lie down, sit up, or get up, is a good share of kata learning. Once absorbed, this knowledge allows you to more fully concentrate on the execution of the techniques themselves. This study is the absolute essential minimum.

You will also do well to read any background information concerning kata that you have access to. It will help you to appreciate what kata is and what benefits you will derive from it. If you read through the technical description of the entire kata before your first practice you will retain much of that information. During the course of your kata lessons, it will be well for you to reread the technical portions periodically, to refresh your memory and refine your physical actions.

It is important for successful kata study to locate a qualified teacher. This is not the simple matter it was to find a qualified Judo instructor who could teach you the rudiments of Judo, which center around *randori* and the contest. Kata, as you know by now, is a specialty in which only the most experienced teachers can claim qualification. The problem of locating a kata teacher may be a tough one; there may be no qualified instructors available. In that case you will have to rely upon written materials such as this book; but continue to do your best to find a qualified teacher.

The qualified kata instructor not only has technical mastery, but stresses the fundamental relationship of teacher and pupil. You will be required, under this type of traditional teacher, to have a strong motivation for learning kata, uncritical acceptance of your teacher, and an unquestioning mind. Nothing more will be asked than that you conscientiously follow what the teacher demonstrates. He will avoid long-winded instructions if possible, but nevertheless kata explanation carries with it more minute details than you have been accustomed to in other phases of Judo instruction. He will not expect you to question his technical knowledge, but you may of course question him if something is not clear or if you are confused. Your teacher will watch your blunders impassively and will wait patiently for your growth and development to kata maturity. Kata must be learned with the attitude that time is not important. There must be no rushed attempt at learning, for rushed learning of kata is impossible. The teacher will not overtax you, and you need not harass the teacher for more information than he gives you. He first will give you an outline from which you can become skillful in the control of the independent techniques. You will be expected to respond with untiring attention to detail and repetition of movements. In time, you will find that the kata technicalities which once oppressed you now liberate you, and, finally, your kata will attain the state which leaves you undecided as to whether your body or your mind is performing.

Which Kata to Practice

Kata, as a major training method of Judo, is clearly an educational process. The place-ment of kata in your overall Judo training program must relate to the wholeness of Judo, if you are to receive maximum educational benefits. This means that at the level of Judo maturity where your interest, study, and practice revolve primarily around *randori* and *shiai*, kata must not only be closely related to these activities, but must carry beyond them to comprehend the totality of Judo, which includes such aspects as self-defense and physical education. At your present level of development you are prone to choose kata only insofar as the skills it imparts are meaningful for what you are now capable of doing, and perhaps insofar as they resemble the skills you need for *randori* and *shiai*. Thus only those skills gain your attention. The Nage and Katame no Kata are sufficient for this purpose, but you should attempt to gain further practice and abilities with other kata, especially Seiryoku Zen'yo, Ju, Kime, or Goshin-jutsu no Kata. All these kata, properly studied and practiced, will bring increased benefits to your *randori* and *shiai* skills, far more than you would obtain from the study and practice of Nage and Katame no Kata alone. But don't misunderstand this advice. The major portion of your kata practice must center on Nage and Katame no Kata.

How to Practice Kata

Kata practice can be approached in three distinct ways and it is necessary to distinguish among them to obtain the most realistic results.

The first approach is the practice of kata in its accepted traditional Kodokan patterns. These are the standard patterns of Judo and among them, in this book only the Nage and Katame no Kata are offered as representative examples. Beyond that, those Kodokan kata outlined in Chapter 2 represent the sum total of standard Kodokan kata. Developed by Kodokan technical boards rather than by individuals, these kata represent the techniques and spirit of the whole span of Kodokan Judo. Your performance of traditional kata, therefore, should be in accordance with the standard technical requirements as outlined in this book, or as taught by qualified instructors.

The second approach is the practice of kata as private variation patterns.

Your performance of these kata must depend to a large degree upon qualified personal instruction, too. Because of the wide variety of personal stylization found in these kata, authoritative, complete, and technically sound written explanations are almost nonexistent. It is outside of this book's scope to detail them, but they are mentioned on pages 36 and 448.

The third approach to kata practice is in the interpreted patterns. The origin of these kata patterns is one of interpretation by the performer or the instructor directing their usage. He takes certain meaningful situations and designs a repetitive process of practice to reinforce the learning of desired skills. There is nothing standard or traditional about these kata, and they also differ from the private variation patterns in that they are not necessarily ever repeated identically from one training session to the next. They are also shorter in length.

However, they are based on characteristics and qualities of kata: prearrangement, ideal conditions of resistance or nonresistance, symmetry, and series arrangement. Since the techniques vary with the needs of the performer, often the whole kata is composed of a single major technique. *Uchikomi* can be considered an example of this pattern. We will cite other examples later in this chapter to more clearly illustrate the pattern (see p. 430).

With these distinctions in mind, you will find the following training tips helpful as you practice kata:

◆ MAKE KATA USEFUL

Too often, through misunderstanding kata is thought of by inexperienced judoists as nothing more than a ceremony and of little lasting training value. Kata is scorned by them as unfit to be included in the training routines of a "fighting judoist." It is only tolerated because, perhaps, it is a basic requirement for advancement in Judo rank. The study and practice of kata is thus often left to the last-minute training rush by students and instructors alike.

While it is true that when kata is used for exhibition purposes only it has limited value, it nevertheless becomes a valuable tool in the development of Judo trainees when properly used. All qualified and experienced instructors respect its importance and use it frequently in the training of student judoists. Judo trainees and instructors who insist that kata does not benefit judoists are making a serious mistake. *The fault for any weakness does not lie in the kata, but in the person who practices or directs it.*

During kata practice, since you are learning a technique and trying to improve your technical efficiency, you are always practicing under controlled conditions. There is at work a kind of cooperation; both you and your training partner have special roles to play, each helping the other. The effect is much like cooperation in music or acting, which exercises each participant and produces a harmonious effect under conditions of correct performance. In spite of this cooperation, however, there must be a sincere and thoughtful attitude regarding each training partner's role. All Kodokan kata are based on the spirit of genuine attack-defense situations. Anything less than this serious attitude tends to weaken the kata as an effective and necessary training tool. Make each movement in accord with the Principle of Judo.

Concentrate on the study of Nage and Katame no Kata. They are the fundamental kata necessary for the development of expert Judo; the study of these kata will be adequate for all examinations up to and including *godan* (fifth-grade Black Belt).

In your study of Nage no Kata, practice the whole kata, but concentrate on the techniques in the hand (*te*), hip-loin (*koshi*), and foot-leg (*ashi*) categories during your first two years of Judo. In Katame no Kata, similarly, you must study the whole kata, but concentrate on the techniques of holding (*osae-komi*). These two kata, with emphasis on the categories just mentioned, will form the foundation for your study of kata requirements for *shodan* and *nidan* (first- and second-grade Black Belts, respectively).

◆ STUDY NAGE NO KATA

Know your role. Whether you are practicing as Tori or as Uke, you must have full understanding of what is to happen: who is defending, and if and when the attack initiative changes hands as each technique develops. It is not just a matter of Uke having the attack initiative until he loses it, or vice versa; the way of transferring attack initiative often varies. You must know who has it originally and just when it changes hands. Without this information and the ability to convey it in physical performance, you cannot consistently practice kata with benefit. In Chapter 8, the description of each throwing technique contains a Technique Summary. If possible, read this before your practice; if this is impossible, read it as soon as you can after practice. Pay attention to the numbers in the Engagement section under each technique; these numbers clearly indicate who has the attack initiative at all times.

As Uke you are able to practice your *ukemi* and improve it, while as Tori you have a fine opportunity to improve your throwing abilities by using the representative throws of this kata. Instantaneous harmony of body actions on the part of both you and your training partner is required as you perform your respective roles. Uke must not be reduced to sloppy or improperly applied *ukemi* actions by an equally incorrect Tori performance. If Uke "jumps" for Tori, it will seriously weaken the value of Nage no Kata. Uke must not try to evade or counter Tori, but must present his body as a target along prescribed lines. Tori must *throw* Uke. Uke, by being overly desirous of cooperating with Tori, can greatly detract from training values by breaking the timing in anticipation of Tori's techniques, thus causing Tori all sorts of technical difficulties which manifest themselves in lack of control.

Take the ceremony out of this kata when you use it in the *dojo* for training. Keep in mind the distinction between kata for demonstration purposes before an audience, and kata where only you, your training partners, and perhaps your instructor are the audience. Taking the ceremony out of this kata does not mean neglecting the etiquette, precise postures, required vigilance, or spirit of your performance; rather, it refers to the effect of your throwing actions. You as Tori may not always be "victorious"; that is, during your beginning attempts with kata, you may not be able to throw Uke correctly—you may never get him unbalanced or off his feet. This is as it should be. You are attempting to acquire skills or polish them. As you progress you will certainly improve your throwing actions and become more efficient. So if during your first attempts to practice this kata you do not handle Uke properly, remember that this is not an exhibition where you have to please an audience; you are performing for your own benefit. As you become more skillful your throws will take on new dimensions of vigor and meaning; you will actually feel them become more powerful and at the same time they will require less effort. Get rid of any remaining casualness that may cloud your opinion of kata; such an attitude divides your energies like a scattered beam of light which cannot be focused on a target. Get the most out of your chances to throw by studying each technique carefully. Find out what makes it tick or why it fails. You will never get a better chance to learn to throw correctly; kata controls everything for you so that you can fully concentrate on what you are doing. To facilitate this, each time you use this kata as a training exercise one or more of the following points should gain your attention. They are all directly translatable to *randori* situations.

As Tori:

1. The *ma-ai* (engagement distance). This is a critical aspect of the throw. Not all techniques operate with the same initial distance between you and your opponent; maintaining the proper distance sets the stage for success, while improper distance spells failure. Positioning yourself too close to the opponent will choke up your entry and weaken your attack; standing too far from your opponent will have a similar weakening effect, and as you overstretch to couple onto him by gripping you may even unbalance yourself.

2. The *riai* (synergy). Some experts consider this the most important lesson that is to be learned in kata. Closely related to engagement distance, the *riai* stands as the Principle of Judo in action. Both yielding and resisting are employed by Tori and Uke to dominate the other by retaining the attack initiative. The *riai* includes the correct way to meet your Uke's strength, to blend your strength with his, to control his strength, and, finally, to subdue him by the application of an appropriate throwing action. This kata teaches you to steal the attack initiative from Uke or to impose it before Uke can seize it himself. It will also teach you a sense of timing in the placement of your attack to make it successful. To accomplish this you must understand the attack initiative (*sen*), who has it originally, and if and when it changes hands.
3. The *taisabaki* (body-turning movement). This is essential to all Judo actions, though it varies in degree. Note the footwork needed to accomplish it and especially note the angle or position your body makes with Uke as each throw develops. Keep in mind that this aspect operates in harmony with engagement distance and *riai*; it must not break those relationships.
4. The *kuzushi-tsukuri-kake* (unbalancing, fitting, and execution of the throw). Pay particular attention to *kuzushi* and *tsukuri*, but don't neglect *kake*. Especially important here is the use of your pulling arm; its direction and manner of pull should be studied for each technique. The entry and placement of your body prior to the finalization of the throw, while Uke is unbalanced, should be a constant object of study. Like engagement distance, *riai*, and *taisabaki*, *tsukuri* and the transition to *kake* should be made with careful study of Uke's foot position; this determines his weak line of balance and the direction in which he can be most efficiently thrown. During *kake*, pay attention to your balance and head position as you throw and in what direction Uke is to be thrown, as well as the area of his *ukemi*. These are all aids to *kake*.

As Uke:
1. The engagement distance. You have the responsibility for determining this distance, thereby clearly identifying yourself as an aggressor, in actual deed or sometimes merely in intent. This teaches you the spirit of your role so that the kata may progress as it was intended. It also points up the seriousness of effect when Tori is able to maintain the correct engagement distance and you do not (or cannot) foil his action.
2. The *riai*. The important thing here is the attack initiative. You always intend to attack Tori; sometimes you actually succeed in doing so. But in

this kata you are scheduled, finally, to lose the attack initiative; in *yoko-gu-ruma*, for example, you have it, lose it, and regain it, only to lose it at last. You are thereby being offered a very good lesson in how Tori obtains the initiative. By knowing how he does this, you have a hint on how to develop a defense for each throw.

3. The *kuzushi-tsukuri-kake*. By knowing how Tori sets you up for each throw, you have a clue to defense against each technique. If you can devise a method by which to foil Tori's actions in these stages, you will be learning something valuable for *randori*. Furthermore, by being the victim of repeated *kuzushi-tsukuri-kake* for each throwing technique, your body learns to feel the approach of the coming throw; instant recognition of that feeling can become a defense in time.

4. The *ukemi* (falling technique). This is vital not only to correct kata performance, but to safety. Concentrate on your form and final position as you settle onto the mat. This kata gives an adequate variety of throwing actions to teach you to fall under any Judo circumstances.

You now have some general hints on what to look for as you practice this kata. The lessons that can be learned in specific form are limitless and all of them can be applied to *randori* and the *shiai*. You should spend your study time for this kata, when you have acquired substantial skill, in looking for new ideas with which to beef up your technical skill; study and find things which are not written in explanations of kata, things which you can carry over beneficially into *randori*. It is beyond the scope of this text to go into detail about them, but they are there, inviting you to discover the "secrets" of Judo.

Practical-minded judoists may be interested in studying this kata with self-defense in mind. But remember that the situation presented by each technique is hypothetical. While these situations can and do exist in self-defense, they do not present a defensive response against any and all forms of attack. They merely exemplify principles which apply efficiently to the prearranged situations and, if understood thoroughly, permit the design of wider applications. To what extent these principles can be carried over into other self-defense situations remains to be studied, but don't expect more out of this kata than is intended.

The spirit of self-defense permeates this kata. Pay particular attention to the development of *zanshin*, which makes every throw a true throw. You need not disregard what has been explained about *zanshin* (pp. 65, 110) as being applicable to self-defense situations; but it can be useful in sport applications of Judo, too. You certainly realize by now that when you apply a throw in *randori* or *shiai*, there is no guarantee that it will score a victory for you. Many a good chance is lost by false assurance or lack of alertness as the opponent slips away from a position on the mat in which he could have been easily overcome. This is due to a lack of *zanshin*. As Tori, your posture and mental concentration should be such that if Uke has not been "ipponed" when he hits the mat, you are instantly in position to continue your attack to a successful conclusion without a break in timing. This example borders on the advanced study of connection-variation techniques (*renraku-henka waza*), and it is based on *zanshin*.

As Uke, while you are cooperating with Tori you may feel like his "guinea pig." Nevertheless, you can get more out of your role than you realize. Think about each technique as Tori applies it against you. Suppose you regard every throw as being made by an opponent in *randori* or *shiai*. Get the feel of each throw, its unbalancing, fitting, and actual execution. Think about your defensive actions or, by prearrangement with your training partner, practice some of your ideas to see their effects. Don't give up as your feet come up off the mat and you go over in midair. This is the time when you must think. Even as you are settling onto the mat, think of how you would avoid this if it were the real thing. Here, too, by prearrangement with your training partner you may try some of your ideas. Experiment with your body, learn its capabilities and limitations. You will not only get over any fear of falling that may remain from your basic training days, but you will also get experience in a wide range of throws, on the receiving end, which will aid you in building a sound defense against throwing attacks.

As a contest or tournament approaches, bear in mind that your training time should be spent in emphasizing *randori* and practice contests. Hard, heavy contact is required to bring you to the necessary state of preparation for the coming *shiai*. In the last five or six weeks prior to the contest, there is less necessity for the use of kata. It is not a matter of learning a technique, but of using what you should have learned earlier; you must use that learning at the speed and in the manner of application appropriate to the coming contest. Prior to this moment, kata should have aided your learning by building a wide variety of skills which you may now call upon for use in competition.

◆ STUDY KATAME NO KATA

Know your role. Whether performing as Tori or as Uke, you must have a firm understanding of what is to happen: who is attacking, who is defending, and if and when the attack initiative changes hands. Without this information and the ability to convey it in a physical performance, you cannot consistently practice this kata with benefit. In Chapter 9, unlike 8 (Nage no Kata), there is no Technique Summary for each technique. Instead, go directly to the Engagement description of each technique. You will note a numbering system similar to what was used for the Nage no Kata. This numbering clearly indicates who has the attack initiative.

As Uke, you have an ideal opportunity to practice genuine escape or neutralization actions against Tori. Primarily use big body movements (but no counterchoking, and a minimum of joint-locking techniques) to escape. As Tori, learn to apply efficient grappling techniques to immobilize your opponent. Body action in both training roles must be instantaneously harmonious as in the Nage no Kata, but it is somewhat more spaced out by Tori's frequent changes in position.

Katame no Kata is really an exercise in immobilizing an opponent, by holding him helpless or by restricting his movement and controlling it with additional threats of unconsciousness or pain. Uke must never make weak attempts to escape from grappling action applied by Tori. If Uke lies dead on the mat, the value of Katame no Kata is seriously impaired, for Tori has no real standard against which to test his control actions. *Tori must apply his techniques with technical correctness and for true effect; Uke must make real attempts to escape from them.*

In the first grappling category, that of the *osae-komi waza*, this is evident enough; it is in the remaining two categories of techniques that this kata often loses usefulness.

In the *shime* and *kansetsu waza*, Tori must strive to restrict and control Uke's escape movements without placing the choke or joint lock into punishing effect. The reasoning behind this goes back to your basic Judo study, when you learned that the basic category of grappling is immobilization in the holding techniques (*osae-komi waza*), and that advanced techniques of choking and joint locking can only be truly effective against a skilled opponent when that opponent is first securely held. So held, he can do nothing about additional action against him in the form of choking or joint-locking techniques. If, on the other hand, he is not held securely, and choking or joint-locking actions are used against him, he is free to escape. Bear in mind this truth: any choking or joint-locking technique which is applied without in some way immobilizing the opponent can be neutralized or escaped from without difficulty. If you cannot hold your opponent, you cannot choke or joint-lock him. So, in practice, Uke must struggle energetically to see if Tori can really immobilize, restrict, and control him without the final application of the choke or joint lock. If escape is possible, Tori's technique is weak because of the lack of control of his opponent, and must be restudied.

Take the ceremony out of this kata when you use it in the *dojo* for training. When you are not performing before an audience, there should be many occasions when you are not victorious in the role of Tori. Taking the ceremony out of this kata does not imply that you should neglect the etiquette, precise postures, required vigilance, or spirit of your performance, but rather it refers to the effect of your grappling actions. In your early study of this kata, many things will go wrong for you. As you acquire skill, your grappling will improve and, in either role, you will make progress. Regardless of how skillful your Uke may become, you as Tori have the advantage of securing a perfect technique, and you will eventually be able to control him in spite of any skill advantage he may possess. If he is able to constantly escape from your techniques, check them by comparing them with the descriptions in the text. Then continue to practice until you can control Uke. Get rid of any casual attitudes about this kata that may remain with you; they will rob you of its benefits. Find out what makes each technique a sound one, or why it is failing for you. You will never get a better chance to learn to grapple correctly; kata controls everything for you so that you can concentrate on what you are doing. To facilitate this, each time you use this kata as a training exercise, one or more of the following points should gain your attention. They are all directly translatable to *randori* situations.

As Tori:
1. The *kogeki no katachi* (attack form). Within this area falls the engagement distance. Not all grappling techniques utilize the same distance between you and your opponent during contact; maintaining the correct distance is absolutely necessary for success. Generally, in the *osae-komi waza* you must make tight body contact with the opponent, while in the *shime* and *kansetsu waza* if you get too close or too far away you weaken your control and final punishing effect. In this kata you, not Uke, are responsible for determining the engagement distance. Also very important is the angle which your body makes with Uke's; maintain it, for it sets the stage for your balance and consequent ability to deal successfully with Uke's actions as he tries to escape. The *riai* operates here, too, and you must learn to utilize any aggressive actions of Uke prior to obtaining the form of your technique; generally speaking, however, Uke permits you to obtain a perfect technique.
2. Control. Control of Uke must not only be established, but maintained. Here is a perfect example of the *riai* with all of its dependence upon the Principle of Judo as it operates in both yielding and resisting, as appro-

priate to the situation. To establish control and maintain it, you must keep Uke unbalanced (*kuzushi*), keep your body fitted to him as he struggles (*tsukuri*), and further execute the finalization of the technique (*kime*), which is similar to the *kake* in Nage no Kata. All of this requires you to perfect your body mobility and turning action (*taisabaki*) as you focus your body power into Uke; study the control points on Uke's body for each technique: his head, his shoulders, his hips.

As Uke:

1. The *bogeki no katachi* (defense form). This cannot be efficient if Tori is successful in maintaining the correct engagement distance; if this distance is maintained, you will be defeated. It is essential that you learn how to destroy this distance and negate Tori's impending technique. This kata teaches you how to get Tori to break the angle his body makes with yours and how to make him lose his balance and with it the engagement distance, which is his key to correct attack form.
2. Control continuity. This kata teaches you what a well-placed grappling technique actually feels like; the points on your body where you are most bothered or uncomfortable as you struggle to free yourself are the control points at which Tori makes good his grappling technique. Locate them by experience and learn to counterattack so that you may loosen, neutralize, or evade control; only then will you stop being Tori's victim.

You now have some general hints on what to look for as you practice this kata. The lessons that can be learned from this kata are limitless and all of them can be applied to *randori* and *shiai*. After you acquire a passable degree of skill in this kata, study it more thoroughly by looking for new ideas which will add to your technical knowledge; then learn to apply them in *randori*.

Zanshin must be evident in Katame no Kata, too. As Tori, you develop it as you position yourself correctly upon release of your technique at Uke's *mairi* signal, but before this, *Zanshin* must permeate all your actions. There is a tendency to lose this important mental attitude when Uke, by reclining, sitting, or facing you in a more or less passive manner, does not provoke the spirit of attack and defense in you. Nevertheless, you must guard against a loose posture and careless attitude as you position yourself in *kyoshi*.

As Uke, you can easily get the spirit of your role, and you should spare no energy in attempting to extricate yourself from Tori's technique. Of course, you must guard against reckless thrashing about or wild flailing of your arms and legs; your escape actions must be legitimate techniques and should not be applied with a defeatist attitude. Make Tori work to control you; give your surrender signal only if he earns it. Look for his weak points in control and go after them quickly and efficiently; if he fails to control you, you may escape. This is the only correct spirit for training with this kata.

Unlike the Nage no Kata, this kata affords a valuable precontest training method for all judoists. As Uke, each time Tori takes a perfect technique, you will have a good chance to test your ability to escape; as Tori, you have a fine chance to test your skill and see how well you can control a truly struggling Uke, especially if you extend the limit of that struggle to a minimum of 30 seconds. You may use this kata up to the time you would normally stop all hard training prior to *shiai*. The advantage is that it exposes you, in either role, to a wide variety of techniques, perhaps more than what you would utilize in *randori*. You should, of course, use this kata as a supplement to normal *randori*, not as your sole training exercise.

The Beginning Role in Kata

Your first attempts to learn kata should be as Uke; obtain a working knowledge of this role before learning how to be Tori. If possible, work with an experienced Tori to make your Uke progress interesting and safe. Early Uke experience develops best when you have full confidence in your Tori and, in the case of the Nage no Kata, your *ukemi* as well. Anything less than full confidence will often destroy not only your learning ability, but also your motivation. If you must work with an inexperienced Tori, both of you in your first sessions should use the self-practice method (see p. 428) and then the form-only method (see p. 429). When you both have acquired familiarity with the techniques of the kata and know each other's body reactions, then perform the kata to its conclusion. This is especially advisable in the Nage no Kata, where potential danger from improper falling exists. The role of Tori in either kata is best practiced after you have reached Brown Belt skill, when it will effectively reinforce your throwing and grappling abilities.

Cautions in Practice

The practice of kata allows no exceptions to the usual training-safety regulations of Judo. Often trainees approach kata with the idea that since it is all prearranged and purely cooperative, there can be no element of danger. Many a beginner has found to his regret that injury is possible and must be guarded against just as carefully as in *randori* or *shiai*.

This is done by ensuring that both Tori and Uke know their roles, that is, what each is to do and what will happen when it is done. In Nage no Kata, Uke in particular must know *ukemi* well. He must additionally know enough about Tori's actions, such as the direction of movement, so that he can predict the direction of his flight, over what shoulder he will fall, on which side he will land, and which arm beats the mat; it helps, too, for Uke to know in what approximate area he is to fall. Tori must control his throws and grappling techniques at all times, using sufficient strength to make the technique work but taking care not to "over-power" it; following the Principle ofjudo, he must apply just enough force and no more.

The self-practice method and the form-only method can be extremely useful in teaching both roles with complete safety. If either performer is unfamiliar with his role, the technique must be talked out and walked through before executing it. Ignorance of the roles is never a valid excuse for injury in kata.

Uki-otoshi and *sasae-tsurikomi-ashi* require similar *ukemi* patterns of trajectory and body handling by Uke. Uke must not hang back and attempt to ride around the side, but must turn over with the motion of the throw. Bending forward by "breaking" at the hips will lessen the chance for a proper and safe *ukemi*, because Uke may lose valuable height and "stick" as he comes down upside down; he may collapse from this awkward predicament onto his head or shoulder. By keeping the body straight and the face somewhat turned up, a smooth trajectory is possible.

The high fall from *kata-guruma* often scares an inexperienced Uke. It comes abruptly from a more or less static, hung-up position high across Tori's shoulders. Uke keeps his body straight, raising stiffly the leg that Tori is not attacking, without draping over Tori. Tori will then be able to shed Uke as a single piece, and can control and guide him to a safe landing.

Generally, *sutemi waza* should not be practiced either as Tori or as Uke by judoists under 12 years of age. *Tomoe-nage* gives the distinct feel of the power of this type of throwing action and produces a potentially difficult and dangerous fall. Uke must turn his body in a big arc. Trying to slow the motion or doubling up to shorten the linear distance generated by the throw may result in a bad landing. Uke must launch himself forward and remember to roll over the correct shoulder in *zempo kaiten* fashion; he must make impact with the mat on the side of his back, not fully on his back. Tori must use his attacking leg correctly; if he pushes too soon, Uke will ride up higher and less far forward, and will have little chance for a good *ukemi*. Above all, Tori must not kick Uke's abdomen with his attacking foot. Tori should relax his grip in both hands as he completes the throw.

Ura-nage is a potentially nasty throw, and it produces an even nastier fall if Uke is unprepared for it. Practice the throw the first few times by having Tori merely sit back and rock onto the mat without much leg lift or arm-heaving action as Uke dives over and tests his *ukemi*; Uke remains lying on the mat. Tori can gradually put more lift into the throw and finally uproot Uke and heave him into space behind Tori. Uke must learn not to let his striking arm (the one over Tori's shoulder) get trapped beneath Tori as Tori settles onto the mat. Note that Uke may assist Tori by pushing downward with the underside of that arm on top of Tori's shoulder; this action will give both partners a better feel for the throw. Do not consider this a fake throw. Finally, Uke should not hang back or dive ahead of Tori's throwing actions: Tori must relax his grip as he completes the throw.

Toko-gake is perhaps the most abrupt and hardest fall in this kata, even when it is correctly performed. Uke must lean forward while bracing backward, allowing his shoulder on the side of his advanced foot to twist inward as Tori sets him up for the throw. There is a definite stiffness to Uke's body and his weight must rest on the outside of the advanced foot as Tori attacks that foot. Do not try to sit the throw out by doubling up; prepare for *a flat landing, square on your back.* Keep your chin tucked tightly in. Tori must pull up with his sleeve grip to protect Uke's shoulder and the back of Uke's head.

Sumi-gaeshi, yoko-guruma, and *uki-waza* require that Uke realize that he will be projected forward circularly, head over heels in *zempo kaiten* fashion, over his shoulder on the same side as his advancing or advanced foot. He must follow the motion of the throw without trying to hang back. In *sumi-gaeshi* and *uki-waza,* Tori can seriously injure Uke by clamping down on Uke's arm inserted under Tori's armpit. Tori must ensure that he releases Uke's arm so that Uke can roll out safely by *zempo kaiten. Yoko-guruma* produces an abrupt trajectory.

In Katame no Kata, the *shime* and *kansetsu waza* are both potentially dangerous if improperly applied. Generally, judoists under 12 years of age should not practice these techniques. Instant release by Tori upon Uke's *mairi* signal is essential. Care must be taken with an inexperienced Uke that neither unconsciousness nor joint injury precedes his signal for surrender. Above all, Uke must understand what the *mairi* signal is and how to apply it correctly.

The Size of Kata Partners

Kata should be practiced with participants of any and all statures for maximum training value. Just as you will surely face judoists with different builds in *randori* and *shiai,* you must guarantee such experience for yourself in kata practice. The use of one type of partner, of a particular height and weight, for the role of Uke should be restricted to the performance of kata as a demonstration or exhibition, where such selection guarantees a simplified performance. As a general rule, in Nage and Katame no Kata, Uke should be a bit taller than Tori to facilitate the throwing and grappling actions and to give a better sense of the spirit of self-defense. A Tori who is markedly larger than Uke can make these kata appear ludicrous, in that Tori appears to be a bully and the audience's sympathy goes to Uke.

The Repetition Method

One of the greatest problems in kata practice is the lack of opportunity to perform enough repetitions of each technique. While separate Judo techniques, especially those of throwing, are usually practiced in *uchikomi* style to guarantee adequate repetition, the practice of Nage and Katame no Kata in standard complete form requires only one application of each technique on the right and left sides or solely on the right side. Time limits will usually preclude more than two or three complete performances at any normal training session. Even if certain categories of techniques are detached from the whole and practiced separately, the value of such repetitions is not as great as that of the "repetition method."

By this method, repetition value approaching that of *uchikomi* style is brought into kata practice. Opening and closing salutations may be omitted (though they, too, may be practiced by this method) and the trainees can get down to matters of technique. Tori applies each technique successively a predetermined number of times (usually no less than five) before moving on to the next technique. In Katame no Kata this poses no problem, but in the Nage no Kata it is better to preserve the symmetry and rhythm of execution by performing each technique normally once on each side, repeating this pattern the desired number of times before moving on to the following technique. Categories may be practiced separately, and it will be found that performing two or three complete categories using at least five repetitions of each technique provides a stimulating workout. Uke may perform to completion of *ukemi* or stop just short of the *kake* stage (see p. 429). This method is useful in initial learning stages or in the correction of technical difficulties at any stage of Judo training. It is also useful to judoists who are polishing their kata performance prior to giving a demonstration.

The Self-Practice Method

Initial kata learning is apt to be difficult when the training partners are equally unskilled. How can either of them expect a harmoniously coordinated performance if each does not know the requirements of his role? If such is the case, practice *without* a partner can be beneficial, and all judoists learning kata will do well to spend some time with this method. Both roles should be practiced in this fashion. By performing either role many times by yourself, you gradually build fluency of movement in the mechanics of kata. You will be able to concentrate on yourself without the distraction of a partner who may also be guilty of many errors. A full-length mirror can be your best "teacher" by helping you to spot technical errors in your practice. Compare what you do in front of the mirror (if you have no mirror, training partners can watch and criticize you) with your understanding of kata performance gained by study of this text. Adjust any differences between this text and your performance and you will greatly improve your skill. This method is not limited to the basic kata trainee, for experts use it, too, perfecting their timing by careful attention to detail.

The Form-Only Method

Circumstances may preclude the practice of a complete Nage or Katame no Kata; the *kake* or *kime* may not be desirable. Among these circumstances are performances by injured judoists who nevertheless want and are able to practice light Judo, the lack of mat space in a crowded *dojo*, or perhaps the lack of a suitable mat surface. In these special cases, the "form-only" method of practice becomes useful. In this method, the initial stationing movements and techniques are performed, but Tori brings Uke to a final position in form only; he does not complete the *kake* or *kime*. No *ukemi* is performed by Uke, nor is there any need for his struggle and ensuing *mairi* signal in grappling. In the *sutemi waza*, Tori may also control his body position by not sacrificing himself to the mat, or by sacrificing himself but releasing Uke from his grip. Judoists beginning kata practice may use this method to familiarize themselves with what they are to do, but it should be discontinued after reasonable familiarity has been achieved.

The One-Sided Method

The techniques of the Nage no Kata are normally performed on both the right and the left sides. Katame no Kata techniques, however, are usually performed only on the right side. However, these kata are flexible enough to permit deviations for legitimate training purposes. In the practice of Nage no Kata, trainees should practice only a right or a left technique if a technical weakness develops on one side, or if temporary physical limitations exist. Such considerations may extend to either Tori or Uke, or to both simultaneously.

In Katame no Kata it is beneficial to practice on the left side to curb any tendency toward a "sugar-sided" grappling ability, which would only be furthered by normal practice in this kata. Modifications to make left-hand techniques possible provide a challenge to the judoist, who must work out the reversals of the "rights" and "lefts" in the text.

Interpreted Patterns

In the interpreted-pattern kata method, it is you, the user, or your coach who determines what techniques to employ. Nothing is standard unless you or the coach want to make it so. You select techniques which have some special significance for you, either at the time of your initial learning or at a more advanced, polished stage of your Judo experience. It matters not whether the techniques you choose are basic styles or not, nor does it matter if you perform them individually or in connection with one another. What matters is that you perform them in kata style, with an Uke who knows beforehand what he is to do and what you will do.

For example, you may wish to develop *hiza-guruma*, *tai-otoshi*, and *hane-goshi*. None of these throws is found in the Nage no Kata. By stepping in kata styles and in directions which you think appropriate, you can practice these techniques and improve your skills.

The interpreted patterns also permit easy learning of connection-variation techniques (*renraku-henka waza*), which you learn about in advanced Judo study. Suppose the combination of *kouchi-gari*, *ouchi-gari*, and *tai-otoshi* interests you. None of these techniques is to be found in the Nage no Kata. After you have developed reasonable skill with each separately, you may practice them in combination through the interpreted-pattern method. Uke moves in a limited manner as agreed beforehand, and serves as the cooperative partner necessary for the initial learning of this combination.

Movement for the throwing techniques applied by this method may be in the manner of *tsugi ashi* or *ayumi ashi* and in a longitudinal, lateral, or circular direction. Thus, this process can be repetitive like *uchikomi*, but with the added benefit of movement. It does not, however, duplicate the value of *yakusoku-geiko*, which you studied during your basic Judo training days, in that all kata movement is prearranged and limited.

Uchikomi can be included under this method but, since you are already familiar with it, it need not be elaborated on here.

Grappling techniques may also be studied by the interpreted-pattern method. Tori can move offensively through various *hairi-kata* (entrance forms) to a conclusion with a technique not in the standard Katame no Kata. Another good idea is the practice of grappling connection-variation techniques in which Tori remains offensive and applies successive techniques to Uke, who can move either in a prearranged manner or under no restrictions in attempts to evade, neutralize, or escape from those techniques. In still another useful practice, Uke performs more or less defensively by taking steps to neutralize or block Tori's *hairi-kata* and the attempt to bring a technique to conclusion. Uke may also make prearranged *nogare-kata* (escape forms) from techniques which have been placed by Tori.

The lessons learned during your first days in the *dojo*, which can be dull and boring, can be enlivened by use of the interpreted-pattern method. The mechanics of standing, kneeling, sitting, getting up, salutations, gripping an opponent, and movement in *tsugi ashi* and *ayumi ashi* with a partner can be prearranged and practiced by this method. This form of instruction not only improves your performances in basic skills, but prepares you for later practice of standard kata. These preliminaries are also good exercise for developing an elastic type of strength. As a personalized training method, the interpreted pattern is not so suitable for demonstration purposes except in showing how training methods may be used.

Private Variation Patterns

Some interesting and valuable training experiences can be achieved by the practice of kata developed by master judoists. Notable here is the Nage Ura no Kata designed by the late Kyuzo Mifune, which teaches a useful series of counterthrowing techniques often encountered in *randori* or *shiai*. This kata serves best at an advanced level of Judo skill, where all the component parts of the kata have been duly studied and an expert degree of skill has been obtained with each of them. These patterns are highly suitable for demonstrations. Many of these patterns exist, perhaps as many as there are master judoists.

Kata as Preparatory Exercise

You already know that all top judoists warm up prior to heavy contact exercise. Kata in any form, since it is a moderate symmetrical exercise, is ideal as either a warm-up or a "cool-down" exercise. Often kata may be substituted for the usual preparatory exercises at the opening or closing of a Judo training session. Thus you not only achieve what normal preparatory exercises permit, but you get additional technical training as well.

Kata in Demonstrations

The best-qualified Tori can be disturbed by a bad Uke performance. Tori cannot make up for what Uke fails to do; however, a good Uke can sometimes support a subpar Tori performance. Since kata is intended as an exposition of certain principles and the spirit of Judo, kata performed as a demonstration before any audience must be technically correct and solid. This is obvious when the performance is before knowledgeable judoists, but it is sometimes not so clear when bringing kata before a lay audience. Kata performed as either entertainment or instruction must never suffer compromise. To assume that the lay audience cannot recognize the blunders which ill-prepared performers may make is inconsiderate and never justifiable.

This is especially true if a gross mistake is made, such as a completely improper response or the omission of a whole technique. These mistakes can and do happen, even for expert judoists, and they clearly show how much Judo training has become a part of the judoist. In such cases, the kata should be carried out to its finish without giving visual sign of error or stopping to indicate chagrin about the technique that was botched or omitted. A technique missed in its natural order can often be spliced in later. An example will suffice to make this point clear.

Toshiro Daigo, an eighth-*dan* Kodokan master-instructor, when performing as Tori in Nage no Kata at the New Year's ceremony (Kagami-biraki) at the Kodokan, ran headlong into a miscalculation by his Uke, a skilled seventh *dan*, who began the *ma sutemi waza* with a striking action instead of gripping in preparation for *tomoe-nage*. But Daigo was not distracted. His normal response of gripping for *tomoe-nage* made impossible, Daigo simply blended smoothly with Uke's striking action and threw him instantly with *ura-nage* (the required second throw of the category), and repeated it on the left side. But the chagrined Uke now realized his mistake. After that, *tomoe-nage* and *sumi-gaeshi* were performed in that order to complete the category. Although Uke had mixed the order of technique performance, Daigo's reaction was so smooth, showing the true intensity and depth of his Judo reflex action, that many spectators believed that they had missed seeing the leadoff technique, *tomoe-nage*. It was not until *tomoe-nage* was performed out of order that these spectators realized what had happened. Daigo's reactions exemplify the perfection of Judo technique.

Partners should be specially chosen and matched as to size when demonstrations are given. Uke should be a bit taller than Tori for best performance and visual appeal in both Nage and Katame no Kata. Further, if possible they should have had ample opportunity to practice together before the demonstration. It is a rare pair of judoists who can, the first time they try, bring off a really technically correct kata.

Unreality in the situations and responses must be avoided. Nothing is so destructive to kata value in demonstrations as a dead performance by Tori, Uke, or both. While Tori must demonstrate control of each situation, Uke must give the impression of vigorous application of his body at the proper moments. The demonstration kata, differing from a pure training exercise, must always see Tori "victorious." Tori must not be turned over or dislodged by Uke. Yet if cooperation is overdone, and it is obvious to the audience that Uke will "lose" from the onset, the kata will fail to convey its intended message.

Finally, kata performed for a lay audience should be explained by a qualified judoist.

Katame Strength-Building Methods

An excellent physical strength-building modification can be made to Uke's role in Katame no Kata. Though in standard practice Uke is permitted to rest his head on the mat as he reclines during the preparatory positioning of Tori, it is better that Uke hold his head off the mat, chin tucked in, for his entire performance while in the lying-ready position. This provides a strong workout for the neck muscles, and the repeated use of this modification by Uke in training is sure to build a powerful neck (see pp. 136; 136, n. 8).

Another valuable strength-building modification which Tori may use, and which at the same time benefits Tori, is a left *kyoshi* with Tori positioning himself on Uke's left side in all techniques. The use of a sufficient number of left techniques provides valuable symmetry.

Extended movement in *kyoshi* is an exercise in itself and a way to achieve strong legs and flexible hip, knee, and ankle joints, as well as graceful movement and good balance. Movement in *kyoshi* can be in a straight line, up and down the *dojo*; or it can be circular, around the perimeter of the mat. Both the standard right *kyoshi* and a left *kyoshi* should be used to make the exercise symmetrical.[1]

---

1. The founder intended movement in *kyoshi* as a method of strengthening the body—a physical education pur-

Developing Muga-mushin

The state of *muga-mushin* is attainable by all judoists who but practice kata sufficiently. It is a quality which has tremendous practical value for application in *randori* and *shiai*. Inexperienced judoists trying to establish *muga-mushin* for a kata performance tend to overdo it by becoming overly tense or overly feeble.

Excessive tension is produced by the mind's trying so hard to do well that it is in a sort of vice; a kind of "mental constipation" develops. This condition can be recognized by awkward body actions and hesitations in performance. The lack of proper body guidance shows a lack of responsive control to the situations imposed by the kata; wild movements with exaggerated attempts at the techniques are the result. The kata becomes a series of unpredictable ill-timed actions, which in extreme cases can be dangerous, especially to Uke. It indicates that the kata is still in a mechanical "thinking-out" stage of development. More experience with kata in training sessions is necessary before this kind of improper performance can be corrected. Concentrating one's breathing, either in meditative fashion (*mokuso*) or while one executes the techniques, helps to alleviate tension.

Weakness results when the mind is trying so hard not to think that it actually approaches a sleeplike state. This condition can be easily recognized in the performer who moves as in a dream, feebly and without alertness. His lassitude precludes spontaneity; weak and undynamic actions characterize his performance of kata. This is, perhaps, somewhat superior to a state of tension, but it shows that automatic responses are not yet developed. This undesirable state is cured by more study and practice. Drastic measures utilizing the element of surprise should be used. Surprise may be injected by a qualified instructor who is supervising the practice, or by one of the performers. The instructor may issue loud commands to punctuate the kata, applying them the moment lassitude develops in one or both performers. Or a more experienced trainee may be teamed with a lackadaisical partner. The experienced trainee should at various times during the practice try to keep his partner alert with unusually fast attacks or, in extreme cases, by mixing the order of the attacks—striking instead of coming into the engagement gripping as expected, or vice versa. Some old Japanese master-teachers, while working with a dreamy trainee, will slap or tap him on top of his head, indicating to the trainee that his defense was inadequate and his *zanshin* absent.

---

pose. He could just as easily have allowed Tori to walk normally to his different locations in the far and near positions.

Kata Tips

Judoists attempting kata practice the first few times often need some visual guides to set the stationing locations, boundaries, and axes of performance. To provide this useful training aid, the mat area may be marked in chalk or striped with removable cellulose tape. Figure (c) on page 76 shows some common markings which will aid beginning trainees. Advanced trainees, too, may need to restudy the markings. Training mirrors for kata study have already been discussed (see p. 446); they must be arranged with full regard for safety.

Inexperienced judoists often become confused at the designation of the techniques of Nage no Kata as either "right" or "left." Officially, the Kodokan identifies each technique according to the side of the body, the leg or foot, shoulder or hip, employed by Tori to effect the throw. This relationship can confuse identification inasmuch as no general rule can be set. It is easier to remember the following procedure: in *ukemi*, Uke will fall to the mat and beat with his left arm from all right-hand throwing actions; conversely, he beats with his right arm after all left-hand throwing actions. This means that techniques such as leadoff *okuri-ashi-harai*, *sasae-tsurikomi-ashi*, *yoko-gake*, and *uki-waza* (where Tori attacks with his left leg or side of the body) and a technique such as *ura-nage* (where Uke rises over Tori's left shoulder) are by Kodokan identification left-hand techniques; in this book, and when we consider Uke's falling mechanics, they are identified as right-hand throws. They all require Uke to beat with his left arm in *ukemi*. By the method of this book, then, there is only one technique in this kata which begins as a left-hand technique. That is *uki-goshi*, from which Uke beats with his right arm in *ukemi* as he is thrown around Tori's left hip.

Uke's position at rest after *ukemi* and the area or point *oi ukemi* are directly related to correct throwing technique. When you need to check *ukemi* positions, the *ukemi* map on page 109 will aid you.

One of the most valuable *ukemi* methods for building the necessary skills in this kata is the partner-support method. You should be familiar with this type of *ukemi* practice from your basic Judo training days. Repeated use will strengthen your Uke ability and give you the confidence you need to perform your role in Nage no Kata. Study Figures 1-4, which are self-explanatory.

The use of Japanese terminology is essential for all judoists from basic training days, but it is especially effective for a better understanding of kata where it is picturesquely descriptive and thus an aid in getting the feel of the techniques. Various English equivalents have been developed over the years to name Judo techniques and the categories they represent. Since the names

1

2

3

4

of the techniques and their English equivalents have been explained in the technique descriptions, only the category names are considered below.

For Nage no Kata, the term *tachi waza* (standing techniques) designates throwing techniques that are applied while the thrower is in a relatively upright position (note that, as in *uki-otoshi*, this includes the kneeling posture). Within *tachi waza*, the subdivisions *te waza* (hand techniques), *koshi waza* (hip-loin techniques), and *ashi waza* (foot-leg techniques) indicate which part of the thrower's anatomy generates and transmits the main force for the throw. The term *sutemi waza* indicates throwing techniques applied while the thrower is in or on his way to a reclining position on the mat. The idea is that the thrower "sacrifices" his body, or "throws himself away" onto the mat; in so doing, he generates the forces necessary for the throw. The *sutemi waza* are subdivided into *ma* (back) and *yoko* (side) *sutemi waza*; these terms indicate on what part of his body the thrower falls to the mat.

In Katame no Kata, judoists must bear in mind that every technique is a method for immobilizing an opponent, whether it be of an *osae-komi, shime,* or *kansetsu waza* nature. The *osae-komi waza* are special techniques for "pressing" or "crushing" the opponent's body so that he cannot escape. They are accomplished by holding the opponent in a particular fashion and applying force to immobilize him on his back on the mat. Thus the English equivalent used in this book to signify *osae-komi waza*—"holding techniques"—takes in the idea of pressing or crushing the opponent to immobilize him. *Shime waza* are special methods for "strangling" or "choking" the opponent to immobilize him. These are given the English equivalent "choking techniques." *Kansetsu waza* are special methods for "bending and twisting" the joints by means of force applied against the joints' normal range of action, in order to immobilize an opponent. The English equivalent "joint-locking techniques" is used to describe this category. Therefore, when you apply *osae-komi waza*, you hold; when you apply *shime waza*, you choke; when you apply *kansetsu waza*, you lock.

When you practice the techniques of either the Nage or Katame no Kata, be certain you understand what category the technique you are executing comes under. With this information you can better understand the intended mechanics and correctly apply your body forces.

Walking between judoists who are practicing kata is a breach of normal *dojo* etiquette. It is not only impolite, but may be dangerous. Always give kata trainees their full right to the area necessary for the execution of their techniques. In an extremely small or crowded *dojo*, kata cannot safely be mixed with instruction of another type or with *randori* going on simultaneously. Organized methods of kata practice must be established, and it must be remembered that kata areas are usually larger than those required for other phases of Judo training.

Conclusion

Kodokan Judo was designed by its founder, a qualified educator, to combine virile fighting capacity with socially beneficial mental and physical training disciplines, by means of healthful athletic endeavor. Kodokan Judo is a system of physical education in the fullest sense.

The quality of a physical education method is, in part, to be judged by its ability to endow mankind with useful, socially acceptable abilities. Kodokan Judo does so only when sufficient kata study and practice are included in Judo training programs.

There is an inseparable relation between kata and physical education which permits Judo to meet the criteria of physical education. Judo without kata, that is, Judo training based solely on heavy doses of *randori* and *shiai*, usually fails to qualify as sensible physical education. Such a restrictive Judo interpretation carries with it the undesirable effects of disproportionate body development, uneconomical use of mental and physical energies, exhaustion, and always the threat of serious injury.

Physical educators must insist on bringing Judo into greater consonance with physical education and must regulate the development of "win-conscious" types of Judo. The present unfortunate tendency in Judo, namely, emphasis on intensive competition for trophies and advancement in rank solely by victory in contest, fails to inculcate wholesome educative values intended by the founder of Judo. The intrinsic scope of Judo involves much more than the mere accumulation of motor skills used to slam someone down or hold him helpless on the mat. It is not possible to accept only some of Judo's component parts and not others without essentially distorting the whole nature of Judo. Those who ignore the kata portion not only break the historical thread of Judo unity but allow the basic directive force of Judo energy to escape them. True kata, as an integral part of Judo, has no championship or contest connotations, but nevertheless does not escape its responsibilities for contributing to the technical growth of judoists in preparing them to enjoy practical achievement, or at least an appreciation of the theory and spirit upon which Judo was founded. Kata meets these responsibilities through those who establish Judo training programs in which kata plays a prominent part.

Appendix
The Historical Significance of Seiza and Zarei

The *seiza* posture has much more significance than judoists usually attach to it. This kneeling-sitting posture has been in use in Japan perhaps since ancient times. It is a convenient posture offering stability to the sitter, but in a combative sense it is a rather "dead" posture that must be quickly abandoned when an emergency arises, such as when a warrior went into action by drawing his sword to deal with an attacker.

When assuming *seiza* from a standing posture it is the *left* leg which is always placed first, knee down, on the mat. Also, the left foot is placed upright, on its toes; the toes are flexed to permit their soles to contact the mat, not with the insteps resting on the mat. With the left knee down, the long sword normally worn or carried on the warrior's left side could be most effectively drawn without endangering the left leg. Thus, in this intermediate position between standing and kneeling-sitting the stability and mobility of the body is maximized and maintained by the upright foot position, which enables the foot to grip the ground or floor. Modern practitioners of the type of Japanese swordsmanship called *iai-do* make use of the kneeling-sitting posture, from which they usually begin the drawing of the sword with the right knee up (Fig. 1).

Kneeling-sitting position (seiza).

Correct kneeling-bowing position (zarei) for Judo.

For combative purposes, the low body position in *zarei* did not absolutely require the person rendering this salutation to lose visual contact with persons near him; an attitude of alertness for purposes of self-defense prevailed. The modern judoist's tendency to bring the back of the neck in line with the spine and to lower the upper body forward and parallel to the mat during *zarei* is combatively weak (Fig. 2). The hand positions on the mat, however, are vestiges of the triangular placement once used to provide a cushion for the face should one's head be shoved down from behind by an assailant.

Glossary-Index

hadaka-jime (naked choke): general, 123, 127–28, 139, 144, 147, 152; mechanics, 346–55

hiza-gatame (knee armlock). *See ude hishigi hiza-gatame*

juji-gatame (cross armlock). *See ude hishigi juji-gatame*

kami-shiho-gatame (upper holding of the four quarters): general, 122, 127–28, 142, 144; mechanics, 306–15

kata-gatame (shoulder hold): general, 122, 127, 144, 151; mechanics, 298–305

kataha-jime (single-wing choke): general, 123, 127, 139, 142, 144, 147, 152; mechanics, 362–69

kata-juji-jime (half-cross choke): general, 122, 127–28, 144, 150; mechanics, 336–346

kesa-gatame (scarf hold), 61. See also *kuzure kesa-gatame*

kuzure kami-shiho-gatame (irregular upper holding of the four quarters): general, 122, 127–28, 142, 144, 151; mechanics, 326–36

kuzure kesa-gatame (irregular scarf hold): general, 122, 127, 144, 151; mechanics, 289–98

okuri-eri-jime (sliding lapel choke): general, 123, 127, 139, 142, 144, 147, 152; mechanics, 355–62

ude-garami (entangled armlock): general, 123–24, 145, 150; mechanics, 380–89

ude-gatame (arm armlock). *See ude hishigi ude-gatame*

ude hishigi hiza-gatame (arm-crush knee armlock): general, 123; mechanics, 405–13

ude hishigi juji-gatame (arm-crush cross armlock): general, 123; mechanics, 390–96

ude hishigi ude-gatame (arm-crush arm armlock): general, 123; mechanics, 397–404

ude hishigi zempaku-gatame (arm-crush arm arm-lock—old classical form). *See* ude hishigi ude-gatame

yoko-shiho-gatame (side holding of the four quarters): general, 59, 122, 127, 142, 144, 150; mechanics, 315–25

General

uge-goshi (lifting loin), 58
Aida, Hikoichi, 52
All-Japan Judo Federation, 50
ashi waza (leg techniques), 34, 60, 108, 98, 206-27, 453
ate waza (assaulting techniques), 28
ayumi ashi (normal stepping action), 94, 118, 131–32, 140, 150, 161, 166, 180, 184, 208, 228, 231, 237, 257, 263, 447–48

bogeki no katachi (defense form), 441
breathing rhythm, general, 68
budo (martial ways), 17, 20
bugei (martial arts), 17, 20
bushi (classical warrior), 18

center performance, general, 76-77, 147,
chikama (near position). See near position
chikara kurabe (strength comparison). *See* combat systems
combat systems: *chikara kurabe*, 20, 24; *hakuda*, 20; jujutsu, 20; *kempo*, 20; *kogusoku*, 20; *koshi no mawari*, 21; *kumi-uchi*, 21; *shubaku*, 20; *sumo*, 20–21, 24, 189; *taijutsu*, 20; *torite*, 20; *wajutsu*, 20; *yawara-ge*, 20; *yawara-gi*, 20; *yoroi kumi-uchi*, 19–20, 180

Daigo, Toshiro, 56, 449
Dai Nippon Butokukai (Japan Military Virtues Association), 29
dan (a graded level of rank), 52–53, 60
do forms, 24
dojo (training area), 15, 49, 59, 76–77, 98, 101, 114, 147, 429, 435, 440, 446

Eishoji (a temple and the first Kodokan), 24 elements of technique: *kiai*, 47, 64, 77, 113; *ma-ai*, 47, 96, 118; *riai*, 54, 57–59, 81, 87, 89, 121; *taisabaki*, 52, 54, 57–61, 95; *zanshin*, 11, 47, 65, 85, 110–13, 121, 130, 163, 165, 170, 172, 177, 180, 186, 188, 194, 196, 203, 205, 210, 212, 217, 437–38, 441, 451
engagement distance. *See* elements of technique, *ma-ai*
engagement position, 75
etiquette, 66, 440; specific examples of, 155-427

far position, 126–27. *See also* elements of technique, *ma-ai*
fudo-shin (immovable mind), 65

gedan Judo (Judo in the narrow sense), 27
Goshin-ho no Kata (Modern Forms of Women's Self-Defense), 35
Goshin-jutsu no Kata (Modern Forms of Self-Defense), 33, 35, 432
Go-no-Sen no Kata (Forms of Counterthrowing). *See* Nage Ura no Kata

hairi-kata (entrance forms), 448
hakuda (fighting method). *See* combat systems
hando no kuzushi (unbalancing by reaction), 34, 228
hane-goshi (spring leg hip), 447
Hasegawa, Hiroyuki, 59
hiza-guruma (knee-wheel), 447

iai-do (sword-drawing system), 456–57
Inokuma, Isao, 59
Ishikawa, Takahiko, 55
Itsutsu no Kata (Forms of Five), 35

jigohontai (defense posture), 89–91; modified *jigotai*, 83, 88, 90–94, 101, 120
Jikishin Ryu, 24
Jita Kyoei. *See* Principle of Mutual Prosperity
jodan Judo (Judo in the wide sense), 27
judogi (judo costume), 66-68; adjusting of, 77, 121, 131, 137, 140; orderliness, 101, 141
jujutsu (a fighting method). *See* combat systems
Ju no Kata (Forms of Flexibility), 25, 35, 52
jutsu (martial) forms, 24

Kagami Biraki (New Year Kodokan celebration), 52, 62, 449
kake (execution of throw). *See* stages of technique
kamae (combative engagement postures), 89, 129
Kaminaga, Akira, 58
kamiza (deity seat), 69, 71, 76, 79, 98–99, 101, 110, 114–17, 121, 132, 147–48, 150, 155
kan (intuitive learning), 22
Kano, Jigoro, 23-34
kansetsu waza (joint-locking techniques), 123, 128, 131, 143–44, 146, 153, 296, 380–421, 439, 440, 444, 454
kari waza (reaping techniques), 34
kata (form): beginning study, 446–50; cautions, 442–44; concept of, 17; a deliberate thing, 38–39; in demonstrations, 448–49; development of *mu-ga-mushin*, 451; as an exhibition, 40; limitations, 49–50; a living thing, 38–39; a medium for self-realization,

427; methods, 445–49; partner size, 444–45; physical and mental aspects, 41; as preparatory exercise, 448–49; private variation patterns, 448; purposes, 43–44, 433–34; selecting, 432; starting role in, 442; as a supplement to *randori*, 428; a symbol, 39; terminology, 452–53; theory, 39; in training, 427–28; two types of, 17; visual aids in, 452

katame-uchi awase (Katame no Kata), 29

Katame no Kata (Forms of Grappling), 13, 16, 29, 35, 41, 52–63, 432; attack-defense theory, 123–26; categories, 122–23; closing disengagement, general, 78, 422–26; closing procedures, 140; engagement distance, 126–27; gripping, 141–43; *mairi* signal, 113–17, 146, 441, 444; opening assumption of *kyoshi*, 139–40; opening requirements, general, 69–75, 283–88; postures, 128–31; rhythm, 148–54; sounds and gestures, 147; stepping movements, 131–35; strength-building methods, 450; study of, 438–42; symmetry and center performance, 147–48; Tori's attack signal, 145; Uke's escape patterns, 145–46; Uke "gives" his body, 143–45; Uke's lying-ready and sitting-ready positions, 135–39

katame waza (grappling techniques), 27, 53, 58, 122

Kawakami, 53

Kawamura, Teizo, 56

Kawano, Masai, 58

kempo (a fighting method). *See* combat systems

kenshusei (special Judo-study Judoist), 56, 58–59

kiai (vital force). *See* elements of technique

kime (decisive effect), 144, 146, 432, 441, 446

Kime no Kata (Classical Forms of Self-Defense), 29, 35, 52

Kimura, Masahiko, 55

Kito Ryu, 23–24

kobo-ichi (attack-defense are one), 85

Kodokan Judo: differences from jujutsu, 25-30; educational value, 25-30; first founding, 23–24; objectives, 26

kogeki no katachi (attack form), 440

kogusoku (a fighting method). *See* combat systems

Koshiki no Kata (Forms of Antiquity), 35

koshi no mawari (a fighting method). *See* combat systems

koshi waza (hip-loin techniques), 81, 98–99, 108, 180, 189, 197, 205, 453

Kotani, Sumiyuki, 52–53

kouchi-gari (minor inner reaping), 62, 447

ko waza (minor techniques), 34

kumi-uchi (a fighting method). *See* combat systems

kurai-dori (movement in high kneeling posture), 133

kuzushi (breaking balance). *See* stages of techniques

kyoshi no kamae (high kneeling engagement posture), 129–30, 132–42, 148–54, 441, 451

kyu (rank of class), 54, 56–58, 61

Ladd, G. T., 28

Leggett, Trevor P., 50

ma-ai (interval). *See* elements of technique

mairi (surrender) signal. *See both* Nage and Katame no Kata

maki-komi (wrap and wind), 61

ma sutemi waza (back sacrifice techniques), 81, 88, 98, 112, 228–53, 449

Matsumoto, Yasuichi, 54

Matsunaga, Mitsuo, 60

Matsuzaka, Takeshi, 62

Disclaimer

Please note that the publisher and author(s) of this instructional book are NOT RESPONSIBLE for any injury that may result from practicing the techniques and/or following the instructions given. Martial arts training can be dangerous—both to you and to others,—if not practiced safely. You should always consult with a trained martial arts teacher before practicing any of these techniques, and ask them to guide you in the proper techniques to be used. Since the physical activities described herein may be too strenuous in nature for some readers, it is essential that a physician be consulted prior to training.